Political Thinking
and
Consciousness

*As soon as an individual's phi-
losophy of life is known, his
personal activities, which taken
by themselves are meaningless,
become understood.*

Gordon Allport

Political Thinking
and
Consciousness
The Private Life
of the Political Mind

ROBERT E. LANE

Yale University

MARKHAM PUBLISHING COMPANY
Chicago

MARKHAM POLITICAL SCIENCE SERIES
AARON WILDAVSKY, Editor

AXELROD, *Conflict of Interest: A Theory of Divergent Goals with Applications to Politics*

BARBER, *Citizen Politics: An Introduction to Political Behavior*

BARBER, ed., *Readings in Citizen Politics: Essays in Political Behavior*

CNUDDE and NEUBAUER, eds., *Empirical Democratic Theory*

COPLIN, ed., *Simulation in the Study of Politics*

GREENSTEIN, *Personality and Politics: Problems of Evidence, Inference, and Conceptualization*

LANE, *Political Thinking and Consciousness: The Private Life of the Political Mind*

LYDEN and MILLER, eds., *Planning-Programming-Budgeting: A Systems Approach to Management*

PAYNE, *The American Threat: The Fear of War as an Instrument of Foreign Policy*

RANNEY, ed., *Political Science and Public Policy*

RUSSETT, ed., *Economic Theories of International Politics*

SHARKANSKY, *Public Administration: Policy-Making in Government Agencies*

SHARKANSKY, ed., *Policy Analysis in Political Science*

STRICKLAND, WADE, and JOHNSTON, *A Primer of Political Analysis*

©Markham Publishing Company 1969
All Rights Reserved
Printed in U. S. A.
Second Printing August 1970
Library of Congress Catalog Card Number: 72-75897
Paperback Standard Book Number: 8410-3036-7
Hardcover Standard Book Number: 8410-3007-3

To twenty-four courageous
and insightful young men

Acknowledgment

I am indebted to the Social Science Research Council for a grant that provided time, books, and secretarial assistance essential to the completing of this book. For four months in the spring of 1966, I enjoyed the hospitality of Nuffield College Oxford where I was free to write up my notes in a pleasant and friendly atmosphere. In the summer of 1967, my wife and I worked on our respective projects at the Villa Serbelloni overlooking Lake Como, a happy and fruitful experience made possible by the Rockefeller Foundation. In the summer of 1968, I revised the manuscript and wrote the concluding chapters on political consciousness on the blooming island of Barbados, where the bounty of God and the lack of summer tourists made the work possible and the living easy.

Contents

Political Thinking
and
Consciousness

Introduction:
Why Are You a Conservative (Liberal)?

If you ask a man why he believes what he does, why he is a liberal or conservative or isolationist or whatever, and if he does not think you impertinent, he is likely to tell you about the world and not about himself. His account may have several components. He is likely to tell you about the facts of the case as he sees them (perception), or as they have been told to him (authority). Buried in this will be bits and pieces of social theory (the causal component), such as the way big business impedes productivity, and also a good bit about why his view is better for others (the moral component), more humane, closer to natural law than alternative views. Perhaps then he will draw some inferences (logic) about what should be done about it (prescription). In the space of a minute or two he will have given you a brief model of the world as he understands it, something of the way he sees, feels, and thinks; but you will go away, perhaps rather sooner than you had planned, with information relevant to only one interpretation of the question.

Suppose you had said, "Yes, but why are *you* a conservative?" tilting the question around so that it faces him rather than the world. He might say, as we are all tempted to, that *he* sees things that way because things *are* that way. But he might be brighter than that, and speak instead about his economic interests served by the conservative view, the gains he gets from it or would get if that view governed society. More than that, he might speak of his sense that the world is properly hierarchical, that there is something natural and therefore personally satisfying about this arrangement, certainly more so than this sticky talk about the equality of man. Perhaps, too, he would say something of the unthinkableness in his circle of being a socialistic New Dealer, suggesting, by the phrase, that event in his life which traumatized the conscience of this conservative. And beyond that, there is the way he became a conservative, at his mother's knee—his mother of blessed memory, who believed in the power of money to solve all family and personal problems. In short, he might, facing inward and backward through time, tell of the rewards to him of his view and how he came by it.

These two ways of explaining a belief, by referring outward to tell of the world and inward to tell of the self, are complementary features of a total explanation for the simple reason that belief is inevitably an interaction between self and world, especially if we speak of ideological constructs as large as "conservatism." These two ways have literatures and histories, one leading back through political philosophy and political science, the other leading back through psychology and sociology, and the two meeting and intertwining whenever the political philosopher or scientist attempts to explain, rarely his own thought, usually the thought of others.

This book takes the inward view; it is about the way men's motivations shape their political thinking, about ideological motivation. The illustrative material comes from the reports of twenty-four young men on how this works for them, the uses of their ideas in their lives, the usefulness of these ideas in meeting their needs. But the analysis goes beyond these reports, interprets them, tries to uncover something of the significance of what they say for the society of which they are a part. The approach I have employed stresses the striving, need-fulfilling character of social thought, as contrasted to an approach that might, for example, reveal the logical aspects of thought, or the associational aspects—the ways in which one thought leads, through processes of conditioning or free association, to another thought. This is not quite the same as saying that it stresses the purposive, for purposes are conscious, and needs and motives, as we shall see, are often unconscious, becoming conscious only through the application of rather strenuous and often painful effort.[1] Bearing in mind the criticism of the concept of "function," the criticism that points out the hidden evaluative criteria in the concept (function for what?), I nevertheless am speaking of "the functions of ideas" in satisfying needs, in serving a personality and a usually hazy plan of life. I suppose the point can be made most simply by saying that, in any ambiguous situation, if an idea is not rewarding it will not likely be adopted; if adopted it will not likely be remembered; if remembered it will not be employed. Why are ideas rewarding?

If one knows what ideas will be useful to a man in his time and situation, with his goals and needs, one knows how he will select from among the available alternatives, and in what direction he will strain them.[2] This is, so to speak, the psychology of the sociology of knowledge. Enough abstraction for the moment; here is De Vita, one of the twenty-four men to

---

[1] For some early distinctions along this line, see Edward C. Tolman, *Purposive Behavior in Animals and Men* (New York: Century, 1932).

[2] The discussion in this book has some parallel features with the work of M. Brewster Smith, Jerome S. Bruner, and Robert White, *Opinions and Personality* (New York: Wiley, 1956). The opening sentence in that book is "Of what use to a man are his opinions?"

clothe the verbal skeleton with flesh and blood. He speaks of the genesis of his ideas as well as their functions.

DE VITA: THE USES OF "LIBERAL IDEALISM"

Tall and thin, a wedge of a mustache on his upper lip, energetic beyond the call of duty, De Vita is now a lawyer in his home territory near Pittsburgh. When he turned to the analysis of his political beliefs in the mid-fifties, he stated his first discovery as follows: "While tracing the formation of my present political ideals, I found, much to my surprise, that not one of my present opinions in an intelligible and expressible form is more than a year old." As he develops his ideas, it appears that he is a strong welfare-state liberal in almost every respect: he favors civil rights, big government serving especially the needs of the poor and unfortunate, a foreign policy marked by even greater economic aid to the developing nations than the U.S. government is presently extending, and all of the trappings of the welfare state. Yet in one respect he finds, like most of our sample, that he cannot be liberal. "Labor, in my attitude, has no claim to power in the American system or any system." With these newly formulated views in mind, he settles down to account for them.

He did not get them from home, at least not directly or by imitation or absorption. For, though the home views were important, as we shall see, in the lower-middle-class home from which he sprang "political events were placed in the realm of the unintelligible, uncontrollable, and therefore unimportant happenings." His parents have a sour view of politics; they are Republican, though probably not for that reason. In this home situation, De Vita says, "I was content for many years to think that I was a Republican, although I really had no idea just what a Republican was."

Nor did he get his opinions directly from school, a technical high school in the Pittsburgh area, where the dull and dusty material on American history stopped at World War II and did nothing more than confirm his view that politics was unimportant. As he says, "I left high school with little more political awareness than when I entered. I still believed I was a Republican." But at Adams College, where I met him, certain lectures and courses and readings awakened him, his interest in foreign affairs was developed, and he received the materials for a fresh approach. But, he asks himself, why should this have made him a liberal, especially the particular kind of apostle of a welfare state he turned out to be? After all, most of the other students were conservative. Why not he?

It is at this point in the story that we come to the analysis of the ways in which De Vita's liberal and internationalist views are, in their various facets, gratifying to him. What do they gratify? What needs do they serve? There seem to be four main ones, which have to do with his liberal orientation, and a fifth, which in some ways explains why he elaborates a political philosophy in the first place. Let us consider that first.

The Need for Orientation. De Vita is a self-made man. The one thing he had to rely on, and the tool he employed in the work of creating the man he is, was his intellect. It has raised him from the dust. Moreover, the insecurities of his vertically migrant life have reinforced his need to know what lies lurking in the unfamiliar terrain, ready to catch him unawares. He speaks of a "strong desire to control through knowing," something to which we shall return, and illustrates it this way:

> I am at a complete loss when I don't know exactly what is going on. I hate secrecy; *it makes me feel weak.* I hate to work on a project in which I am asked to do only a portion of the work and never told the ultimate goal of the project. I spent this past summer in a research laboratory on a project which no one seemed to understand except the company executives. I had a miserable time simply because I didn't know what was going on. For another example of my need to know I can cite the planning of this paper. The outline is perhaps as long as the paper itself. Although there was much revision along the way, I always had the plan for the whole paper in mind. [My emphasis.]

Consider, in the light of this need for orientation, some of the uncertainties of his situation, as he describes them.

> I have at present no real social-class connection. My family is in the lower middle class. They own a small paint store. I have inherited many of the values of this class. . . . Then on the other hand I see many of the negative aspects of this lower-class life. I'm out of my home environment; I can't go back. Adams College has educated me out of my class, has changed many of my social values, and has given me a ticket to a way of life which my parents, at my age, would not have dreamed possible. I'm out of the lower class, yet I can't at present claim membership in an upper class. Two factors keep me hanging in a virtual no-man's-land between the upper and the lower classes. The primary, and I hope temporary, impediment to my upward movement rests upon the fact that I have no money. . . . Secondly, I find that I cannot accept some of the upper-middle-class values which I find most readily adhered to here on the campus . . . I am in a period of transition. . . .

In this ambiguous and unsettling situation, and with his felt need to orient himself, to have a plan, it is not surprising that De Vita, more than most, has developed something of a political philosophy, a little more elaborate, a little more detailed than others':

I have now a criterion for the analysis of political information, and also, because my liberalism pervades other fields, a
criterion for the analysis of almost any information. I have a
knowledge of what my value system is, and therefore can tell on
the conscious level why certain information irritates me, while
other information pleases me. This may sound trivial, but none-
theless until quite recently I hadn't realized that I have a definite
pattern of values. . . . The satisfaction which I gain from knowing
definitely answers to one of my major psychological needs.

I suspect this is true about De Vita, for he seems to have taken great
satisfaction in discovering himself, and to have experienced a sense of delight
and relief in exposing some element of his personality which helped him to
account for his opinions:

I now know that my self-image of independence was only a
defense used to cover a thwarted drive for dependence on others.
. . . My one successful attempt at free association in connection
with this paper produced a very good example of my dependency
upon women . . . I am indeed glad that I grasped the opportunity
to do a work of this type [that is, writing the ideological self-
analysis].

He needs to have an intellectual grasp of things, as we shall see, to be able
to defend his ideas and beliefs and values, to protect himself against the great
unknown.

Autonomy from the Past; a New Identity. In his search for orientation, De Vita, like any other man, is guided by his own past experiences;
his feelings about these experiences tell him whether or not to accept them.
At first it seems he is rejecting his family, his ethnic and class culture, those
aspects of himself which are so clearly marked by the scars of his childhood
and youth in lower-middle-class Pittsburgh. But as the tale unfolds we see
that he is in fact torn, ambivalent about them. This ambivalence is clear as
he speaks of the lower-class culture he has now abandoned; it is also clear,
though somewhat concealed from himself, as he speaks of his parents. I
shall argue that his liberal orientation in politics is a reaction to this ambivalence and that his forceful rejection of the politics of his childhood gains
momentum from his need to keep down the doubts that may arise from time
to time about the rightness of his views, gaining strength from the energy
invested to resolve his own conflict. That is one theme. Another has to do
with a punitive element in his personality, a desire to punish his parents and
his old "bad" self for the misery they caused him. First, a look at the cultural ambivalence.

On the one hand, the standards under which I was raised
include a tremendous emphasis upon the value of hard work, a

somewhat puritanical moral code with strong inhibitions in relation to drinking, social activity, and partying, a concern for thrift, and a scorn for almost any sort of social indulgence. Moreover, my experience with and observation of human relations in this lower-class environment have impressed me with a warmth and depth of feeling of man for man that I note nowhere else. It could probably be called an "everybody is in the same boat" feeling.

He contrasts this with what he perceives to be some parallel features of the middle-class culture into which he has moved but in which he cannot feel at home:

The middle-class social system [which De Vita sees illustrated at Adams College] seems to be so very shallow, very artificial, and so lacking in the warmth and feeling that characterized my home environment. I can't accept the easygoing attitudes toward work, the strong emphasis upon group conformity, the open striving for status, the surface nonchalance that really covers up intense competition, and the judgment of people upon very superficial, and to me unimportant, bases. The lower-class values of sincerity, nonindulgence, hard work, and close personal relationships, still very much a part of me, seem to pull me away from this upper-class way of life.

Now a look at his views of his parents. Here I infer something that De Vita, not quite liberated, cannot or at least does not say: that he has strong resentful feelings regarding them. At first he is effusive, but even here the careful reader will detect a surreptitious note of complaint:

I can probably be categorized as the "spoiled child," for I cannot recall a time when my parents really refused to give me anything I wanted. My parents were always loving, warm, and permissive. . . . My parents always seemed very interested in what I was doing and always insisted upon helping me. I never really did anything, as a child, completely by myself, because I always had so much ready help from my parents. I came to depend upon them very much and strove always to please them. Although I can't recall an instance when love was withdrawn, I know that I've always feared to go against my parents' wishes. I received too much love and came to depend upon it.

Psychologically, it is a clever device, damning by great praise: "They were too good to me." But the critical themes are revealed more clearly elsewhere:

Conflict with my parents meant, or appeared to mean, the withdrawal of love. . . . Since I had no opportunity to vent my hostility at home, the fear of the withdrawal of parental affection being too great, I therefore turned my more aggressive desires on my playmates. . . . I tried to carry the domination-submission relationship which I found in my relations with my parents into my relations with other children. In my relations with my playmates I could cast myself in the dominant role. I could impose myself upon them just as my parents had imposed themselves upon me.

Then, as he speaks of his parents' political views, he tells us, again indirectly, that they were ignorant, suspicious, prejudiced, and narrowly provincial. Like another young man whom we examine later (Demming), who in similar circumstances reported how he came to resent his parents' poverty, De Vita probably resents his parents' poverty, meanness, and way of life. Yet there was that solicitous mother and that supportive father, whose nurturant spirit created bonds that, deep and strong and comforting as they are, cannot easily be severed. Again, ambivalence.

But something must be done, and since it is clear that he cannot go home again and that some set of ideas appropriate to his new situation is called for, a clean break is required. It must be sharp and drastic, so irreversible that it will force him to maintain his new identity and not permit him to slip back into the old outworn, unhappy collection of thoughts and behaviors associated with his family and his rejected status and way of life. His new political ideas will help to make of him a new man.

To show this opposition I have set forth in parallel columns De Vita's statements about how it was in the old way and how it is now with him.

The Old Way

My home environment . . . is almost anti-intellectual and is characterized by a deep distrust of those who possess knowledge.

Political information came [in the family] in the form of rumor, myth, and value judgment, occasionally mixed with scraps of fact.

Government was at most a necessary evil, run by corrupt politicians

The New Way

Superior intellect and its manifestation in superior policy formulation is the only legitimate claim to power which I recognize.

My desire for power most readily manifests itself in my strong desire to control through knowing. . . . My decision to enter the field of law was made primarily on the assumption that my knowledge of government, of society, of behavior, and of people will give me great power.

I favor big government, government welfare programs, govern-

The Old Way (continued)
who would try at every opportunity to squeeze the utmost from the citizens.

Prejudice, based upon myth, is strong and bitter. The government is corrupt, the Negroes all carry razor blades, the Jews are cheats, etc.

The whole atmosphere reflects an attitude of stagnancy and the feeling of being caught in a huge trap that perpetuates lower-class status.

In school the student learns, in superpatriotic detail, of the founding of our country and of its greatness. An "America can do no wrong" atmosphere prevails. . . .

The New Way (continued)
ment use of all the tools of monetary policy . . . and expansion of government regulatory services.

The many prejudices which I inherited from home life have caused contradictions in my civil rights opinions. For the most part, I can, upon reasoning, weed out the false prejudices and support a policy of equal rights for all groups.

Facts and figures can be altered in the future. Why be satisfied with things as they are when we know how they really should be? . . . Political thinking for me is conscious dreaming, and the dreams are always cast in situations in which I can be "the man on the white horse."

I see the bullheadedness of nationalism as the basis of world unrest. . . . My ideas on foreign policy [are] enough to make any America-firster shudder.

Surely, the direction of these ideas, and especially the intensity with which they are held, helps De Vita to reject his past; and they are the more needed because of his ambivalence about his parents and their values, and his former self and former friends, and because of his uncertainty of the new man he is fashioning in his lonely upward climb through the lush fields of Adams College to some yet unclear destination.

The Need for Affection (and the Fear of Hostility). De Vita entered into the task of studying himself with zeal, commenting at the end, "Needless to say, the work has been extremely rewarding." He finds three main needs served by his liberal ideology:

My basic drive seems to be (1) a striving for affection which leads to a considerable amount of dependency upon other people. To protect this dependency pattern I have developed (2) a drive to

avoid competition in order to keep myself from rebuff and alienation.

With these two drives in hand—and it seems to me that they merge so
nearly into one pattern of behavior that they may best be treated together—
De Vita had a problem:

> On the basis of these two drives alone I could not fully ex-
> plain my liberal political idealism. I searched further and finally
> uncovered a highly repressed but nevertheless very strong drive
> for power, control, and prestige. Moreover, I've found that
> whereas this drive is quite beneath the surface in my dealings with
> everyday reality, it manifests itself much more powerfully in my
> political idealism. . . . My attack upon the status quo is perhaps
> the most important outlet for my repressed power drive.

In the rich detail of his account, however, one can see much more than
these drives at work, as was indicated in the interpretation of his reaction
to his past self. Nevertheless, let us take two themes here: the need to be
liked and the accompanying fear of provoking hostility in others (and, of
course, an even greater fear of his own aggressive feelings), and the need to
dominate, control, be on top, something he interprets as a way of winning
admiration (enhancing his self-esteem), but which might be found to have
other components as well. The need to be liked is the item here on the
agenda; we treat it briefly because it is featured in a later chapter. How
does De Vita's liberal idealism meet this need? He states the need this way:

> I had always imagined myself to be a very independent type
> and had, therefore, believed that I could always turn to myself
> for reassurance in time of stress. However, while tracing through
> moments during which I had been forced to turn to myself, I found
> that always these were times which were accompanied by frustra-
> tion and depression. I found that these were times which followed
> an occurrence in which I was rebuffed by someone upon whom I
> depended. . . . I turned upon myself the aggression which I had
> refrained from turning upon the other person, thus producing the
> depressed feelings, for I felt that an open show of hostility on
> my part would mean the withdrawal of affection on the part of the
> other.

He documents this in many ways; he has thought about it a great deal.
Among other things, he finds that this pattern of needs has meant that
"I am never really doing things for myself. I am always working to please
someone else"; at first parents, then teachers, then girls: "My sex relations have not been entirely satisfactory because I fear that an advance on
my part will meet with disapproval and withdrawal of affection. My striv-

ing to gain affection involves always a considerable amount of hostility."

This affection-hostility problem, the need to obtain evidence of the one and to express and conceal or legitimize the other, has, I think, four effects: (1) the need to disguise strong hostile feelings gives his political philosophy a critical, hostile tone; (2) it affects the manner and circumstances of his political expression; (3) it affects the content, leading to utopian abstraction; and (4) it favors his stand on foreign policy and civil rights. On the first point, the critical quality of his political philosophy, the following paragraph is illustrative:

> I want reform both below and above me. Thus I am against any policy which seeks to preserve a status quo that has been of no benefit to me. [But he has been rescued from his "miserable trap" by a scholarship to Adams, one feature of the status quo.] I can't support things as they are because I myself fit nowhere into the present system. From the point of view of an outsider looking in, all I can do is to criticize—that I do. I believe that in the future the radical fringe will probably be clipped from my liberal idealism. An extreme dissatisfaction with the status quo certainly answers to my social needs.

The hostility engendered by the frustrations of his youth have found a set of targets that his "liberal idealism" makes legitimate. But, wise young man that he is, he foresees that the claws of this philosophy may, as he finds a place in the status quo, be clipped—the claws, I think, and not the wings.

The second effect that this need complex (it has as much to do with the control of aggression as the drive for affection) suggests to De Vita is not in the substance of his views, but in the manner in which he expresses them, the occasions and the grounds for political expression. To express them is both desirable and dangerous: "I've often been challenged to defend my liberal position. To make a stand implies entering into competition, and either to alienate myself from another's approval by defeating him or to alienate myself from the approval of my liberal friends by allowing myself to be defeated. . . . Hence I avoid heated political discussion." Better still, however, "I bring my ideas into formal debate where the rules keep the exchange of real aggression at a minimum. . . . If I cannot gain the affection of my opponents, I can certainly gain their admiration." He needs to win (dominate) but fears to alienate, and compromises by hoping to impress.

The third effect has to do with the tendency toward abstraction in his philosophy, a tendency encouraged by his problem in coping with situations in which hostility, his own and others', may be let loose. The idealistic posture of his thought, its future orientation and utopian quality, serve to help him remove himself "from the little details that people are forever arguing about. . . . I can avoid conflict by making my point unattackable. I merely take my political picture out of the realm of [realistic] discussion."

And finally, a point to be made later in greater detail, the need for affection leads De Vita to argue for a foreign policy modeled on the posture of an ingratiating man, a policy of winning friends and seeking affection. Further, along the same lines, "my attitudes toward civil rights and basic freedom reflect my drive to win affection." Love of mankind seems not to be De Vita's strong point; the humanitarianism in his liberal idealism does seem to have this other affection-striving source.

The Need to Dominate.   De Vita's world is tripartite:

> My image of the world is clearly divided into three sections: the world of those superior to me, whom I must please; the world of those equal to me, with whom I must avoid conflict; and the world of those beneath me, who should recognize and admire my claim to power.

De Vita is tired of trying to please people and is distressed by his fear of competition (because he wants to win, something hard to do without competition), but the domination of others, as he interprets this, is a pleasant experience. He interprets it so that he does not appear in a cruel light, for it is his purpose to gain admiration, which he regards as the reward of domination, in benign ways: "One can gain admiration by holding himself as a model of excellence before his subordinates." This is not destructive, for "in destroying a person I would destroy also the source of the admiration and affection which I really seek. I turn instead to a form of intellectual domination, a form of control which derives from having a knowledge of the entire situation at hand and all its implications." Naturally, this drive to dominate and control others runs head on into a competing need, the need for affection and the fear of generating hostility in others:

> Where one drive serves to draw me away from people into a position of power over them and the other drive pulls me toward people in order to gain the affection derived from close relationship, it is most understandable that either the one or the other will have to be repressed. . . . Hence my drive for power usually suffers under the load of inhibitions connected with my tendency to withdraw from conflict. . . . I've found it ever more necessary to repress these drives toward power because they conflict with my social adjustment, which is becoming increasingly important to me.

But in childish games of cowboys and Indians, "I was always the man on the white horse," the dominating figure.

How does De Vita's "liberal idealism" serve these needs? At first they do not seem to be the natural source of a point of view marked by themes of freedom and equality. Or do they? Here De Vita is more insightful than many a student of authoritarianism, for he sees a close relationship between an intellectual's need to dominate and to control and a liberal position. By grasping the relationship between the need to know and the need to control, by further seeing the way in which futuristic and utopian thought permits the domination of these thought materials, and, finally, by seeing the implicit dominating role of the intellectual in a liberal society, he makes, I think, a contribution to a more general understanding of character and ideology. He does it in this way:

> Liberalism gives me a pattern by which to understand the political world. I can understand it because I create it. My drives to know, to understand, and to control are satisfied. Liberalism is a tool with which I can fashion a political order to my liking. I want to change the present order and I want to institute a new order which I can understand, and, by understanding, control. Knowledge is my claim to power, and hence the new order will be open to intellectual domination by me. Liberalism is itself, in my estimation, a much more intellectually oriented movement than is conservatism. Whereas the conservative must only seek to preserve, the liberal must create and reform. Liberalism is inherent in my claim to power—knowledge. It is the best medium for venting my drives to know, to understand, and to control.

Moreover, the plastic aspect of an ideology that need not be so intimately tied to reality gives one scope for imagining a different self in this different world. It is an invitation to remodel that tired self-image, giving it, with grace and generosity, some quality dear to the heart, but lacking in the here and now:

> The farther from reality my idealism carries me, the more dominant becomes my striving for control and power. Because my political ideals do not support reality as it is, but rather as I would like it to be, my personality enters into my attitudes, not as it [my personality] is, but as I subconsciously would like it to be.

There follows that phrase quoted earlier and resonant with memories of a childish game of cowboys and Indians: "Political thinking for me, then, is conscious dreaming, and the dreams are always cast in situations in which I can be 'the man on the white horse.'"

The drive for power and control guides specific policy choices, often through an anthropomorphic device in which De Vita sees the government as behaving like a person—like himself, for example—as we shall see in more detail later on.

> As I have won my positions of power by establishing a record of works which have pleased my superiors and stimulated the admiration of those beneath me, I no doubt cast the United

States in a similar role. We, for the most part, deal with our subordinates, powerwise at least, when we deal with the rest of the world.

Hence, argues De Vita, we should control, as he seeks to do, through knowledge and generous conduct. De Vita favors big strong government, a regulatory and welfare state, but he is skeptical of populistic theories of government, in which policies are a close reflection of popular wishes:

> I have a distaste for what is called "popular opinion" as a dictate to policy. . . . Popular opinion is generally wrong. As I've controlled groups through understanding and organizing situations, so I believe government should control society. Policy can be based on what is right rather than what is popular. As I attack the status quo, then . . . I am creating a system that I can control. My drive to dominate becomes dominant in my dream of government, because I can identify with a position of power in government. Here is my chance again to be "the man on the white horse."

And then, bringing in the other need he feels so strongly, he adds, "Here is my chance to win the affection and admiration of a whole nation."

With these views it is not surprising that De Vita admires the New Deal, but he surprises himself with the intensity of his respect for this government and period. He finds an explanation in the resonance of the themes of the New Deal with his own inner strivings:

> The New Deal probably appealed to me on an unconscious level long before I knew what a New Deal liberal was. I've never realized until now why I praise the government actions which some of my friends labeled as despotic. . . . The New Deal was a large extension of government control. To me, the New Deal means a strong executive grinding its way out of a national depression. Here I had an example of the betterment of society through intellectual central control.

It bothers De Vita that he cannot adopt one of the usual tenets of the liberal, support for a strong labor movement. As may be seen clearly enough in what has gone before, equalitarianism is not the portal through which De Vita enters the liberal domain; he is not really thinking much about the workingman, or the problems of long hours, low pay, monotonous jobs. Perhaps it might be said that the labor movement does not speak any longer for the weak and poor and dispirited, but that is not why De Vita does not accept it:

> I have no sympathy for labor and a disgust for the labor movement. Ever since I began to think about labor, I have always considered it to be intellectually inferior. In my attitude

toward labor the generally repressed hostility incorporated in my drive for domination is unleashed. Labor, in my attitude, has no claim to power in the American system or in any system. They are usurpers who seek to control the intellectually justified power positions which are held by management. . . . My image of labor greatly thwarts my drive to power through knowledge and therefore labor receives the brunt of my hostility.

The nouveau intellectual, like the nouveau riche, exaggerates his "wealth" and demeans those who do not have it and cannot make it. But De Vita will change—a little. In the meantime we have captured him, a sensitive, intelligent, and above all striving young man of twenty, whose needs for orientation push him to think through his political values and beliefs, and whose need to reject his past and to create a new identity make opposition to the status quo and support of liberal idealism both feasible and appropriate. Beyond this, his need for affection and fear of hostility (in himself as well as in others), combined with a need to dominate and control people, where he can do this safely, lead him in the subtle ways we have seen toward a form of critical liberal idealism, at least as he uses the term. De Vita is a real person, not a psychological abstraction, not a "type"; but his case illustrates the functional need-serving character of political ideas.

Economic and Career Needs.   Lest it be thought that the point of view I am expressing is ignorant of the powerful effect of economic interests or career advantages upon political thought, we must note that De Vita's politics do not run counter to his career interests, for he has in mind a career of work either in the government, in which case "big government" is an advantage, or in teaching, where his political views are not directly relevant, or in law, where "liberal idealism" can at least find a home. Had he anticipated a career in business, surely his politics would have been different; but at his stage of career choice, an ideology and value system such as his might more readily guide his choice of career than be guided by it. More generally, in interpreting the results of the discussion in this book, the modest attention to economic and career needs should be seen as the result of catching men before career commitments are made.[3]

THE TWENTY-FOUR MEN

De Vita is one of twenty-four men who attended Adams College (where I once taught), each of whom was invited to write an "ideological self-analysis." Adams is a private, elite university, drawing largely from middle- and upper-middle-class families. Thus the human milieu in which these

---

[3] See Ralph Underhill, "Values and Post-College Career Change," *American Journal of Sociology,* 72 (1966), pp. 163-72.

men went to college was, for the most part, composed of an economically secure group of young men, more Republican than Democratic, more than ordinarily intelligent, anticipating "success" in worldly terms, intending to do some graduate work (chiefly business, law, or medicine). In this environment, a certain upper-class humanity prevails; it is bad form to be blatantly anti-Semitic or anti-Negro, though a certain discreet prejudice is common; and it is bad form to be totally without concern for the underprivileged, although ambition for the self, properly disguised, is each individual's main interest. Compared with other universities, Adams has a kind of internationalist norm. The faculty is more liberal than would be true at church-affiliated or technical colleges; the students anticipate and to some extent discount this.

The particular twenty-four men were in no sense a random sample of the college population; they were students in certain political science classes. Hence, to some extent, they were more than ordinarily interested in politics and political ideas. Three came from Catholic families, but only one was a practicing Catholic at the time the biographies were written. Five were Jewish, though only one seemed to take his religion as a guide to behavior. Of the sixteen "Protestants" (that is, men from neither Catholic nor Jewish families), only a few mentioned their religious beliefs as relevant to their social judgments.

Six of the group made a point of their identification with the poor or oppressed or underprivileged, and believed in governmental protection and support. In this sense six were liberal. Five indicated their belief in inequality and the values of a society with a differentiated elite (of which they would be members), and a government whose main function is to keep order and protect property. In this sense they were markedly conservative; perhaps "reactionary," in spite of its propagandistic tone, conveys a better sense of their position. Characteristically, the main line of differentiation between the two is this: the liberals stressed greater opportunity for the poor, the very conservative stressed greater opportunity for the able. The remaining thirteen were about evenly divided between moderate liberals (expressing some concern for the less privileged but doubtful about the role of the government) and moderate conservatives (expressing a general approval of hierarchical society, a positive value for personal wealth, but hoping for a vague "progress" in which all can share and not generally repudiating the New Deal). There were ten Democrats in the group, nine Republicans, and one "states' rights" advocate. Four did not indicate their political affiliations or preferences, speaking of themselves as independent, or as guided by their preference for liberal ends but conservative means, or by a moralistic view that neither party is satisfactory, or simply agonizingly unable to make up their own minds.

Their fathers had a variety of occupations, but the dominant one was business (fourteen), with such professions as lawyer, schoolmaster, doctor, scientist, and engineer also represented. Three came from distinctly lower-middle-class homes, while some of the others were the sons of "self-made men." Two were from homes with old-family names of a patrician character.

And, of course, all were between the ages of nineteen and twenty-two and all were well-educated and intelligent.

Twice I have mentioned "ideological self-analysis" without explaining the term. Briefly, it is the analysis of one's own political values, opinions, and beliefs, and the functions they serve in one's personality and life situation. It is an extended response to the questions "Of what use to me are my political ideas?" and "How did I come to have these political ideas?" More specifically, in the cases to be analyzed here, it is a response to questions about a man's liberalism or conservatism, or, in a few cases, his Republican or Democratic party preference. The aim in asking for an ideological self-analysis is to invite a clarification of views that are normally quite vague and inconsistent, often below the threshold of consciousness, often accepted up to that point without examination, often quite unrelated to a person's life purposes. In some ways, too, this self-oriented inquiry seeks to make the student more aware of the relationship of personality to ideology, of basic needs to social thought. Further, the analysis is intended to reveal the hidden anchors of opinion and thus to permit a mobility and flexibility of thought which is otherwise impossible.

Over the years I have explored this process of ideological self-analysis through student essays, through individual extended interviews with selected graduate students, and through group sessions of three men each. The material on which this book is based comes, as I have said, from twenty-four undergraduate autobiographies. No student could, I think, write autobiographies as revealing as these without preparation; the very notion that ideas are acquired for their gratification values, rather than (or in addition to) their truth value, is foreign to the formal training the students have had, though it is implicit in much of their thinking and in the lore of politics. Hence they were selectively exposed to a growing literature on this point,[4] and were then instructed, in their own investigations, to avoid

---

[4] Among other readings assigned and discussed are: Smith, Bruner, and White, *Opinions and Personality;* T. W. Adorno, Else Frenkel-Brunswik, Daniel J. Levinson, and R. Nevitt Sanford, *The Authoritarian Personality* (New York: Harper, 1950); Erich Fromm, *Escape from Freedom* (New York: Rinehart, 1941); Harold Lasswell, *Psychopathology and Politics* (Chicago: University of Chicago Press, 1930); Abram Kardiner, *The Psychological Frontiers of Society* (New York: Columbia University Press, 1945); Hadley Cantril, *The Psychology of Social Movements* (London: Chapman & Hall, 1941); G. M. Gilbert, *The Psychology of Dictatorship* (New York: Ronald Press, 1950); Robert Lindner, *The Fifty Minute Hour* (New York: Bantam, 1955); David Riesman, *The Lonely Crowd* (New Haven: Yale University Press, 1950); Gabriel Almond, *The Appeals of Communism* (Princeton: Princeton University Press, 1954). From time to time articles and books by Nathan Leites, H. V. Dicks, S. M. Lipset, Margaret Mead, and David Levy were also assigned.

theorizing, to avoid psychologizing, and to write out of their own experience, testing their reports by the internal "feel" of the relevance of what they reported. This was a novel experience for most of them, and, as it turned out, both painful and, as De Vita said, enormously interesting and informative. The autobiographies were produced in the fifties and early sixties; the names and other identifying references have, of course, been changed to ensure anonymity.

In my interpretation, not everything these men say is taken at face value, for of course they deceive themselves and often are out of touch with their own deepest needs. For the most part, however, they can report quite a bit of the need-gratifying function of their thought, and on this level, not too far below the surface, they are quite accurate, candid, and insightful. I thought they proved to be, in the face of self-revelations that most men shirk, brave men.

WHAT GOOD IS THIS INFORMATION?

Perhaps this information about the need-gratifying character of a person's political ideas is useful to the man himself (De Vita certainly thought so), but what good is it to anybody else? Have we here only a kind of political therapy? Or is it like the clinical therapy it vaguely resembles, also a basis for learning about the way the mind works—in this case, the political mind? It is the possibility that these self-examinations tell us something about the nature of the political mind *in general* that stimulated this book.

The first part of the book is devoted to a brief discussion of the nature of human motivation, the energizing sources of action. Here, as elsewhere, there is a kind of physical analogy that runs through the discussions of motivated decisions; perhaps we always think in metaphors about the unseen. The need-gratifying force, like hydraulic pressure or electric current, or, more concretely, like the spring in a pin-ball machine, which forces the ball to the point where gravity does the rest, is, in the analogy, "triggered," "channeled," "blocked," or "reinforced" by something. This analogy with the physical world is, I think, evident in the "model" of ideology formation which follows the general discussion of motives. These parts of the discussion are designed to "place" and give enlarged meaning to what comes next.

The discussion of the way certain special needs are served by their associated political ideas comes next. The needs thus treated are: (1) the need to be liked (something we saw in De Vita's case), and the way this is reflected in defensive and self-validating behavior; (2) the need to express aggression (a need that De Vita shared with others), and, equally important, the need to control and inhibit aggression; (3) the need to present a moral appearance to the self and others; (4) the need to restore one's self-esteem, damaged through feelings of physical inadequacy and low status; (5) the need for continued affiliation with the family (identity continuity) as a source of orientation and support, and, in contrast (6), the need for autonomy from the family and the establishment of a separate identity.

If, as must be obvious, the material at hand does not permit us to talk about the incidence of these needs, or to prove an association through the use of correlations, or to prove some causal sequences through other statistical devices, we must make our contribution in other ways. This is done through an investigation of the nature of the needs as these are experienced by the young men themselves, differentiating types and themes from something that at first seemed undifferentiated. Then, through showing the channels and mechanisms employed to make political ideas rewarding to these specific needs, I have sought to develop some minor contributions to the theory of political thinking. And, occasionally, it has seemed that there was something about a given need that, whenever it might occur in a context similar to the one here examined, had conservative (hierarchical, freedom-constricting, privilege-protecting) or liberal (equalitarian, freedom-enhancing, privilege-destroying) implications. Often, however, the needs I have isolated for treatment have a greater influence on the style and manner of expressing ideas than on their content. This discussion is intended, as I said at the outset, to help us understand something of the way in which political thought, like other "acts," is a self-serving activity, part of man's striving nature, functional for his life purposes as he experiences them.

Psychological information of this kind always has social implications if we can but discover them, for social institutions must employ and set to work men's motives, skills, and purposes, and must interrelate persons in ways congenial to their own concepts of appropriate interpersonal relations. Still, the leap from information of an individual nature, or even from information about habitual mental processes, to an inference about social functioning is often hazardous. In a speculative mood, I shall attempt in the final chapter to say something about the way in which an enlarged understanding of the need-gratifying function of ideas, as developed in this study, alters our picture of social and political institutions. At the very least, it leads, wherever politics is studied, to an initial question: "What do the actors want?"

2

Human Needs, the Energizing Sources of Political Thought

VALUES

An outsider cannot see another person's values the way he can see his behavior, but he can find out about them in two ways. One is to observe that person's choice of goals, to see what they have in common. If that common property is a conception of what is worth striving for, it is a value. Or one can ask that person to reflect on his own behavior and thought, so that he can say for himself what is worthwhile, what is a value. There is scarcely any other way to find out.

Some have used the term to indicate what people actually *do* desire, and others to indicate what a person feels he and others *ought* to desire. Lasswell and Kaplan illustrate the first of these usages: "A value is a desired event—a goal event."[1] Clyde Kluckhohn illustrates the second: "A value is a conception . . . of the desirable which influences the selection from the available modes, means, and ends of action. . . . The cue words are 'right' or 'wrong,' 'better' or 'worse.' "[2] Both are important for analyzing political thinking, but, curiously, the values specified by these and other authors may be treated in either way: as something people *do* want or as something they think they *ought to* want.

To flesh this out, so that we can see how this approach might illuminate political thought, let us consider several of these value schemes. An early

---

[1]Harold D. Lasswell and Abraham Kaplan, *Power and Society* (New Haven: Yale University Press, 1950), p. 16.

[2]Clyde Kluckhohn, "Values and Value-Orientations in the Theory of Action," in Talcott Parsons and Edward Shils, eds., *Toward a General Theory of Action* (New York: Harper Torchbooks, 1951), p. 395.

one is reported by Gordon Allport in his analysis of E. Spranger's "ideal types" of men, each expressing the dominance of some particular value.

The Theoretical. The dominant interest of the theoretical man is the discovery of *truth.*

The Economic. The economic man is characteristically interested in what is *useful.*

The Esthetic. The esthetic man sees his highest value in *form* and *harmony.*

The Social. The highest value for this type is *love* of people, whether of one or many, whether conjugal, filial, friendly, or philanthropic.

The Political. The political man is primarily interested in *power.*

The Religious. The highest value for the religious man may be called *unity.* He is mystical, and seeks to comprehend the cosmos as a whole, to relate himself to its embracing totality.[3]

There are parallels and differences here in comparison with Lasswell's eight values: power, respect, rectitude, affection, well-being, wealth, skill, and enlightenment.[4]

Surely, if a man allowed any one of these values to dominate his purposive behavior in a variety of situations, his political thought would be shaped and colored and saturated with that value. The theoretical man would devise a government by experts (of which he would imagine himself to be one), just as we saw De Vita do, although De Vita, like others, has multiple values. But the point is that if one knew a man's dominant value, in this sense of actual desire, one would have an entry into his political thinking. In fact, as we shall see, these concepts of value are not so very different from the way psychologists have conceived of basic motives. Many of them we shall examine again.

But now, as we shift the concept somewhat from "value" to "value orientation," a somewhat different range of concepts comes into view. A "value orientation" is, according to Kluckhohn, "a generalized and organized conception, influencing behavior, of nature, of man's place in it, of man's relation to man, and of the desirable and nondesirable as they relate to man-environment and interhuman relations."[5] These value orientations are answers to the questions: Is man good or evil, or a mixture? Is human nature mutable or not? Is man subjugated to nature, in harmony with it, or master over it? What is more important: the past, the present, or the future? Are men properly active or passive? Who are the important people: one's elders, one's peers, or oneself? In most cases, though not in all, one can ask both how an individual prefers things to be and how he thinks they

[3]Gordon Allport, *Personality* (New York: Holt, 1937), pp. 228-30.
[4]Lasswell and Kaplan, *Power and Society,* p. 87.
[5]Kluckhohn, "Values and Value-Orientations," p. 411.

ought to be. Value orientations do not designate the objects of striving, but guide striving and thought, as we shall see below in Chapter 5.

There is no doubt about the utility of these approaches; but two points must be made. First, if one asks about preferences, about what is desired, as we have seen, one is getting close to asking about human needs and motives, with this difference: the values and value orientations may be thought of as part of the ideational scheme of things, while the needs and motives are part of the personality system. This may seem like a formal distinction, but the usual way to analyze the relationship between two ideas is to note their consistency, their intellectual relationship, the way one implies another, or overlaps with another, or is subsumable under another. Thus the burden is placed on logical analysis, and the energizing force is the drive toward consistency, perhaps a mixture of logical and emotional consistency, as in what are called "balance" or "dissonance" theories. At this common level of ideas, we lose something of what we are looking for: the energizing source of political thought. And, aside from the important satisfactions to be gained from consistency, one cannot answer questions about the rewards to the individual in "choosing" one idea over another.

Furthermore, there is some risk of tautology in limiting the analysis to this one level, as when a person explains, "I believe in a free society because I value freedom." It is true that reference to needs and motives can be no more illuminating ("He values freedom because he has a need for autonomy"), but a focus on the individual who produces the ideas is less likely to run into this difficulty. For these reasons, values treated as desires seem to me to offer less explanatory power than a direct attack upon the problem: What needs or motives does an idea satisfy?

If, on the other hand, one treats values as the desirable, as embodiments of "the ought," another difficulty comes into view. Here, instead of logical consistency, the energizing force must be the need to appease a conscience that embraces not only ethically good and bad, but also aesthetic and epistemological standards, internalized in such a way as to produce guilt when they are violated. There is no question at all about the force of this drive in influencing political thought. Political ideas are inevitably normative in this sense; almost every aspect of political life is evaluated in these good-and-bad terms. This is true not only of the clear rationalization of economic self-interest, but also of more distant, symbolized, and personally unfamiliar domains of thought, like foreign policy, the role of the judiciary, and treatment of the poor and dispirited. But, and this is the point, one must go beyond the rationalization to the rationalizing person in order to account for this intellectual product. Again, in some sense, an understanding of why a person rationalizes in this way must depend upon more than a knowledge of what he thinks is an ethically better scheme. Beyond this is the complex of needs that shape his conscience and relate his conscience to his desires.

There is one further problem in employing values as the main instrument for explaining political thought: sometimes the values fail to *engage* the topic. M. Brewster Smith found this when he asked people about their views on the Soviet Union. Those for whom "freedom" was a high priority value did relate their views of the Soviet Union to this value; it seemed to inform and guide their attitudes. But those for whom "security" was a priority value seemed not to relate their information or opinions about the Soviet Union to this value at all. Smith argued that something about the values and the kinds of people who hold each value was responsible for this difference: the freedom value was more easily engaged, and those who held it were in some way more ready to use it on distant material of little personal relevance.[6] It is true that this problem of engagement is not eliminated by referring to the personality system, but there is a language to take care of this problem. A "need" is regarded as a latent condition, and, at least in some vocabularies, a "motive" is an engaged need. (Though one should add that there is often much discussion of "motive arousal" as well.)

For these reasons, then, it seems at once safer (because of the lessened risk of rationalization, and the lowered emphasis on logic and, when values are used as "oughts," guilt) and more satisfying (because of the more fundamental—earlier, more powerful—nature of the explanations) to rest an account of political thought on concepts of motivation than of values. Hence the need- and motive-oriented question: "Of what use to you is your liberalism (conservatism)?"

THE FUNCTIONS OF AN IDEA IN A HUMAN LIFE

"What adjustive functions of personality are served by the formation and maintenance of an opinion?" ask Smith, Bruner, and White. They answer their question this way: "There are three functions served by holding an opinion, and we shall call them *object appraisal, social adjustment,* and *externalization.*"[7] The first of these, object appraisal, means the usefulness of the opinion in sizing up objects and events in the environment from the point of view of one's major interests and going concerns. The function of the opinion is to guide a person through the real world and to help him get

---

[6]M. Brewster Smith, "Personal Values as Determinants of a Political Attitude," *Journal of Psychology,* 28 (1949), pp. 477-86.

[7]M. Brewster Smith, Jerome Bruner, and Robert White, *Opinions and Personality* (New York: Wiley, 1956), pp. 39-41.

what he wants. The second function, social adjustment, refers to the way opinions help a person get along with others, identify with them and with his reference groups, differentiate himself from others, or even express his hostility toward them. And the third function, externalization, refers to the way in which opinions (often through displacement and projection) help a person to legitimize his unacceptable feelings, to act out some inner problem in a way that helps to liberate his energies and reduce his anxieties.[8]

The first point to be made against this example of what is, I suppose, the leading psychological approach to the explanation of political thought is that it is too blunt a set of "functions," too undifferentiated in its conception. To lump all functions together under "object appraisal," "social adjustment," and "externalization" is too costly; one gives up too much information in the process. As we shall see shortly when we examine various concepts of men's needs and motives, one might think of ideas as functional, in the sense of serving felt needs, in many situations obscured by these blunt categories. Among these might be consistency needs, where logical rules are given moral force; needs for appeasing the conscience and for presenting to the self and others some moral image; curiosity and the need to learn and understand and give meaning to the world and purpose to life; needs for economizing thought and effort; needs for relieving the sense of pain and for rationalizing one's hardships; needs for expressive acts, tension release, giving vent to impulsive sentiments.

But this is not to undermine the functional approach in general; in spite of its difficulties, I do not want to do that. Granted that functional argument implies some evaluative criterion, so that the functional and the dysfunctional may be sorted out, and, further, that such criteria are often supplied on vague and subjective bases by the observer;[9] granted, too, that cause-and-effect language is often more precise, more likely to incorporate references to two important ingredients of causal inquiry: necessity (could the "effect" have come about without a given "cause"?) and sufficiency (whenever a given "cause" is present, does it always produce the same alleged "effect"?); nevertheless, it is often useful, as I think is made clear in the above illustrations, to think of need-filling, purpose-serving cause-and-effect relations as contributing something to a system (personality, organism, life)—and that is what functional analysis does.

---

[8]*Ibid.*, pp. 41-44.

[9]It is a common observation, for example, that people hold ideas that seem to impede their efforts and frustrate their goals; indeed, they not only hold such ideas, but may cling to them in the face of overwhelming contrary evidence or pressure. In such cases the observer may decide that a person's ideas are dysfunctional. If he should be a psychoanalyst, he may try to get the individual to view a competing set of ideas as indeed more functional to his "real," that is, longer term, needs. The point is that a person's concept of what is functional for him is not always the best criterion of what is good for "the system," that is, for his self.

But what are the needs? That seems to be a first question, and we shall address ourselves to it in just a moment. The drive to satisfy motives and fill needs is the energizing source of thought; without recognizing this, one does not understand the function served. And then, how are these needs met, by what means, through what thought processes? These are the questions to which we seek answers.

SOME CATEGORIES OF HUMAN NEEDS

As necessity is the mother of invention, so, more generally, human needs are the parents of social thought; the effort to gratify these needs or reduce their urgency stimulates and shapes thinking.

No one can write political philosophy without stating or implying what needs people strive to satisfy, often confusing real needs with some idealized version. It is unclear in *The Republic,* for example, whether Socrates believes most men do experience a need for that harmonious balance of reason, appetite, and spirit that he calls "justice," or whether he believes merely that they ought to. Nor is it clear in Rousseau's *Social Contract* whether he holds that men are in fact motivated by a desire for the public interest, that all men would be so motivated under appropriate conditions, or merely that men should be so motivated. But even if the "is" and the "ought" were separated out and clarified, the confusion on the basic roster of motives to be accounted for would remain. We associate Hobbes with a belief that an overwhelming popular need for peace and security, combined with strong aggressive tendencies, leads (and must lead) eventually to the acceptance of more or less absolute government; Machiavelli with the premise that rulers above all seek to satisfy their needs for power and glory (as well as for security); Locke with a belief in the primacy of men's needs for "esteem" and the avoidance of disgrace; Mill with an aversion to men's growing need for popular acceptance and conformity, and his approval of their need for self-development. Each philosopher has taken this ambiguous object, man, and found in him some needs or sets of motives which seemed to him more important than others and more useful to the philosopher himself in constructing an edifice of social thought congenial to his purposes.

Modern psychologists, turning to the problem of motivation and the satisfaction of human needs, have tended first to look to the demands of the body, the conditions of existence and relief of pain, as a means of anchoring their systems in something material, and hence apparently observable, measurable, real. Such physiological drives or needs are surprisingly varied. Murphy, for example, classifies these in terms of visceral drives (hunger, thirst, rest and sleep, oxygen drive, sex, etc.), activity drives (restlessness, perseveration, rhythm, curiosity, impulse to cope with environment), sensory drives (drive to experience: sights, sounds, touches, etc.), and then the drive to express emergency responses (excitement, fear, rage, disgust, shame, grief, etc.).[10] Are these irrelevant to our interest, the gratification provided by political ideas? I do not think so. Here, for example, is a report on the thoughts of a conscientious objector preparing for postwar relief work, who in 1944 was put upon a semistarvation diet.

> By the twelfth week not only his dreams but his conscious thoughts revolved around food as steadily as the earth around the sun. . . . He became more restless, irritable, and—in one of the ominous and universal symptoms of starvation—increasingly apathetic. He had difficulty concentrating on any activity for very long. He lost self-confidence to the point where he sought more control by the experimenters, saying, "I think it is a good idea to put strong checks on us." Writing in his diary during the twelfth week, he observed that he enjoyed being alone, that his thoughts and moods had turned inwards, that his interest in other individuals and in post-war relief work overseas declined, and that what he now dreamt of was being an architect and leading a "personal home life" in a small town or rural environment.[11]

In fact, so powerful was the egocentric effect of starvation that this young man did give up his intention to do war relief work and went back to an earlier interest in architecture. Apparently, adequate diet is a condition for a sense of social responsibility, or, put another way, preoccupation with the self serves, so far as any thought can, the needs of the hungry.

Later we shall see how a young man's sex drives, expressed in thoughts about the "uncomplicated sex life of working-class people," created a kind of ambivalence in his attitudes toward the working class. For most people such fantasies are unconscious, hence their links to social thought are rarely spelled out; but they are sometimes there and may be important. We are only now discovering the ways in which physiology affects thought, through such drugs as mescaline and LSD and tranquilizers, through implanting electric circuits, through experiments on sensory deprivation, and through surgery on brain-damaged individuals. But the way in which social thought reflects body states and in some way perhaps serves body needs has yet to be explored.

Learned motivation is what we are interested in. If motivation is derived from physiological needs, the derivations are often tenuous and obscure,

---

    10Gardner Murphy, "Social Motivation," in Gardner Lindzey, ed., *Handbook of Social Psychology* (Cambridge, Mass.: Addison-Wesley, 1954), p. 609.

    11James C. Davies, *Human Nature in Politics* (New York: Wiley, 1963), p. 13; see also "The Effect of Different Intensities of the Hunger Drive on Thematic Apperception," in John W. Atkinson, ed., *Motives in Fantasy, Action and Society* (Princeton: Van Nostrand, 1958), Chap. 2.

but even where they are reasonably clear, their usual basis in animal experiments makes inferences about the motives behind complex thought patterns difficult. I must pass over this literature, therefore, somewhat reluctantly, and go directly to a figure who seems to be a parent of much contemporary thought and research, Henry Murray.

In his *Explorations in Personality,* Murray developed a list of about twenty-seven needs. (There is some overlap and inclusion of one with another, and Murray expresses skepticism about the utility of some, while certain others, it seems, are merely the opposites of those listed earlier and hence rest on a different footing, especially if one uses for each need an approach-avoidance scheme of analysis.) These needs are organized in terms of postures toward inanimate objects (acquisition, order), ambition (achievement, recognition), defense of status (inviolacy, defendance), human power (dominance, deference, autonomy), aggression and abasement, avoidance of blame ("blamavoidance"), affection (affiliation, rejection, nurturance, succorance), play, and the needs to know and to tell.[12] This rich, insightful list will suggest the origins of much of the empirical work on motivation done in the past twenty years, especially the work of David McClelland and those who, in turn, have worked with him and followed him.

There are other lists and, inevitably, competing schools. Maslow thinks of the basic human needs as best classified in the following way:[13]

The Physiological Needs, which he says can be almost any number one wants, depending upon the degree of specificity desired, come first, but when they are satisfied, "higher" needs emerge.

The Safety Needs include not only the need for physical safety, but also, in some degree, the need for familiar routines, for order (as Hobbes said), for protection from noxious stimuli and their threat. When invoked, these needs may be "a strong determinant not only of . . . [a person's] current world outlook and philosophy but also of his philosophy of the future."

The Belongingness and Love Needs, says Maslow, come after the physiological and safety needs are more or less satisfied, but they are no less important, since their frustration can also produce a "sick" individual.

The Esteem Needs (especially *self*-esteem) may be classified in two groups: those dealing with "the desire for strength, for achievement, for adequacy, for mastery and competence, for confidence in the face of the world, and for independence and freedom," and, second, those dealing with "the desire for reputation and prestige . . . status, dominance, recognition,

⎯⎯⎯⎯⎯⎯
[12]Henry A. Murray, *Explorations in Personality* (Oxford and London: Oxford University Press, 1938), pp. 80-85, 109-15; reprinted in David C. McClelland, ed., *Studies in Motivation* (New York: Appleton, 1955), pp. 63-70.
[13]A. H. Maslow, *Motivation and Personality* (New York: Harper, 1954), pp. 80-98.

attention, importance, or appreciation." It is here, in the main, that we find the sources of gratification afforded by a wide range of political ideas.

The Need for Self-Actualization, a need that may be pithily expressed by the aphorism "What a man can be he must be," expresses the need behind the drive for self-fulfillment which emerges when other needs are satisfied.

The Desires to Know and to Understand are in part conceived as instrumental to the satisfaction of the more basic needs, but Maslow says there is something left over: "there are reasonable grounds for postulating positive *per se* impulses to satisfy curiosity, to know, to explain, and to understand."

The Aesthetic Needs represent an area on which little research has been conducted, but which Maslow feels is related to but separate from cognitive needs, and may be seen in desires for order, for closure, for symmetry, indeed for beauty itself, however defined.

This is one man's attempt to give order and achieve a kind of closure on the proper basis for interpreting the striving nature of man. Here is another, limited to learned or acquired needs, but similar to Maslow's in some respects, created at about the same time. This one is by Rotter:[14]

Recognition-Status: the need to be considered competent or good in a professional, social, occupational, or play activity; the need to gain social or vocational position—that is, to be more skilled or better than others.

Protection-Dependency: the need to have another person or group of people prevent frustration or punishment and provide for the satisfaction of other needs.

Dominance: the need to direct or control the actions of other people, including members of family and friends; to have any action taken be that which the subject suggests.

Independence: the need to make one's own decisions, to rely on oneself, together with the need to develop skills for obtaining satisfactions directly, without the mediation of other people.

Love and Affection: the need for acceptance and indication of liking by other individuals. In contrast to recognition-status, this need is not concerned with the social or professional position of friends, but seeks their warm regard.

Physical Comfort: a learned need for physical satisfaction that has become associated with the gaining of security.

14Julian B. Rotter, *Social Learning and Clinical Psychology* (New York: Prentice-Hall, 1954), p. 132.

Still other scholars, developing measures of certain motives thought to be important, have explored one or a few of these in depth. David Mc-Clelland first developed an instrument for measuring needs for *affiliation,* for *power,* and for *achievement,* as expressed in storytelling and fantasy life, and then, on the basis of further work on the achievement motive, linked this particular motive to economic and social development.[15] Crowne and Marlow have created an instrument for measuring people's need for social approval, and have written a book on *The Approval Motive,* showing how the motive is aroused, when it is expressed, and with what sad consequences for those who harbor it.[16] Sears has explored the need for *dependency* in children, finding it a motive that leads girls to achieve an appropriate feminine role, but leads boys to social maladjustment.[17] Much is said today of the loss of and consequent search for identity, a situation revealed in acute form in developing societies; this identity confusion is thought to be the crucifix of adolescence, the scourge of marginal man. "Identity and ideology," says Erikson, "are two aspects of the same process": the process of self-discovery, self-development, self-maintenance, and self-acceptance, all wrapped up in the designation "identity formation."[18] Ideas serve important identity needs, helping to define the self, not just for others, but for the observing, striving, thinking self itself.

In these and other discussions of the nature of men's needs there are certain recurrent problems that must be faced, one of them being a two-stage problem: (1) What is the relation of the physiological condition of man to his needs? (2) What is the relation ,of a given physiological state to the genetic endowment? Treated simplistically, it is a "nature versus nurture" problem. On the one hand there are those who, like Machiavelli, Rousseau, and Freud, believe that motivational drives are given at birth, the problem being to channel them, and if necessary to restrain them, through education. On the other hand, there are those who, like Locke and Mill, believe that the individual is more or less plastic at birth, and can be taught to want almost anything, for better or worse. Plato, it seems, lies somewhere in between these views: men, like metals, have intrinsic qualities, but they can be taught to fill social roles. The modern equivalent of these contro-

15 See David C. McClelland and others, *The Achievement Motive* (New York: Appleton, 1953).

16 Douglas P. Crowne and David Marlowe, *The Approval Motive* (New York: Wiley, 1964).

17 Robert Sears, "Dependency Motivation," in *Nebraska Symposium on Motivation, 1963* (Lincoln: University of Nebraska Press, 1963), pp. 25-64. See also Glen Heathers, "Acquiring Dependence and Independence: A Theoretical Orientation," *Journal of Genetic Psychology,* 87 (1955), pp. 277-91.

18 Erik Erikson, "The Problem of Ego Identity," in Maurice R. Stein, Arthur J. Vidich, and David M. White; eds., *Identity and Anxiety* (New York: Free Press, Macmillan, 1960), p. 81.

versies is revealed in the conflict between physiological psychiatrists and psychoanalysts, between the Sheldonian somatotypists and the social psychologists. The modern posture is to ask, first, what is the contribution to a tendency for a given type of behavior (and thought) of the physiological endowment and what is the genetic character of that endowment? And second, what is the social learning that shapes and uses this endowment to produce that behavioral (and thought) tendency?

The second persistent problem is an evaluative one. Put simplistically, again, it asks, "Is man 'good' or 'bad'?" and at first it seems to be a quarrel among those who believe that the important social drives are inherited or given, that is, those who speak of "original nature" or "natural man." Rousseau says men are "good," but made bad by society; Freud and the Christian church (and some would say Hobbes, though I disagree) have said that he is impulse-ridden, selfish, and sinful at birth, but can be taught to restrain his evil impulses and, with help, to desire the good of others. Yet even among those who focus primarily on learned needs and drives, the designation of some drives as "good" and others as "bad" is evident; one can see in Maslow's discussion of "esteem needs" a "good" component, "the desire for strength, for achievement, for confidence," and a "bad" component, "the desire for prestige, status, dominance, attention." More than that, the social philosophies competing for acceptance inevitably seek to encourage some needs (which are often regarded as more "natural" or more "basic") and discourage others, as when the social Darwinists encourage dominance and aggressive needs and discourage dependency needs, while utopian socialists encourage "belongingness and love needs" and discourage "recognition-status" and, usually, "physical comfort." One might say that the problem of education was to channel bad needs (aggressiveness) into socially useful outlets (economic competition).

Some acts and thoughts are instrumental, that is, they yield their satisfactions in their capacity to bring about a satisfying result, and some are consumatory, that is, they are satisfying in themselves. An authoritarian, who sees the world in hierarchical terms, may express equalitarian ideas without conscious hypocrisy in order to preserve the good opinion of his equalitarian friends. The functions of these particular ideas are *extrinsic* to his personality; they serve a need not related to the content of the ideas, his need for social adjustment. Any other idea would have done as well. But, as may well be imagined, these equalitarian ideas do not sit well in the psyche of such a person; they have no resonance with his inner needs, his deepest and enduring values. Under other circumstances, where he is not so constrained by the requirements of the situation and hence is free to choose resonant, inner-need-meeting ideas, he would select ones reflecting his sense that the world is a jungle, that power over others is enjoyable, that many people are unworthy of equal treatment, that a social pyramid is indeed a lovely piece of architecture. The functions of these ideas, we would say, are *intrinsic,* for their content matches his personal needs. In the analysis of the functions of ideas in the lives of the students reported below, we attempt to confine the analysis to intrinsic functions, the ways in which these ideas meet the inner needs of the young men under the microscope.

Finally, there is the matter of the number of needs or motives with which men are endowed. There are those who think men have many basic irreducible needs, and those who believe there are relatively few, with perhaps many disguises. On the one hand we find Thorndike listing more than fifty needs [19] and Murray listing more than twenty-seven; on the other hand, Freud was content with only one at first, gratification of the libido, or Eros, a lonely motive later to be joined by another, the death wish, Thanatos. As the study of motives developed, this question of few or many was seen to turn in part on the fruitfulness of linking social motives to some physiological source, an inclination that naturally reduced the number of motives, contrasted to the value of focusing more specifically on the way motives are socially learned. Perhaps even more importantly, in the current state of knowledge, the question of numbers of motives turns on the difficulty of working with a long list of relatively homogeneous categories balanced against the advantages of a shorter list of less homogeneous categories of motivation. This problem of parsimony *cum* bluntness versus multiplicity *cum* differentiation poses a difficult choice. McClelland and his associates suggest two criteria for inclusion of a need in a basic list: (1) the motive must be very widely distributed, perhaps in some form almost universal, such as, in their glossary, needs for affiliation, for power, and for achievement; and (2) the motive must depend upon anticipated emotional gratification based on previous experience. In this latter sense, a person might have a "need to be liked" if he expected that he could win the affection of others because in the past he has done so and found it rewarding. [20] On the other hand, much experimentation shows that frustration of a drive or need seems to increase the drive to satisfy it. The two themes are not incompatible over time; indeed, they work together. A person learns a need through rewarding experience, but it may be intensified through frustration. McClelland does not, in fact, enumerate the motives that satisfy these two criteria, but says that "with these two limiting criteria, it should be possible to come out with not too long a list of motives common to all

---

19E. L. Thorndike, *The Original Nature of Man* (New York: Teachers College of Columbia University, 1913).

20McClelland and others, *Achievement Motive,* pp. 75-77.

men."[21] Perhaps. As we shall see, we come out with a list of ten needs useful in the analysis of the gratifying qualities of political ideas.

NEEDS SERVED BY IDEAS: AN INTERPRETED APPRAISAL

Each man's concept of human needs reflects his interests, his research, and the general state of working thought on the subject at the time. With more than a glance over the shoulder at Murray, Maslow, and others, let us set out the array of human needs that seem, on reflection, most adequately to account for the political thought, at least of young middle-class men, and perhaps of a much larger group as well. Here they are: (1) cognitive needs: learning, curiosity, understanding; (2) consistency needs: emotional and logical and veridical, the kinds of needs satisfied by the reduction of dissonance; (3) social needs: affiliation, approval, being liked; (4) moral needs, satisfied by the appeasing of conscience and/or by giving the impression of rectitude to others; (5) esteem needs: worth, status, importance; (6) needs for personality integration and identity clarification; (7) needs on occasion (but for everyone at some time) for the expression of aggression: the desire to injure; (8) needs for autonomy, freedom, the removal of constraint, and the experience of choice; (9) the need for self-actualization: development, growth; (10) the need for adequate instrumental guides to reality, object appraisal, and attainment.

    1. Cognitive Needs. The need to know and understand, which Maslow thinks is an independent basic need, could be interpreted as merely instrumental to such other basic needs as the need for safety or the need to earn a living, somehow, but the evidence seems to be against this instrumental view. There is an independent need to interpret experience, a persistent curiosity, a desire for knowledge, a need for cues in placing oneself in the social universe, defining rights and duties and expectations, reciprocal relations, and more than that, for giving these "placings" meanings or rationalizations. By classifying things and each other, men add properties to what they see, enlarging its significance, giving themselves cues for proper feelings and perceptions. We say of a certain state that it is a "dictatorship," suggesting, to Americans, that one should be against it and see the associated acts as restrictive of freedom. How should one feel? What should one "see"? The individual seeks cues on these matters. They are, in one sense, the meaning of meaning.

    The apothegms and cliches that pass for theory among ordinary citizens (most of us most of the time) give cues for a "useless" understanding, an

---

21*Ibid.,* p. 81.

understanding that wants to know *why* in matters that hardly affect us. The child's persistent "Why?" and the primitive mythologies relating things beyond man's control illustrate this pursuit, this drive. Similarly, as every storyteller and historian knows, men want to know "what happened next," even in Wonderland, even in ancient Cathay.

At more elevated levels of education and understanding, the pleasure of creating larger intellectual constructs embodies the exercise of a skill, something said to be satisfying in itself.

Murray suggests that there is a need for *play;* is idea manipulation a form of adult play? Is there something in political discussion and thought that satisfies some of the same needs as anagrams and Scrabble? Beyond this, perhaps, *curiosity* is a motive in itself, for that great animal experimenter, Harry Harlow, found that "monkeys can and do solve mechanical puzzles when no motivation is provided other than the presence of the puzzle."[22] Harlow believes curiosity is an independent motive. Achievement needs, the need to meet some internalized standard of excellence, may be enlisted in all forms of thought; certainly the construction of a better argument would qualify. Perhaps, too, some quasi-aesthetic sense aroused by an "elegant" solution, where parsimony combines with logic to give a form of gratification, is at work. There is even a theory that as one goes up the phylogenetic scale, as one moves from primitive to more advanced civilizations, and as a child matures, there is apparent to the observer a development from concrete (taxic or stimulus-bound) thinking to abstract thinking.[23] It is almost as though there were some force in life urging it toward more complicated and more abstract and more useful ideas, ideas with better fit to reality; in Smith, Bruner, and White's terms, a force toward better and better "object appraisal."

"Cognitive needs" are composite, including, as suggested, (a) a placing or orienting function, which tells both what to see and how to feel and respond, (b) a play function, (c) a curiosity function, (d) an achievement function, (e) some aesthetic functions, and, overall, (f) a security function, all guided by some continued search to make ideas and reality, words and things fit together better.

One might say, too, that one seeks knowledge in order to seek further knowledge, a metacognitive function, for in order to collect new information a person needs, as it were, bins in which to put it, labels to tag it, handles

---

[22]Harry F. Harlow, "Mice, Monkeys, Men, and Motives," *Psychological Review,* 60 (1953), pp. 23-32; reprinted in McClelland, ed., *Studies in Motivation.*

[23]K. Goldstein and M. Scheerer, "Abstract and Concrete Behavior: An Experimental Study with Special Tests," *Psychological Monographs,* 53 (1941), whole no. 239. There are some closely related concepts in Jean Piaget's *The Moral Development of the Child* (New York: Free Press, Macmillan, 1965).

to grasp it with. Men need the concepts appropriate to the information they would acquire. Thus it is that one idea can serve to improve memory and give utility to sensation and observation. Moreover, since ideas draw meaning from other ideas—as when, say, the concept of "welfare state," through antitheses and discrimination, gives meaning to the concepts "capitalism" and "socialism"—learning serves as the basis for further thought and for further learning. Everyone, in a hit-or-miss fashion, engages in a kind of programmed learning, where one thing must precede another to give it meaning and make it usable. So it is with political ideas.

Finally, political ideas, like other kinds, are the means of economizing time and effort, for they give the means for habitual and easy responses (if a man is a Democrat, he is, some might say, associated with undesirables; if he is for civil rights, he is probably for urban redevelopment as well). One cannot be rethinking these matters all the time; ideological reflexes are essential to daily living. Men are curious for that piece of information that tells them "the rest," often, paradoxically, stifling further curiosity.

In his list of values, Allport suggests a type of man, "the theoretical," who is interested in truth and draws his satisfactions from searching for and perhaps finding something he regards as "true," whatever it may be. Lasswell suggests that one of the eight values of man is enlightenment and another is the employment and enjoyment of a skill. Men not only need to know, they appreciate knowing and knowledge; they value it.

2. The Need for Consistency and Balance. If the mind undertakes this search-and-seizure operation on the world, seeking to know it and give it meaning, however primitive, however minimal, the intake is perception mingled with thought from which concepts or "cognitions" emerge (to guide further perception). These elements or cognitions must somehow fit together; if they do not, a person is uncomfortable with what he knows, and seeks to readjust the elements so that they do fit together in a way that reduces the strain. "The existence of nonfitting relations among cognitions," says Festinger, "is a motivating factor in its own right," producing a drive like hunger or avoidance of pain.[24] Broadly speaking, there are three ways in which ideas must fit together: (a) The cognition should fit reality (theories should fit the evidence, effects should follow causes, established expectations should be confirmed); this is termed veridicality. (b) Statements must follow the rules of logic, avoiding fallacies recognized in Western thought, the undistributed middle, contradiction; this is called logical inconsistency. And, in a somewhat different vein, moved by somewhat different but no less strong motivating forces (and one more universally experienced), cognitions

---

[24]Leon Festinger, *A Theory of Cognitive Dissonance* (Stanford: Stanford University Press, 1957), p. 3.

should have emotional harmony or balance. While this will be explicated at greater length in the discussion on motivational conflict (Chapter 4), the basic idea rests on men's preference to have favored objects or concepts (like the self) positively related to favored concepts, qualities, or events (like good looks or success) and disfavored objects or concepts (like a political opponent) negatively related to similarly disfavored concepts or qualities. With two concepts each of which may be favored or disfavored and related conjunctively or disjunctively to each other, eight combinations are possible, of which half are dissonant or unbalanced and painful.

One wonders about the propriety of including such a need among the roster of basic needs energizing thought; somehow it seems not to be on a plane with the need to get along with people, or the need to express anger. Our ambivalence is reinforced by the realization that dissonance reduction often reflects a kind of characterological weakness, like the intolerance of ambiguity which is said to characterize authoritarians, for it implies an inability to face unpleasant "facts" and a drive to rearrange the world so that one's predilections are flattered. Yet, in a larger sense, it might be seen as part of the need to achieve some harmony of the emotions consonant with the rules of the intellect, combined with an economizing of effort or avoidance of the difficult and painful task of thinking things through anew every time the familiar order is challenged. Many of the works on basic needs and values and on the functions of opinions in the personality were developed before the theories of cognitive dissonance or balance were given much currency; perhaps it is for this reason that the need for consonance or harmony is slighted.

One often sees the principle at work in ideological discussions. S. M. Lipset, an old socialist and clearly an academic liberal, sets forth a reasonable and persuasive case on the "authoritarianism" of the working class,[25] a case that, if believed, would create a cognitive dissonance among socialists and communists everywhere: the working class (a favored concept) is positively related to authoritarianism (a disfavored attribute), and a howl arises from these quarters. One of their own has turned on them, and heresy, not skepticism, hurts most. Former Vice President Hubert Humphrey, a historic liberal, supports the American war effort in Viet Nam; antiwar liberals, in order to reduce their dissonance, first disbelieved the reports, then attributed them to the requirements of the office ("The real Hubert Humphrey is not for it"), reducing dissonance in two of the ways most commonly employed. Could it be said that Rousseau, clinging to his theory of the goodness of mankind and his democratic inclinations in the

---

[25]S. M. Lipset, *Political Man* (Garden City, N.Y.: Doubleday Anchor, 1963), pp. 87-126.

face of man's evident fallibility and selfishness, reduced the dissonance by reconceptualizating "the will of all" into a vague concept of "the general will," not to be tested by observable vote or decision?

3. Social Needs and Values. Perhaps, to an American audience at least, one hardly has to stress the ways in which ideas serve men's needs for "belongingness and love," for "love and affect," for "affiliation," so familiar are we with the problems of conformity, of the "other-directedness" of the "organization man" and the "marketing personality." This "social adjustment" function is stressed by Smith, Bruner, and White, as it is by others who have thought about this problem. It is a feature of many studies of small groups, in which men have adjusted their attitudes toward Russia, their perceptions of the length of a line, the movement of a point of light, the pitch of a tone, so as to fit their ideas in with those of others, even, sometimes, against the clear evidence of their senses. For some men, this is quite conscious—as we shall see, for example, in the case of a young man who says that when he got to college he quickly decided he would have to adopt the prevailing norms of that college because, being Jewish, being from a little-known school, being physically small, and having no real dynamic qualities of his own, he would need to do this in order to get along. But, too, we shall see the opposite: men who become radical in the presence of conservatives and create an image of themselves as "angry young men" in defiance of the pressures around them. Moreover, since the social functions of ideologies—their functions for society, not the individual—are so often said to be the improvement of interpersonal relations, providing means of cooperative work, improving group morale and solidarity, and rationalizing sacrifices and restraints, it must be the case that political ideologies tend to have these functions for individuals as well. It could not be otherwise.

Yet, of course, political ideas are also partisan, generated and maintained in conflict, organized to support the group interests of contending factions. Thus, at the same time that they serve to improve some interpersonal relations, they must also damage others. One might say that it is their capacity to meet both needs that gives them their power to satisfy; they meet the need for affection and belonging *and* the need to express and legitimize hostile feelings, the antagonisms built up in a life inevitably met with frustrations. The nature of the politics of a society will, in some measure, depend on just this balance of needs served, the need to express love and the need to express hate, the need for consensus and the need for dissensus.

But, as so much contemporary writing tells us, the pattern of conflict in society, like the pattern of association and friendship itself, does not simply separate one man neatly from his opponents and rivals and associate him with his friends and fellow partisans. Rather, he has a number of reference groups, ideal and real, whose opinions differ in such a way that if he adopts one set of ideas to accommodate to a valued group, he threatens to make himself less popular with another.[26] It is at this point of internal conflict that the social adjustment problem becomes interesting, for here the man must devise strategies of thought and evaluation which take into account (a) the importance of an idea to him, (b) the risks of losing the good opinion of some group, (c) the gains promised by ingratiation with another; and in doing this, he must consider not only (d) what these groups believe, but (e) how they value him on other grounds, (f) their likely reaction to disagreement, and (g) what it would cost him in consistency and self-respect if he changed his ideas, or, alternatively, if he changed his group allegiances.[27]

Maslow says that those who have most nearly satisfied their needs for love and belongingness early in life can later, when some question of, say, personal integrity is raised, best do without such evidence of the love of others.[28] Thus needs are, here as elsewhere, complexly related to a person's history of need satisfaction. The social adjustment needs seem to come in an infinite variety of shapes, sizes, and colors, ranging from the "neurotic need for affection" which Horney says is associated with an inability to give affection in return, through the search for popularity, as a symbol of affection without the real thing, or the need for and fear of intimacy, reflected in several of our cases, to the varieties of altruistic love, some of them reflected in Murray's term "the need for nurturance," that is, a desire to give help to others. And, as it is expressed in the language of needs, so also, perhaps preeminently, love is a value, the core of religion and morality, not so much in the getting as the giving ("Love thy neighbor," not "Seek love from thy neighbor"). It is in this form that Allport's list has it: "The social man prizes other persons as ends, and is therefore himself kind, sympathetic, unselfish";[29] but in Lasswell's list the emphasis is on the value of love received, of affection gained.

It is, I think, in this area of love and hate, affection and its opposite, that the distinction between the intrinsic and the extrinsic properties of ideas is most important. For it is here that a man may gain the affectionate support of his comrades by expressing a philosophy of hate, a situation that

---

[26]See Herbert H. Hyman and Eleanor Singer, eds., *Readings in Reference Group Theory and Research* (New York: Free Press, Macmillan, 1968). Some of the properties of the group milieu and reference groups for the Adams College men are discussed below in Chaps. 4 and 5.

[27]For additional theoretical interpretations of conflicting reference groups, see Leon Festinger, "A Theory of Social Comparison Processes," in *ibid.*, pp. 123-46.

[28]Maslow, *Motivation and Personality*, pp. 89-90.

[29]Allport, *Personality*, p. 229.

must have occurred many times in the barracks and beer halls of Nazi Germany. On the other hand, a person who really loved and trusted his fellow men might, in his pacifism or equalitarianism or civil rights advocacy, alienate his companions, at what cost to himself it would be hard to say. (But, of course, there are pacifists who adopt their views to provoke their parents to anger, and advocates of interracial brotherhood who are filled with anger and hate.) This dual function of ideas, their capacity to move others and to express one's own love-hate impulses through their content, requires the most careful sorting out; but, at least in ambiguous situations where social conventions are somewhat obscure, the matching of content and inner needs is likely to give greater weight to the idea that serves this intrinsic function.

4. Moral Needs and Values.   It is a curious thing that neither Maslow nor Rotter, neither McClelland nor, indeed, Murray, stresses a need for propitiating the conscience, slighting, so to speak, that element of Freud's basic trilogy, the superego. Murray, it is true, refers to people's defenses against blame in the term "blamavoidance," by which he means "to avoid blame, ostracism, or punishment by inhibiting asocial or unconventional impulses. To be well-behaved and obey the law,"[30] and elsewhere the needs to "preserve one's good name," and "to avoid shame and humiliation," but these are not the materials out of which that inner state of guilt is made; they do not suggest internally enforced ethical codes, but only a desire for moral appearances. In referring to moral needs and values here, I intend to cover both guilt and shame, both the propitiation of the conscience and the sense that it is dangerous to violate a conventional moral code.

Is there such a need? John Stuart Mill says that there is no such primitive or original need for morality, but only a learned association of one's own happiness with that of others. Rousseau suggests that men are born with what might be called a conscience. Freud says that men are born with a need for love but not morality; that is the product of the internalized social codes and prescriptions learned from the parents. Cahn, divorcing the sense of justice, a major ingredient in any moral system, from concepts of natural law, indicates that in some form the sense of injustice is universal.[31] As social constraint, morality is indeed universal, and the attempt to make its strictures part of the personality is a feature of every educational system. Lasswell includes "rectitude" as one of the eight values, but Allport does not mention "ethical man" among his six types, although "religious man" is not supposed to be ignorant of morals. Certainly, with this degree of agreement and support, it does no violence to common belief

---

[30] Murray, *Explorations in Personality,* p. 65.
[31] Edmond Cahn, *The Sense of Injustice* (Bloomington: Indiana University Press, 1964).

to include morality among the basic needs for which ideas are functional, are gratifying.

Political ideas are functional for this feature of the human system by their capacity to legitimize, rationalize, moralize a man's own acts of *obedience,* which might otherwise offend his sense of independence; his acts of *aggression,* which otherwise might offend his sense that hostile acts are immoral; his acts of *sacrifice,* which he might otherwise resent, considering them collective depredations against his purse and person; and, of course, his acts of *revolt* against authority, which otherwise might offend a deep-seated inhibition against challenging parental surrogates. In this sense ideologies are indeed the springs of action, the levers whereby ideas prompt movements.

Politics is the area where men seek something for themselves, usually presented at least as something for their group or faction, and probably also as something in the public interest. It is an arena of selfish interests, yet it is the domain where talk of the public interest has its greatest currency, not only as rationalized self-interest, but also, at the official level, because some concept of what is better for more people must enter into the calculations of responsible officials if the polity is to survive. The function of political ideas, then, is not only to help displace private emotions onto public objects and rationalize these in terms of some concept of public interest. Political ideas deal with interests, clearly conscious and fully accepted, and place these within the framework of some overall concept of the general welfare. They relate self to others, and in doing so call on moral codes and conventions to give legitimacy and "meaning" to political life.

Contrary to popular belief, it is, I think, easier for most men to believe that their positions in society are somehow "just" or merited than otherwise.[32] It saves them what they most dread, an obligation to attack the foundations of the system, to alienate themselves from the values of the society, to cut themselves off from the nourishing flow of sentiment and solidarity which pours from the established religious and secular authorities. This is true for most men; but some, particularly those isolated from the main cultural stream or bulwarked behind the social barriers divorcing their group from another, or marginal in some way to the main group affiliations, are more relieved to find corrupt the society that dealt them their hands. In either case, the rationale that accounts for a man's place in society is a moral one, and political ideas express these moral sentiments better than almost any others. They fill that need.

5. Esteem Needs and Values.   Somehow self-esteem seems to be bound up with all activity; it seems to be an ingredient of all other needs.

---

[32]See my *Political Ideology* (New York: Free Press, Macmillan, 1967), pp. 161-86.

Certainly a person's self-esteem hinges on his concept of himself as moral; guilt might be described as the disappointment with the self over the failure to live up to some moral code. Self-love and self-esteem may be validated through the affection of others. Careers are the vehicles of self-esteem. But it has never seemed enough to leave this need as merely the spirited ghost of other needs; it has had to be given a status of its own—as Maslow does with his basic esteem needs, as Rotter does in his use of "recognition-status" as a basic need, as Crowne and Marlowe do in seeking to measure the approval motive, that is, a fairly widespread "tendency to avoid self-criticism," and in their test conditions "to choose self-evaluative statements which . . . portray a stereotypically acceptable self-image."[33]

The relationship between a person's self-esteem and the way he thinks other people perceive him is intimate because, inevitably, over the long haul men do tend to see themselves as others see them. They have, as Robert Burns requested, that gift. It has often been remarked that the problem of self-respect for those who are discriminated against by society, preeminently the American Negro, whose status is flagged by his skin color for all to see, have great difficulty in achieving that level of self-respect which would enable them to believe in their own capacities and so to utilize them to the full. It is a matter of timing; genuine self-esteem, built with loving care into the structure of the plastic psyche early in life, seems to reduce the craving for evidence of the esteem of others in adulthood. For it is doubt about the self that creates that craving. Just as the Calvinistic code made doubt about one's predestined state of grace a lever for the hard work and striving characteristic of the Puritan ethic, so doubt about one's worth creates the striving for ever refreshed evidence of worth reflected in the deference or plaudits of others, those little reassurances that still the qualms of doubt. Certainty of low worth breeds apathy; doubt breeds striving. As Adler pointed out, a modest inferiority complex is one source of ambition; as we shall see in our cases, it is the germ of a politics of status, and it is a great help to the Republican party.

Almost everything that one does is freighted in some measure with an increment of self-esteem or a decrement thereof; or, if the act be public, it will imply some change in the esteem of others. How, then, shall we isolate those features of behavior and thought which are, more than others, expressions of this need? Crowne and Marlowe, as we have seen, sought to measure the "approval motive" by testing people's tendencies on attitude tests to "fake good," that is, to say they liked or did certain things they thought they ought to like or do, but which in fact people rarely did like or do, and to say they did *not* do certain things that people usually did do, but

---

[33]Crowne and Marlowe, *Approval Motive,* p. 189.

felt guilty about. This would be one way to measure the need for social approval or respect, the need for the esteem of others.

Another way is to see what aspects of life are stressed in talking about oneself; whether or not a person is paying special attention to "what other people will think," whether or not an act is fraught with "loss of face," or, to employ the Greek phrase, with jeopardy to his *philotema,* or to his honor, or to his prestige. Does income buy experience or sensuous gratification, or does it buy esteem? Does a promotion bring opportunity for the exercise of skill or power or opportunity to carry out some purpose, or status and respect? Does achievement satisfy some "instinct of workmanship" or achievement motive, or does it prove something to others?

There is a third way: ask people to speak directly about their sense of self-esteem. With enough insight, they may say something important about the part it plays in their own lives, the things that diminish it, the way they earn it. These last two methods are the ones I used.

The enjoyment of the exercise of power over others might have its source only in the fruits such power brings, money or the advancement of some goal, but there might be more to it than that. There may be something about imposing one's will over others which, as in the case of Woodrow Wilson, gives satisfaction of a secret, almost intrinsic kind.[34] It is for this reason, no doubt, that Rotter lists "dominance and power" as one of the basic, but of course not universal, human needs; and Lasswell lists power as one of the eight values, a value yielding deference; and Allport and Sanger list "political man" as a basic type, interested in power. But there is also wisdom in the common interpretation of the man who "likes to throw his weight around," acts bossy, or engages in unnecessary show of authority and power. The common interpretation is that this behavior "makes him feel big"; it is a restitution to the small man of the sense of bigness he cannot find, unaided, in himself. It is often a feature of the official's desperate search for self-esteem, under the borrowed mantle of government or other institutional authority.

Again the extrinsic facets of political ideas meet men's needs in one way, the intrinsic in another. Men gain, or think they gain, the esteem of others by expressing greater love of their country than another, a greater willingness to sacrifice, a greater appreciation of the founding fathers, or, given a different audience, a greater daring in criticism, a greater sophistication regarding corruption, or, again with a shift in circumstances, a greater knowledge of the way the government works. But the intrinsic satisfactions that come with ideas resonant with the need for esteem are of another

---

[34] Alexander L. George and Juliette L. George, *Woodrow Wilson and Colonel House* (New York: Dover, 1964).

character, and are reflected, for example, in a set of ideas that places one's own group at the pinnacle of honor, as when a scholarly political scientist devises a government in which the experts have the greatest authority, or when a philosopher elaborates the reasons why philosophers should be kings. The concept of popular sovereignty is accepted by most people and, I think, helps to keep governments stable because it helps to put the people, their self-esteem flattered, one notch higher in their own eyes.

6. Personality Integration and Identity Formation. The Burmese politician, struggling to achieve some consistency in thought and action, some interpretation of himself in the role he has chosen at a time of national troubles, experiences one kind of "identity crisis."[35] In that case we are looking at the problems of a man in a role, caught between the demands of two cultures. But if we take a view of men as men, of their human condition, we will find generic conflicts not associated with any special role or cultural situation, for it is the nature of man to oppose one tendency to another, one need against another. Were it not this way, each appetite or need would require external restraint to bring it to a halt, as the Russians are said to ask the government to provide for them a "moral corset" to protect them against their own self-indulgent tendencies.[36] Or, one might say, the man who does not schedule his satisfactions, by opposing tomorrow's needs against today's desires, is sick as well as feckless, just as he is sick if his restraints overwhelm his desires. Inner conflict is inevitable; it is the way they are worked out that measures a man's "wholeness," his health and capacity for fulfillment.

Given this situation, I am surprised to find so little attention to "personality integration" or "ego synthesis" in the discussion of motivation, although one can see its shadow in the term "self-actualization," meaning the realization of a man's potential. Lasswell's "well-being" refers to the inner sense of satisfaction that comes with health and fulfillment; it is certainly a value, but it is not the same thing as personality integration or a successful identity formation. Smith, Bruner, and White speak of the function of an opinion in externalizing just such inner conflicts as we have in mind, but this is less for the purpose of healing or reducing these conflicts than to express them, to bind them, to contain them, as when a man responds inappropriately to an authority because he is externalizing some long buried hostility to authority arising in his relations with his father.

The most common kinds of disintegration are those arising from six sources: (a) conflicts developing from the repression and maldirection of the

---

35 See Lucian Pye, *Politics, Personality, and Nation Building* (New Haven: Yale University Press. 1962).

36 Henry V. Dicks, "Observations on Contemporary Russian Behavior," *Human Relations,* 5 (1952), pp. 111-75.

sex drives, (b) those emerging from unacceptable hostile and angry feelings, (c) conflicts over tendencies to retain some dependency (irresponsible) status of which one is ashamed or which are inappropriate to one's responsibilities, (d) conflicts over one's posture toward authority and those who embody it, (e) the related but separate conflicts over demands for autonomy and choice in interdependent situations, and (f) the inevitable and ceaseless conflicts over the tendency to indulge the self versus the moralized need to care for and share with others. Then, to extend this harassing list, there are the scheduling problems already mentioned, the weighing of now against tomorrow, combined with the natural conflict created by consideration of the cost, in sacrificed alternatives, of every act, every expenditure, every option chosen. All of these, at every level, involve the overall problem: restraint against indulgence, a defining characteristic of personality.

The resolution of these conflicts with a minimum of repression (that is, the stuffing of some need down into the dark hole of the unconscious, where it rarely sleeps, but rather finds another outlet, illegitimate, uncontrolled by conscious processes of reason) is an important part of the identity-formation process, for such minimum of repression permits a person to describe himself to himself accurately, to know himself in depth. The other most important part of identity formation is the social placing of the self, something we referred to in describing the need to orient oneself in the world, but which here, with the concept turned to reveal another facet, refers to the way in which a man seeks to know what properties are appropriate to himself through knowing what groups he belongs to, what roles he occupies, what cultural traits are indisputably his own. If personality integration is largely self-referential, identity formation is, in addition, inclusive of the self-in-society theme, the understanding of "who I am" through understanding "where and what I am." It is in this way that a man is helped to a party identification by an identification with a social class, for, he will reason, if the Democrats are the party of the workingman, and I am a workingman, then I am appropriately a Democrat; they are for me and I am for them. A person thus consumes and uses ideas, such as loyalty to party, to fill out his identity, to make it resonant with his image of himself in society, and to reduce the need to account for discrepancies that might, if challenged, bother him. They justify his position in society ("It is lack of education that accounts for my relatively low status"; "It is hard work that accounts for my being better off than others"), they reduce the "absurdity" of pain and suffering ("I suffer for a cause: my children will be better off"). Ideas give continuity to life, and identity is a vehicle for self-continuity. To change the language, political ideas contribute to the pattern maintenance of the self by linking the self to an ongoing social purpose, beyond the self, enlarging the self.

   7. The Expression of Aggression.   Aggression is behavior and thought aimed at the injury of an object where the injury is the point of the act.[37] It emerges from anger and may be learned through the usual processes of rewarded effort, or may be imitative, or may be what seems to be the natural outcome of frustration. There are more or less aggressive individuals, and, since group norms vary, more or less aggressive populations; that is, individuals and populations who, although not chronically aggressive, are more easily aroused than others. And, of course, there is a variety of restraints against this mode of expression, especially fear of the consequences and guilt over the violation of a moral inhibition. Yet, in spite of fundamental differences in aggressive feelings and in spite of the power of the restraints, the need to express these feelings is powerful and universal.

Politics invites the expression of aggressive feelings because it is an area of conflict, partisanship, frustration. It is that domain of thought and action where rival interests confront each other, and where rival policies must be "thrashed out." There is always an "opposition," legitimate or otherwise; there are always rival candidates for that scarce resource, power. At the same time, politics is an area of moralized sentiment, as in patriotic songs and verse; it is where expressions of solidarity are quite meaningful; it is where common history is made.

For these two reasons, then, the ubiquity of aggressive feelings and their special relevance to politics and political thought, that I include this need and motive in a basic list.

8. Autonomy and Freedom.   If we think of the crux of the question of lack of freedom as resting on restraint of choice, and if we include in this restraint three things—lack of opportunity or resources, coercion in its various manifestations, and psychological inhibition or incapacity—we shall have, if not a single meaning, an area of meaning sufficient for our purposes. Is the need for such free choice widespread, intensely felt, basic, that is, developed early and dominant over other needs on occasion? Readers of *Escape from Freedom* may doubt this, but they should recall that Fromm was referring to a setback in a process that he said had been going on for four hundred years.[38] For these times, one might give the need a higher place than for other times. But in all times, I would argue, the child has, year by year, successively broken through restrictive barriers; the adult has been restive over the restrictions over some domains of traditional or expected choice, even in traditional society. It is a strong motive force and one that is so intimately related to problems of authority and its internalized components as to produce internal conflicts and guilt.

And, of course, it is, like aggression, woven into politics, so that hardly a fiber does not imply some theme of governmental restraint, coer-

---

[37] Here, as in the later analysis of aggressive thought, I rely heavily upon Leonard Berkowitz, *Aggression* (New York: McGraw-Hill, 1962).

[38] Erich Fromm, *Escape from Freedom* (New York: Rinehart, 1941).

cion, impediment to "doing what I want to do." This is the other side of the concept that government, as the source of frustration, is the instigator of aggressive feelings. Frustration is exactly what we are talking about: the interruption of purposive behavior. More than that, the relationship of imperialist or colonizing countries to their dependent peoples is fraught with restrictions on the sense of freedom. Whatever they do, because *they* do it, these metropolitan nations are seen as deprivers of freedom, of autonomy. Government is law and law is prescription and restraint, however lightly worn.

There is something more in this relation between the need for autonomy and political thought. Some men work together easily as teams of co-operative and more or less equal partners, while some find the constraints of compromising their own purposes, of dealing with independent personalities, difficult. It is reasonable to suppose that these differences in need for independence of others or need for interrelations with others should find their way into political thought. Almost all utopian philosophies, for example, create images of totally harmonious interacting individuals, and hence the means for reconciling conflict are undervalued and underdeveloped. So devious is the mind, however, that a perverse principle prevails: those utopias are more likely to be invented and accepted by persons who have difficulty in getting along with others. The utopian solution expresses their need for something they cannot achieve now, or, it seems, even in the faction-ridden societies of utopian radicals.

It takes no further argument, I think, to convince one that the need for freedom and autonomy is both a strong and enduring motive and preeminently relevant to political thought, realistic or utopian.

9. Self-Actualization. After the conflicts are dealt with and contained, if not resolved (because, as we said, it is a condition of life to be torn between competing needs), and after an identity is shaped and made usable in life's struggles, there is that further need to achieve, to be fulfilled and to fulfill oneself, to "become" something. I am combining here the thoughts of others and synthesizing them under the term Maslow and Rogers employed in a larger sense, "self-actualization." It embraces the need for achievement that seems to be such an important ingredient of social and economic development and is defined by its apostle and student, David McClelland, as the desire for "success in competition with some standard of excellence."[39] Rogers speaks of "self-actualization" in the following terms: "Rather than many needs and motives, it seems entirely possible that all organic and psychological needs may be described as partial aspects of . . . one fundamental need." "That need," he says, is "to actualize, main-

---

[39] McClelland and others, *Achievement Motive,* p. 110.

tain, and enhance the experiencing organism."[40] While rather vague, this concept means, among other things, self-knowledge, autonomy from external forces, development of various parts of the self. Allport, in a literate and moving essay on *Becoming,* speaks of this concept as follows:

> We maintain . . . that personality is governed not only by the impact of stimuli upon a slender endowment of drives common to the species. Its process of becoming is governed, as well, by a disposition to realize its possibilities, i.e., to become characteristically human at all stages of development. And one of the capacities most urgent is individuation, the formation of an individual style of life that is self-aware, self-critical, and self-enhancing. . . . Becoming is the process of incorporating earlier stages into later; or when this is impossible, of handling the conflict between early and late stages as well as one can.[41]

All of these center on "the need to grow," to develop, to employ the teachings of experience in a progressively more fruitful manner. There is something serendipitous in this, something melioristic, but also something recognizable and real.

But is it the kind of need that can be gratified by ideological manipulation, by thought and imagination? Here I would refer the reader to the concepts of human nature in the works of the classical political philosophers. One of the criteria for sorting out these concepts is just this: the educability of mankind, the possibility of growth, the plasticity of a basic material that is not instinct-ridden or inherently aggressive or distrustful. Is it too exotic, then, to believe that, because men populate their vision of the world with creatures like themselves, those who are themselves aware of a self-actualizing need, and not frustrated in this, will think of political man as a self-actualizing developing person, and so will conceive of political systems that promote individuation and growth, giving them that quality of freedom in which this is possible? For John Stuart Mill, the criterion by which a political system is to be judged is this, and only this: the kind of intellectual and moral growth (self-actualization) it produces. Democracy is a better system than any other just for this reason.[42] Through encouraging people to take responsibility for their own and others' destinies, it develops their faculties. And who will deny that Mill himself experienced a dominating need for self-actualization?

10. Instrumental Guide to Reality (Especially Economic Reality). One need merges with another. Earlier I suggested a need to know and

---

[40] Carl R. Rogers, *Client-Centered Therapy* (Boston: Houghton Mifflin, 1951), pp. 487-88.

[41] Gordon W. Allport, *Becoming* (New Haven: Yale University Press, 1960), pp. 27-128.

[42] See especially his *Representative Government* in the Everyman edition (New York: Dutton, 1910), which includes *Utilitarianism* and *On Liberty,* p. 193.

understand expressed in self-orientation, curiosity, speculative play, the pleasure of consistency and logical relations, creativity, considering these to be somehow satisfying in themselves, not merely for their usefulness in helping a man to get what he wants. Here I have in mind the usefulness of ideas in helping to get what one wants, a utility criterion, especially since, whatever other needs they satisfy, men must "make a living," must satisfy some of their economic wants. Maslow lists physiological needs and safety needs; merging these, I am saying here that ideas gratify these needs by guiding men correctly in their groping with nature and society, things, and men. Allport lists "economic man," whose criterion is utility; Lasswell lists wealth (and well-being) among his values; Rotter, limiting his list to learned needs, lists comfort ("learned need for physical satisfaction that has become associated with the gaining of security"). And Smith, Bruner, and White make "object appraisal" one of their three functions of opinions, for "the holding of an attitude provides a ready aid in 'sizing up' objects and events in the environment from the point of view of one's major interests and going concerns."[43] I mean more than appraisal, however; I mean guiding a man in getting the object. It has always seemed to me that the term "object appraisal" was too passive, possibly because it was developed to deal with opinions on Russia, about which the respondents couldn't do very much, and not about taxes and playgrounds and pensions, all of which are much more important as well as accessible to their own influence for most Americans.

Political ideas are guides to reality and instruments for getting what one wants. There are whole theories of political behavior built around the single hypothesis: the individual seeks through his vote, and through the opinions and "ideologies" that support his vote decision, to maximize his gains, generally interpreted as economic gains.[44] The interest theories of political life are generally of this persuasion: interest groups seek "more" for their members; parties are coalitions of interests. Here is where the thought associated with a well-informed "felicific calculus" (Bentham) would find its power to gratify; here the ideas behind a rational ends-means chain find their rewards.

In the analysis of the case material that follows, I have selected certain needs on the basis of one criterion, the needs revealed as the young men talked about the use to them of their political ideas. I do not exhaust the inventory given above, but rather have selected from it those needs that

---

[43]Smith and others, *Opinions and Personality,* p. 41.

[44]See, for example, Anthony Downs, *An Economic Theory of Democracy* (New York: Harper, 1957). Downs, more than others, allows for nonmaterial utilities, but, since these must be measured in common units for the theory to work, there is always a tendency to return to the units of utility measurable by money.

are illuminated by the material. The needs to be explored are: (a) the need to be liked, a kind of social adjustment, (b) the need to express and control aggression, (c) the need to appear moral to the self and others, and (d) the esteem needs or the need for status, particularly among the young men who suffer from marked feelings of inferiority. I shall then deal with the way men's relations to their families generate strivings that affect their political views. First we shall consider those whose continued identification with their families serves a variety of needs, most of which seem marked by the advantages of continuing the struggle for identity within the family orbit, a search for (e) identity continuity. Then we shall explore the needs and motives served by disidentification with the family, the rewards of (f) autonomy. Often I shall refer to needs for wealth and status, but these are best interpreted as the means whereby men serve more basic needs, such as self-esteem or autonomy with respect to others. But before entering upon this analysis, let us consider how these motives work in the general economy of the personality.

3

Guide to the Selection
of a Congenial Political Idea

Tracing an idea to its "source" in some energizing motive is difficult even with the aid of thoughtful ideological self-analyses. To most people both their own political belief systems and their motives and needs are relatively unknown. In the hope that it will serve in linking "source" and political expression, I offer the paradigm set forth below; it is not a "model," but rather a convenient scheme for guiding exposition.[1]

MODEL OF A POLITICAL "IDEA MACHINE"

Some Internal (remembered) or external (heard or seen) (1) *message or cue* (involving perception of both source and content)

engages or arouses (2) one or more *motives or needs,* stimulating goal-attaining or need-reducing efforts, which are

shaped by a person's (3) *modes of conflict resolution and strategies of defense* (ends-means rationality, withdrawal, projection, reaction-

---

[1]Compare the following paradigm, devised to account for belief systems in a social group or society: "For any society: an *existential base* creating certain *common experiences* interpreted through certain *cultural premises* by men with certain *personal qualities* in the light of certain *social conflicts* produces certain *political ideologies"* (Robert E. Lane, *Political Ideology* [New York: Free Press, Macmillan, 1962], pp. 415-16). In the present paradigm I focus much more on the "personal qualities"; the emphasis is not on political beliefs, but on political thinking.

formation, etc.), and sets in motion a process of search for and selection among ideas promising to satisfy these needs.

The Person's Consequent search and selection is guided by:

(4) other features of his *personality,* including his concept of himself (definition and appraisal—that is, his identity: self-awareness, internalized models, self-esteem) and his "objective self" (intelligence, capacities, energy, emotional balance, perseveration, unconscious tendencies), and

(5) the engaged elements of his *philosophical and operational belief system,* including his concepts of reality (time, place, cause), concepts of authoritative knowledge, concepts of morality and other values (as relating to and embodying his needs), and concepts of scarcity and abundance (reflecting his mood); and

(6) his *learning strategies,* including his curiosity (embodying his "need to know"), tolerance of ambiguity and dissonance, openness to dissent, use of concrete and abstract modes of thought; and

(7) his concepts of "the world of people for him"—his (frequently conflicting) *references to groups and persons* serving as models, audiences, antagonists, communities of life space, and his characteristic mode of interaction with them; and

(8) his characteristic *definition of the situation,* specific to each occasion, including his interpretation of what is expected of him, what is at stake for him in terms of motives, values, and goals; all to produce

(9) his *political and social belief systems,* including both doctrine and styles of belief.

In the use of the paradigm, I think it will be most helpful to explicate first the beliefs themselves (9), the products of the "idea machine." With these in mind, we shall then turn back to the beginning to discuss the arousal of a motive (2) and some of its properties. In Chapter 4 we shall discuss motivational conflicts (3) and in Chapter 5 refer to elements of identity and personality (4), philosophical premises (5), learning strategies (6), the social milieu (7), and the situation (8) as these men may define it for themselves.

THE BELIEFS THEMSELVES

Political Doctrines.   The general problem of linking motivation with political interpretation as shaped by personality, mind, and milieu is often made more difficult by the perceived lack of relevance of politics and government to the things people care about and strive for. This became most clear to me when I asked the working people of Eastport, an eastern industrial city in the United States, about the ways in which government affected their lives. They were living in a government-supported housing project, drawing occasional unemployment benefits, sending their children to public schools; most of them were veterans of World War II. They said, "It don't affect me," or, after much thought, they said slowly and doubtfully, "Well, roads and schools, I guess," or perhaps, simply, "Taxes." The relevance of public affairs to their own welfare, the very grounding of their lives, was not perceived.[2] This strikes from the news much of its meaning.

What is required, then, is a set of bridging concepts about politics and self, the self as a citizen, as "subject," a user of public facilities, a beneficiary of freedom and justice, as well as a voter and, perhaps, a cousin of a man who knows somebody. The conceptual framework for linking an individual's life to political phenomena is often missing, although history, in the form of war, and racial disturbances, and depression, sometimes supplies the missing link. A political ideology or belief system forges many such links.[3] It is these links in the minds of students which we shall examine.

One set of bridging concepts between self and politics is provided in the themes common to the history of political philosophy: equality, freedom, justice, power (concentrated or fragmented or shared), violence and revolution and war, and, most recently, alienation and allegiance. Another set is provided by the themes and concepts employed in the current dialogue between communism and democratic capitalism: property, colonialism, representation, exploitation, social class, and much more. But the issues in contest between communism and democratic capitalism are not, in this framework, the salient ones for the population of students we have examined. These young men are not political philosophers dealing with traditional issues in order to clarify them, even in their own minds; they are American students trying to frame a social philosophy that has relevance to them, now, and "now" means personally on the threshold of a career and historically in the period of an expanding but challenged welfare state

---

[2] *Ibid.,* pp. 131-200.

[3] The relationships between political belief systems and "value orientations" are obscure. See Florence R. Kluckhohn and Fred L. Strodtbeck, *Variations in Value Orientations* (Evanston, Ill.: Row, Peterson, 1961).

and a contested set of international responsibilities.

Under these circumstances, the important dimensions of social philosophy are, with some overlap:

1. *Opportunity for the able versus opportunity for the underprivileged.* This is the one dimension of conservatism-liberalism (and it has many) that is salient for this group. It is the dimension that, I believe, most nearly serves as the axis around which other issues cluster.

2. A sense of *exclusiveness,* of belonging to a variously defined elite group with a right to special privilege, power, and respect, versus a strain toward *inclusiveness,* which accords to others (Negroes, labor) similar rights and respect. Perhaps the central theme here lies in the assumption that "I am (we are) different and better," contrasted to the theme that legally and morally "I am (we are), or should be, the same." For many, legitimacy for feeling "different and better than others" comes through the concept of education.

3. There are no isolationists in this group, but for some the question of internationalism versus nationalism or chauvinism is salient. The three opposing themes here are *support for a world of more or less equal nations versus a world in which the American nation dominates others, versus, again, a world in which only the American scene seems important.*

4. *Government (usually called "big") as a threatening force* manned by "politicians" (bad) and "bureaucrats" (dull) *versus government as a useful instrument,* more or less benign or at least neutral, for solving social problems. The fear of government, which foreign observers have said characterizes American political culture, is sometimes apparent in this young elite stratum, whereas it was not at all apparent in the lower-middle-class and upper-working-class Eastport group.[4] Both groups feel that government should be "strong," but some want it to be more limited than it is.

5. Focus on the going order: *continuity and tradition and stability* (applecarts all right side up) *versus the need for reform, change, and efforts to solve insistent problems.* In this contest of opposing views, each individual shares some ambivalence: there are no proponents of reform who do not worry about continuity and stability, and the advocates of the going order allow an escape clause for "progress"— something that gives them trouble.

6. *Identification with the concept and symbol "capitalism" (or "free*

---

[4]Lane, *Political Ideology,* pp. 131-200.

enterprise") versus neutral or nonsalient orientation to this concept and symbol. Few men reject "capitalism," but some, including moderates and "liberals" (their own term), invoke it, defend it, attack its attackers. The extent of endorsement of the status quo in this group is reflected in the fact that the rallying point and symbol of the reformers is the New Deal. The hallmark of the first group is identification with "business," while the second group tends to identify more with the professions.

7. Allied to the defense of capitalism is the emphasis upon *competition, initiative, risk-taking, and managerial skill*—personal qualities reflecting and testing one image of man—*versus an emphasis upon humanity, compassion, duty toward others.* In this way concepts of personality and of economics tend to be fused.

Even though the men are reluctant to claim that they have well-developed political belief systems, they do refer to themselves as "liberal" or "conservative," and these references suggest the clustering of their beliefs in some systematic way. Upon examination, one can see that these dimensions have a liberalism-conservatism theme, and that they cluster in the following manner:

Liberal	*Conservative*
Opportunity for all, especially underdogs.	Opportunity for the able.
Inclusive personal and social orientation toward ethnic and other groups.	Exclusive personal and social orientation toward ethnic and other groups.
Greater equality for other nations in world affairs.	Focus on priority of American interests and rights.
Belief in positive government.	Suspicion of government, restrictive view of government.
Capitalism as a neutral symbol.	Capitalism as a positive symbol.
Greater acceptance of social change.	Greater faith in the status quo.
No identification with business and businessmen.	Identification with business and businessmen.

In reviewing this short list, we are surprised to find that certain of the staples of political philosophy are missing, even if we grant that these men are writing their "belief systems" and not their "philosophies of government." For example, there is little reference to the preservation of *freedom,* even though one of the personal needs we shall discuss is a kind of autonomy and liberation from certain controls. Apparently the engagement of the need with the perceptions of government is not made.[5] There is some discussion of *order* and *stability* in society, but rather little. Everyone wants it, of course, but these biographies were written before the rash of student protests, urban disturbances, and foreign-policy protests; the government's role in keeping order was taken for granted. *Justice* is rarely mentioned; it is rather subsumed in the issue regarding opportunity for the able versus opportunity for the underprivileged. The organization of government, the *constitutional* arrangements, are ignored. Political philosophy is indeed truncated in these reports of political belief systems—a matter for reflection.

Stylistic Properties.   The distinction between style and content in expression leads to some confusion, since every change in style affects the message content. Nevertheless, there are stylistic facets of belief that are different from the doctrine itself. Often, it seems, the content is more likely to be structured by a situation, or by convention, whereas the form or style of the belief is more directly affected by the personality of the believer. Sometimes these stylistic properties refer to the way a doctrine is expressed, sometimes to the way in which its expression is affected when the believer is challenged, or to the relationship of a belief to action, again a property of the believer. We turn here to a brief analysis of this ambiguous area of the stylistic properties of beliefs and believers.

Abstract versus Concrete.   All nonproper nouns are abstractions, but those with wide scope and those distant from sensory experience we term abstract. Abstract thinking is less reflexive, less stimulus-bound, more analytical than concrete thought.[6] There is, I believe, a tendency for men with difficult motivational conflicts frequently to employ exclusively abstract thinking, to give distance between ideas and their own immediate and conflictful experience.

Normative versus Descriptive.   Between the "is" and the "ought" there is, we are told, an unbridgeable gap; one cannot derive an "ought" statement from an "is" statement, or, of course, vice versa. Political thought is traditionally normative. There is something gained if in the political dialogue of a nation there is a balance between these two modes of expression, but the balance need not be the same in every individual. The common view that conservatives are more familiar with "reality" and at home in talking about what *is* while liberals are more at home in discussing what *ought to be* has very little support in the Adams College sample.

5On the theme of engaging personal values with political opinions, see M. Brewster Smith, "The Personal Setting of Public Opinions: A Study of Attitudes toward Russia," *Public Opinion Quarterly,* 11 (1947), pp. 507-23, and "Personal Values as Determinants of a Political Attitude," *Journal of Psychology,* 28 (1949), pp. 477-86.

6For a discussion of this dimension, see O. J. Harvey, David E. Hunt, and Harold M. Schroder, *Conceptual Systems and Personality Organization* (New York: Wiley, 1961), pp. 24-49.

Rather, it is my impression that the nature of the dominant motive, while it may not alter the balance of descriptive and normative statements, defines the targets of the statements. For example, the desire for wealth and status tends to make both kinds of statements self-centered; both descriptions and evaluations have more to do with "me" and less with society. The need for moral self-imagery, of course, leads to more normative thinking.

I can illustrate one of the complex interrelationships between abstraction and normative thinking by quotations from the biographies of two of the men who have been experiencing intense motivational conflicts. De Vita explains his preference for idealistic (abstract and normative) thinking as follows:

> Liberalism answers my need to avoid competition. Because it is idealistic it is, therefore, out of reality and really above the little details that people are forever arguing about. I needn't worry about any argument that attacks me on the level of everyday reality. On the ideological level I am strong. I can avoid conflict by making my points unattackable. I merely take my political picture out of the realm of discussion.

De Vita likes to dominate but fears conflict, especially when he might lose. By talking about what ought to be in more or less abstract terms, he reduces his risks.

Mintz, another Adams student, favors the "idea" of working-class power, but does not like individual members of the working class, whom he finds vulgar. He, too, finds abstract and idealistic discussion congenial. He says, "I am a visionary of a sort in that my interest in politics arises largely out of how much improvement I can promote in the status quo."

Personification versus Impersonalism. Some statements of political belief systems read like a play or opera; they are about people. In other cases the belief system deals with impersonal entities like "the state," or "society," or "constitutionalism." Either may be democratic or authoritarian; that is, their substantive content may have many equivalencies. Yet there are subtle distinctions here. For example, there is some evidence that liberals who need to be liked personify "the government" so that it behaves like a person in an ingratiating or warm and human manner. On the other hand, the belief systems of certain conservatives often refer to the essence of government as a "strong man" at the controls. The impersonal state becomes personalized by giving it human attributes; the references to the "strong man" are impersonal, making him the symbol of order and control.

Partisan Decisiveness versus Qualified and Hedged Opinions. It is often said that the authoritarian has an inability to tolerate ambiguity and reveres decisiveness and the will, and there is some evidence for this in the biographies. On the other hand, the sources of indecisiveness and an unwillingness to make even a tentative political commitment are less clear, for they reflect a sense that too much is at stake and also a sense that too little is at stake, conflict between the opinions of parents or other reference individuals and groups, and chronic states of indecision where nothing ever seems much superior to anything else. In this connection, concepts of "independence" and "alienation" and "withdrawal" need to be reevaluated to illuminate their inner meaning and the sources of the underlying conflicts.

Assertion (Sense of Authority in Self) versus Citation (Search for External Authority). Some men believe that their opinions are worth something because they are based on their own conclusions; others give weight to an opinion because it is based on someone else's conclusion, with which they agree. Research has shown that a sense of the low worth of one's own opinion is, not unexpectedly, rooted in low self-esteem,[7] and the biographies bear this out. Further, there is some suggestion in our material that those who wrap their views in the authority of a doctrine (Thomist, Burkean, Freudian) tend to be politically conservative. It is as though the conservative's self-serving stance needed the support of an external authority, while the middle-class liberal, apparently somewhat less "selfish," takes responsibility for his own views.

Personal Responsibility for Society versus Nonresponsibility. Students have, or used to have, little power to effect social change or to prevent it, yet they differ greatly in their allocation of responsibility for what must be done. There are nonalienated observers who make judgments but who view the world as somehow disengaged from their own efforts and lives. In some sense they care about the outcome, but do not see it affected by their own action.[8] These are not necessarily the men who cannot make up their minds on their party affiliation; rather they are men whose ambitions are defined exclusively in private career terms. Others, including some ambitious for wealth and status, see themselves as guiding the nation in some vague capacity. It is a matter of linking one's own self-concept to social concepts in such a way that it is an appropriate expenditure of effort to *do* something about what is happening all around one. Social critics, of course, are not necessarily responsible actors in the social drama.

Other stylistic properties will be discussed as the various needs are explored, but these are some of the most important ones.

---

[7] Carl I. Hovland, Irving L. Janis, and others, *Personality and Persuasibility* (New Haven: Yale University Press, 1959).

[8] Compare the concept of "political divorcement" in Lane, *Political Ideology,* p. 173.

MOTIVES: THEIR PROPERTIES AND
IDEATIONAL PRODUCTS

If these are some of the main political beliefs that people talk about, think about, care about, how may we link them to the underlying motives that they serve? To do this, we must first outline some properties of the motives themselves and their relationships to ideas. We are assuming here that motives are not narrowly topic-bound, but rather are more or less characteristic of the individuals in many situations. The men say this of themselves, characterizing their *personalities* in this general way, and not at all limiting their self-descriptions to their relationships with politics.[9] But, to be clear on this point, one may distinguish between a *chronic* need or motive and a low *threshold* for motive arousal.[10] The latter is a better description of the nonphysiological motives we are discussing: certain needs are latent, but easily aroused. Thus, when Caplan, one of our sample, says, "There is what some people call a 'Napoleonic complex' which seems to seize us short ones, which makes us more aggressive," we take this to mean not that he is always aggressive, but that aggressiveness is easily aroused in him. As it happens, his early socialization into radical politics by a beloved socialist grandfather gives political themes a high stimulus value for him, and he is especially (but not exclusively) aggressive on political matters.

Motive Arousal.   If people's motives are best conceived as a characteristic readiness to respond in a certain way, what kinds of stimulus situations elicit motivated responses? We know that experimentally one can arouse fear,[11] anger and aggressiveness,[12] sexual drives,[13] achievement motivation,[14] and other motives,[15] but perhaps motive arousal revealed in

---

[9] In the series of studies edited by Hovland and Janis, the concept of "topic-bound" responses to communication is developed. See, for example, p. 4 of *Personality and Persuasibility*. The matter obviously relates to the question of "motive extensity," treated below under "strength of motivation."

[10] The difficult question of whether a motive is, as the psychoanalysts say of primary motives, "constant," or whether it is best characterized in terms of latency and easy arousal, need not concern us here. Attention is called to the psychoanalytic formulation discussed in Chap. 4. So far as I can see, whatever consequences this distinction has for the theory of motivation, they do not affect our inferences on political thinking. Hadley Cantril, among others, seeks to ground motivation in "the appetitive systems": "Sentio, Ergo Sum: 'Motivation Reconsidered,'" *Journal of Psychology* 65 (1967), pp. 91-107.

[11] Irving L. Janis and S. Feshbach, "Effects of Fear-Arousing Communications," *Journal of Abnormal and Social Psychology,* 48 (1953), pp. 78-92.

[12] W. Weiss and J. B. Fine, "The Effect of Induced Aggressiveness on Opinion Change," *Journal of Abnormal and Social Psychology,* 52 (1956), pp. 109-14.

[13] R. A. Clark, "The Effects of Sexual Motivation on Fantasy," in David C. McClelland, ed., *Studies in Motivation* (New York: Appleton-Century-Crofts, 1955), pp. 44-57.

[14] David C. McClelland and others, *The Achievement Motive* (New York: Appleton, 1953).

[15] Charles N. Cofer and Mortimer H. Appley offer a bibliography on motivation of almost 2,000 items in their *Motivation: Theory and Research* (New York: Wiley, 1964).

life histories is different. We find some suggestions in our biographies of the ways motives can be aroused to guide political responses. Rather than focus on "objective" properties of the stimuli, as persuasion experiments do (message content, communicator characteristics, media characteristics, situation),[16] we turn to the "functional" properties of the stimuli, that is, the relationship between stimulus and predisposition. In this context, what is most important in motive arousal is the way in which a situation or topic or person (a) enters into old quarrels and identifications with parents, (b) facilita'tes or frustrates current life strivings, and (c) threatens a fragile portion of a person's self-image. Of course, these three are closely interrelated. In the following vignettes we see how *general* latent motives are stimulated by *specific* political themes and stimuli.

Old Quarrels and Identifications with Parents.   When Svenson is confronted with "anti-intellectual" arguments, he responds in ways he regards as uncharacteristic for him. He links these to an enduring and bitter quarrel with his father, who is prone to anti-intellectual statements. He responds aggressively in these situations, with an aggressiveness linked to his intense desire to be autonomous from home influences and the implied dependency status.

Confronted with questions of tolerance toward all religious groups, Simpson admits to anti-Semitic feelings. He believes this may be due to his envy of the reputedly assertive qualities of Jews, for his relations with his mother have led him to believe that he lacks an appropriate assertiveness. He fears this passivity in himself; the fear is aroused by thoughts of the successful assertiveness of Jews.

Facilitation and Frustration of Current (and Anticipated) Life Strivings.   Niven, whose parents have risen from lower-middle-class status, builds dream castles in Scarsdale. Confronted by questions of party choice, he associates Republicanism with policies that will permit him to realize his dreams of wealth and with partisanship appropriate to the status to which he aspires.

Ransome has been taught by parents with whom he identifies that socialism inhibits competition; his own experience in competitive situations has led him to believe that he can succeed in an open competitive society. He associates certain Democratic regulatory policies with socialism and an inhibition of competition, and consequently he responds to these topics with a moderate hostility, strengthened by his identification with his father.

Threats to Self-Image (Identity).   Mintz is uncertain of his "true sexual motivation" and worries about homosexual tendencies. He believes the working classes have a kind of earthy sensuality and wholesomeness in

---

[16] These are the characteristics of the "observable communication stimuli" studied in the Hovland and Janis series mentioned in n. 9, above.

this regard. His attitude toward working-class "underdogs" is one of fear of intimacy and distant empathy. His mild socialist inclinations permit him to rationalize and bind these feelings, while the boisterous, self-confident, bourgeois campus leaders threaten them.

Buenello is a strong, hostile, and, by his own admission, authoritarian personality who admires strength in others. A Catholic who once considered the priesthood, he has developed a moral facade of "walking in the image of Christ." Interested in politics, he is ambivalent about the mixture of power and "corruption" he sees there, responding with a denial of partisanship and withdrawal of political activity until he can join (lead) a moral crusade in politics.

Dobb, the wellborn son of a prosperous Republican family who has been given "all the advantages," believes that his wealthy grandparents have tended to "bribe" him and rob him of his independence. Several times he mentions his "desire to stand on his own two feet" and to avoid all "crutches," including religion and parental help in finding a job. He chooses roommates with much less wealth than he has and limits himself to their standard of living. Conservative Republican politics evoke these old quarrels, frustrate his striving for independence, and threaten his self-image as a man who "sides with the less fortunate" and "stands on his own two feet."

In this perspective, the important feature of the stimulus that arouses a motive or engages a need is the characteristic of the communication, the cue, or the topic that engages a pattern of striving already laid down. The importance lies in the way it is assimilated to an older and more enduring life problem: what an individual was, is, might be, and wants to be.

Strength of Motivation.   Certainly motives vary in their strength, their power to dominate other motives or to change ideas. Yet the concept of "strength" is ambiguous. McClelland employs it to mean three things: (1) motive dependability, that is, the probability that a given motive will occur during a day or week or some other period of time; (2) motive intensity, that is, the degree of emotion that is aroused when the motive is enlisted and the intensity of feeling about the response the motive elicits; and (3) motive extensity, that is, the variety of cues or situations that touch off this motive, as, for example, the variety of different kinds of situations interpreted as power-threatening, or likely to deprive one of affection.[17]

We have little evidence on the first of these (motive dependability), but motive extensity is revealed in several ways. Those who seek affection or "need to be liked" are sometimes quite selective; if the need is mixed with status needs, the arousal of this need depends upon the status of the individuals whose affection is at stake. Trumbull and Novak need acceptance

---

[17] *Achievement Motive,* p. 69.

from high-status groups; Lamb seeks acceptance and affection from the working-class men on a maintenance crew; De Vita needs to be accepted, respected, or liked by everyone, but his competitive (power-seeking) needs create conflicts for him. So also with the need to express aggressive feelings. Those who are most aggressive toward their fathers tend to be aggressive in their political thought; but Svenson, torn by his need for human warmth, is eclectic and unsure in his aggressive thought.

As for motive intensity, the language employed is a clue. Some of the expressions of needs reflect what seems to be a *cri de coeur,* a desperation for need fulfillment, while others seem relatively cool. Contrast these two passages:

> I also am troubled by various feelings of general "unlovable-ness" which are diffused and not so easily described as feelings of sexual inadequacy. The history of my relationships with girls is a long string of failures, ineffectiveness, and inertia   [Mintz].

> I am always trying for general approval or for someone's special approval, but it must be obtained on my own. This striving is evident in my relationships with people . . . but it must be achieved without the aid of a crutch [by which he means favors and ingratiation]   [Dobb].

Mintz's need to be liked is apparent throughout his biography; it arouses deep emotion, as the above words imply, and it is evoked in a variety of situations. This is not true of Dobb.

Unfortunately, it is not the case that the greater the need intensity, the greater the effort to satisfy the need and the greater the chance of success.[18] For example, McClelland found that too strong an elicitation of the achievement motive prior to tests of imagination and storytelling usually had a freezing effect; it reduced the subject's capacity to set the fantasy processes in motion.[19] Similarly, Crowne and Marlowe found that those who needed social approval most and tried hardest were least likely to succeed.[20] To be effective, it seems, striving must be tempered by some kind of perspective, control, patience, perhaps consideration of countervailing values.

Similar Needs Often Have Different Inner Meanings.   I can illustrate this point with two instances of underlying variation in the meaning of a motive or need as the individual expressed or revealed it. (a) Novak and Rogers, two insecure, ethnocentric reactionaries, need status, the kind that

---

18McClelland, ed., *Studies in Motivation,* p. 438.

19McClelland and others, *Achievement Motive,* p. 103.

20Douglas P. Crowne and David Marlowe, *The Approval Motive* (New York: Wiley, 1964), p. 165.

money buys. Both are explicit about their sense of relative financial deprivation in childhood; their friends had bigger houses, better cars, belonged
to better clubs. The need for wealth is probably symbolic of many things,
but in an important sense it is a restitution of childhood deprivations, a fulfillment of childhood wants. This is quite different from Simpson's desire to
be rich; for him it seems to be a symbolic measure of an assertiveness that
he feels he lacks. Relatively prosperous, he fears he is too passive; his
mother has told him so.

(b) Both Lamb and De Vita want to be liked by others, but find this
very difficult; both say they are lonely, both feel a sense of strain in intimate
personal relations. Their need to be popular and to win social approval
serves, when it is gratified, to relieve doubts about their likability. But Mc-
Donald, who also wants to be liked by his peers and fears loneliness, seems
genuinely to enjoy the company of others. He is an adopted child and isolation raises archaic fears of not really belonging.

Consciousness.   Speaking of the seven needs on his list, Maslow says,
"These needs are neither necessarily conscious or unconscious. On the
whole, however, in the average person, they are more unconscious than
conscious."[21] In part it is this very point that makes ideological self-
analysis so useful, for at the same time that it brings political beliefs
struggling into the light of the conscious world, it does the same for certain
needs and motives; we see them blinking in the daylight to which they are
newly exposed. But, of course, much still remains at the unconscious level.

One of the most interesting and, in the long run, most important
characteristics of modern society is the increase of consciousness; consciousness of the roots of religious thought, the conventional bases of our
institutions, the immoral foundations of our race relations, and, not least,
the psychological sources of political thinking. If this is so, what are the differences in political thinking between those who are self-consciously aware
of their needs and motives and those who are not? Self-awareness is a
capacity for introspection, a consciousness of the self-serving nature of one's
own ideas, a capacity to reflect on one's own inner conflicts, a familiarity
with the unrationalized version of the self, a knowledge of one's goals and
values, and a willingness to engage seriously in ideological self-analysis
(reflected, for example, in De Vita's immense satisfaction in his own discoveries about himself).

In my study of the working-class and lower-middle-class men of Eastport, I found that these men had what seemed to me to be a tendency to
"treat the self as a somewhat impersonal object with needs and qualities to
be appraised from an outside perspective," although, of course, the men

---

[21]A. H. Maslow, *Motivation and Personality* (New York: Harper, 1954), p. 101.

differed from each other in this "objectification of the self." Comparing those who reported at some length on their inner emotional life and those who could not, or at least did not, I concluded that "the best of the citizens were *not* intimately or sensitively self-aware, while some of the undemocrats and alienated men were much more concerned with what was happening inside themselves."[22]

A close content analysis of the twenty-four cases, scored for self-awareness in this sense, reveals several things about the relationship of self-awareness to political thought among these better educated and more intraceptive men. For one thing, the elements of self-awareness do not cluster: those who were most aware of their own areas of insecurity and anxiety were not likely to be more aware of their own life goals or the direction of their ambitions. On reflection, this seems reasonable: the very anxieties reported tended to prevent the clarification of goals and purposes.

The second point is that a complex and subtle analysis of one's own conflicts and problems does not seem intimately related to a complex and subtle analysis of society and politics. In spite of my experience with working-class men, this was contrary to my expectation, for I had thought that the injunction to "know thyself" was preliminary to the civic injunction to "know thy society."

Third, I had anticipated that liberals would be more introspective than conservatives, but the evidence for this is very slight indeed. The reactionaries, those who limited their social goals to whatever gave them, the better educated elite, opportunities for wealth, were just as likely to be introspective and intraceptive as the liberals, defined as those who sought greater opportunity for the disadvantaged.

Yet if self-awareness of one's own motives and conflicts (but not necessarily life goals) is not related to complexity of social analysis or to liberalism, it does seem to have one political implication: it seems to help a person develop a political belief system with a better psychic fit, one that responds to his inner needs and hence is likely to be more stable than the political belief systems of the unaware. As I read the statements, there is less pretense, less projection and reaction-formation and other unconscious defenses reflected in political beliefs among the self-aware. And I think this is as true of those who express doubts about their political beliefs as those who are quite certain, for the doubts are couched in terms of the weighing of alternatives. The capacity to look at and write and talk about the less attractive side of one's own personality, the tolerance of the seamy side of self, is, as it should be, related to the tolerance of doubt and ambiguity in politics.

Reinforcement. Is it necessary to reward efforts to satisfy a need

---

[22]Lane, *Political Ideology,* p. 410.

for that need to persist in a person's arsenal of motives? Perhaps there is a need for reinforcement for such learned motives as affiliation, autonomy, cognitive balance. On this point, two things are likely to be true. Unless a person has had some experience that leads him to think that motivated behavior (such as striving for achievement, power, or affiliation) will be rewarding, the motive is unlikely to be operative, that is, to guide behavior and thought. Second, it seems to be the case, with people as with rats, that uncertainty of reward is a positive incentive toward need-satisfying effort. Crowne and Marlowe suggest that it is doubt about social approval that increases efforts in that direction;[23] Lasswell and others have suggested that it is doubt about one's power or significance or worth that leads to striving for public offices.[24]

The point is important for several reasons. One of the two men in our sample who were certain to be rich was not at all interested in making money or in taking his parents' money (at least not now). Those who mentioned wealth and status were those whose parents dedicated their lives to the effort to attain them, or who saw wealth as a validation of their assertive qualities, or who were insecure on other grounds and saw wealth as a means to security and self-validation. (In all of these cases, the men tended to be appropriately conservative.) Their doubts drove them on. On the other hand, given their background and current status, there was a high probability that they would become wealthy. Thus in these cases, and in those where the young men needed affiliation and acceptance by others or a moral public image, both doubt (uncertain reinforcement) and some realistic anticipation of success were present. Further, when one of the men found that realistically he could not attain his aims of achieving power and status as a member of the Adams "in-group," he switched to the "out-group" and became a rebel leader. At the same time, he switched from Republican to Democrat, indicating his belief that a liberal ideology was more congenial to his current efforts. Uncertain (not negative) reinforcement shapes the motives that then find their own appropriate supportive belief systems.[25]

Control.   There are several theories of the way in which needs or drives or motives are controlled and limited. One is that a drive is reduced by achieving its aim; it becomes satisfied. Thus the man who needs to be liked may satiate this need by the experience of being liked and then turn to other goals. The second is the catharsis or discharge theory; aggressive

---

[23]Crowne and Marlowe, *Approval Motive,* pp. 162-65.

[24]Harold D. Lasswell, *Power and Personality* (New York: Norton, 1948), pp. 39-58.

[25]"Attention to the factor of possibility of attainment is crucial for understanding the differences in motivations between classes and castes within our own population and between it and other poorer countries and cultures" (Maslow, *Motivation and Personality,* p. 77).

[26]This view runs contrary to considerable theory and research on aggression. See Leonard Berkowitz, *Aggression* (New York: McGraw-Hill, 1962).

feelings are reduced by expressing them.[26] If Trumbull could have told his father what he thought of him, he would have felt better and reduced his chronic anger. The third runs counter to these: a person with multiple needs pursues those that are rewarded; the appetite grows by what it feeds on. The limits of striving toward impossible (unrewarding) goals are found in satisfying goals reflecting other needs (sublimation, perhaps). All three seem to be at work, but they work differently for different motives, and have different resolutions for different intensities.

Those who were made to feel inferior in childhood because of their lack of stature or athletic ability may have turned instead to intellectual pursuits. In college, these are rewarded, and their sense of inferiority seems noticeably to decline. They do not express their feelings of inferiority in their current political thought; their radicalism or conventionalism (depending on how other needs combine with their inferiority feelings) loses its edge. This is a combination of the satiation of status needs and the substitution of one domain of striving for another.

The aggressive personalities tend, in some ways, to continue their aggression, and the matter of controls becomes crucial. As we shall see, those whose aggression is limited by a feeling that "aggression does not pay"—that is, it is not rewarding *to them*—remain conservative. Those whose aggressive feelings are inhibited by some sense that aggression hurts others tend to be liberal. Aggressiveness is not related to the direction of thought, but the mechanisms of control—guided, of course, by other qualities of personality—are important in shaping political thought.[27]

Those who need to be liked seem insatiable, for their very efforts at being liked are often dysfunctional. Yet their entry into careers and work life with other payoffs may provide other satisfactions, and later, no doubt, their political ideas will be shaped more by economic interests than by concern for the opinions of others. Some of them, worried about their conformist tendencies in college, indicate as much.

Motives and Milieu.   The social psychologist Clark showed pictures of nude women in an art class and found that overt sexual responses were inhibited in elicited responses, whereas covert and symbolic sexual themes were increased. He showed the same pictures in a fraternity setting and found a substantial increase in overt libidinous expression.[28] The point is clearly made: some motives need "licensing" in order to be openly acknowledged and expressed, and situations differ greatly in this respect. In the biographies, the need to achieve dominance over others—the power motive—is rarely (though occasionally) mentioned; it finds its expression in

---

[27]See Chap. 9, on "The Inhibition of Aggression."
[28]See n. 13, above.

political thought somewhat obliquely: as an emphasis on "strong" government, in which the individual plans to play a part. The conservatives stress
their roles as members of the educated elite who will share in power, while
the liberals stress their participation in a welfare state that will regulate
others. Other motives, like striving for wealth, were treated more openly in
the fifties than they were in biographies written in the later sixties. Men
moved by an avowed need for wealth and status tended to be directly conservative and open about their reasons for their conservatism. In college,
men will acknowledge their need to be liked and popular; it is a licensed
motive. But the implication that they tailor their political thoughts to this
end is treated ambivalently by some (though surprisingly candidly by
others). The need to be liked is usually divorced from its political implications, or, often, the implications are discussed and, after some worry,
denied.

Channeling.   The process of growing up is one of channeling and
directing the diffuse motives as they emerge. [29] There is usually considerable
choice in the channels open to need-satisfying action and thought, especially
in an area of thought as ambiguous as politics. In the most general terms,
an individual will seek some ideas that are socially sanctioned or at least
not punished, and at the same time personally congenial, in the special sense
that idiosyncratic and little-known features of his own personality are
matched with ideas that serve and express these personality elements,
modified by experiences of reward, punishment, or substitution-sublimation,
and culturally available in the material he reads and hears.

But, since people have multiple motives and needs, we must turn to the
resolution of the conflicts that this multiplicity occasions.

---

[29]Gardner Murphy refers to the "canalization" of motives, suggesting something like the
psychoanalysts' concept of primary unbound id-related motives as the energizing power behind
the secondary motives such as those we are here considering. See his essay on "Social Motivation" in the first edition of Gardner Linzey, ed., *Handbook of Social Psychology* (Cambridge:
Addison-Wesley, 1954), p. 612.

4

Motivational Conflict and Political Choice

Without some consciously conflicting motives, a person is sick; he is in the grip of an obsession (a special kind of conflicted state). Everyone has a variety of motives that he seeks to satisfy and which must somehow be reconciled or scheduled. In doing this he is shaping the demands to be made upon the political world and the gratification available in political ideas of different kinds. A brief examination of the interrelationships of motives, then, will give insight into the processes of conflict resolution.

THE INTERRELATIONSHIPS OF MOTIVES

"One of the things we mean by personality," says Murphy, is "the tendency for certain *syndromes* of motives to appear in one personality rather than in another."[1] Briefly, then, let us review some of the relationships between motivation and personality. In the first place, personality itself, with its traits and habits, interests and values, defenses and complexes, self-images and identities, is created around the need-satisfying, striving activities of the individual.[2] The motive is the message. In the second place, motives, like values, are both ends and means, consummatory and instrumental, hence "one motive may work through another." The relationship of a consummatory motive to an idea is intrinsic; the instrumental relationship is ex-

---

[1] Gardner Murphy, "Social Motivation," in Gardner Lindzey, ed., *Handbook of Social Psychology* (Cambridge: Addison-Wesley, 1954), p. 611.

[2] Although the characterization of personality as a construct built around a set of motives is central to psychoanalytic thinking, where the motives are in the first place instinctual, this is also the view of such psychologists as Maslow, Rotter, and McClelland. See A. H. Maslow, *Motivation and Personality* (New York: Harper, 1954); Julian B. Rotter, *Social Learning and Clinical Psychology* (New York: Prentice-Hall, 1954); David C. McClelland and others, *The Achievement Motive* (New York: Appleton, 1953).

trinsic.[3] In the third place, motives may be characteristic of an individual, but may have, so to speak, a limited engagement, engaged by one situation and not another (as we shall see); hence dominance relationships among motives change with time and place and circumstance.[4] It is for this reason we discuss social roles and the definition of a situation. Fourth, those motives laid down earlier are more likely to be stronger than those acquired later, and this is especially true of motives learned in the preverbal stages of life.[5] Fifth, those motives with social support are more likely to control behavior than those that must be expressed idiosyncratically and alone. Sixth, although there may be some general tendencies cross-culturally for the hierarchy of need priorities outlined by Maslow to prevail, the resolution of conflicts within the sample of young men here examined is not made easier to understand by ordering them according to physiological needs, safety needs, and social needs. On the other hand, it may indeed be useful to consider that it is only when these are met that the freedom to experiment, grow, and develop to one's capacity (self-actualization) can be found.[6]

More specifically, certain kinds of relationships among motives are discernible in the case material: (a) the conflict between conscious and unconscious motives, (b) the conflict in scheduling need-satisfying behavior, (c) ambivalence about a motive, (d) incompatible motives, and (e) self-defeating motives, as revealed in self-defeating behavior.

Conflict between Unconscious and Conscious Motives.   In the sex-arousal studies mentioned above, the men exposed in the classroom to pictures of nude women repressed their libidinal thoughts in order to satisfy their needs for social approval and perhaps also their sense of themselves as sophisticated, self-controlled students, an identity and a role they prized.[7] In our own material we often find men stating a motive they are ashamed of and denying its force and implications almost in the same breath. Thus Trumbull, a very conservative and ethnocentric member of an elite family, says: "Probably as a reaction against and shield for my admitted feelings of inferiority and insecurity I have developed a trend which I would classify as ethnocentrism," and, within the same paragraph, "I might add, in conclusion, that I firmly believe that most of my prejudices

[3]Maslow, *Motivation and Personality,* p. 106. See above, in Chap. 2, the discussion of "extrinsic" and "intrinsic" relations between motives and ideas.

[4]See M. Brewster Smith, "Personal Values as Determinants of a Political Attitude," *Journal of Psychology,* 28 (1949), pp. 477-86.

[5]See David C. McClelland, *Personality* (New York: Dryden, 1951), Chap. 12.

[6]Maslow, *Motivation and Personality,* especially Chap. 5; see also Maslow's *Toward a Psychology of Being,* 2nd ed. (Princeton: Van Nostrand, 1968).

[7]R. A. Clark, "The Effects of Sexual Motivation on Fantasy," in David C. McClelland, ed., *Studies in Motivation* (New York: Appleton-Century-Crofts, 1955), pp. 44-57.

are true on an absolute scale of values." He has brought up from his unconscious a need for status and esteem. Now he sees, but cannot accept, that this need leads to an idea he cherishes: Jews, Catholics, and Negroes are inferior to him. We catch him at the moment of conflict over this self-discovery. Here, then, lies one of the values (perhaps all too ephemeral) of ideological self-analysis.

Motivational Priority Conflict. It is often the case that men need compatible things, but cannot pursue them simultaneously. The motives must be given some order. Perhaps a person wants high academic achievement and popularity, or the symbols of what might be called "secondary affection" to distinguish it from intimacy and close friendship. It is the scarcity of time and energy that creates the conflict. Everyone has experienced this conflict, for it is a condition of life. What varies is the strategy developed to cope with the problem: tension, fatigue, incompleted tasks, irresponsible behavior, "omnivorousness," or, perhaps, scheduling of life to reward both motives. Novak *had* to get on the crew of the college radio station; he also *had* to achieve high academic standing to outshine his father, whose college yearbook he had virtually memorized. He sought the first to the exclusion of the second and was forced, by his poor grades, to leave college.

Incompatible Motives. Some motives, by their very nature, are incompatible with others. It is not possible to win affection and maintain a constant critical attitude toward the sources of the desired affection at the same time, as Lamb discovered. A man with high standards of "perfection" which he imposes on others as well as himself and a strong "need to be liked," Lamb says, "Quite obviously one cannot object to people the way I do, express it very often, and still expect to be liked." Similarly, King, a politically minded young man, needs to think of himself as independent and autonomous of group pressures at the same time that he needs evidence of his popularity and acceptance. A liberal Democrat, he nevertheless joins the Conservative party in the Adams Debating Society, and then worries about his conformity. He denies that he is a conformist and differentiates himself politically in minor ways, but he becomes self-contradictory in the process.[8]

Ambivalence. A motive may carry two emotional charges, one positive and the other negative. On the one hand, one wants to gratify it; on the other hand, perhaps not. This is most likely to occur when in a given culture the motive itself is under a cloud. Dominance over others is such a motive. Goldberg, a vigorous champion of the Jews *and* of the American culture, reports that he likes to lead others and is uncomfortable when he

---

[8]There is another form of incompatibility discussed briefly under social reinforcement and cross-pressures, below. This occurs when a person is torn by his identification with two or more groups, each of which values a different object of striving.

must follow; he says he plays unnecessarily rough in physical-contact games and throws his weight around. But he does not like this about himself and partially excuses himself by his belief that this aggressive tendency developed through his protection of younger children in the ethnic wars of his neighborhood. Similarly, De Vita discovers in himself a need to dominate others; but this domination is pursued through intellectual superiority and, he says, is never intended to be destructive. Yet he wishes he did not need this quite so much.

Self-Defeating Motives.   People sometimes "stand in their own way"; they seek some immediate goal that blocks their long-run interests, or they behave compulsively, achieving catharsis at the cost of some more enduring goal or purpose. At such times they may ask themselves, "Why did I do that?" Novak reports how he drove away the people he wanted to cultivate by "talking too much," yet he did it time and again. His desire to impress people and be the center of attention was, as he recognized, self-defeating. MacGregor reports that as a boy he wanted favorable recognition from his father, and sought this by trying to best his father in argument, a procedure that merely exacerbated the tension between them. But perhaps this is equally a case of ambivalence, in which he wants also to provoke a war with his father. The situation was a developing one; he acknowledges that at one point this was indeed his motive.

POLITICAL EXPRESSION AND CONFLICT RESOLUTION

There are four important sources of theories on the ways in which people resolve their motivational conflicts: (a) rational decision-making theory, infused with economic modes of analysis; (b) social psychology, emphasizing social reinforcements and the treatment of cross-pressures; (c) concepts of cognitive dissonance and cognitive balancing; and (d) psychoanalytic theory, dealing substantially with the conflict between conscious and unconscious desires. Each of these, of course, suggests ways in which people in conflict situations "choose" their political ideas.

Rational Decision-Making. [9]   The rational way to resolve conflicts among needs (say the need to be liked and the need to assume an independent identity) is to assign net values (gains minus costs) to each course of action or idea, make a transitive list of these evaluated items, calculate the risks and probabilities of satisfying the need, and choose the one with the

---

[9] The rational decision-making described here is an abstraction from economic theories of choice, as seen, for example, in Kenneth Arrow's *Social Choice and Individual Values* (New York: Wiley, 1951). For an important modification of this view see C. E. Lindblom, *The Intelligence of Democracy* (New York: Free Press, Macmillan, 1965).

highest value and preferred risk schedule. It is all conscious, informed, calculated. Ends and means are matched according to probable payoff and loss. Long-term gains are considered along with short-term gains; secondary gain is not allowed to take precedence over or obstruct a longer term and more enduring satisfaction. Time is taken into consideration through an appropriate discounting schedule. Everything is compared with everything else so that the world of values and the world of costs have all been included.

Competing motives may be regarded as an economic problem, or a problem suitable for cost-benefit analysis, where a variety of satisfactions are purchased by expenditures of time and effort and something of value, and the opportunity cost of satisfactions forgone by gratification of the chosen motive is appropriately included in the calculation. Any one good (motive) is pursued until some increment of another competing good (motive) affords greater satisfaction. Thus the motives could be scheduled on a set of indifference curves; that is, in a two-motive system, a set of curves each of which represents the preferred mixture of motive indulgence at the given rate of exchange. Brian Barry suggests that society often must consider equity and efficiency in this light, so much equity being given up in return for so much efficiency according to the quantities of each available and the terms of exchange.[10] In the same way one could think of a rational person bottling up anger in order to win the affection of an individual; he exchanges the momentary pleasure of catharsis (telling the man off) for the pleasure of an enduring friendship or favor. Or, alternatively, a man seeks the gratifications of autonomy (freedom from being told what to do) up to the point where greater achievement is more rewarding; he then pursues achievement satisfactions until some other motive, perhaps his need to see himself as moral, is set out of balance, whereupon he gives time to civic causes. This assumes, according to the curvilinear shape of most indifference curves, that there is a declining marginal utility for each increment of satisfaction from pursuing a given motive, and under some circumstances this is no doubt true.

There is some evidence in our case material to support this theory of rational choice among need-fulfilling activities. For example, Caplan, an aggressive, attention-seeking young man, reported that he pursued a strategy of calling attention to himself up to the point where he found he was losing friends. It took him a little while to realize this (and the inference is that his need schedule changed over this time), but in his later years in prep school he decided that he had surfeited his need for attention and would like more respect from people who were put off by his showmanship. He changed his behavior and moderated his attention-seeking activities.

---

[10] Brian Barry, *Political Argument* (London: Routledge & Kegan Paul, 1965), pp. 5-6.

To the extent that men can make decisions about their need-satisfying activities by economic calculations such as these, one has little trouble in linking ideas and motives, given the information on motive "syndromes" and the features of a belief system that offer "payoffs." This is not readily available information, but the principles to be followed in selecting a set of beliefs up to the point where another set would be more gratifying suggests, for the man with plural motives in considerable strength, moderation and balanced views on almost everything. Few ideas would be "bought" at the cost of alienating friends, few that would seem "immoral" to many people, few that deprived the individual of opportunities to achieve success in his line of work; for in every case, the benefit to him of any given idea carried to some extreme would be less than the benefit of a more moderate idea. He would balance his idea budget as he does his life, and, no doubt, his bank account as well. This is not a necessary consequence of the rational decision-making process of the resolution of conflicting motives; but I suggest that empirically it would work out that way. Intensity of belief (passion) seems to go with extremity of belief,[11] and passion and the system of rational budgeting of indulgences seem unlikely to go together.

Side by side with Caplan's case, however, there is the case of Novak, mentioned above, to illustrate self-defeating tendencies. Novak was also an attention seeker; he sought attention as a child by clever talk, but people said he talked too much. He desperately wanted friends and wanted to impress older boys, but his talkativeness drove them away. Yet he went on talking. Something went wrong with his rational calculation and scheduling of motive satisfactions. Similarly, experiments in motive arousal hardly confirm the theory of rational choice among need-fulfilling activities. Men exposed to frightening films on the effects of tooth decay were less likely to go to a dentist than those who had been less frightened;[12] men who were exposed to messages that greatly excited their desires to tell interesting imaginative stories were less able to do so than those whose achievement motives were less strenuously stimulated.[13] We must put this theory in perspective.

Anthony Downs and other economists imagine that people generally calculate gain and loss to themselves in this way because sometimes they do almost manage to do it.[14] But the conditions that encourage this sort of thing are greatest in economic calculations and diminished in many kinds of

---

[11]See, for example, "The Intensity Component in Attitude and Opinion Research," Chap. 7 of Samuel Stouffer and others, *Measurement and Prediction,* Vol. 4 of *The American Soldier* series (Princeton: Princeton University Press, 1950).

[12]Irving L. Janis and S. Feshbach, "Effects of Fear-Arousing Communications," *Journal of Abnormal and Social Psychology,* 48 (1953), pp. 78-92.

[13]McClelland and others, *Achievement Motive.*

[14]Anthony Downs, *An Economic Theory of Democracy* (New York: Harper, 1957).

political thinking. The conditions facilitating rational decision-making are greatest where cause-and-effect relations are clearly discernible, where gain and loss are measurable in common units (money), where links to old recurring quarrels are slight, where interpersonal relations are contractual and contractual relations are socially approved, where appetites for more of what is at stake (money?) are accepted, and where a variety of motives can be satisfied by the same act, with power, status, wealth, sensuousness, and even respect all linked together. But that is often not the case in political behavior and thought, especially as these deal with distant things.

Social Reinforcement and Roles in College. The particular social setting in which the conflict takes place will reinforce certain outcomes and penalize others. For our sample, the setting is a divided one, for the men come from families whose influence, determinative in childhood, still remains substantial, and yet the arena in which they are working out their current conflicts, the college, requires them to move beyond the family domain. In both situations the class structure, the institutional expectations and interpersonal relationships, and the roles the men are required to play are influential. A few of the social influences on the strategies of the resolution of their motivational conflicts may be mentioned.[15] Their college arena has these properties:

1. It provides a moratorium on consequences, time for indecision and the consolidation of feelings before commitment, lessened penalties for both hesitation and change. It is in this context that one must read the indecision of Trueblood, who believes he must perfect his knowledge before he chooses, and yet declines to inform himself so that he can make the choice asked of him. It is the function of college to give leisure for choice—career choice, moral choice, political choice—and it is the further function of a college to provide diverse information to guide those choices. Conflict resolution takes on a special leisurely and exploratory character in college.

2. College provides distance but not total separation from the home culture; for many of the men it was their first prolonged stay away from home, and for all of them it was the "replacement depot" that disengaged them from one permanent setting and prepared them for another. They were thus "free" to repudiate old beliefs and motives and try on new ones; and they were also "free" to cease the rebellion that may have characterized their home situations and come to terms with a less frightening, less demanding, less coercive, and more equal set of parents. Simpson, for example, feels he cannot choose a political party until he is completely away from home domination, but he is preparing himself now, in college, for that choice.

---

[15] The effects of college education on attitudes and beliefs is summarized in my "Political Education in the Midst of Life's Struggles," *Harvard Educational Review* 38 (1968), pp. 468-94.

MacGregor, on the other hand, finally has his quarrel with his father under a degree of control; only now can he agree with his father's politics without feeling that these are necessarily dictated by the stern and forceful older man.

3. The lack of career creates a kind of "interest gap," in the sense that there is a weakening of the tie between ideas and the way men earn a living, their relationship to property. This opens up the possibility of expressing in political thinking such noneconomic motives as the need for moral imagery and the need to be liked. Indeed, college life is marked by a kind of free market in affiliation, creating opportunities and anxieties that give this motive a dominance it may not have again in a man's lifetime.

4. Along the same lines, the ties between college students and the institutions and elites that have come to be referred to as "the establishment" are loosened; at least, that is true if one acknowledges that although the college is part of "the establishment," considerable disaffiliation and latitude of opinion and behavior are allowed in the student-college relationship. This situation permits, even encourages, a detachment toward conventional arrangements, beliefs, relationships. In these circumstances, combined with the new distance from parental culture, the needs for autonomy and the sense that "no one can tell me what to do" are encouraged, as they may not be under other later circumstances, and certainly have not been up to the college period. For some, this is frightening; the opening up of unstructured choice is purposefully not perceived, or perhaps a new dogma is chosen to fill the gap. Buenello, his mind closed to much of the world around him, is a Thomist; Silver, fearful of change, is a latter-day Burkean; Donaldson finds institutional and ideological answers in union power. More frequently the answer to the new relaxed institutional bonds is to behave and think as though the fetters were still on the ankles and wrists; the hobbled gait and manacled gesture persist.

5. The homogeneity of the society in terms of age, status, and, to a larger extent earlier than now, social and ethnic origins, limits the range of conflicting group references. In the traditional literature on electoral behavior four theories on the influence of social memberships over political choices are common: (a) people who are cross-pressured by conflicting group references (Catholicism, a Democratic-associated religion, versus middle-class status, a Republican-associated status) tend to make late decisions and to withdraw from emotional involvement; (b) if a person takes a deviant position for a given group, under stress he is very likely to come back to the orthodox position; (c) the more homogeneous a community in attitudes and behavior, the stronger the influence on any individual who has deviant inclinations to accept the community norms; and (d) the longer the term of

group membership, the more powerful its effect on decisions.[16] I suspect that the shaping of needs and motives follows somewhat similar rules; men learn from others what to want in life, as well as from their own interpreted experience.

Yet in spite of these general findings, the college community is different from others, and the homogeneity is more apparent than real. In their college years students become less conformist and more individualized.[17] As we have said, the college licenses deviant thought more than other communities. Demographic similarity is not necessarily ideological or motivational similarity: the community is made up of people who will be musicians, engineers, businessmen, army officers, poets, scholars—never again will they come so easily together. A radical rooms with an orthodox man (Simpson), and the latter says of this experience, "I roomed with a very bright boy, but irreligious, immoral, and cynical—a pseudo-Bohemian attitude. We didn't get along . . . [but] I secretly admire this boy now, and have come to realize what an influence he has had on me." Life styles, concepts of the good life, the good society, will diverge. Motivations, under these circumstances, will be given social support from several conflicting sources, and motivational conflict may be much more encouraged than the demographic homogeneity would suggest.

6. The roles these men play include "son," "friend and peer," and "student." As we know from much research, the "part" learned for a given role tends to be adopted, especially if the individual has had to improvise his own script.[18] Thus we would expect that here at college, certain features of the student role would structure the conflicting goals and striving, making a permanent change in need priorities. At the same time, one must be aware of considerable research suggesting that the friend-and-peer role works contrary to this assumption, and that among students, student values tend to have greater weight than faculty values.[19] In our own sample, however, there is substantial evidence that, at certain junctures of life, when the on-

---

[16] These are some of the theories in Bernard R. Berelson, Paul F. Lazarsfeld, and William N. McPhee, *Voting* (Chicago: University of Chicago Press, 1954); and Angus Campbell, Philip E. Converse, Warren E. Miller, and Donald E. Stokes, *The American Voter* (New York: Wiley, 1960).

[17] See Harold Webster, Mervin Freedman, and Paul Heist, "Personality Changes in College Students," in Nevitt Sanford, ed., *The American College* (New York: Wiley, 1962), p. 824.

[18] Irving L. Janis and B. T. King, "The Influence of Role Playing on Opinion Change," *Journal of Abnormal and Social Psychology,* 49 (1954), pp. 211-18; also I. L. Janis and Leon Mann, "Effectiveness of Emotional Role Playing in Modifying Smoking Habits and Attitudes," *Journal of Experimental Social Psychology,* 3 (1967), pp. 334-48. A later study shows that changes persisted eighteen months after the original experiment.

[19] See Lane, "Political Education."

going life struggles provide the occasion, the student role is internalized and needs are changed. Thus Demming, failing in his fight for recognition as an in-group leader, became impressed with the way in which the faculty went about thinking through problems, and the method of inquiry and evaluation characteristic of a scholarly community was given a high priority (and, indeed, he went on to do some teaching later in his career). Similarly, De Vita, as we have seen, found reinforcement in college for his view of knowledge as power; seeking power and dominance, he internalized the scholar's role and became a legal scholar.

In commenting on this, let us recall two of the needs mentioned earlier in Chapter 2: the need to know and the need for cognitive balance (dissonance reduction). The social support at Adams provided reinforcement for the need to know and the capacity to tolerate ambiguity or dissonance. At the same time, the role of student, requiring rehearsal in veridical perception and reporting, helped to structure the expression of this need to know and the capacity to tolerate cognitive imbalances in politics as in other areas of life.

In this special setting, then, certain modes of conflict resolution are encouraged. Men are made more conscious of their competing needs and a greater variety of motives are licensed or reinforced; the consequences of exploratory behavior and thought are reduced both by the lack of immediate career pressures and by the looseness of ties with the establishment; the student role tends to reinforce curiosity or the need to know and to shape the need for cognitive balance so that men more easily tolerate dissonance, solving their problems of cognitive imbalance more by reconceptualization than by withdrawal or incredulity.

Cognitive Balancing. Most concepts or cognitions have not only references (the things in real life they stand for or designate), but also emotional valences, that is, positive or negative feelings that they generate in a person. In politics this is especially true, for it is an area of thought marked by conflict and partisanship. Thus concepts such as voting, segregation, President Nixon, Bill of Rights, all have valences, as the reader can discover by self-examination. The simplest kinds of statements, sometimes called "bands," would then be made up of two concepts (an object and a subject) held together by a relationship (or verb). But the relationship often itself implies some kind of positive (harmonious) or negative (inharmonious) or neutral state between the two elements. Rosenberg and Abelson offer the following examples of these valences attached to a relationship between elements. [20]

---

[20] Milton J. Rosenberg and Robert P. Abelson, "An Analysis of Cognitive Balancing," in M. Rosenberg and others, eds., *Attitude Organization and Change* (New Haven: Yale University Press, 1960), pp. 112-63.

Positive	*Negative*	*Neutral*
Likes, supports.	Dislikes, fights.	Is indifferent to.
Uses, advocates.	Opposes, undermines.	Is not responsible for.
Possesses, aims for.	Inhibits, aims against.	Does not affect.
Brings about.	Prevents.	Does not lead to.

One can designate the valence sign of the elements by a plus or a minus sign, the positive, negative, or neutral relationship by the letters "p", "n," and "o." Thus in 1964, say, the sentence or band: "President Johnson favors integration" would be, for a pro-Johnson Democrat who himself supported integration, "$+p+$," and for a Democrat who opposed integration, "$+p-$." The first does no violence to a person's emotional harmony or consonance, for someone he likes favors something he approves of, but the second, the sentence as experienced by the anti-integration Democrat, creates a kind of emotional dissonance, for someone he likes supports something he dislikes. The theory of cognitive balancing, and now much research, too, states that he is motivated to change some element of this sentence to reduce this dissonance. A moment's thought will reveal that, given these elements, there are eight possible states, four of which are consonant and four dissonant. The consonant states will be those where:

1. two concepts of identical sign are believed to be positively related ($+p+$ or $-p-$), or
2. two concepts of opposite sign are believed to be negatively related ($+n-$ or $-n+$).

Similarly, dissonant statements would be those where:

1. two concepts of identical sign are believed to be negatively related ($+n+$ or $-n-$), or
2. two concepts of opposite sign are believed to be positively related ($+p-$ or $-p+$).[21]

It is the fact that ideas have affective signs, that cognitions have both references and valences, that makes it necessary to combine veridicality, logic, and consonance in a single theory of motivation. The fusion of things normally kept separate gives power to descriptions of the ways people actually do use ideas, the needs served by them.

The Need to Be Liked. An individual may argue, quite simply, "All my friends voted for Johnson. If I criticize him, I risk their good opinion."

---

[21] *Ibid.*, pp. 119-20.

The positive charge on the concept Johnson comes from the need to be liked (by partisan friends) and may be changed by the dominance of another motive or an altered perception of other people's attitudes, or by changed perception of the risks involved in disagreement. Our evidence shows that this kind of thinking and conflict resolution is close to the surface of consciousness, hence available to conscious thought and rational decision-making as discussed above. But the problem is rarely so simple; I believe that some men deal with distant political figures in a kind of subliminal dialogue. In this political fantasy the most important ingredient is the answer to the question "Does [would] he approve of me? Does [would] he like me?"[22] Clearly, if the individual has such a fantasy relationship with the former President, he hesitates to criticize him for fear of forfeiting this good opinion. Prior to the balancing of this sentence the individual must balance some unspoken sentences that are "articulated" in the twilight of the unconscious.

The Need to Express (and Control) Aggression.   An expressively aggressive man may easily explode in anger over an unwelcome message such as our old example from the days of a previous administration, "President Johnson favors integration." But consider two possible outcomes from this angry response. First, this message is useful in legitimizing a chronic state (low threshold) of anger which the man cannot otherwise justify—the negative evaluation of Johnson persists. The fact that the sentence is unbalanced is a minor matter in this context; in a sense, the unbalanced sentence helps him to balance his own emotional state ("I have a right to be angry," "I am irritable for a good reason"—two balanced if unspoken sentences). Or, second, suppose that he worries about his outbursts; the expression of anger is a problem for him, for he is concerned about his hostile impulses. His angry explosion then must be undone, and he goes about discovering reasons for saying good things about Johnson, proving to himself that he is not really an angry man, that he can see good in people with whom he disagrees, that his explosion was a momentary thing. The negative charge given to the concept Johnson is deliberately reversed so that he can balance his own self-image ("I am not an angry man," "I can see good in my opponents"—two balanced sentences).

The Need for Moral Self-Imagery.   A man caught up in what Myrdal called "the American dilemma" experiences it as a moral dilemma. For reasons that are only partly conscious he does not want his children to go to an integrated school; but he appreciates the intellectual and moral argu-

---

[22] This inference regarding fantasied personal relations with the President emerges from material gathered in extended interviews with fifteen working-class men in Eastport. The material on this aspect of the interviews was not published in the main report on this study, *Political Ideology* (New York: Free Press, Macmillan, 1967).

ments supporting integration. He hears of Johnson's stand. He applauds it, gives Johnson an overt increment of positive emotional credit, but forces are set at work which will undermine this later. The sentence remains balanced at an overt level, but the concept Johnson takes on ambivalence with a positive conscious charge and a negative unconscious charge. Now his balancing problem has shifted, and over time he must cope with his ambivalence toward Johnson in such a way as to meet his needs for moral self-imagery.

These illustrative problems of the relationship of some enduring need-fulfilling orientations to cognitive balancing reveal some of the problems in dealing with short-range "thinking" and in proceeding without further intimate knowledge of the personal functions served by the emotional valence of a concept. Yet given these complexities in both short- and long-range (life-history) terms, the analysis of the mechanisms of cognitive balancing is illuminating. Let us examine several, illustrating them from our sample of cases. This list is taken from Abelson's analysis of "Simulation of 'Hot' Cognition" (by "hot" he means affectively loaded).[23]

Stopping Thinking (Withdrawal).   In the course of his ideological self-analysis, Trueblood says, "I do not follow public affairs"; a positive concept, "I," is associated with a negative concept, "lack of information gathering in public affairs." This thought is painful to him, for he feels he ought to be informed, and, upon analysis, his reason is also painful to him: he fears saying something wrong and believes that pleading ignorance will excuse him. He finds it better not to think about the whole matter.

Denial.   In his self-analysis Silver produces the thought "I am prejudiced against Negroes." He is ashamed of this at first, and attempts to deny it and to prove to himself the veracity of his denial by joining the local chapter of the National Association for the Advancement of Colored People. (It does not work and he later tries rationalization.)

Differentiation.   In his discussion of his prejudices Trumbull says: "I feel that Catholics as a group are objectionable, but I refer only to their religion, not their persons." In making this distinction, he can relieve himself of some guilt over the prejudice implied in condemning "Catholics as a group" by making his objection doctrinal. Indeed, he has the authority of the Christian religion in this: he hates the sin but not the sinner.

Transcendence.   Abelson illustrates this device graphically as follows:[24]

---

[23] Robert P. Abelson, Chap. 17 of Silvan Tomkins and S. J. Messick, eds., *Computer Simulation of Personality* (New York: Wiley, 1963), p. 288.
[24] Robert P. Abelson, "Modes of Resolution of Belief Dilemmas," *Conflict Resolution,* 3 (1959), p. 348.

The house of Montague $(-)\rightarrow$ n $\rightarrow$ The house of Capulet $(-)$.

This is an unbalanced sentence, since two negative concepts are negatively related to each other (the two houses are quarreling). The device for transcendence is to lump them together and relate them positively to a negative concept: "a plague."

A plague $(-)\rightarrow$ on (p) $\rightarrow$ both your houses $(-)$.

Similarly the concepts "omniscient God" and "evil" seem in this world to be positively related, an unbalanced relationship. The device of "free will" may be employed to relate them and balance the sentence.

God $(+)\rightarrow$ gives men "free will" to choose between (p) $\rightarrow$ [good $(++)$ and evil $(-)]$ $(+)$.

In our sample, Buenello, who seeks advancement within the capitalist system, also wishes to follow the teachings of St. Thomas, who condemns usury and working for profit to the self. By linking this proscription of the profit motive with interest in a larger concept of "a modern Christian order" and the benefit to others of working for profit, he is able to transcend the specific negative unbalancing concepts, including them in larger, positively charged concepts.

Rationalization.   This is defined by Abelson as "the acceptance of the truth value of the sentence, but somehow deflecting its evaluative implications."[25] This is done by finding acceptable euphemisms for the unfavorable terms, by altering the perceived consequences, by changing the cause to avoid blame, and so forth. We find King, a moderate liberal Democrat, joining the popular Conservative party in the Adams Debating Society. He worries about his conformism and asks himself whether he did this to make himself more acceptable to others, a painful (unbalanced) thought. He changes the evaluative implications by (a) noting that the consequences to his integrity were not so bad, since he rarely voted with the Conservative party, and (b) observing that he joined the Conservatives in order to avoid the "extremism" of the Liberal (Democratic) party.

Bolstering.   When the acceptance of a valued concept is threatened by its occurrence in an unbalanced sentence, men may save it by giving it additional emotional support. Thus the concept "not conformist" in King's implicit sentence is bolstered by discovery of his independence on other occasions. Similarly the concept "not prejudiced" in Silver's feelings about Negroes is bolstered by his belief that there is a natural principle that

---

[25]Abelson, Chap. 17 of Tomkins and Messick, eds., *Computer Simulation of Personality,* p. 288.

makes it appropriate for each group to live with its own kind. In these cases, it seems, bolstering and rationalization have much in common.

Changing Emotional Charges. Finally, of course, men do change their feelings about concepts, people, events. Demming, confronted by the implicit sentence "I cannot be accepted by the Adams in-group," changed his attitude toward the in-group and made a determined effort to oppose its members and institutions. It was a radical change, for it involved changing many of the other implicit and explicit sentences by which his life had been guided.

Indeed, the analysis of Demming's case, in Chapter 8, reveals some of the difficulties in reducing dissonance where important concepts are involved. For one thing, each of a person's ideas is imbedded in a matrix of other ideas, and changing any one may threaten others with a chain of dissonant relationships. Certainly this is likely to be the case with party identifications, just as Demming's *volte face* with respect to "the establishment" caused him to change his party preference and other attitudes. "Commitments," as we have said, restrain certain efforts at cognitive balancing. Also, the two other themes in this whole question of balance and consonance are implicated; there is the veridical constraint ("Johnson *did* say on television that he supported integration") and the logical constraint ("He can't be both for it and against it at the same time"—at least not without concept differentiation). In general, the theory says, the dissonance reduction is made so as to do the least violence to one's preferences (the weakest valence is changed first), within the constraints of veridicality, logic, and salience of the matter at hand, the salience limiting the withdrawal tendencies of the individual.

In this brief analysis I have tried both to suggest the way in which a long-term view and a focus on motivation may affect theories of cognitive balancing and to reveal how these theories may be useful in explicating specific efforts at conflict resolution. The attention to cognitive balancing mechanisms should not be allowed to obscure the fact that in the long run it is the balanced psychological condition, not the balanced sentence, that will receive men's greatest effort and attention.

Unconscious Motives and Conflict Resolution. Both in Freud's work and in the works of others in the psychoanalytic tradition, motives are regarded as enduring pressures on the individual leading toward behavior designed to discharge the pressure.[26] The source of the pressure is the id, that is, the unbounded, anarchic, largely unconscious set of impulses that

---

[26] See, for example, David Rapoport, "On the Psychoanalytic Theory of Motivation," in M. Jones, ed., *Nebraska Symposium on Motivation* (Lincoln: Nebraska University Press, 1960), pp. 173-247.

provide the energic source of all behavior and thought. Rubinstein, speaking of "motive pressure," says that

> perhaps the most fundamental postulate of psychoanalytic theory [is] the constancy principle. In its application to the theory of motivation this principle states in essence (1) that psychic energy emerges continually through the impact of specific somatic stimulation on the mental apparatus, (2) that in its primary (i.e., its unbound, unneutralized) condition it is continually pressing for discharge, (3) that the discharge takes place primarily by the operation of a set of basic motives, which constitute the id class of motives, and (4) that secondarily other avenues of discharge become available.[27]

The most important motivational conflict is that set up through the mechanism of repression, the conflict then occurring between some motivated act or thought prompted by the id, and the learned repression of that act or thought by the ego or superego, cued by anxiety and forcing denial or disguise of the anxiety-producing motive. Those motives that are thought to be instinctual, parts of the original id, are related to sex and aggression, with dependency or succorance motives sometimes included.

Without entering further into psychoanalytic theory, let us consider two possible strategies of conflict resolution in these circumstances: projection and reaction formation.[28]

Projection.   The mechanism of projection has two important qualities: first, it involves the attribution of unconscious unacceptable impulses to others. The individual cannot project an impulse he does not have, and generally does not need to project one he finds acceptable. Second, the person generally applies to these (real or imagined) impulses in others the same moral repudiation he applies to his own impulses. Projection, unlike empathy or person perception, is an entirely unconscious process. The person is not aware that he has the projected impulses himself. He is only "aware," or believes, that others have these forbidden impulses in great strength and number, and that steps must be taken to contain their actions.

A social attitude often thought to reflect the use of projection is anti-Semitism, that recurrent pariah among social attitudes. Ackerman and

---

[27] Benjamin B. Rubinstein, "Explanation and Mere Description: A Metascientific Examination of Certain Aspects of the Psychoanalytic Theory of Motivation," in Robert R. Holt, ed., *Motives and Thought,* Vol. 5 of *Psychological Issues* (New York: International Universities Press, 1967), p. 44.

[28] The following discussion is greatly influenced by a draft chapter by David O. Sears for our joint work, *Public Opinion* (New York: Prentice-Hall, 1964). Owing to space limitations the chapter was not included. I must not saddle Sears with responsibility for the construction I have put on his ideas, but the basic concept of the way in which Christian doctrine and Marxist-Leninist theory are supported by the two defense mechanisms discussed is his.

Jahoda analyzed the anti-Semitic attitudes of forty patients in psychoanalysis, finding that "None of the cases manifested a genuine, deep *depression.*"[29] This is significant because depression results when hostility is turned inward rather than being expressed in direct or diluted form toward another person, and one of the ways to discharge aggression outward, rather than upon the self, is to project it, to accuse someone else of being hostile. Negro prejudice works through the same projective mechanism. For example, Silver, an Adams College junior, fearful of dirt and his own impulses and believing sex to be somehow unclean, retains his anti-Negro feelings in spite of his conscious recognition that prejudice of this kind is wrong and, for a Jew, dangerous. He cannot help feeling that Negroes are somehow "dirty" (he will not bathe at the same beaches with them), and likely to contaminate him in ways that overtly have to do with his status but covertly suggest something less available to his conscious mind. He solves his motivational conflict by partial repression and projection.

Reaction Formation.   Perhaps the second most important mechanism for managing conflicts involving an unacceptable motive, denying, containing, and using it at the same time, is reaction formation, a device whereby a person behaves and thinks, in his conscious mind, along lines directly opposite those indicated by the motive he fears and despises in himself. In this way the conflicted person can maintain his self-image as one totally dissimilar to the person he fears unconsciously that he really is, and can summon and channel energy enough to keep repressed the motive he hates or fears in himself.[30] We see it in our cases when a young man protests too much that he loves everything about his home and parents, but reveals, inadvertently, the constant friction and hostility he is disguising and trying to repress.

Perhaps the commonest political example of reaction formation is an altruistic or philanthropic attitude, such as is evidenced by the outspoken champion of minority groups, of the poor or crippled or sick, of the unemployed and all those derelict on society's shores. A person who says, "All I want to do is help others" is very likely repressing his very natural desires for self-aggrandizement and/or hostile retaliation against others. Among our group Donaldson illustrates the operation of reaction formation of this kind. He reveals subliminally throughout his biography a need to assert his will aggressively against others. For example, his vision of his own future is one of a labor organizer, and in one illuminating glimpse of his fantasy life

---

[29] N. W. Ackerman and M. Jahoda, *Anti-Semitism and Emotional Disorder* (New York: Harper, 1950), p. 25.

[30] See, for example, the discussion of reaction formation in Irving Sarnoff, *Personality Dynamics and Development* (New York: Wiley, 1962), pp. 251-53. Sarnoff suggests that cynicism is a reaction-formation defense against unacceptable feelings of affection.

he sees himself addressing "almost vituperatively" a mass of leaderless workingmen in order to enlist them in a *cooperative* way of life. He says he goes out of his way at parties to befriend the lonely and unhappy person, making a point of his kindness toward others. He does not *say* that the managing classes are hostile and aggressive or that the other people at parties are callous and inconsiderate, but he implicitly draws the contrast between his own philanthropic mission and loving behavior and theirs. Certainly this seems to be a case of denial and reaction formation, one we shall deal with at length in Chapter 11.

The matching of idea with strategy for dealing with motivational conflict is influenced by the content or meaning of the idea itself; some ideas or ideologies lend themselves better to projection, some to reaction formation, and, of course, some seem to invite rational conscious choice. The Christian doctrine, for example, which promises that "the meek shall inherit the earth," and asks us to "turn the other cheek" toward the enemy who has slapped the first one, and proposes that we should "love thine enemy," seems to make a strong appeal to a reaction-formation strategy of coping with hostility.

The Marxist-Leninist doctrine, on the other hand, lends itself more easily to conflict management through projective mechanisms. The image of the bourgeoisie as exploiting the proletariat, selfishly using the workingman to increase his own personal fortune, and plotting with other capitalists to overthrow socialist states, is congenial to the man who wishes to accuse all others of misdeeds but to picture himself as the model of altruism, morality, and concern for the welfare of others. Both projective and reaction-formation mechanisms, if hooked up with their appropriate ideologies, will give strength to intellectual conviction.

Fungible Goals.   When engaged, needs become motives, and motives have goals or targets. Some goals may serve to fulfill a variety of motives simultaneously, and the most important of these "fungible goals" are wealth and status. No doubt it is partly because they serve so many ends that they appear so important in many people's striving efforts and so important in the biographies of these young men. One seeks to know the deeper meaning of wealth and status for those who strive for them, but uncertainty about which needs should be given priority may be one source of their precedence. Certainly they aid powerfully in resolving motivational conflicts by providing multipurpose answers.

The Reconciled Motive.   To be "successful" in the sense of giving long-term satisfaction to striving and comprehensive fulfillment to the whole personality, the strategy of conflict resolution should give the set of motives certain properties: (1) Are an individual's motives *balanced,* in the sense that they embrace all relevant motives, and especially long-range and enduring satisfactions as contrasted to immediate ones? (2) Are they *realistic*, in the sense that they take into account his own capacities as well as the probable events in the environment, especially the way others will respond to his pursuit of the indicated goals? (3) Are they *conscientious*, in the sense that they acknowledge the difference between desire and the desirable, his own wants *and* the nagging dictates of his conscience? (4) Are they *ego-syntonic*, in the sense that they are in harmony with the deepest trends in his own psyche and not at war with some unknown impulse life that might at some time take him unaware and frustrate his pursuit of happiness?

5

Personality, Mind and Group References

PERSONALITY: SELF-IMAGE AND OBJECTIVE SELF

In the choice of an idea a man inevitably "chooses" something he thinks becomes him, fits him, an idea that goes with his other qualities, his other ideas. All of this depends on how he sees himself, for "appropriateness" and "fit" are meaningful only in terms of the self for whom the idea is chosen. [1] For example, a young man by the name of Gardiner, the cousin of an industrial tycoon, affianced to the daughter of the Republican candidate for governor, sees himself as destined to succeed, modestly but appropriately garbed with power and status. He chooses ideas that have none of the garish stripe of extremism; they are conservative, humane, tenderly protective of the status quo. Donaldson, on the other hand, sees himself as a rough-hewn advocate for the underprivileged, something of a hero to them; his ideas speak of power collected in his hands and used for the benefit of others.

The biographies reveal a variety of self-images. It seems to me that the following features are especially significant for the study of motivated political thought.

Peer Acceptance versus Marginal Man versus Young Rebel. If a person sees himself as generally popular and accepted by the peers that

---

[1] The most seminal piece on identity and self-image is, of course, Erik Erikson's "The Problem of Ego Identity," *Journal of the American Psychoanalytic Association,* 4 (1956), pp. 58-121. Following Erikson's scheme, one might define the dimensions of adolescent identity problems as: time perspective versus time diffusion; self-certainty versus identity consciousness; role experimentation versus negative identity; anticipation of achievement versus work paralysis; identity versus identity diffusion; sexual identity versus bisexual diffusion; leadership polarization versus authority diffusion; ideological polarization versus diffusion of ideals. While these are suggestive terms, Erikson himself quickly abandons them as the ingredients of a working scheme, and I must confess I do not find them resonant with the problems of the sample of late adolescent men I am dealing with here.

count for him, one of the great problems of adolescence, and indeed adult life, is solved. His political thinking does not have to be framed so as to serve the purpose of gaining friends or of making enemies; he can rely upon the "resonance" of his ideas with his other needs, or can treat political ideas casually if he is not interested in politics. He can, in the terminology employed earlier, rely upon their "intrinsic" properties, not their extrinsic ones.[2]

Independence versus Conformity.   Whether or not they see themselves as acceptable to others, men may value independence and fear conformity. It may be important for their self-image that they see themselves, like Dobb and Demming, as "standing on their own two feet," or that they experience a sense of that independence from authority of all kinds that Rogers said was the most important value in his life. Under these circumstances, men very likely prefer to ground their views in "facts," not in what is commonly believed. Perhaps the most frequently mentioned concern, though not the one with the deepest psychological implications, was "conformity." Many of those who worried most about their conformism were indeed conformist in their thinking.[3]

Active (Assertive) versus Passive (Dependent).   Those who saw themselves as assertive tended to worry about their aggressive tendencies; those who saw themselves as too passive worried about their lack of leadership, spirit, dominance. The dimension is an important one in shaping one's self-image; it colors attitudes toward governmental authority in a subtle way. The assertive ones feel confident toward government power, although they may, if they are conservative, oppose it. The passive ones are fearful of government power, even though they may support it. I suspect the difference is caused by two different feelings: (1) the sense of a capacity to "fight back" if the government tries, as Rogers put it, "to enter my private preserve," and (2) the sense that one could use (where "using" is an assertive act) government power for one's own purposes as De Vita planned to do.

Moral Consciousness versus Unconscious Morality.   Men who see themselves as "moral" and talk about it frame their political views in moral terms, usually terms designed to earn them moral credits. Most of the men simply assume their own morality and, although they may refer to the corruption of politicians or of big business, they do not frame their thought along moralistic lines. No doubt ideological self-analysis in the nineteenth century would have employed moral rhetoric to a greater extent than do

---

[2]See Chap. 2.

[3]The discussion of conformity in America sparked by David Riesman's *The Lonely Crowd* (New Haven: Yale University Press, 1950) has taken on other dimensions. For a discussion of research findings in this area see Robert E. Lane and David O. Sears, *Public Opinion* (Englewood Cliffs, N.J.: Prentice-Hall, 1964), Chap. 8.

those written by the Adams men. The decline of "sin," the low-tension morality of the American public,[4] together with and perhaps caused by the acceptance of sex in this generation, may be sources of this change.

Intellectuality versus "Being Regular."   The self-images of those who, often because of their poor athletic abilities, see themselves as "intellectuals" (or have done so in their childhood) occasionally lead them into abstract and elevated views of political discourse, but the tendency is not especially marked. Surprisingly, there is no more reference to political literature in their statements than in the statements of others, no authors' name-dropping to speak of. The influence is apparent in another direction. They take to the task of analysis more readily and write longer biographies; they organize their biographies less as chronologies and more as analytical essays; they give less "what" and more "why." In short, the self-image of intellectuality is revealed not only in their reference (often embarrassed) to their early reputations, but also in their performance.

Feelings of Inferiority versus Confidence of One's Own Worth.   A surprising proportion of the men refer to feelings of inferiority, either in their current lives or in their childhood, and perhaps only now receding. Such references do not seem to be related to diffidence about stating their political views (some of those who reveal these feelings are reluctant to make up their minds and state their views, but others are not). Although the political implications are to be found more often in relating the source of these feelings (physical size and awkwardness, parental denigration, social marginality) to political thinking than in trying to ascertain differences between those who have (state) such feelings and those who do not, there is a recurring effort by those who feel inferior to use political ideas to give themselves an increment of status.[5]

We have been speaking here of self-images, self-conscious identities, self-awareness, but the subjective self and the objective self are not the same thing. The objective self includes such properties as intelligence, energy, capacities to persevere, self-control, and some elements of the personality that are inaccessible to the conscious mind. The method employed here limits our data in this domain. Suffice it to say that if a man's self-image and his "real self" are grossly out of line, he is destined to frustration. The short, fat candidate for the ballot is not more an object of pity than the chronically hostile and withdrawn candidate for political office. In such a situation, of course, one looks for the source of the propensities to self-defeating acts, perhaps in an appeal to martyrdom.

---

[4]See Chap. 21, "The Lost Sense of Evil," in Robert E. Lane, *Political Ideology* (New York: Free Press, Macmillan, 1962).

[5]See below, Chap. 13.

THE PHILOSOPHICAL PREMISES
OF POLITICAL BELIEF SYSTEMS

The energy source of thinking must set in motion a train of thought employing the basic premises of belief which color and shape any particular conclusion or inference about politics. These basic premises are, as has been argued elsewhere,[6] the elements of a philosophy: metaphysics (what is real), especially time, place, and cause; epistemology (what is true), especially the nature and uses of knowledge, that is, evidence, inference, logic—matters touched upon in the strategy of learning; ethics (what is good), the contents of a conscience and the precipitate of the struggles that take place there, and, by a complicated extension, the ethical life for self and others, and the ethical society. Beyond this, there are the objectified and rationalized concepts of what is worth striving for, in the sense of the objects of desire for self and others—some of the ingredients of a *value* system (power, wealth, status, enlightenment).

Without discussing individual differences, we may briefly characterize the group in these terms, drawing a few implications regarding the consequences to their political thought of the dominant themes.

As might be expected, most of the young men are future-oriented in the following senses: The importance of their current status and problems lies in the effect they have on their futures, their careers. They place things in a developmental construct. Social institutions draw their significance not so much from the way they affect present interests or family interests, but rather from their effect on still uncertain career interests. Even if the men have not decided what careers they will undertake, what is important is that society provide a set of open choices for them.[7] This is, incidentally, in marked contrast to the working-class men of Eastport interviewed at the same time, who saw their futures as extensions of their present situations, with the important addition that they expected to be moderately "better off" in the future. Partly, of course, this difference in time orientation is due to age differences, but more importantly it is the difference in seeing the world as a ladder to be climbed compared with a view of the world as an escalator where the motive power is supplied by society. Buried in this concept of the future, then, is the concept of government as facilitating individ-

---

6See my *Political Ideology,* Sec. 5. Compare Florence R. Kluckhohn and Fred L. Strodtbeck, *Variations in Value Orientations* (Evanston, Ill.: Row, Peterson, 1961).

7Compare the discussion in Chap. 4 on the lessened importance of economic interests or beliefs in a college setting. The emphasis given to future orientation here and the emphasis on the moratorium on the consequences of belief in the earlier discussion are reconciled by the lack of *immediacy* and *specificity* of economic interests and consequences in the present situation. The future is important, but the essential concern about the future is that it be open.

ual effort; the conservatives see the facilitation as "applying to me," the liberals as applying to underdogs (but not ignoring "my" claims, either).

The stage for the important events that happen or will happen is sometimes the local home community, but the significance of what happens there is national, that is, generalized to some important larger group. International affairs are important, not because these men see themselves on an international stage, but because the rest of the world is "real" and its population is made up of people whose fates are matters of conditional interest. In this sense, the egocentrism of the adolescent, based on a belief in the cosmic importance of "my problems now," is somehow compatible with an other-regarding concept of distant and alien others. Those with unresolved identity crises are neither more nor less likely to pay attention to American foreign policy in a world of nations. On the other hand, it must be said that the attention to personal futures and ambitions tends to give primary importance to national policies affecting career choice and success.

Men are dominant over nature and the social order; change is a product of effort, not fate; causes may be impersonal (population growth, natural resources, depression), but, because men can guide nations' destinies as well as their own, something can be done about "problems." More or less realistically, these young men identify themselves with the leadership class that can effect change; thus it is not so much a matter of what "they" do to "us," but what "we" do about events. The scholarly ones believe that by manipulating ideas they affect the course of events. This reduces their capacity for utopian thinking while it increases their capacity for handling the next step in a changing society.

Truth is determined by a reading of experience (their own and others') combined with selective acceptance of authoritative opinion. Universities are sources of authoritative knowledge, as are government commissions, prestige papers (like the *New York Times*), and professional advice. Political truth is colored by but not determined by partisan interest; the truth about distant events is determined more by the source of the report than anything else; usually someplace, if one only knew where to look, there is somebody with pretty good answers, and very likely he is "the man on the spot." I think it is the case that for the liberals more than the conservatives knowledge is tentative, but for virtually all of the twenty-four men the world is knowable. Both concrete knowledge and abstract knowledge (theory) are true.

"Goodness" consists of attention to three things: the work ethic, the demands of the community when these conflict with one's own desires, and the individual needs of others. Of these, the attention to work as opposed to play is the only one that is ever really talked about. It is a living issue. While the decencies of a person to others, his kindness and sacrifices, are observed and approved, there is little attention to the concept of the "good man" as such. No doubt this is due to the very real tension between study—the work of the student—and "goofing off," while there is not much felt tension on matters of being decent to others. As these topics are reflected in social thought, the work ethic is shared by both liberals and conservatives, but the conservatives tend to make this *the* good, whereas the liberals see social ethics in terms of assistance to underdogs. Since none of the men know very many underdogs, the question of social ethics rarely is reflected in problems of personal conduct. (With the emergence of "the urban crisis" and student involvement in race relations, there may have occurred a merger of social and personal ethics in this area for an increasing number of students.)

As we shall see, there is some ambivalence about the values that are worth striving for. In general, all the men want achievement (career success), few speak of enlightenment or a desire to achieve through scholarship (though De Vita does, as we have seen), few speak of moral achievement (though Buenello and Donaldson care a great deal about their moral images), and few speak of the homely virtues of family and fatherhood (in contrast to the working-class men of Eastport). There is some ambivalence about striving for wealth and power, but, given the setting, it is surprising how many name wealth and status, if not power, as their goals in life. For the most part these are the conservatives, but the order of cause and effect is not clear; are they conservative because of these life goals, or do they pursue these life goals because of their conservative business-oriented philosophies? Those who speak of "independence" as a life goal mean, at this time in their lives, autonomy from the family, for it is the constraints and unpleasant relations in the family, not the constraints of government or the dominance of big business, that bother them.

While concepts of reality, truth, ethics, and value are significant in shaping political thought, there are several other premises that are not so easily placed in traditional philosophical thought. One of these is the concept of abundance versus scarcity. Several studies have shown the importance to political thinking of the underlying premise of this dimension. Those who believe that goods and values are scarce are likely to believe the following: (a) what someone else gets deprives me of something; (b) prudence and caution in holding on to what I have (and, by extension, what society now has) are desirable; (c) the future is characterized more by danger than by opportunity; (d) other people, especially strangers, proceeding on the same scarcity assumption, must be regarded with suspicion as sources of threat and deprivation. In the Eastport working-class sample, those who had been

most deprived as children were most likely to be worried about the government's unbalanced budget and largess toward the poor.[8] In Malaysia, the
assumption of scarcity by civil servants impeded mutual trust and, ironically,
measures toward economic growth.[9] In contrast, the Adams College men
have an assumption that there will be abundance and growth in their life-
times; opportunities for them are waiting if they can recognize them; hence
success depends on their own efforts and skill. Few see their own success as
depriving anyone of anything, although the conservatives are likely to see
governmental favoring of labor and underdogs as somehow detrimental to
their class interests.

This general belief in abundance has three important effects. It helps to
account for the view that change is not only inevitable, but also not risky;
the perils of a mistake are not disastrous. If change can be so defined, it
becomes "progress," and we have here one of the root causes of the American attitudes toward progress. After all, we are the "people of plenty."[10]
Second, it colors mood: from black to rosy. Mood is hardly a "concept" or
a "belief," although it may be so phrased: "Tomorrow will be better";
"Things are going from bad to worse." Its basic dimension is optimism-
pessimism. Yet at the same time, mood (probably an inference from preverbal training, or perhaps an outcome of the "Oedipal phase")[11] affects
belief in opportunity and abundance. Both optimistic mood and belief in
abundance affect such important political beliefs as those dealing with the
consequences of new welfare legislation, the outcome of a policy of free
enterprise (in a scarcity society, the devil takes the hindmost), and the shift
from policy shaped by government regulation to one shaped by giving and
withholding grants and contracts. The conservative Adams College men
(perhaps in contrast to men in colleges catering to the sons and grandsons of
immigrants and the insecure white-collar classes) seem not to fear the
welfare state, while neither conservatives nor liberals (with one exception)
fear the competition of all against all. Conservatives, however, do have a
nameless fear of "big government."

Third, belief in abundance helps support the natural-harmony theory of
conflict, for under these affluent circumstances the "unseen hand" has something in it. This is only to state in other terms the idea that it is possible for
each to gain and none to lose under the best circumstances, and that under

---

[8]Lane, *Political Ideology,* Chap. 16, "Money and the Conservative View of Life."

[9]James C. Scott, *Political Ideology in Malaysia* (New Haven: Yale University Press, 1968).

[10]David M. Potter, *People of Plenty* (Chicago: University of Chicago Press-Phoenix, 1954).

[11]The deep and enduring pessimism of *The Uncommitted* Harvard college students in the fifties is said by Kenneth Keniston to be due to their "seduction" by their mothers, followed by the realization that it was only a passing liaison (New York: Harcourt, Brace & World, 1965).

the worst the collective gains exceed the collective losses. It will be noted that both Adam Smith and Abbé Sieyès made their statements on the virtues of individual and unregulated efforts to gain something for themselves in periods of rising income. Translated into political terms, the free play of interests striving for favors from government can, where there is an increase in things to be given, work in an atmosphere of moderated hostility and mutual suspicion.

LEARNING STRATEGIES

Since a political belief is directly or indirectly learned, and since men learn in different ways, is there something we can say about the manner in which learning "strategies" link motive and belief? The contribution of these cases to an overwhelming literature on learning lies in three areas.[12] In the first place, let us consider the point about "cognitive needs" mentioned in Chapter 2, the need to know. Here the analysis must focus on the question put by Lynd: "Knowledge for what?" The general point is that the political knowledge sought is that which is useful in certain life struggles: (a) identity formation, (b) interpersonal relations, and (c) career or task achievement. It is *motivated* learning.

Identity Formation. When Demming discovers he cannot achieve leadership positions in conventional and conservative organizations at Adams College, he suddenly *learns* the liberal philosophies of his professors, switches from Republican to Democrat, and employs the ideas so discovered in rationalizing his position as a rebel leader on the campus. The process helps him to think of himself as a different and more worthy individual. When Mintz finds in high school that his lack of athletic ability, small stature, and diffident manner keep him from general acceptability, he *learns* about Shavian socialism and advances these heretical views among his associates. As a defense against his "outcast" status, he gives himself a radical identity. De Vita, separating himself from his old lower-middle-class family identification, *learns* a liberal political philosophy at Adams that helps to establish his new identity.

Interpersonal Relations. Svenson, whose father is a nativist and anti-intellectual, quarrels constantly with his father and *learns* his mother's

---

12A very useful but not quite up-to-date summary and interpretation of the literature is provided by Ernest R. Hilgard, *Theories of Learning* (New York: Appleton-Century-Crofts, 1956). Recent studies of cognition and cognitive processes have added much to the material interpreted by Hilgard. For reviews of this and other material, see the new edition of G. Lindzey and E. Aronson, eds., *Handbook of Social Psychology,* 5 vols. (Cambridge, Mass.: Addison-Wesley, 1968-69).

more internationalist and intellectualized values. He uses these as weapons against his father. King, a liberal Democrat in his home town, *learns* a more conservative view at Adams College, where he feels it is advantageous to side with the Conservatives in the Debating Society. Dobb *learns* the arguments for the Democratic party so that he can become a Democrat in opposition to his parents' Republicanism.

Career and Task Achievement.   MacGregor, having rebelled against the family conservatism, *learns* to come out of his "liberal idealistic shell" when he confronts the need to enter business on graduation. Gardiner, destined to become a business leader like his father and cousin, *learns* to associate with "people like himself" and to adopt ideas appropriate to his destiny. Silver, eager to make the right contacts at Adams, *learns* the "correct" prejudices and political views that make him acceptable.

These processes conform to well-established learning theories, grounded as they are in a matrix of rewards and punishments; in occasional detail, they reveal how it is that one set of communications rather than another was persuasive. Moreover, where the information is supplied in sufficient perspective, they reveal the stages of concept development that are made explicit in developmental psychology. Yet in each case, it is useful to know just what the young man is striving for, what he wants, what his needs and motives are. For it is in understanding these needs and goals that we see why one piece of information or a different attitude is useful to him and another is not.

Learning strategies, of course, deal with the way information is processed and used, a matter on which there is much research. One of the common and most useful concepts in this area is that of the "open mind" as contrasted to the "closed mind." The open mind uses information as a tool of exploration rather than as a mechanism for defense of established doctrine; bits of conflicting information are allowed to rub up against each other rather than kept compartmentalized and isolated; the open mind is tolerant of ambiguity and permits dissonance, such as an unwelcome statement from a favored source.[13]

What our material reveals in this connection is the complexity of openness. One of these complexities was treated in my discussion of Eastport working-class belief systems: the problem of contextualizing ideas without ideologizing them, that is, putting them into a framework of other ideas to give them "meaning" without having that framework become a prison cage.[14] Openness for some of the Eastport men meant the lack of a framework of ideas; they lost in meaning what they gained in flexibility. Here let us look at the "openness" of three men who say they have not made up

---

[13] See Milton Rokeach, *The Open and Closed Mind* (New York: Basic Books, 1960).
[14] See "Conceptualization in Political Discourse," Chap. 22 of my *Political Ideology.*

their minds as to which party to support; they are open to new information and to new arguments. It could not be said of them, in politics at least, that they are ideologues or blind partisans, or that they have "closed minds." And they are interested in politics.

Trueblood believes that in all things he must make the most careful discriminations and correct decisions. He worries about his parents' good opinion and is uncertain which party they support. He can see reasons for believing that the Democrats have the best policies, but he thinks the Republicans attract the best people. The decision is too much for him and he prefers to be generally neutral.

Cohen's parents, whom he detests, are Republicans; his aunt and uncle, whom he greatly admires, are also Republicans. He has "an obsession to be rich and successful" and believes that being a Republican will help in this striving process. On the other hand, he admires certain members of the faculty who are Democrats. At the moment he is a Republican but declines to discuss policy issues and believes he could change parties very easily.

Simpson is an internationalist and associates that position with the Democratic party. On the other hand, he too (like Cohen) has a "reverence" for wealth and status, and believes that those who have achieved them are Republicans; he would like to be associated with them. He is contemptuous of his Republican father and likes his more liberal Democratic mother. He cannot choose a party while he is under the family influence, but believes that later on he will be able to make this choice.

Each of these men seems to hear both sides and weighs arguments on both sides, some of the arguments having to do with party positions and some of them (not inappropriately) with their own identifications and future careers. They tolerate their ambiguity reasonably well. Yet are they learning more and assimilating their learned material better than the partisans, especially the partisans who can yet hear the other side? On the whole, it seems to me, the advantages lie with what might be called the "open partisan," the man who has a tentative commitment to one side of an issue, but is continually reassessing this commitment as new information comes in. The virtues of the open mind, the tolerance of ambiguity, the entertainment of alien ideas need something else or they risk paralysis. They need a capacity to summarize and hold a point of view, however tentatively, while new information is processed. And for such a tentative commitment, such men as Trueblood, Cohen, and Simpson need (a) a clearer set of priorities in their reference ideas or reference individuals than they now have, (b) a greater willingness to assert the self against the world, and (c) a greater detachment of ideas from self so that a wrong idea does not necessarily imply a wrong and sinful and, especially, unsuccessful self.

The third point has to do with learning in a field where coherence has never had much of a chance. One learns patriotism as one learns religion, and children confuse the two;[15] one learns civics as a set of copybook facts and rules, moralized but distant and bookish; one learns "politics" as a matter of moral ambivalence. Participation in local affairs involves imposing oneself on others in a partisan context, uncongenial to many, unfamiliar to most. Policy issues, especially issues of foreign policy, have remote bearings on the individual; he cannot calculate loss and gain to himself, only to some party or person or ambiguous principle (collective security; America first). The coherence of ideas so learned is hard to perceive; the weaving of their interrelationships into a pattern of thought that becomes an ideology or a belief *system* in the sense that theology can be a system of ideas, or physics, is unlikely and difficult. Learning politics therefore follows eclectic strategies enforced by the nature of the way the subject is introduced and the diffuseness of the material. We have "dissonance" instead of logic. Instead of first principles, one has reference groups.

THE WORLD-OF-PEOPLE-FOR-ME (REFERENCE GROUPS)

Unless one knows to whom or for whom or against whom a man is formulating his views, one hardly knows what direction these "processed" motives will take. If he seeks status, in whose eyes will he look for a reflection of his new status? If it is autonomy, it must be autonomy from some person or group, however narrowly or widely defined. Perhaps in the case of such motives as the achievement motive, where satisfaction lies in meeting an internalized standard, one might say the reference person is the self, but it is the rare person for whom this is enough; one wants others to know about a job well done.

The nature of the reference is important, for people and groups serve a variety of reference purposes. Among our young men, Cohen, rejecting his parents, chose an uncle as a *model* for life style and politics. Trumbull cared what a certain elite group thought of him; its members served as the only important *audience*. De Vita chose to work out his needs to dominate in the *arena* where he could excel, among intellectuals and professional men. Demming and MacGregor selected their views in part because they would challenge their *opposition;* for Demming this opposition was the college in-group, for MacGregor it was his father. This last case illustrates the

---

[15]See, for example, David Easton and Robert D. Hess, "The Child's Political World," *Midwest Journal of Political Science,* 6 (1962), pp. 229-46.

importance of negative reference groups.[16] Altogether such reference groups and persons provide standards of behavior, cues for the appropriate thing to do and say, audiences from which to extract attention and approval, antagonists against whom to measure one's strength and from whom to get revenge or to retrieve one's "honor," arenas within which to work and strive, communities in which to develop a sense of belonging once again.

But again the simplicity of a scheme is confounded by the complexities of life: a person does not have one reference group, but many; he is not accepted or rejected for one attribute, but for several, and they may be in conflict, creating what is called "status inconsistency"; his life, especially if he is young, as our men are, is fluid, and what is appropriate to the stage he is leaving may be inappropriate to the one he is entering; his concept of his social place may be at war with reality. The adolescent who would like to please both parents and friends may not be able to do so. Further, a man's reference may be ambivalent: many a young man insecurely accepted in an elite school hates its inner character but derives satisfaction from the prestige this connection gives him back home. Reference groups and persons generate a variety of conflicts, so here again the modes of conflict resolution will sluice his energizing motives into one social outlook or another as these motives are guided by his various social references.[17]

DEFINITION OF THE SITUATION

It is useful to differentiate "personalities," "minds," and "opinions." The properties of the personality are more or less enduring qualities that permit men to cope with the world: their internal conflicts and the way they solve them, their dominant drives and needs, the habitual ways in which they relate to people, their consciences and regulatory mechanisms, their moods and affective states, their concepts of self and ideal self. The concept "mind" refers to the ways in which people cope cognitively with the world, their stores of knowledge, their analytical capacities and styles, what they believe and how they believe it, and their strategies of learning. Opinions are the products of personalities and minds as these respond to situations, but the way the situation is defined affects the opinions given.

---

[16]One of the failings of an otherwise great book on the employment of family and college reference groups by Bennington girls in the late thirties is the slighting of *negative* references. See Theodore Newcomb, *Personality and Social Change* (New York: Dryden, 1943). I suspect the negative reference to the family is stronger among men than among women, a factor accounting for the difference in findings at Adams and at Bennington.

[17]See Herbert H. Hyman and Eleanor Singer, eds., *Readings in Reference Group Theory and Research* (New York: Free Press, Macmillan, 1968).

All personalities are "plural" in the sense that in spite of the basic unity of selfhood, there are various and sometimes incompatible facets that come to the fore under different situations. In the repertoire of identities, one may find the image of the self as "victim" (some of the Adams men's reports of their childhoods arouse this image), as a "leader of men" (Coleman says that only gradually he came to think of himself in this way), as an "easygoing, live-and-let-live person" (Svenson says this is his dominant trait, but at certain times he loses his easygoing quality and becomes an avenger of the ethnic underdog for reasons not quite clear to him), and a variety of other self-perceptions. As men define situations differently they engage different facets of their personalities.

Partly for this reason every individual has a variety of opinions on a given topic: perhaps one for his parents, shaded toward the acceptable or, equally likely, the distinctive; one for his roommates, with whom he has been having a running quarrel in which they call his friends "hicks" and he calls them "playboys" and "preppies"; and maybe one for "formal" use, when he has an audience (if only himself) who asks what he "really thinks" about something or other. Opinions vary with audiences and reference groups; they also vary with what the individual regards as the stakes involved in an occasion. Is he called upon to defend his consistency? Or to show that he is a congenial, unopinionated person? Or to employ his views instrumentally to gain some objective for which they serve as guides to reality?

It is his definition of the situation that guides a man in his selection of self-images to put forward and groups to whom he should address his thoughts, his evaluation of the stakes involved in something he cares about. Geoffrey Gorer says that Americans are generous with their money until the situation is defined as a business or bargaining situation, in which case they feel that their "shrewdness" or "acumen" is at stake and their whole frame of reference changes.[18] Similarly, the Adams men select a political point of view among those "available" to them, according to the way in which they perceive the situation:

"Superior Group."   Goldberg says that his whole personality changes when he thinks he is in a group that has high status or great popularity or power. Among equals he is relaxed and talkative; in the superior group he is awkward and silent. He thinks of Republicans as representing such a superior group and avoids them, preferring to be among Democrats, and, of course, to be one himself.

"Joining the 'Big Men.'"   Caplan says that when he went to prep school he was the only radical among 300 Republicans. He made a point of

---

[18]Goeffrey Gorer, *The American People* (New York: Norton, 1948), pp. 178-81.

his radicalism: "As a freshman I debated the Taft-Hartley law with a senior. . . . I was a little boy but all the big guys knew me." As he grows older he is admitted to positions of power and orients himself toward equals. He becomes less dogmatic, more "mellowed."

"Grand Old Man."   Novak was forced to leave school because of poor grades due to his intense extracurricular activities. After a year at another school: "I returned to Adams without any widespread recognition. I hoped to become a 'grand old man' to whom younger students would turn for advice. I became extremely conservative in my political attitudes. Some labeled me 'reactionary.' I rather enjoyed this."

"Angry Young Man" versus "Up-and-Coming Adams Man."   Coleman feels that, in comparison with his social success in high school, he has not been successful in making a name for himself at Adams. Therefore, he says, "I have tended to seek strength in 'rebelling against the system.' . . . I paint a picture of myself as the 'angry young man.' The more conservative the people around me are, the more liberal I become. . . . A victory for me is always an underdog upset brought about by my own political abilities, despite the deck's being loaded against me." But back in Arkansas, where Coleman has political ambitions, he sees himself in a very different situation. There, he says, he drops his "pseudo-Marxist doctrine, something I feel no need for when I am at home, when I have a position as an 'up-and-coming young Adams man.' "

There are certain kinds of discussions, audiences, topics, situations calling for characteristic responses, shaping opinions:

(a) A task-oriented group calls for narrow, relevant, "hard" opinions; a group of acquaintances calls for nonserious, noncontroversial opinions; a "bull session" may call for "way-out" or provocative opinions, with nothing lost if one is "proved" wrong.

(b) Opinions expressed at home (for most of the men, but not for Ransome, Gardiner, McDonald, Lamb) should serve to differentiate the individual, to reveal an independent stance; opinions among friends (whether provocative or congenial, as above) should serve to cement relations.

(c) Opinions expressed formally to the faculty (in essays and ideological self-analysis) should serve to "impress" the instructor. This may be done by literary skill (rarely successful), playing up to the instructor's prejudices (sometimes successful, if discreet), or displaying knowledge and analytical skill (often but not always successful).

(d) Opinions about politics revealing a knowledge that "there is more than meets the eye" tend to score, psychoanalytic opinions (even by amateurs) which go to a "deeper level" and have initially implausible assumptions tend to score; opinions on matters of taste implying high standards and superior critical sense—that is, negative opinions—tend to score. Here the definition of the situation is, in substance, a classification of the subject matter.[19]

A GRAPHIC VIEW OF POLITICAL THINKING AMONG ADAMS MEN

The paradigm in Chapter 3 was intended to outline the elements of the political "thinking machine" whose energy is provided by the relevant drives or needs or motives of an individual. But, with a little more specificity, and some suggestion of flow that must not be taken literally, I am appending a chart to summarize what the paradigm began.

---

[19]The context prompts speculation on how these men defined the situation in which they wrote their ideological self-analyses. They could "score" by revealing the worst about themselves, by referring to the impact of my course upon their ideologies, by making themselves "liberal" and "tolerant." On the basis of later discussions with the men and internal evidence in their biographies, I think they wrote them as much to satisfy themselves as to satisfy their instructor. Perhaps, however, there was a tendency to believe that revelations of their failings were more likely to fulfill their mission than revelations of their success—a counterweight to their established life habits.

SOURCE OF ENERGY	ELEMENTS OF A POLITICAL "IDEA MACHINE"					OUTPUT: POLITICAL BELIEF SYSTEM	
Motives and Needs	Strategies of Conflict Resolution	"Personality": Identity and Objective Self	Philosophical and Operational Beliefs	Group Milieu, Reference, and Role	Definition of the Situation	Stylistic	Substantive
Need to be liked and self-validation through others	Rational decision-making	Accepted vs. marginal vs. rebel	Future orientation	Home vs. college	Locating self in system	Abstract vs. concrete	*Liberal:* Opportunity for all
Aggression and inhibition of aggression	Group reference and role modeling	Independence vs. conformity	Local + national/international theatre	High status vs. low status	Assessing stakes in situation	Normative vs. descriptive	Inclusiveness
Need for status and overcoming "inferiority"	Cognitive balancing (denial, reconceptualizing, rationalizing, attitude change)	Active vs. passive	Dominance of man (self) over nature and events	Definition of reference group or individual as:	Identifying roles and groups in situations	Personification vs. impersonalism	Equality of nations
Need for moral self-imagery	Repression and sublimation, projection, reaction formation	Moral consciousness vs. unconscious morality	World as knowable in concrete and abstract terms	model	Learning "scoring" procedures	Partisan vs. nonpartisan	Positive government
Motivated striving for identity continuity through family	Withdrawal	Intellectuality vs. "being regular"	Goodness of work and people	audience		Assertion vs. citation	Capitalism a neutral symbol
Motivated striving for autonomy from family		Inferiority vs. self-confidence	Abundance, optimism, natural harmony	arena		Responsible vs. nonresponsible	For social change
				opposition		Focus on self vs. focus on society	Not identified with business
				Relation of group values to each other			*Conservative:* Opportunity for the able
							Exclusiveness
							U.S. priority
							Restriction of government
							Capitalism a positive symbol.
							Faith in status quo
							Identified with business

6

The Need to Be Liked

CONCEPT AND SOURCE

Some people need reassurance about their likability; more than others, they need to be liked and are uncertain about whether or not they are liked. How do they tend to "select" their political opinions? The trait I have in mind here is expressed by the men themselves in such terms as these:

> I have fallen short of my standards (including my relations with other people) so often that I have a lack of self-confidence and therefore can see no real reason why anyone should be very interested in me. At times it could be said that I am scared of people. I have a great desire to be liked   [Lamb].

> I am troubled by various feelings of general "unlovableness" which are diffused and not so easily described. . . . The history of my relationships with girls is a long string of failures, ineffectiveness, and inertia   [Mintz].

> My basic drive seems to be a striving for affection which leads to a considerable amount of dependency upon people. . . . I depend upon these people [roommates] for affection and I therefore cannot stand the chance of losing this affection by turning my aggressive impulses outward   [De Vita].

These are the statements of those who experience this need most acutely, hence are anxious about the issue. If one takes the references of all those who, whether or not their likableness is a critically anxious issue for them, express some need for popularity or other evidence of their likability, one finds that it is the most commonly expressed need in the sample of some fifty biographies (of which twenty-four are analyzed here), just as it was the most frequently mentioned motive among the Syracuse students studied by Arthur Combs right after the Second World War. [1]

The Political Style of Those Needing to Be Liked. In a simpleminded way, one can formulate certain hypotheses about the shape of the political beliefs of men in the embrace of this particular need. More than others, they would tend to look at things as follows:

1. Government should adopt policies that ingratiate the various publics. It should offer maximum aid and services, avoid hostile acts whenever possible, be nice to people. These ideas follow from men's tendencies to *project* their own dispositions onto others, seeing others behave as they themselves behave, and from their tendencies to *generalize* their own view of the world in such a way as to think others share it.

2. Government and public officials should yield or withdraw when threatened. Crowne and Marlowe found that people who need social approval do, as a matter of fact, behave this way. [2] If they themselves behave this way, it would follow that they would see the government, as well, appropriately behaving this way.

3. Representative government might be especially congenial, on the grounds that the authorities in such a form of government are obliged to be responsive to their constituents. And since members of Congress, and indeed members of all legislatures, have a variety of styles, the person with a need to be liked would at the same time demand and expect his representatives to act in a responsive, propitiating way.

4. The person who needs social approval and seeks evidence of his likability avoids risks; [3] hence he might be expected to prefer a government that limited itself pretty much to what was generally approved, the conventional as well as the "nice" performance.

5. Not the charismatic leader, but the conventional and superficially charming person is the one to whom these men might be expected to be drawn. He would have no rough edges, no barbed wit, nothing to disturb or upset or create conflict.

6. The conflict-laden elements of politics would, I think, be overlooked, attention being drawn to ritual and form, state occasions, the unifying symbols of government, themes of historic tradition. These men would prefer the language of ambiguous but pleasant inference, the platitude and cliche.

---

[1] Arthur W. Combs, "A Comparative Study of Motivations as Revealed in Thematic Apperception Stories and Autobiography," *Journal of Clinical Psychology,* 3 (1947), pp. 65-75, reprinted in David C. McClelland, ed., *Studies in Motivation* (New York: Appleton-Century-Croft, 1955), pp. 89-101.

[2] Douglas P. Crowne and David Marlowe, *The Approval Motive* (New York: Wiley, 1964), pp. 133-49.

[3] *Ibid.,* pp. 166-85.

These brief notes represent a caricature, or an idealized model, of some expected ideological tendencies among those who need to be liked. Could it be said that in some way they describe the politics of the United States? After all, it is believed both in the United States and abroad that American aid to other countries represents an effort to buy their friendship, that American politics is more ritualistic and empty of genuine conflict than others, that American political leaders lack the definition and sharp edges of those on the Continent, that American congressmen are, above all, glad-handers. But is it true that Americans do care more about being liked than citizens of other nations?

There is indeed some evidence to show that Americans are especially graced or cursed with this motive. Gorer has suggested that for Americans, love and success somehow are equated, and that the success drive is thus linked to the need to be liked, or at least to a demand for evidence of being liked by others.[4] Farber, in a comparative study of British and American insurance clerks' attitudes toward bringing up children, finds that Americans mention a number of special social skills that are "all subordinate to the broad all-important one of 'Getting Along with Others,' a quality not mentioned at all by the British." Moreover, "the American stress is upon adjustment of the child *to other children,* while the British are much more concerned with their behavior toward adults. . . . Finally, *love* appears as an element in several American responses, both in the form of the child's 'Receiving Love' and to his being 'Loving.' "[5]

When contrasted with a very different population, post-World War II Russian refugees, a matched group of Americans again revealed somewhat greater concern about their own acceptability. The tests given to these two groups consisted of projective thematic apperception tests and some projective questions and stories to be interpreted, all designed to reduce the cultural specificity of the material. In contrast to the Russians, the Americans were more likely to characterize and evaluate a person in any of these stories or pictures "in terms of his positive or negative attitudes toward the subject himself." They were less likely to deal with the person in terms of "those characteristics that could be more properly called the person's own." "Americans much more frequently than Russians ascribed to the

---

[4]"Because the [American] child is pushed to the very limits of its capacity, because the conditions for its success are often so vague, or so far outside its control, the child becomes insatiable for the signs of love, reassuring it that it is worthy of love, and therefore a success" (Geoffrey Gorer, *The American People* [New York: Norton, 1948], p. 107).

[5]Maurice L. Farber, "English and Americans: Values in the Socialization Process," *Journal of Psychology,* 36 (1953), pp. 243-50, reprinted in McClelland, ed., *Studies in Motivation,* pp. 323-40.

actor the wish to be liked and esteemed by his friends."[6] Whether or not the need to be liked is increasing along with the urbanization and industrialization of the world, it seems that Americans are richly endowed with it.

Concepts Related to the Need to Be Liked. A concern over one's likability and acceptance by others is measured by self-reported worries on this score, plus the revelation of concerns that may not be openly stated. It is clearly not an easy thing to say whether or not the needs underlying such concerns, or the concerns themselves, are congruent with the need for affiliation, or for social approval, or for guidance by others (other directedness) as these have been developed by other students of this subject.

Some measures of "affiliation tendencies" devised to study the "sources of gregariousness" are based on a simple test: does a person choose to be with others or to be alone, or is it a matter of indifference to him? This research indicates that a person seeks others to help him validate his own emotional states, that is, to determine, when he is in doubt, the appropriateness of his own fear or insecurity.[7] Just how should he feel, in a given situation? Our men's biographies reveal that they too need acceptance or friendship to give them cues on how to behave, what to think, even how to feel. But there is a difference here. The men we have in mind are *worried* about their relations with others, hence they may not seek others, except in fantasy, because they are not sure how they will be received. This problem can be put in terms of what is called approach-avoidance theory, a theory that says that as people approach a goal offering at the same time the promise of reward and the threat of disappointment or punishment, both hope and fear increase—but in a special way. Much research indicates that, as one moves closer to an ambivalently perceived goal, fear increases faster than hope, so that under many circumstances there comes a point, short of the goal, where a person no longer pursues it. But then, so the theory goes, as it becomes more distant again, hope exceeds fear, and the cycle starts on another round. Often, it seems, this is the case with our men: they need people, but become anxious as they approach them. We cannot, therefore, guide our expectations along the lines developed by the work on *the psychology of affiliation.*

What is called the "need for affiliation" or the "affiliation motive" is a broader concept, since it includes fantasy life and measures concern and

---

[6]Eugenia Hanfmann, "Social Perception in Russian Displaced Persons and an American Comparison Group," *Psychiatry,* 20 (1957), pp. 135-36. See also Eugenia Hanfmann and Jacob W. Getzels, "Interpersonal Attitudes of Former Soviet Citizens, as Studied by a Semi-Projective Method," *Psychological Monographs,* vol. 69, no. 4 (1955).

[7]See, for example, Stanley Schacter, *The Psychology of Affiliation: Experimental Studies in the Sources of Gregariousness* (Stanford: Stanford University Press, 1959).

anxiety about interpersonal relations, as well as choice to be with others. Research and speculation about the nature of this motive rests on work with a set of projective tests based on ambiguous drawings (thematic apperception tests), about which the subjects are asked to tell freely imaginative stories.[8] The coding system for these stories gives us a clue to the meaning of the need for affiliation. A statement is coded as affiliation imagery "when a story contains evidence of concern, in one or more of the characters, over establishing, maintaining, or restoring a positive affective relationship with another person(s). Concern of this sort is immediately evident if the relationship is described as friendship." Further information is gathered about "statements of liking or wanting to be liked, accepted, or forgiven, or wanting understanding or sympathy," about frustrations of these desires, instrumental activity to secure affiliation, and, of course, whole plots turning on such activity.[9] As might be expected, when people's feelings of insecurity about their own place in a group is aroused, they score high on this measure of "n-affiliation."

While there is much in common between the need for affiliation as conceived in these terms and the need to be liked, including a concern about social approval, there are some difficulties. In the first place, the "need for affiliation is an approach motive"; that is, those who score high on this need have "a disposition to move toward others to elicit positive affective responses from them."[10] Some of our men are "shy"; they do not easily and casually move in this direction. More important, those with a high need for affiliation are described by those who know them as "self-assertive and confident (indicative of positive anticipations)," and also as "egotistical."[11] This would not be the way either I or, I think, others would describe men with a need to be liked. Certainly they do not reveal themselves this way in their biographies.

The need for affiliation, defined this way, is different from the need for social approval, as defined and measured by Crowne and Marlowe. These psychologists devised a test including items describing thoughts and acts that people rarely adopt but feel they should ("I never hesitate to go out of my way to help someone in trouble") and others (scored in reverse) describing thoughts and acts that people often adopt but feel they shouldn't ("I like to gossip at times"). A high score then indicates that most probably a person is trying to make himself look good because he is asking for and needs the approval of others. People who measure high on this test tend to

---

[8]See especially Chap. 4 and 5 in John W. Atkinson, ed., *Motives in Fantasy, Action, and Society* (Princeton: Van Nostrand, 1958).

[9]John W. Atkinson, Roger W. Heyns, and Joseph Veroff, "The Effect of Experimental Arousal of the Affiliation Motive on Thematic Apperception," *Journal of Abnormal and Social Psychology*, 49 (1954), p. 406, reprinted in Atkinson, ed., *Motives*, pp. 95-104.

[10]*Ibid.*, p. 103.

[11]*Idem.*

be susceptible to persuasion, tend to be conformist, seek popular responses on ambiguous questions, and avoid taking risks. Their way of dealing with conflict or challenging situations is typically to avoid them; their response to aggressive people is to become propitiating; above all they tend to try to conceal their true nature from others, a matter that makes a study of the thoughts of people with a high need for social approval quite difficult. A further, and rather tragic, feature of this syndrome is that "approval-dependent persons seek affiliation but tend to be disliked. Awareness of how they are evaluated seems to emerge only on a fantasy measure."[12] One would expect from such persons, and indeed one seems to get, stereotyped social thought, conventional and unoriginal politics; the middle of the road is their path to safety. Perhaps, among other reasons, this helps to explain why persons who rate high on the McClelland n-affiliation measure do not score high on authoritarianism; they would be likely to hedge on extreme statements of any kind.

This social approval motive seems close to the need to be liked, although it does not necessarily imply the need for positive *affective* responses by others; at least the questions on the scale do not imply the need for "warmth" and friendship, which is the quality desired (and in some ways also feared, as we shall see) in the men here at the focus of our attention. Social approval is colder, more distant, more concerned with impressions than with friendship.

Finally, there is the question of other-directedness. As Riesman conceives of it, it does not imply the need to be liked by others or the worry over likability that we find in the Adams men. Riesman says:

> What is common to all other-directeds is that their contemporaries are the source of direction for the individual. . . . The goals for which the other-directed person strives may shift . . . it is only the process of striving itself and the process of paying close attention to the signals from others that remain unaltered throughout life.[13]

Thus the goals need not include the friendship or affiliation of others; the goals might be whatever the significant others prescribe.

Nevertheless, there is a conceptual overlap here, which might help us; but the evidence is not favorable. Elaine Graham devised an inner-directed—other-directed values scale, two parts of which seemed to Miss Graham to be most closely allied to Riesman's concepts.[14] They are:

12Crowne and Marlowe, *Approval Motive,* p. 190.

13David Riesman, *The Lonely Crowd* (New Haven: Yale University Press, 1950), p. 22.

14Harriet Linton and Elaine Graham, "Personality Correlates of Persuasibility," in Carl I. Hovland and Irving Janis, eds., *Personality and Persuasibility* (New Haven: Yale University Press, 1959), pp. 69-101.

Work-oriented values such as efficiency, control, competence, and meeting high personal standards (ID) vs. needs for
friendship, popularity, intimacy, group adjustment and cooperation, and a responsiveness to social pressure on the basis of these
needs (OD).

Concern with self, with inner drives and preferences which
may be unconventional, with strivings toward creative achievement and personal recognition, and with independence from
social restrictions (ID) vs. needs for security, social approval,
participation in the community, and a responsiveness toward
conformity pressures on the basis of these needs (OD).[15]

On the whole the other-directed values and needs in this list do not adequately describe those men who report and reveal their need to be liked.
As we shall see, some of them are nonparticipants because they are
worried about giving offense to others or doing the wrong thing; they also
fight against their conformity tendencies with a fierceness, if not always
with a success, that makes this version of other-directedness inapplicable.
Finally, Miss Graham's other-directeds were more persuasible than others.
At least some of ours, it seems from their biographies, take principled
stands and cannot be moved by friends or family.

Because our data come from biographies, rather than questionnaires,
we can see the varied personalities caught in our net. They have one thing
in common: they are worried, probably more worried than others, about
their likability, and they do want, indeed need, to be liked.

Origins and Meanings of the Need to Be Liked.   The way in which
a need to be liked expresses itself in politics depends on its "meaning" to
the individual, which in turn depends on how it is learned. There are very
good reasons for believing that the most enduring and strongest motives are
learned early in childhood, often before a child can use symbols or think in
words.[16] This is important, because a motive acquired at this time, through
unmediated (unverbalized) experience, cannot be easily clarified; the
stimulus situation is "messy," as McClelland says, very unlike the labora-
tory situation, where all extraneous matters are excluded, and unlike adult
situations, where things can be "explained." Therefore, the motive (affective state) does not become extinguished by the removal of a particular
stimulus or reward, for the affective state is not connected with anything
particular. It emerges from an inchoate condition. Furthermore, the motives
learned at this early stage seem to be especially closely connected to a more
primitive, archaic part of the "brain," the autonomic nervous system, and

---

[15]*Ibid.,* p. 81.
[16]See David C. McClelland, "The Importance of Early Learning in the Formation of
Motives," in Atkinson, ed., *Motives,* pp. 437-52.

once these connections are made, the motive is harder to reach through the cognitions of the cortex, a part of the brain that developed later phylogenetically and matures later in the life span. For these and other reasons, a motive, unlike habits (which are learned in specific stimulus-response-reward situations), is likely to endure for a long time, and is unlikely to lose its force when its object is attained. A person who needs to be liked does not therefore lose his affection-seeking drive when he discovers he is liked, as he might lose his hunger when he is fed. At least, he will not do it so quickly. This suggests that political thoughts satisfying needs or motives of this kind are likely to be relatively enduring in their main thrust. These enduring thoughts will probably not be topical issue opinions (on candidates, on urban redevelopment, on the war in Viet Nam); rather, they will be attitudes toward violence, authority, moral appearances, autonomy. It is the "latent function" of the attitude in serving the basic motives that ensures and guides this perseverence: it avoids conflict, expresses high moral sentence, protects privacy.

But this internalized experience, this affective state that time and again drives a man to seek one kind of gratification rather than another, has a pale shadow: imitation. People of all ages, but especially the young, learn through imitation, that is, through modeling their behavior on someone else's behavior. The reward lies in solving an immediate problem of what to do, how to behave, what to say, as well as eliciting the approval of others. A man might respond to others in an "overly friendly" way because he has seen his father behave that way. That friendly kind of behavior may have been greatly rewarded at some time, and from then on it may have become part of that person's repertoire of interpersonal styles. But it has a different meaning for him than such friendly behavior has for the person who constantly must test his likableness. The imitated behavior plays a different part in the economy of a personality than does the need-dominated behavior of the men we have here in mind. The imitated behavior is more accurately described as a "habit," the need-dominated behavior as a "motive." While habits and motives share a similar manifest expression, a habit, if not rewarded, is more likely to drop out of the repertoire of thought and behavior than a motive. A habit, therefore, is more open to change.

Now let us turn to a brief consideration of the nature of the reward. Ingratiating behavior may, in the first place, be simply instrumental to another goal. Thus, a person wants to be liked because this may enable him to win office in an election, which in turn will enable him to do something he wants to do, perhaps exercise power over others. The affection-seeking is not based on a need for affection, but on a need for something that affection brings; the reward is extrinsic to the particular affection-seeking character of the behavior. We call this kind of reward an "instrumental" reward.

Second, as with the need for affiliation, the need to be liked may reflect a need for self-validation.[17] When men need to be liked they need to be told, often again and again, that they are "all right," that their opinions, their emotions, their actions are right. Affiliation does this by giving cues and models for behavior and thought. Being liked does this by providing an individual with some sense of positive approval from others. Festinger puts it this way: "The subjective feelings of correctness in one's opinions and the subjective evaluation of adequacy of one's performance on important abilities are some of the satisfactions that persons gain in the course of these associations with other people."[18] And if this is true of association, it is even more true of being liked by others.

The third basis for desiring to be liked is a special form of this self-validation and, most likely, less available to the conscious mind. People concerned about their hostilities and critical attitudes toward others may both assert how much they like others and demand evidence that others like them. It helps to reassure them that they have not offended and that they are not offensive.

As I mentioned, these various bases for a need to be liked are important, because, most superficially, if the need to be liked masks an underlying hostility, then much of the ingratiating and risk-minimizing political thought mentioned early in this chapter will be overlaid and undercut by hostile references.

OBSTACLES TO EASY FRIENDSHIP

Intellectuality, particularly at an early stage, presents certain problems in the attainment of an easy, natural, tension-free relationship with others; and then, too, it is a product of these problems. The matter of social uncomfortableness where elite figures are concerned also directs both friendship and thought. The fear of intimacy, whatever its cause, channels political thought, I believe, into a rather special mold.

In this analysis the *dramatis personnae* and their problems are as seen in Table A. With this evidence of the way the "blockages" are distributed, there is no reason to claim that they form a syndrome, although of course when they accumulate, their influence on political thought will be especially

---

[17]This theme seems to have increasing acceptance among psychologists. See Leon Festinger, "A Theory of Social Comparison Processes," *Human Relations,* 7 (1954), pp. 117-40; Schacter, *Psychology of Affiliation;* and, especially, Albert Pepitone, *Attraction and Hostility* (New York: Atherton, 1964).

[18]Festinger, "Theory of Social Comparison Processes," p. 135.

TABLE A

Impediments to Easy Relations with others
(Blocking the Need to Be Liked)

Name	"Intellectuality"	Uncomfortable Relations with Elites	Fear of Intimacy
Lamb	Yes	Yes	Yes
Mintz	Yes	Yes	Yes
De Vita	Yes, but there is no evidence that this impeded friendships in childhood	Yes	Yes
Trueblood	Yes	No	?
Goldberg	No	Yes	No
Demming	Yes, but not part of self-image and may not impede friendships	Yes	No
Svenson	No (defense of "intellectuality" is not related to friendship problems)?	No	Yes
King	No	Yes→No	No

noticeable. Since a partially thwarted need increases striving, for Lamb, Mintz, and De Vita political thought reflects the need to be liked to a high degree, as may be seen in the summary of Chapter 7.

Intellectuality. People like others who have values similar to their own for several reasons, among which are the opportunities this "value-homophily" provides for congenial talk, the lack of areas of sensitivity and conflict of which one must beware, and, not least, the "validation" by each partner of his own evaluations, implying the "rightness" of the person himself. But not all values lend themselves equally to this congeniality, and the qualities associated with intellectuality may be of this less congenial kind: affective neutrality and a cognitive approach to things, always asking "Is it true?" not "Do I like it?"; preciseness and correctness, bookishness (tropisms toward books rather than people?), learning worn too publicly, and other similar qualities. If this is a problem for the adult, it is a much greater problem for the "precocious" young man who turns to books and academic achievement instead of (as compensation for a deficiency in) affective engagement with his fellows, a melancholy turning point for many a young "scholar." How, then, does such a quality channel the need to be liked into social thought?

In youth, at least in American high schools, intellectuality is not often a successful avenue to popularity; nor is the popular person likely to turn his talents to things intellectual (though, of course, he may get "good grades"). It is a mutual affair. This problem of popularity and intellectuality is illustrated by the early difficulties reported by three Adams men, Mintz, Trueblood, and Lamb. Here is the way it seemed to Mintz, concerned about his "lovableness" and highly intelligent as well as moderately intellectual:

> In high school, athletics, good looks, success in being an "all-around guy," and popularity with the girls became all-important. Unable to meet the challenge, I withdrew within myself and narrowed my social contacts to a small group of friends of the same age and sex. Because of my apparent preoccupation with studies and my inactivity in sports and extracurricular activities, I became known as an intellectual and just missed being voted the most intellectual in the class.

Mintz resented this label and his assignment to this position, and, partly for these reasons, "agitated for reforms":

> I wrote my senior-year source theme on Shavian socialism and became much impressed by equalitarian political theories. For my efforts, I received little support and gained nothing but the label "revolutionary," which, along with "intellectual," was neatly inscribed in the school yearbook when I graduated. My bitterness toward the high school persists, as evidenced by the fact that I have never revisited it since the day I departed with my diploma.

Trueblood, whose sister was considered by their parents to be more aggressive and daring than her brother, and whose history of "physical inferiority," glasses, and lack of athletic ability added to what he calls "my sense of weakness and inferiority," sought various means of compensation for these deficiencies in boyish prowess. One was development of his "artistic ability," and another was "feeling more intelligent":

> This led me to application in my schoolwork and to a desire to show off my knowledge to others. The latter caused a particular smart-alecky phase about my second- and third-grade years.

For a period of a few years he attempted to withdraw and became "introverted," but, gradually finding this unsatisfactory, he later sought more social contacts. This was difficult:

Being a scholar was in many other people's minds the anti-thesis of being an athlete. Therefore, the more I tried to gain superiority through brains, the more I felt others disassociated me from brawn; thus the policy [of intellectuality] which possibly increased some superiority feelings was also heightening inferiority.

While Mintz's early intellectuality was touched with a reformist radicalism, and Trueblood's was in part aesthetic, Lamb's was moralistic:

I enjoyed stories about great Americans such as Washington and Lincoln, and the books I liked the most stressed the moralistic side of their lives, Washington and the cherry tree, and Lincoln and the few cents he walked miles to return. These books show that throughout my life I have always put great emphasis on setting and living up to high standards.

And of course, this was especially true of schoolwork: "I have always thought that to study was morally good, and I think that, speaking objectively, I overdo my homework." Pursued without conflict, such "perfectionism," as Lamb calls this trait, might have led to a scholar's life, or some professional dedication, where the anxiety associated with this pattern of high standards might have been assimilated and actually employed for satisfying work. But there is further conflict; there is that "need to be liked" mentioned in Lamb's quotation above. And the conflict between his "perfectionism" and his need to be liked exacerbates the stituation: "Since I never fulfill my goals, I lose self-confidence, and this causes me to redouble my efforts to live up to my standards. It also causes in me a desire to be liked in order to assuage my lack of confidence."

The intellectual product of this pattern of a need to be liked confronted with a compensating or at least intruding intellectuality is hard to ferret out of the data, but, since these are speculative essays, I shall hazard a guess. Empirically it has been found that bookishness is associated with liberal tendencies in the sense used here: equalitarian, internationalist, reformist, inclusive.[19] One of the reasons for this may be the tendency of intellectuals to transcend their own immediate case in order to look at larger patterns of events, the tendency to generalize, the movement from particularistic to universalistic modes of thought.[20] These universalistic

---

[19]Gardner Murphy and Rensis Likert, *Public Opinion and the Individual* (New York: Harper, 1938).

[20]Max Weber, "Politics as a Vocation," in Hans H. Gerth and C. Wright Mills, eds., *From Max Weber: Essays in Sociology* (New York: Oxford University Press, 1946), pp. 93-95.

modes are, *in the current culture,* supportive of equality of opportunity, inclusiveness toward minority groups, internationalist. The culture orients them in this direction because of the way categories are defined and employed; *all* men have equal rights, race and creed are illegitimate legal categories, all nations are sovereign. More importantly, and more intimately, the disaffection created by the attitude of schoolmates toward the bookish youngster creates incipient rebellious feelings, as we have seen in Mintz's case, and these may be harnessed to reformist (equalitarian) causes.

But the fact is that Trueblood withdraws from his liberal tendencies because he wishes to associate with the rich and powerful men in the Republican camp. Mintz is for the underdog, but he is disgusted by the vulgarity of the working classes. Lamb is for liberal ends, but is, he says, a conservative about the means to be employed, and frankly admits the satisfactions he gains from the status quo. The intellectuality does not come through as a strong liberalism in these cases, though the men may be more liberal than they would have been if they had only sought to gratify their needs to be liked.

Something else is more clearly at work. The conflict between affect and cognition, between being liked and being more learned than others, produces a kind of anxiety, with a special political style: *hedging and indecision.* Mintz's indecisiveness is reflected in the following quotation:

> I review my life and am amazed at the small number of decisions that I can truly call my own. . . . Even now, making ordinary, petty decisions is an effort, and I often seek to shift the choice to another, usually on grounds (and with some truth) that it makes no difference to me how the matter is resolved. . . . Even less significant decisions such as are involved in reading menus provide a perpetual source of anxiety and uncertainty.

Trueblood is in the same leaky boat, bailing all the time. He lives by the motto, which was born, he says, of a sense of inferiority, "Be ye perfect in all things." But this makes decisions extremely difficult for him:

> No decision ever turns out perfectly, and disgust with producing more inferiority eventually results in . . . an excessive meticulousness in making decisions lest any details be overlooked . . . and a dread of making any decisions. . . . A leaning toward Republicanism is continually being undercut by a few successful individuals who may be Democrats. The measured consideration of the present party social standing, etc., is being undercut by what one thinks may be their future social standing. There is no end to the factors which can be introduced and weighed in making the decision.

Lamb, somewhat more decisive, yet hedges in ideological orientation:

> I am *liberal and conservative* on political, economic, and so-
> cial issues. . . . [My] goals are liberal in that they are based on
> the liberal premise that all men should have equal opportunities.
> . . . Despite these liberal goals, I believe that the way to ac-
> complish them is through conservative means.

And explaining this conservatism, he says, "My whole life is regularized
and organized and . . . I find it very difficult to do anything that has not
been planned. My setting of high standards and trying to follow them
involve a striving for the security of having a set pattern of life." Under
these circumstances, for Lamb, as for Mintz and Trueblood, decisions come
hard, and the net result for all of them is a highly cautious, tentative,
indefinite approach to politics, especially partisan identification.

Now it is not the case that people who are purely intellectualistic, if I
may use that term, are usually politically neutral or withdrawn. On the
contrary, the American campus, at least, is a source of ideological and
partisan political activity, even though economic interests are less likely to
be engaged in American political struggles. Therefore, it seems to me, the
conflict between the need to be liked, the yearning for some kind of affective reassurance, and the intellectualistic tendencies described is the source
of the hedging, indecisive style just described. And the fact that this conflict has a long history has created, in each case, a characterological inhibition against political (or other) commitment.

Uncomfortable Interpersonal Relations with Elites. Let us suppose
that for those who need to be liked the criterion for turning in a liberal or
conservative direction (and the point is the "turning," not the destination,
for many other things enter into what seems to be an appropriate place to
stop) is the selection of people one somehow feels comfortable with, either in
actuality or in fantasy. Say a man likes to associate with elites because he
so clothes himself with the properties of elitism that he sees himself as bigger
or better because of his important connections; then surely a Republican and
a conservative are congenial things to be. One looks "up," face warmed by
this elitist sun. Or, alternatively, a person may be uncomfortable in the
company of important people, suffering from a sense of comparative inferiority; they seem so self-assured, so self-confident, they have so much
one wishes one had (in personal or material qualities), one imagines slights.
How easy, then, to moralize the preference for the humble and lowly as a
principled choice and to erect upon it a structure of liberalism and humanitarianism! The grounds of this choice are some complex personal problem
(of which insecurity and feelings of inferiority are parts in *both* selective
turnings) and include one's preferred dealings with people.

Here we shall examine those made uncomfortable by elites to see if perhaps they show the effects of this downward-glancing posture in their political thought. There are five of them: Mintz, Demming, De Vita, Goldberg, and I include Lamb because, while he wishes to be nice to everyone and wants everyone to like him, he has special troubles with the rich and self-confident. These men are all hostile toward the dominant figures of the social worlds in which they live; in the conventional terms of their societies, they are non-status-seekers, though in other terms they seek recognition and "narcissistic supplies" like everyone else.[21] This is not just the liberal's antagonism to the "establishment," but rather an uncomfortable feeling created by the apparently integrated and secure representatives of the dominant groups in their milieus. It is more specifically interpersonal than economic or political.

Mintz is explicit on this matter: "I consciously avoid the BMOC's [big men on campus] because, while I cannot always detect it, I feel that they must be somehow phony. I particularly dislike persons who are highly self-satisfied and self-centered." At the same time he "envies" their purposeful behavior. Lamb says: "Our family belongs to a club and I don't like to go there because of the presence of a few snobs who feel that they should be acclaimed as wonderful people because they have money." He goes on to account for this: "The fact that I am uncomfortable with and dislike people who act superior is that, because I lack self-confidence, I am scared of them." Goldberg says:

> My belief that the Democratic party is for the "little guy" has its basis in my background, where it is reinforced both by my position in a minority group, which is discriminated against, and by feelings of inferiority in certain social situations which I subconsciously may think would arise more frequently in my dealings with members of the Republican party, whom I probably associate with a "superior" group.

In these three cases, it is the interpersonal uncomfortableness of association with social elites that reinforces, if it does not prompt, an aversion to elitism and elite attitudes. In Demming's case it is a little different; he has been rejected by the elite. Having fought against the Adams Broadcasting System (dominated, he thinks, by an elite in-group) and the College Council and lost, he says of himself: "At this point my hostility began to spread to other university groups which seemed also to represent the college elite. My hostility resulted from a desire to be accepted into these

---

[21] I don't know if he invented it, but the term is Otto Fenichel's. First he speaks of "narcissistic needs," and then, a page later, of "narcissistic supplies of affection." See his *The Psychoanalytic Theory of Neurosis* (New York: Norton, 1945), pp. 40-41.

[prestige] groups . . . [but also] was intimately connected with a deep sense of inferiority." Unable to "make it" with the elite, he finds companionship with the out-group, where he is comfortable, feels accepted and rewarded for his ideas and organizing talents, and where his lack of the appropriate in-group traits is not a source of embarrassment.

Finally, De Vita represents another variant of this interpersonal strain. As we have seen, he is a lower-middle-class boy in an elite school, marginal, transitional, a man without a social identity—something of which he is acutely aware. Yet the interpersonal problem predates this situation, for it applied to the boys' clubs and school groups he knew before coming to college. This is the young man who has said, "My image of the world is clearly divided into three sections: the world of those superior to me, whom I must please; the world of those equal to me, with whom I must avoid conflict; and the world of those beneath me, who should recognize and admire my claim to power." But the world of those in a "superior" position was not a comfortable one for De Vita. He says, "I have always had a feeling, which up to now I couldn't understand, that I am never really doing things for myself. I am always working to please someone else. . . . I worked for the affection and praise of those upon whom I depended," something he resents. Furthermore, among his contemporaries, "I have never been able to gain very many friends among the fellows in my own position. I always felt I was competing with them," and he dreads open competition. As a consequence, elites, and those who threaten to be more successful in competition than he is, make De Vita uncomfortable, and, as he reports, "my drive to control pulls me away from people from whom I cannot really gain affection. If I can't gain affection on their level, I have to rise above them and gain their admiration." Thus he is drawn into groups where he can gain control, admiration, and the respect of others. He identifies with the underdog because the underdog cannot compete and does not make him feel uncomfortable. The frustrated need to be liked leads to a relatively more successful effort to be admired.

Yet one further case will reveal the complexity of anticipating the political expression of this need to be liked addressed to a lower-status audience. King is a spare young man from a middle-western city who reports himself as liberal and a Democrat partly because that is the party of "the common man." But, he insists, he is moderate and "well within the extremes." He loves his parents, follows their wishes, and seeks success on their terms, devoting much energy to getting good grades. Of his high school life, he reports feeling somewhat out of the "ruling clique," and yet

In spite of this I wanted to be popular, and be elected. I really wanted most of all to be elected student mayor. I set out to

> organize the "plain folks" and form a coalition. . . . My general
> policy was to say "Hi!" to a lot of people. Even though I wanted
> to displace the [ruling] clique, I did not attempt to crusade
> against it, for that would have made me stick out and classed
> with the odd balls of the school.

He won the election and organized a political machine based on his "plain
folks" coalition.

> To me this [policy and victory] symbolizes my connection
> with the "common man" concept, which I associate with just one
> party. My association with this concept has brought me strength
> and acceptance, just as I feel it has brought the Democratic party
> strength and acceptance.

Yet when King comes to Adams College and joins a multiparty debating
society, he finds it advisable to join not the Liberal party, but rather the
Conservative party, whose positions in the society debates he nevertheless rarely supports. He takes this curious step, he says, "to avoid extremism . . . I have a fear of extremism." The need to be liked, combined with
moderate opposition to an elite group in high school and identification with
the common man, would, if King were like the others, lead him to move in a
liberal direction. But he does not move that way. Rather, this situation leads
him to move in a conformist direction at Adams College, where the thought
of alienating the moderate conservative majority shifts him nominally to the
right.

The lesson is an important one. The anxious person who needs to be
liked and who for one reason or another excludes the elites from his
audience is bound to his liberalism only so long as he feels hostile or ill at
ease with the elites, whether or not he is in fact excluded by them. But the
binding may come loose; the nature and exclusiveness of the elites may
change, and then the drive for popularity, or perhaps only for the symbols
of popularity, might push gently and with well-rationalized effectiveness
toward some middle position, some hedging, some further distance from the
feared extremes, rightward to a more conservative or ambiguous public
image.

All of these men are glancing downward in their search for audiences,
at least when we first see them; the downward glance, prompted by fear of
and dislike for elites in interpersonal situations, leads to support for the
underdog, not out of some moving empathy, but because it rationalizes this
uncomfortableness with elites, helps to "get even" with them for causing
these uncomfortable feelings, and explains otherwise inexplicable behavior.

FEAR OF INTIMACY AND THE BID FOR THE AFFECTION OF UNDERDOGS

In what form does the person who needs to be liked want this need satisfied? Take, for example, the question of intimacy. Does a man want real reciprocal warmth and closeness in his relations with others? Does he want to reveal himself completely? Does he want to share his "deep heart's core"? Lewin says, comparing Germans with Americans, that Germans reveal themselves and open up their personalities to relatively few, but with these few they achieve a high degree of intimacy. Americans, on the other hand, are much more open with many more people, but never so intimate with their close friends.[22] While, for example, the socioeconomic status patterns of friendships have clear political implications because politics is organized on status lines, the intimacy of friendships has no such clear reference. Yet it is not irrelevant, for the world of politics is laced with close interpersonal relations; in some sense, that is what much of it is all about. Let us consider first some glimpses into the nature of the problem as we see it in these biographies.

Here I am sorting out a rather special problem: a combined desire for and fear of close and warm personal relations, the *intimacy complex*. This is not a mere desire for popularity, for unless the desire for popularity is combined with the desire and fear of closeness or intimacy, it may not play the same part in the complex economics of the personality. Equally, it is different from the thirst for acceptance and the fear of rejection in a group, for this often has social roots not related to the intimacy complex at all. There are four men who betray this complex in sufficient outline for us to identify it: Lamb, Mintz, De Vita, and Svenson.

Lamb, whose thin body and full face form an incongruous mixture, reports with regret that he "never had a close friend," but seems to frustrate his own inclinations to build up such a friendship by being too "nice" and then by criticizing his associates, and building up a circle of acquaintances instead of friends. In the dining hall, for example, he says he passes by boys he knows well in order to cultivate some boys he hardly knows at all. Following this observation, he says:

---

[22] Kurt Lewin, *Resolving Social Conflicts* (New York: Harper, 1948), pp. 1-31. Gorer also takes this view about American social relations: "Generally friendship has extension rather than depth, and is founded more on common interests than congeniality of character" (*The American People,* p. 132). In *Political Ideology* (New York: Free Press, Macmillan, 1962) I find that those who seem to have absorbed the democratic ethos most integrally tend to prefer an arm's-length friendship; it is the "homeless" men looking for some political utopia who seek greater intimacy (pp. 466-67).

It should be noted that in school I was president of my class every year except one from the fourth grade on. I was also voted most generous by a landslide in our senior poll. A number of people thought it really should have been "most gullible." There is an element of truth in this, because with my great desire to be liked, I would go considerably out of my way to be liked, and I probably felt that if I didn't do favors people asked of me, they would not like me. This is partly due to my distrust of others and my inability to have close friends.

His interpersonal ambivalence is rather openly stated; the intimacy complex is one that Lamb acknowledges of his own accord.

For Mintz, the problems of personal relations are more intense and express themselves somewhat differently. Where Lamb has a large number of friendly associates and few (he says) close friends, Mintz has few acquaintances and several intimate friends. But the matter is troublesome, with reference to his ambivalence regarding both underdogs and personal friends:

My yearning to help people who are in unfortunate situations . . . contrasts sharply with another trait, a coldness, remoteness, and hostility toward these same people on the level of personal contact. . . . In order to explore my further attraction to remote objects and fear (it is—I think—a fear) of intimate contacts, I shall have to penetrate deeper. . . . For years prior to adolescence I was disturbed about the diminutive size of my genitals and general physical smallness . . . and although I have outgrown these fears to an extent, they still retain some hold over me and contribute to an overall sense of inferiority and inadequacy. . . . I am also troubled by various feelings of "unlovableness" which are diffused and not so easily described as feelings of sexual inadequacy.

As a consequence Mintz shuns a variety of personal contacts, as we have seen. He does not like the "ultra-enthusiastic, purposeful, 'well-rounded' individuals." He avoids the "highly satisfied and self-centered." "Superficiality is a characteristic of which I am intolerant in my personal associations." And yet, in spite of the intimacy complex, this sensitive, intelligent, humane young man has friends: "It has always been close friendships that I have sought and gained, and, without intending to sound hypocritical, have been simultaneously the best friend of five different boys." Observe, however, that he has kept a count, and that he knows his priority in the friendship hierarchies of these five boys.

De Vita shows both sides of the intimacy problem. Speaking first of his ambiguous social situation somewhere between a lower-middle-class origin (his father runs a paint store) and his upper-class associates at

Adams College, he says, "The middle-class social system seems to me to be so very shallow, so very artificial, and so lacking in the warmth and feeling that characterized my home environment. . . . The lower-class values of . . . close personal relationships [are] still very much a part of me." Remember how De Vita explains the complications of this "part" of himself:

> As a result of my drive to win affection, I have developed also a drive to win admiration through seeking to control and dominate others. . . . I've never been able to have any real friendships with fellows my own age because I tend to view those in my position as potential competitors for the affection and approval I need. I've never been able to be one of the group . . . [but] if one can gain affection through pleasing his superiors, one can gain admiration by holding himself as a model of excellence before his subordinates. . . . I can't gain affection on their level; I have to rise above them and gain their admiration.

But it should be observed that this is not the kind of admiration based on social status, social rank. Perhaps this is because circumstances have not opened this door to De Vita; perhaps, too, it is because he retains a basic humanity to which this kind of rank is uncongenial, a humanity complicated by aggressive feelings and related to his desire for the warm, close relationships he cannot achieve. The intimacy complex is evident here and shapes his substitutes for close friendships, admiration and control, in a special way.

Svenson is a little less self-revealing, a little less self-aware, and a little more eager to cover up his hostile feelings than the others. Rather than reporting his self-discovery, we must reveal it in his half-conscious statements about himself. He says, first, making the case for his need for a certain kind of interpersonal relation:

> I find great pleasure in what the Germans call *Gemutlichkeit* —the spirit of good-fellowship, friendliness, brotherhood, etc. I have always felt somewhat proud of the fact that I could "get along" with nearly any personality. It seems impossible for me to hold any sort of grudge whatsoever.

At a later point he reports having been the "fall guy" for some practical jokers, and goes on to say, "My credulity and trust in my fellow man fit, of course, with the desire for friendship and fraternal spirit which I discussed earlier." Now, while this is not the same as a desire for intimacy, it is suggestive of some such desire, and since it forms a central feature of Svenson's analysis, one may infer that he places it high on his list of priorities in values and desires.

But the other side is there, too, the fear of intimacy and the desire for the "distancing" of people or of neutralizing the free flow of emotions in personal relations. One must read between the lines:

> As I see my personality, the thing which characterizes it most is an almost complete lack of aggression and a profound unwillingness to do violence or injustice to anything. My philosophy is, indeed, "live and let live," and I very often cast myself in the role of peacemaker among my friends. Most differences between people seem to me petty and unimportant.

At this point one's suspicions are aroused; it is all too bland, the self is being held in check at some cost, cost to the individual and to the friendships he seeks. Intimacy is certainly inhibited by this style, a revelation that, together with some political implications, is further seen in the following passages:

> For the most part, my political identifications follow this easygoing trend also. If asked to characterize the way I feel about the majority of politics, I would say "indecision and indifference." . . . When I discussed my feelings on the labor question, I was unsure which group to identify with. This is one particular example of a general trend in my personality—a dislike of positively committing myself to anything. [Does he mean people, too?] . . . In conversation I very often leave sentences unfinished, preferring to let the listener draw the conclusion. My ability to engage in verbal controversy in political matters is thus rather handicapped. I dislike arguments, anyway, even friendly ones, and often keep silent though I disagree with what is being said. . . . Naturally, with this sort of attitude, I do not identify with any particular political party.

One does not achieve intimacy, as a rule, or even "brotherhood," with this sort of diffidence; one does not reveal or share one's personality if one avoids arguments and adopts the chronic role of peacemaker. The fact is that Svenson has very substantial hostilities to carry around with him ("My father's dealings with me invariably carried, to my way of thinking, a marked injustice and incapacity for understanding. . . . I was always belittled for one thing or another, seemingly so my father could have something to criticize"). Thus, reading between the lines, as we must, I would say that Svenson's search for "brotherhood" involves a frustrating ambivalence about intimacy, something he desires and fears and does not know how to attain.

Now it is a curious and I think significant observation that these four men all go out of their way to protest their affection for various underdogs, members of religious, ethnic, or economic minorities. It is true that, except for Svenson, they all have reasons for not identifying with elites, and hence may seek identification elsewhere, but I think something else is at work, something related to their intimacy complexes. The origins of these complexes are, of course, lost in obscurity, but we have reason in several instances to suspect that it is an intervening hostility that is at work, and even more, a fear of their own hostility. Lamb speaks of his too frequent criticisms of his friends, De Vita speaks of his view of peers as competitors, Svenson shuns conflict and protests his "almost complete lack of aggression" a little too strongly. Only with Mintz does it seem to be something else—something we shall see in a minute. It is plausible to believe that the intimacy complex might help to shape a political philosophy of tolerance and goodwill toward underdogs, minorities, and distant groups. The distance is important because it helps to solve the problem of intimacy: these others are out of reach. Support of civil rights and goodwill toward minorities are a kind of symbolic ingratiation. Under this stimulus, one might frame a view that says to "the people," the disadvantaged, and especially the objects of prejudice or denigration, "I love you all," thus bidding, again symbolically, for their reciprocated and safely distant affection. In this way a person's need for affection shapes a kind of offer: "I will be for you if you are for me," or perhaps, negatively, "I will not reject you if you do not reject me."

It is in this spirit of tolerance that Lamb frames his views on the treatment of people he hardly knows:

> The fact that I want to be liked can be applied to my relations with all peoples regardless of income, religion, or race. At the present time I have had so few relationships of this sort that my views are more theoretical than anything else, but I don't think my opinions would change if I were really exposed to a large number of people of lower income and lower educational level.

And De Vita says, "To discriminate against a group is to alienate yourself from any affection which might be gained from that group." Moreover, what applies to "tolerance" also applies to equalitarianism: it is a way of being liked and of avoiding the alienation of affection, all safely with distant others.

We have seen that Svenson cannot make up his mind on his party preference and prefers to avoid controversial subjects generally. Yet on one matter he is outspoken:

> Perhaps the strongest political opinions I possess are centered in one particular field. I am very much against "America first" attitudes in almost any degree. This seems to stem from a

belief that all nations, persons, and ethnic groups are politically equal, and deserve to be judged under the same standard of justice. . . . The problem of desegregation is one of the most important social issues of our time.

In view of his "easygoing" indifference to most issues, this stand puzzles Svenson: "My feelings on these subjects [nativism and civil rights] seem a little too strong and too firmly entrenched to fit completely the patterns of indifference and indecision." He explains them biographically: a radical childhood acquaintance, a reaction against his father's views. Yet in the perspective of the entire record, including, incidentally, the fact that "I find it difficult to express emotion," it seems likely that his frustrated desire for brotherhood and intimacy among friends is working itself out through these symbolic expressions of affection for distant and denigrated others.

But Mintz is still more complicated. On the one hand, his attitude toward the working class is, as we have seen, disgust. On the other hand:

> I particularly envied their rugged, earthy, unfragile appearance and the uncomplicated sex life which I imagined they must lead, and their apparent lack of worries. I also tend to equate a certain simplicity and untarnished quality with the lower classes as opposed to the superficiality that I generally associate with the middle classes.

Does Mintz seek the affection of this group? There is an ambivalence here which he cannot easily resolve. It is connected with his "substantial uncertainty in locating the sources of my true sexual motivations." He explains this as follows:

> Occasionally I am troubled by fears that I might possibly have homosexual tendencies. I try to test myself by picking out a boy on the street and imagine myself involved in sexual activities with him, and then notice my reactions. With the boys, while I do not find the prospects of sexual activities appealing, I do sometimes envy their good looks and feel myself puny and inadequate by comparison. My reaction to the girls is mixed and thus quite disturbing. Some I find distinctly appealing, some to which I have no positive reaction, and a few which I immediately dislike and, perhaps, am even afraid of.

For Mintz, therefore, the working man (and woman?), or an unknown boy or girl on the street, means something special, and the possibility that he desires their affection in a special way must be acknowledged. There is something there that, in his fantasy life if not in reality, draws him to these people. At one level he certainly wants—and fears—their affection. Thus, to repeat, he finds his sympathies with the underdog contrasting "sharply with a . . . coldness, remoteness, and hostility toward these same people on the level of personal contact." The intimacy complex, openly with Mintz, perhaps more subtly with some others, has sexual overtones as well as the more dominant theme centering in a set of unacceptable feelings of hostility.

The point, then, is this: A need to be liked which is somehow complicated and constrained by a fear of intimacy tends to work itself out in social thought in the form of bidding for the affection of distant groups, safe because they can be seen more as symbols than as persons. What goes into this intimacy complex is another matter, but some element of unacceptable hostility is a very likely ingredient, hardly known to the cook who prepares this dish for his own table.

7

Validating the Self Through Being Liked

This corrosive need to be liked seems often to reflect a special kind of uncertainty about the self, an uncertainty about one's rightness or correctness in style, manner, and thought. It reflects, that is, a need for self-validation. The energizing need, mediated by some interpreted experience, personality traits, beliefs, or conflicts, leads to the selection of political ideas that promise to be rewarding in this context.

WINNING VOTES: THE SYMBOLS OF ACCEPTANCE AND THE SUBSTANCE OF POWER

What is it that tells a person he is likable, has been accepted, is making a go of it among others who look, from the outside, to be so secure and purposive and all of a piece? The term "popularity" is on the tongues of these men, but how does this popularity show itself? By invitations, for example, when they were younger; Mintz writes: "I was always invited to a few less parties than most of my friends and, when I did receive an invitation, I usually believed I did either (1) because the hostess needed boys and chose me to equalize the party, or (2) because one of my friends had requested that I be asked." More likely now the cues lie in being included when the fellows make up a party to go out for a beer, for a trip to Bennington or wherever. It is revealed in rough greetings, jokes, friendly demeanor, horseplay. In a very real sense, the absence of these cues leads a man to search for substitutes, symbols of acceptance: votes. King tells at length of his campaign to get elected; as we have seen, Lamb explains that he was the "president of my class every year except one from the fourth grade on." Mintz has to go back to the third grade for this kind of satisfaction,

124

but "it was there that I received one of my most cherished experiences—being elected president of the student council." Citing such electoral success as a proof of popularity, a validation of the self, is common. Electioneering represents an occasion for intermingling the techniques of "winning friends" (or so it seems), the techniques of political maneuver, and, sometimes, discussing the substance of political issues. It is King who says, "In a sense, both myself and the [Democratic] party have exploited the common man since we have taken his vote to gain power. But we have both benefited the common man with the gains from this exploitation. The party gives welfare programs, and I give appointments and recognition."

Politics deals with the symbols of acceptance, often in lieu of the real thing; the drive to collect votes comes from doubts about one's popularity, but not everyone with these doubts takes the vote-collecting path. Generally only those people with sufficient skill and strength and "plausibility" to achieve some success along these electioneering lines pursue them. Not always, of course, but often, at least in school, where it all goes on under the eye of the teacher, it is the "nice" and clean-cut types who make a success of it, and they may not at all be the young men who are most often sought in high school for a Coke party and in college for a night on the town, an exploration of the sinfulness of liquor, a "mature" movie, the drama of sex. But the themes change in real life with real money at stake and real power to be won. Perhaps, disguised by the years and the hardening effect of experience, the two types can still be seen in politics, the clean-cut reformer and the party regular, touched by sin, who was never, ever, president of his class in high school or college (and perhaps a third type who mixes a love of power with an interest in policy).

Browning and Jacob's research on the need for affiliation among politicians tends, in a modest way, to support this interpretation, for they found that it was the policy-oriented men in politics (reformers?) who had the highest need for affiliation, that is, who were working through problems of "establishing, maintaining, or restoring a positive affective relationship with another person."[1] Policy orientation, as is evident in the class presidents described here, seems to go with, and not be a substitute for, concern about friendship, the need to be liked. And when this interpretation is placed side by side with Crowne and Marlowe's finding that people who most desire social approval have the most difficulty in winning friends,[2] a portrait of a political style and the meaning of school elections in the lives

---

[1]Rufus P. Browning and Herbert Jacob, "Power Motivation and the Political Personality," *Public Opinion Quarterly,* 28 (1964), pp. 86-89.

[2]Douglas P. Crowne and David Marlowe, *The Approval Motive* (New York: Wiley, 1964), p. 165.

of these young men comes to light. Their policies are contained by their fears of alienating substantial groups (Lamb is a liberal-conservative; King is a liberal who joined the conservative group in college; and Mintz favors the underdog but is repelled by the underdog's vulgarity). Their need to be liked, and worry over this aspect of their lives, provides their motive force and at the same time provides, each within the boundaries of his own belief system, constraints on the choice of policies deemed admissible. Is this the germ of a political type: the "nice guy in politics," clean-cut, reformist but not radical; amateur and not "regular"; not a self-dramatizing man; a Lindsay, not a La Guardia; a Henry Cabot Lodge, not an Alben Barkley; rarely at the top (this kind of modest social anxiety does not quite provide the personality base, the drive, for real eminence); not a man of the people, a role that calls for more color and flair than one finds here; rather the candidate of the League of Women Voters and the Municipal League, white collar down to his shoes, "principled," eager, restrained, always running for president of his class with teacher not quite out of sight?

Yet, lest the discussion seem to suggest that schoolboy politicians are all of a kind, let us explore the case of Coleman, distinguished from the other three by the instrumental nature of his desire for popularity: he wants it not to validate his likableness, about which he seems to have no doubts, but to validate his *strength,* about which self-doubts were planted early. In high school he was, in his own terms, "a highly successful campus politician," being elected president of the student body at age fourteen; and at the time of writing he was running, in absentia, for the position of precinct chairman of his native Arkansas. Commenting on this political drive, he says:

> My background had given me the desire for position, the ability to appeal to people, and an interest in history. It was only natural that I should go into politics to find the security of strength that I sought, the only security possible for me.

Yet this remarkable young man is not merely seeking security; he is seeking greatness, and politics is the vehicle. In a memorable passage, which marks him as more vain or more candid than others, he says:

> From the age of about fourteen I have had a feeling of destiny in my life. I have felt that I was chosen, by God, if you like, for greatness. It is quite possible that this idea came about as a compromise between my need for power and the Christian ideology which forms part of my superego [his father is a minister]. This destiny has been the most salient feature of my life since I was about fifteen. Since that time most of what I have said and done has been in terms of what effect this will have upon my future. My political career has in large part been mapped out in my mind

since I was sixteen and is being started this year. Such a belief cannot be explained in terms of my need for security.

. . . It is I who feel the hand of destiny and I just do not believe that the psychological explanations are applicable. My background has been what it has because I needed the personality and talents that I have. Perhaps the nature of American democracy has forced me to clothe a need for power in a cloak of God-given destiny and humanitarian goals, but the same answer applies. No, I do not know what that goal is, but I have always felt that I will know when I arrive at my positional goal. I don't dash around plotting the conquest of the world, this is just something that is seriously and quietly within me.

At any rate, you can see that this belief to a large extent affects my feeling about political labels such as liberal and conservative. They become more means and less ends, though not completely so.

This man has fire in his guts which is not calmed by being liked, by mere popularity; *he will be and must be* somebody, somebody with power. Perhaps a deviant case of schoolboy politician, but with so small a sample we hardly know how deviant.

One might say the "nice guy in politics" (Adlai Stevenson) is the former student class president who needed reassurance about his likableness; the driving, ambitious politician, his eye to the main chance, is the former campus politician who needed, as Coleman says, "the security of strength," a resolution of doubts about his power and will (Hubert Humphrey? Barry Goldwater?). And neither of them is the "party regular," who rarely achieves eminence, but works, in cloakrooms and back rooms and convention halls, to lubricate (with jokes and money and favors) the political process.

"LOST GLORIES"—SELF-VALIDATION IN A DECLINING MARKET

If political ideas, properly expressed, are used as means for getting along in some preferred way with those others one cares about, then the rightness of one's views are indeed measured by how one gets along. Gardiner, a child of privilege, inducted into his current conservative ideology by the patient attention of a sensitive, conservative father, puts the matter well:

Actually, I feel that the years that I have spent at Adams have done little to change my political or general ideas. They have, instead, served to convince me that I was right *because I was able to make friends and achievements at Adams by maintaining my principles as they were.* [My emphasis.]

Similarly, those without "friends and achievements" may change their politics for that reason. When Demming failed in these respects at Adams, he saw himself as victimized by an in-group establishment and switched from conservative to liberal, Republican to Democrat, overnight. People test their ideas by whether or not these ideas are associated with successful experiences.

What happens, then, when the evidence of "success" is intermittent; when, looking backward over his short life, a young man sees, for example, some golden years marked by what everyone must have referred to as "promise," and then some years of drift or even relative failure? When it is the other way, as it was with Trumbull, whose high school years were marked by "a definite lack of self-confidence and a need to prove self-superiority," followed by several years at Adams, "which undoubtedly have been the happiest and most fruitful of my life," the temptation to see change as "progress" and to anticipate more such "progress" in the future is very great. But when a man in college looks back on a better period, he is made uncertain about the future, the problem of self-validation is worrisome, and, according to much established research, uncertain rewards lead to greater striving and a greater sensitivity to the conditions of success. Here are three men (Coleman, Simpson, and King) who look back upon their high school days as more successful than their college days, in part because of a sense of higher standing among their student colleagues in high school than at Adams.

Coleman, whose sense of destiny we have already examined, is a moderate liberal (on all issues except the power of labor) partly, he says, because he has had the sense of being an underdog at Adams, compared to being top dog in high school:

> I came from a high school in which I was easily the "biggest man on the campus." . . . I had the position and the recognition that I needed. But at Adams most people are in higher economic levels than I. I cannot easily be at the top of my class and my athletic prowess did not meet the competition. . . . I have no doubt that much of my liberalism is due to the fact that I feel I cannot realize the ideals [top status, recognition] of Adams as I see them, and thus to have stature must deny these goals. The more conservative the people around me are, the more liberal I become.

Nevertheless, back in his home state, Coleman maintains a moderate, eclectic, even opportunist position, one that will serve as the basis of a political career.

Simpson, a lad with a rather pale character, worried about his assertiveness and yet contemptuous of weakness in himself and others, also looks back upon a bright past, in his case in an English school. There, he says, "I had the feeling that for the first time I had been a complete and unqualified success." But in college things are different: "With the slow realization that I have not been so successful at Adams as in preceding years, I have become increasingly cynical." Yet, in saying this, he finds he only half means it.

> I am beginning to develop two sets of values. On the one hand, I have a strong desire to make money, to achieve social prestige, and to have my children have the very best of everything. Yet, on the other hand, I realize that this is a very superficial set of values and the real accomplishments of life are not dependent on wealth. I want to leave the world a better place than it was when I arrived.

Then, without warning, but with a clear implicit train of thought associating his values to his capacities, he says: "I think I am quite bright, yet in some ways seem rather slow-witted, and not shrewd enough to succeed. [Is this the source of his idealism, offering, as it does, an excuse for not achieving wealth and prestige?] I tell myself that I have not been successful at Adams, yet tell myself that I haven't really tried and that Adams criteria are immature." Then, shifting values again, almost as though "being liked" were a *substitute* for success along other lines, he says, "The result has been that although I present a very ingratiating outward appearance, I have a sort of inner 'schizophrenia.' "

Is it any wonder that Simpson says that "I am as yet unaffiliated with either party, largely because I feel that it makes little difference to my way of life which party is in office"? And yet he also says, "I have an affinity to the Republican party, which traditionally is symbolic of the financially successful men in the nation. It is because I am trying to climb that I tend to identify with those that already have 'climbed' and reached the top." These have been the assertive men, and "Wealth and social prestige have come to mean for me both symbols of assertion and the reward for assertion."

Perhaps Simpson sees "social service" as an ideal that, along with other values and advantages, rationalizes failure and provides a legitimate way out. Further, "being nice" is in line with this set of ideals and congenial to a nonassertive personality. At Adams his life situation has provided insufficient support for a clear choice; asking himself, "How'm I doing?" he must answer truthfully (a strength), "Not so good"—and his political ideas are, therefore, somewhat fluid.

King (the liberal who joined the Conservative party in the campus debating club at Adams in order to avoid any appearance of "extremism"), remembers his high school days as a period of former glory, and, like Simpson, contrasts these to the rather modest success he has achieved at Adams. But musing on this, he sees it differently; he sees it as a possible indication that his success in high school had assuaged certain anxieties about himself and therefore his current lack of striving may be seen as a sign that he no longer feels he must be powerful and popular. He has come to rest. But has he, therefore, lost his ambition? This worries him; but let him tell the story:

> I believe that there are primarily two reasons why Adams has not caused me to change my party preference. The first is that I plan to return to Blank City [where the Democrats are in control of things] and possibly enter politics there, and therefore I regard Adams as an untypical situation. But more important than this, I believe, is the fact that at Adams I have never felt any real drive to be popular, and have power, in the sense that I did in high school.

Observe the implication that had he felt these drives, he would have changed parties and, so he implies, his supporting beliefs.[3] But this would be hard to say, and he does not say it explicitly. Rather, here he worries about something much more important to him: What is happening to these drives? "I do not believe that this desire [to be powerful and popular] has left me for the rest of my life, in fact, I am certain that it has not." Then he worries about the source and nature of the drives: Are they really "his," really internalized?

> It may be because I am no longer near enough to my folks that they can push me, but I do not believe that this is the case, because I have continued to do well scholastically here, never being off Dean's List. This is all that they expect of me.

Following his parents' wishes in the academic sphere, would he not also have done so in the extracurricular one, if he were "their man" and not his own? The slowing down of his drives must have been his own choice; hence he can pick them up again when he needs them: "I like to think that it [his relaxation of ambition for popularity and power] is because of the fact that I was able to reach the goal of power and acceptance which I set for myself in high school, and therefore do not worry about these things as much at Adams." This is his preferred view, but then again, perhaps he is the victim of a changed environment, not "his own man" after all: "The

---

[3]Actually, there is some reason to believe that the upwardly mobile switch their party identification to that of the class of destination before they change their ideology; there is often a lag in this regard. See Eleanor E. Maccoby, Richard E. Matthews, and Anton S. Morton, "Youth and Political Change," *Public Opinion Quarterly*, 18 (1954), pp. 23-39.

change may be a result of the fact that the atmosphere at Adams is not conducive to such worries." But no: "I would imagine that this is not the case, since I think that some people here are concerned with such problems." And then, in a state of confused exhaustion, in which a truer picture of his situation emerges: "Perhaps the answer lies in one, or a combination, or none of these assumptions. At this point, I feel that I am too close to the problem to judge." Thus does he end his account, "the true story" of the way in which, once again, the drive to be popular and the need to be liked are joined to the everlasting question "How'm I doing?" which in turn is referred back to a previous period when, so the young man believes, he was doing better. His political views reflect the basic doctrine of the period of his success, a moderate Democratic party liberalism, with an overlay of uncertainty, reflecting his feelings that recently he has not been doing too well.

Consider now these three young men, about age twenty, who look back upon their high school careers as somehow embodying glories now lost, not sustained at Adams, where they have not reached "the top." All three are bothered by problems of assertion and the need to demonstrate their strength, two of them interested in politics as a career (Coleman intensely so, King in a more distant hypothetical way), all of them using interpersonal relations and signs of friendship and support as more of an instrumental value than a terminal consummatory one, thus validating themselves and proving, again and again, that they are "all right." In this sense, doubt about the answer to that troublesome and vital question "How'm I doing?" moves them in three separate directions, yet with something in common:

Coleman: assertion of a high mission and quasi-divine destiny, for which his political views, liberalized in college but still plastic, must be employed.

Simpson: ambivalence regarding his two-valued choice: self-assertion and conservatism, on the one hand, and service to mankind and some liberalized idealism on the other. But while this ambivalence prevents a party identification, the clear foreshadowing of the conservative choice in his identification with successful men and need to test himself is plain. The liberal inclination goes, as is so often the case, into internationalism, a safe as well as congenial outlet.

King: a sense that politics and political ideas are in the service of getting along and getting on, moderately liberal in his home community, where the Democrats are in power, and more conservative in the Adams Republican milieu. He is more worried about the inner state of his drives, including his conformist tendencies, than about the content of his beliefs.

What all three have in common, though in devious guises, is the affirmation or reaffirmation of the will to succeed, after some loss of momentum in college. And, since this is, at the moment, a larger head of steam than is available for any other driving purpose (service to others, enjoyment of life, love, and family), one expects politics to bear to this engine the relationship of a freightcar to a locomotive, a state of dependency. Among the others especially marked by a need to be liked, Mintz, Lamb, De Vita, even Demming (the man who shifted a cosmology to gain a place in Adams' life struggles), political ideas might have more of an autonomy of their own. But among those who are worried about their *loss of momentum* at Adams, and what this portends for their future, politics is a pale prisoner of the need to assert oneself against life. *Declining fortunes,* I would argue, *inhibit political choice on political grounds.*

VALIDATING THE AMBIVALENT SOCIAL IDENTITY

A person's identity, that which he feels he is and somehow must be, is a mixture of things *sui generis* (properties he feels to be special to himself) and things shared with some group—a family, a religious body, a community, a nation. [4] These latter shared qualities comprise his *social identity* and, like the things special to himself, may be viewed with mixed feelings, a certain ambivalence. As a man may not like his tendency to "blow his top" when he gets angry, he may not like his race or nation (a xenophile, perhaps), or, more likely, he may be uncertain about his feelings. [5] When his social identity is made up of positive identifications, he is fortified by an ease of reference to the ideas, the styles and manners of those with whom he identifies; his validation in the outside world—that is, his search for evidence that he and his are acceptable, somehow "right"—is made easier by these circumstances. And, after all, if the outside world should fail, there is the in-group of his shared identity to restore this feeling—their views weigh more heavily in the scale.

But if he should himself doubt the rightness of his group memberships, his social identity, and if these are immutable (as they are in racial groups and to a considerable extent in religious and nationality groups), this matter of self-validation becomes infinitely complex and painful beyond words. So

4See Erik H. Erikson, "The Problem of Ego Identity," *Journal of the American Psychoanalytic Association,* IV (1956), pp. 58-121, reprinted in Maurice R. Stein, Arthur J. Vidich, and David M. White, eds., *Identity and Anxiety* (New York: Free Press, Macmillan, 1960), pp. 37-87.

5See Robert E. Lane, *Political Ideology* (New York: Free Press, Macmillan, 1962), pp. 381-99.

happy a concept as "assimilation" turns out, on examination, to be anything but happy for those who must do it. Can we learn something from our biographies about the way in which a search for acceptance, for signs of affection, by those with ambivalent social identities affects their social thought?

There are two men of Italian extraction in the group, both from Catholic backgrounds, De Vita and Buenello. Buenello mentions his Italian upbringing and ardently asserts the importance to him of his Catholicism. His religion is especially related to his rejection of *all* present political parties, for he would make Christianity the basis of a new party that he would like to see organized. De Vita mentions neither his Italian nor his Catholic roots. De Vita slips out of this part of his social identity and rests everything on personality and class; Buenello flaunts it, defies the world, moralizes it, bases his social thought on it. For neither is it a tension-free area of thought: flight (and acceptance of the role of an intellectual with the appropriate political postures) versus defiance and exaggerated claims for its validity—these are the two themes.

But it is among the Jews that the problem of self-validation by the bearer of an ambivalent social identity is most clearly seen. There are five Jewish men in the sample, and their patterns of adaptation may be summarized as follows:

Silver: Surrender to the standards and views of the dominant Gentile society, minimize all distinctions; ignore signs of discrimination, but (as if in compensation) preserve and defend, at least among Jews, the Judaic *religious* heritage.

Goldberg: Maintain a vigorous defense of the two parts of one's social identity, the Jewish ethnicity and the American culture, maintaining their mutual reinforcement, emphasizing the secular features of each, bounding the inevitable conflict by a lively, if occasionally wounded, self-confidence.

Caplan: Admit the immigrant heritage (embodied in the person of a beloved grandfather) but ignore the "Jewishness"; assert the self as a person (with, as it happens, some charm) to bend the environment; yield only what is necessary, and in this way establish a counterforce to discrimination.

Mintz: Look the other way (inward, perhaps, to one's own troubles; outward toward non-ethnic social distress); repress the ethnic identity conflict; meet the world through competence and understanding and sympathy. (Mintz did not repress his dependency needs or his sexual conflicts—only his conflicts over his Jewish identity.)

And finally there is the case of Cohen, who "works through" in candor and pain the problem of affiliation for one who has an ambivalent social identity, revealing some of the ways in which it affects idea selection. He writes in the third person, as though he were interviewing himself, giving a name to his other self ("Alex")—a form that only he adopts and which already reveals this divided identity as well as giving his painful conflict some little distance. The problem is central: he starts his biography with the question, "What right has a Jew got to be a Republican?"

Slightly built, with an attractive, sensitive face, he answers this question first with a melancholy glance at his social situation: "Alex told us that he feels very insecure; it does not seem to him that he belongs anywhere or that he is in a particular group of friends. He feels alone." His feeling is complicated, of course, by his rejection of his family, but the business of being a Jew is crucial to his problem:

> Alex becomes very anxious when he has to introduce himself to non-Jews—his name is "so Jewish." The subject believes he developed this fear during a summer which he spent working in a resort hotel frequented largely by wealthy non-Jews. . . . On a number of occasions that summer he said he noticed a much more unfriendly attitude toward him when the guests discovered his name; he also overheard many anti-Jewish remarks and regrets working there. He has given serious consideration to changing his name.

He worries about his own anti-Semitism, revealed to him rather starkly by his reaction to "the bearded gentlemen of the lower East Side in New York." He "experienced a real hate for these people and at first blamed them for the anti-Judaism which some people have." But, of course, his own ambivalence was not solved by so simple a measure of scapegoating. He continues, in the third person:

> Since he has attended Adams, he has had the desire to disassociate himself from Jews, but finds himself working enthusiastically for the Hillel organization and giving strong support for the state of Israel. He also finds that he is more at ease with Jews and is not "on guard" with them. . . . The subject says that his relatives and their Jewish friends have always talked as if the Jews were surrounded by hostile nations. Alex thus finds that he is trying to associate with a group which he does not completely trust, while trying to disassociate from another group to which he is drawn by common background and fear of other groups.

Alex—Cohen—is ambitious; whatever else happens, he feels he must be a "success," which for him implies wealth and status, as well as acceptance:

> In Alex's quest for success he desires to be associated with the most successful groups in the United States and these are mainly white Protestants; therefore he does not want to be identified with Jews, and the "lower East Side". ones in particular. . . . These Jews are largely poor and Democrats, and this is another impetus in the desire to disassociate; these Jews make bad impressions on Christians and they think that all Jews are the same. Alex wants to show them that all Jews are not the same, that they are not all Democrats. Then he will be accepted and will be a success.

Filled with doubts and uncertainties about his own motives, moved by "a certain fear he has about" Christians, anxious lest, in his support for Israel, he be called a "traitor" by these Christians (something his father once called him when they disagreed), "Alex" Cohen shapes a tentative political orientation precariously fitted to these conflicting forces and the needs they represent. "We believe," he says, in his role of interviewer of "Alex," his other self, "that the subject could change his party affiliation without too much difficulty." His role as representative of the assimilated Jew leads him into a wilderness of ideological and political ambivalence and doubt.

The case is illuminating as well as humanly moving, for it reveals the way in which an ambivalent social identity can, so to speak, follow a tortuous political path, now trespassing on social ground belonging to the preferred group, now on the ground of the rejected group and, of course, marked by the sense that the preferred group is threatening enemy territory, while the rejected group is, in some sense, home base. With national origins, with race, with some elements of social class, with regional or communal loyalties it is no different, and sometimes equally paralyzing. There is no peace at the margins.

Cohen is a moderate and rather precarious conservative; Silver, the young man who sought desperately to go along with the "big men" at Adams, is a strong and somewhat extreme conservative, in the sense in which we have been using the term (rewards go to the able, inequality is necessary and not so bad, social and economic distinctions based on race [but not religion] are quite permissible, tradition should be encouraged above all); Goldberg is a humane but certainly nonradical Democrat, Mintz a liberal Democrat, Caplan a leftist moving from the Henry Wallace Progressives to the liberal Democratic camp. An ambivalent social identity, on this showing, certainly does not command any preference for a certain section of the political spectrum, although Jews generally are more liberal than communicants of other religions.[6] Nor can it be said with con-

---

[6] See, for example, Lawrence H. Fuchs, *The Political Behavior of American Jews* (Glencoe, Ill.: Free Press, 1956).

fidence—and this is contrary to my expectations—that ambivalent social identities make men more introspective, more sensitive to their own conflicts; often they seem to do so, but sometimes not (Caplan, Buenello); the tendency is weak, at best. But what does seem to be the case is that the political thinking of men with ambivalent social identities is cast in the form of a *dialogue,* an inner conversation where "the other side" is taken into account. This other side may be vigorously, even ruthlessly, rejected, but there is a sensitivity to the possible rejoinder, there is an awareness of what others think, there is a preparation for some feedback, if not a capitulation to it.

Moreover, while the positions these men currently hold seem sometimes fixed as though by act of God (Silver, Caplan, Goldberg), each of them has a history of change: Silver changed from Democrat to Republican; Goldberg had a Republican period and a radical period before becoming a moderate Democrat; Caplan had been a Progressive before his current Democratic partisanship; Mintz had defended Shavian socialism before becoming a Democrat; and Cohen—well, Cohen has not changed, but we saw him report that he could easily switch to the Democratic camp. The Protestants have also revealed considerable flexibility, for we are dealing with men in a life period marked by fluidity, but to a lesser extent—about half of them have changed, or indicate, like Cohen, that they might easily do so. I would speculate that the greater flexibility of these Jewish and Italian students may be accounted for by their ambivalence regarding their social identity, and within this framework by the conflicts arising from their need for acceptance, their need to be liked.

The process of maturation is marked by periodic "crises" for everyone, that is, periods when a confrontation with one's past and present self is thrust upon the growing person. At such moments an ambivalent social identity contributes to one's political flexibility. Goldberg's excursion into Republicanism coincided with his rebellion against continuing his religious education. But Caplan, the assertive one who never mentions his Jewish affiliation, reveals some of the interpersonal forces at work:

> At prep school I stubbornly held to a view and withstood all fire. My radicalism amidst 300 Republican sons won me quick renown in the political club. As a freshman I debated the Taft-Hartley law with a senior. . . . I was a little boy, but all the big guys knew me. As I grew older, however, and closer to the top, I mellowed. I began to hold political discussions with my own classmates—and this took on a new tone. With your equals, an element of friendship and familiarity enters all discussions. You can't impress them—they know you too well; but you can alienate them. I was still given to sweeping dogmatisms, as, indeed, I still

am, but they have receded somewhat both in vigor and in fre-
quency.

The need to be liked causes someone with an ambivalent social identity to
respond positively to the opportunity for "friendship and familiarity." In
the end "Sammy" may slow to a walk, and Caplan's tone of voice, if
hardly muted, becomes less shrill.

"CONFORMITY": A LICENSING OF
UNACCEPTABLE THOUGHTS

Living with a Prejudice. Silver, a small, sober young conservative
with a serious face and some reluctance to speak about his inner life, puts
the first canon of his political creed this way: "Belief that a divine intent
rules society as well as conscience, forging an eternal chain of right and
duty which links great and obscure, living and dead. Political problems at
bottom are religious and moral problems." As this suggests, he takes his
Judaism seriously, but he also wants very much to be accepted, and something happens to his interpretation of this "divine intent" as he changes
schools and then goes on to college. He speaks clearly and candidly for
himself: "Some of the boys at the day school were very anti-Negro, and in
order to get close with a particular group of the 'important' boys, I was
forced to accept some of their beliefs and prejudices." A little later on he
refers to his partisan political preferences; he comes from a Democratic
family:

> At Country Day School I was about the only Democrat in
> the student body, although at the time I had never made a real
> effort to study the policies, individuals, etc. of either party. . . .
> Now [at Adams College], however, since I have made an attempt
> to analyze my political beliefs, I feel that I am a true believer in
> the Republican party. All of my friends at prep school as well as
> at college have been Republicans.

The family has been upwardly mobile, but his parents were not oblivious
of the more intense inward mobility of their aspiring son. They urged him
not to forget his former lower status friends, something that was not easy
for him: "Even with such teachings from my parents, I was still very
pleased that I had been accepted to join the fraternity and become a member of the 'better' group. Soon we moved to Green Lawn [a better sub-
urb], and this made my new conservative beliefs all the more firm."

To report these feelings about status, an achievement for anyone and especially for one who, as we shall see, prides himself about his morality, is difficult, and there is evidence that Silver struggles with his problem, though he sees it through a prettied-up and rationalized perspective. His problems at college revolve around acceptance and conformity:

> At college, the big problem for me would be conformity. . . . Coming, as I did, from an unknown school in the Midwest, being Jewish, and not having any real dynamic qualities, I was faced with the problem of friendships. Having read and heard what the patterned Adams man was to be, I quickly decided that I must fit the proper typology in order to be a successful undergraduate. . . . Even in prep school I was an "outsider" trying to become intimate friends with the boys who had been together in school since the elementary grades. Thus with my feeling of being an outsider, of being too inferior in size, and of being of a minority group, I felt that I had to grasp onto the ideas and mores of the "big men."

And he proceeds to do so, meanwhile teaching us three things about this thirst for acceptance and hunger for acceptability. First, observe the *"in-out"* dimension; Silver's desire is accentuated by his sharp sense of coming late to the feast of fellowship, of being stigmatized by his Jewishness, hence even more of an outsider, of being from a middle-western and unknown school, of not belonging, not primarily because of any quality of personality, but because of unfavorable birth and circumstance. Adoption of the right opinions helps to erase or erode the differences, at least to bridge them, to make him more like the insiders, hence not conspicuous as an outsider. Second, there is the *"up-down"* dimension, symbolized pathetically in his reference to his inferior size and the ideas of the "big men." He grows in stature by associating with elites among these insiders. Being low in the hierarchy, he acquires status within the system of insiders, of those who belong. And finally he acquires a substitute for "dynamic qualities" or a compensation for their lack, which he feels so keenly; he cannot make a mark or even make friends by relying on personal qualities, but appropriate absorption of the ideas, and perhaps the goodwill, of the elites will make up for this sense of inadequacy. He wants not merely the external symbols of status, but also evidence that *personal deficiencies are somehow made good.*

But let us pause for a minute. What seems to be a strong drive for conformity, motivated by the need to be accepted, if not enthusiastically liked, has a lower depth. Is Silver really motivated in his racial prejudice and his economic conservative elitism by a desire to conform, or are these only excuses, means to legitimize and make acceptable to himself ideas he seeks to hold on other grounds? Anti-Negro sentiment, which in one place

Silver says he adopted for conformity reasons, in another place he reports in different terms:

> My only prejudice, and I am quite ashamed that I have such a prejudice since I belong to a minority group, is one which deals with the Negro problem. I have tried to search my past for reasons for my prejudice, but I have never succeeded in obtaining an answer.

He then tells about his association with Negroes in the past (mostly as menials), and cannot find any incidents to base his prejudice on. Rather he bases it on a "belief that men segregated themselves in society according to race in obedience to a basic natural law which decrees that like shall seek like." When he goes to an integrated beach, he will not swim in the water; he reports that "I have always had a hatred of filth, and the color of the Negro might have been a source of dislike," although now he has outgrown "such foolish reasoning." As we have seen, he joined the National Association for the Advancement of Colored People in order to help himself get over the prejudice, but to no avail. Is it any wonder, therefore, that he allowed himself to be "persuaded" on this point by the elite students at the Country Day School? Indeed, was it any persuasion at all? And if this is true of his color prejudice, might it not be that his conservatism and his adoption of elite ideas were already latently there, waiting for an occasion to show themselves in some more legitimate dress? This becomes more plausible in the light of Silver's remark that he "has always had the desire to be better than such a working class [as porters and truck drivers] and therefore have tried to avoid a close association with such a group." In short, it was not so much the pull of conformity as the push of inner, intensely felt, and barely conscious drives toward racial purity and elite status that motivated Silver in this way. His need for acceptance was not so indiscriminate as the needs of some others; it was guided by these ego-defensive needs whose force gave a special elitist direction to his striving.

Release from Radicalism. If Silver was, in some sense, "forced to be free"—that is, found conformity congenial to some values he believed to be illegitimate, if not downright dangerous—what shall we say of McDonald, struggling with problems of his political acceptability on totally different grounds? McDonald had been given over for adoption at the age of two, and after a brief spell in a foster home had been adopted by a childless, loving, professional couple with left-wing leanings. He seemed to make friends easily, for he reflected some quality of acceptance of and acceptability to others. Nevertheless, even for him, the question of shaping his beliefs so as not to forfeit this social acceptance is a problem. Can he be a socialist without giving up the good opinion of his friends?

> The Democratic party is accepted by the American people. Although I see in the party the political expression of my basic beliefs, I see it also as an upholder of the general American society and culture. It is for this reason that I identify with this party rather than some lefter wing party.

He then tries to explain what this ambiguous phrase means and why he chooses the more conservative option.

> First, I see the socialists as people without a country. They are cut off from society. When I see them on the street corners passing out handbills, they appear to me as lonely men without friends, save for their political associates. My socializing experience has been one of anxiety and loneliness; I have found that to relieve the tension caused by conflicts between myself and the society, my behavior had to be patterned so that I would be acceptable to my peers and superiors. . . . I had to act in a certain way that would appeal to the others around me. . . . I cannot detach myself from my friends in order to devote myself to leftist political activity.

But, as with Silver, one wants to know the cost of conformity, the satisfactions of conscience or aggression or whatever that must be given up to remain within the sphere of acceptable political thought. There are hints throughout the discussion of beliefs which suggest that these are not, after all, so very great. He is not, he says, "destructive," he sees the advantages of "mass production" by big business, he speaks of the "cooperation" of labor and management. His father, whom he accepts and, indeed, recalls in concrete illustrations with some affection and pleasure, is only a moderate leftist; his conscience is not seriously bothered by his "apostasy," his reference groups are not tearing him apart, his identification with the going order is substantial. And so it is easy to be a little more "evolutionary," a little less leftist, and, half conscious of the compromises he has made, he picks up the mantle of the Democrat and wears it without feelings of constraint.

The general point is an important one. The need to be liked and hence to make one's opinions acceptable to people can work either with or against other needs. It may appear to the individual that he is adjusting his opinions to the group's, but, almost without his knowing it, he is often being unburdened of a view he did not want to hold, or licensed to express a view that can be expressed without guilt only when so licensed. What seems to be a confession of conformity is really only partly that. Like a screen memory in analysis, the false confession hides and prevents a deeper confession, another need striving to express itself.

PROJECTING AND GENERALIZING THE NEED TO BE LIKED

There is a process that of necessity comes up over and over as we trace through the way these needs express themselves in political thought: the projection of a need in such a way as to see political agencies through what might be called "need-colored glasses." The aggressive man sees the government as aggressive, while the dependent person sees the government as somehow serving his dependency. Here we have men projecting or generalizing their need to be liked, so that government officials are seen to be in the grip of this same need, and government itself is appraised with a special concern for the way in which it elicits affection.

Lamb hints at this, suggesting that government should behave as he does: "In my personal life I put a high value on being good to others, and so too I believe in public affairs all people regardless of income, race, color, or religion should have equal opportunities." De Vita is more explicit in this regard: "In the externalized form of the drive for affection I substitute the United States for myself, and in so doing, I believe that the policies of the United States should be directed to winning friends and gaining the affection of other people all over the world." Both Lamb and De Vita state or imply that the government is (should be) like them: it should be nice to people; it should seek friends everywhere.

But this interpretation of government as "a person who should be endowed with the qualities I cherish for myself" is only part of the political picture, for political *parties* are also sometimes so endowed. For example, McDonald, whose fear of isolation keeps him from espousing a more radical view, and whose basic identification with the going order limits his drive to express radical sentiments, is, like Lamb and De Vita, an affection-seeking person, particularly toward his parents. He has repressed, he says, his aggressive impulses toward them, and now identifies strongly with them and their liberal-to-socialist doctrines. He fears a cold, restrictive authority, and one reason he prefers the Democratic party to the Socialist party is that he sees it as more latitudinarian. This puts him on the point of a dilemma: Is the New Deal a giant bureaucracy, as some say, restrictive and impersonal? He solves the problem this way:

> This aspect of seeking love from the authority figures precludes a figure that is cold and impersonal. Thus I cannot accept the bureaucratic implementation of most political measures, yet I see in the welfare economics of the New and Fair Deals, i.e., the welfare state, an intense consideration of human problems. It seems to deal with society not as some mechanistic object with which to be toyed, but as a living, breathing mass whose interests

must be furthered. I see in the Democratic party an expression of parental love which is demanding yet permissive.

While De Vita and Lamb want the government to be like them, McDonald wants the government and the Democratic party to be like his parents, and so to satisfy his need for a nonrestrictive, love-giving object.

Let us look at one further variation of this theme: taking the chosen party as a model for one's own political behavior, and also, perhaps, creating the party in one's own image. King, who fears extremism and the rejection this implies, and who has collected votes to reassure himself about his own likability, makes a comparison between his own behavior in gaining and using power and that of the Democratic party. Recall the passage in which this is expressed:

> My association with this [common-man] concept has brought me strength and acceptance, just as I feel it has brought the Democratic party strength and acceptance. In a sense, both myself and the party have exploited the common man, since we have taken his vote to gain power. But we have both benefited the common man with the gains from this exploitation. The party gives welfare programs, and I gave appointments and recognition.

But while the overt argument is a statement of a similarity, one suspects that there is a two-way identification process in motion here. On the one hand, I am like the Democratic party, strong and kind. On the other hand, the Democratic party is like me, reliable, trustworthy, and familiar, therefore unlikely to surprise or offend me.

There are good reasons for such projective thinking (attributing one's own qualities to others) in politics; one validates one's own personality traits and life style by having the government adopt them. Such projective thinking, in this relaxed sense, gives sanction to something (like needing to be liked, or trading votes for favors) about which a person may have harbored grave doubts. And on the other hand, it makes for a congenial image of government, a predictable one, one readily accepted, honored, and obeyed.

SUMMARY

The need to be liked is a pressure, a push from inside. When it pushes or moves or, as we say, motivates a man, it engages other attitudes, emotions, values, skills, and then together, so to speak, they emerge from the "black box" of the unknown personality into some observable political thought or act. Diagrammatically, and oversimplified to be sure, our discussion might look like this:

A. Obstacles to Easy Friendship

Need	Mediating Element	Political Expression
Need to be liked ←→	Intellectuality, especially at an early age, where cognitive responses stifle casual, playful, affective responses; both cause and effect of social anxiety. →	Painful indecision in politics; ambivalence; hedging but rarely withdrawal.
Need to be liked ←→	Fear of intimacy combining with need for reassurance about likability; tendency to maintain distance between self and others and to symbolize people. →	Bid for the affection of distant underdogs; religious, racial tolerance, and symbolic equalitarianism.
Need to be liked ←→	Blockages and strain in interpersonal relations with self-confident elites (possibly reflecting one kind of authority tension). →	Selection of lower status, less "important" clienteles, audiences; welfare policy targets.

B. Validating the Self

Need	Mediating Element	Political Expression
Need to be liked ←→	Self-doubt and intense need for self-validation combined with self-conscious interpersonal skills. →	*Popularity:* Vote solicitation on "clean-cut" reform lines. Votes as affirmation of acceptability. *Dominance:* Vote solicitation and policy as vehicle of career advancement; self as a mission.
Need to be liked ←→	A sense of lost momentum in the drive for "success," especially status among peers, memories of former glories, fears of loss of drive and motivation. →	Political choice less "autonomous" and more in the service of ambition and opportunity.

B. Validating the Self

Need	Mediating Element (continued)	Political Expression
Need to be liked ←→	Ambivalent social identity creating and reflecting social anxiety; identification denied, flaunted, used in "the social encounter." →	Political thought reflecting (1) elements of a dialogue with an internal opposition; (2) a flexible, but often intense, commitment.
Need to be liked ←→	Rejection (and quasi repression) of unacceptable thoughts, hence search for resolution formula. →	Pseudoconformity to license the guilty idea; screen confession of "weakness" in face of pressure.

C. Projective and Generalizing Tendencies

Need	Mediating Element	Political Expression
Need to be liked ←→	Projective tendencies, not so much for getting rid of the projected material as for making it acceptable; also (and different) generalizing tendencies to see government and parties as like the self. →	Images of government and political parties as propitiating and inviting, reflecting, in this case, the need to be liked.

8

The Politics of Aggression

AGGRESSIVE POLITICAL THOUGHTS

Aggression is behavior and thought aimed at the injury of some object; it implies hostility and is mediated by "anger."[1] It may be acted out or merely rehearsed in the mind; hence it embraces fantasy, thought about distant objects, people, institutions, symbols. The most common aggressive political ideas are those that denigrate such political figures as judges, politicians, civil servants, political opponents, and, of course, the institutions they inhabit, the rules they employ, the values they espouse or perhaps merely represent. Not all political criticism is aggressive in this sense, for much of it aims to help a man to do his job "better," not to injure him or denigrate him. Criticism may seek to correct a policy, not destroy it. The presentation of "constructive alternatives" is one ingredient of nonhostile but critical discussion; another is the interpretation of something regarded as wrong (a man, a policy, a decision) in terms of error rather than evil.[2] Nihilism, destructiveness, cynicism are embodiments of aggression-laden thought, thought designed to denigrate, aimed at the injury of many objects.

Consider these modes of aggressive political thought:

"Politicians are all corrupt"; "Intellectuals are all pinko" (denigration and abuse).

"I wish all politicians would drown in the bottom of the ocean" (fantasy of injury).

---

[1] This definition and much of the following discussion follows Leonard Berkowitz' *Aggression* (New York: McGraw-Hill, 1962).

[2] See my discussion of "The Lost Sense of Evil," Chap. 22 of *Political Ideology* (New York: Free Press, Macmillan, 1967).

"Membership shall be limited to persons of the Protestant faith" (injury by discrimination, ranking, exclusion).

"Let's burn the embassy" (hortatory; plan for injury).

"I heard that Johnson planned Kennedy's murder" (malicious gossip).

"Have you heard the one about Jackie . . ." (malicious joke).

"Godless Russia . . . " "Capitalist exploitation . . . " "Red tape . . . " (pejorative language).

"War brings out the best in man" (violence as a value).

Then there are those thoughts or arguments whose implications are deliberately callous: "Let the devil take the hindmost"; "People get what they deserve"; "I'm looking out for number one"—all have an aggressive element. Sometimes partisan conflict is aroused *in order* to do injury ("We'll wipe up the floor with them"; "They'll never rise again"). Finally there is the expression of loving ideas designed to irritate or wound, as when a California wife became a Communist as a means of revenging herself against her businessman husband. All of these represent aggressive political behavior and thought.

There is a looseness about the objects of aggressive political thought, a breadth of target that deserves notice. The civil servant who denies a tax exemption, the congressman who votes against a civil rights bill rapidly become symbols of government itself. The entire apparatus of government, the "whole kit and kaboodle," "the lot of them," "the mess in Washington," "the City Hall crowd" are likely to be lumped together, for it is characteristic of aggressive people that they fail to make distinctions, employing instead broad categories any element of which evokes their anger. In one sense this is stereotyping; in another sense it is generalizing the reaction to a specific stimulus so that the reaction is set off by a broad range of "similar" stimuli—stimulus generalization.

Here, then, are some of the themes of aggressive politics, much of it cast in the American idiom, but in thought and mood a worldwide phenomenon.

Aggressive Political Thought *(seeking to injure)*	*Conciliatory Political Thought* *(seeking to avoid injuring)*
1. Justice as revenge and retribution; talonic law; sentence as punishment.	1. Justice as future-oriented, reconditioning of a personality.

*Aggressive Political Thought
(seeking to injure)*

*Conciliatory Political Thought
(seeking to avoid injuring)*

2. Political partisanship based more on defeating (hurting) the opposition than helping one's friends.

2. Political partisanship based on policy or patronage gains to be derived from victory; identification stronger than disidentification.

3. All effective opposition (frustrators and creators of conflict) regarded as somehow illegitimate, suspect; *ad hominem* argument employed.

3. Opposition accepted within the framework of a constitutional system; there is a right to oppose; in this sense opposition regarded as legitimate.

4. Government and its officials regarded as exploitative and corrupt; hence to be treated with fear and contempt.

4. Government as possibly (but not necessarily) "fair," honest within limits, doing what it is supposed to do, hence drawing on a greater repertoire of emotions and expressions.

5. Everything the government does is interpreted as "politically motivated," something involving a "payoff" or patronage, or unprincipled pandering to a selfish public, all of which justify a critical, hostile posture.

5. Government responds to a mixture of social needs and political force, both of which are legitimate considerations for political leaders.

6. Bureaucrats are those who fail to make good in society, hence inefficient. They are likely to be corrupt; they are also rigid, bound up in red tape, impersonal, officious.

6. Bureaucrats may be all kinds of people; they are like anybody else, but they can be damn annoying and don't always do what they can to help.

7. Behind the appearances of democratic government and popular elections there lies a cabalistic controlling power.

7. Things are more or less what they seem; money and power go together, but numbers, organization, friendship ties, and

Aggressive Political Thought *(seeking to injure)*	*Conciliatory Political Thought* *(seeking to avoid injuring)*

Rightists see this as an "Eastern intellectual establishment" or as "Communists"; leftists see a business and military "power elite."

even ideas have influence. Elections make a difference.

8. The electorate is "a bunch of sheep," untrustworthy, fickle, impressed by the wrong things; hence elections are farcical.

8. The electorate is made up of many elements, most of whom vote their self-interest as guided by habit, but some respond to changed situations with a changed perception of what is good for what might be characterized as self-in-society. Whatever the determinants of electoral choice, the electoral process is beneficial over the long run, and anything but farcical.

9. Rules and laws are manipulable by insiders and, if one is lucky, even "by me." There is no real rule of law.

9. With some exceptions, the laws are for everybody; their enforcement is equal enough so that the chances are good that if one offends, he will be "caught," and (except for pariah peoples) if one is "caught" he probably has offended.

10. Any dealing with government (access) is characterized as "the runaround."

10. Any dealing with government is likely to be slow, frustrating, tedious—but possibly instrumental to some intended goal.

11. News of public affairs is opaque, deceptive. "They are holding back"; "They never let you know what's going on"; "Don't believe what you hear or what you see in the papers."

11. News is news, perhaps hard to follow, perhaps biased, incomplete, rarely giving "both sides"—but, read with skepticism (not cynicism), it is sufficient to give orientation—

Aggressive Political Thought (seeking to injure)	*Conciliatory Political Thought* (seeking to avoid injuring)
	if you only had the time to follow it.
12. Foreign nations are wily, untrustworthy, selfish, and ungrateful. They will get you one way or another.	12. Foreign nations, like the United States, pursue their national self-interest, which may include honoring treaties (up to a point), living within an international code, trading and communication for mutual gain.
13. Labor unions are run for the benefit of union bosses. The rightist version holds that unions keep their membership by coercion and by protecting their "right" to featherbed. The leftist version holds that the union leaders are in collusion with management.	13. There are all kinds of labor unions; some are "crooked," most provide protection and genuine collective-bargaining gains for their members. But strikes that endanger or greatly inconvenience the public should be discouraged.
14. Across the ethnic barriers (whites seen by Negroes, Negroes by whites, Italians by Irish, etc.) are groups of people who are (a) out for themselves in some "gross" (not like "us") manner; (b) "pushy," "dishonest," "unclean," "cliquish," "irresponsible," etc.; (c) strange, hence (d) dangerous. One must "draw the line"; "if you give them an inch . . ." Jokes and offensive names (Kike, Wop, Nigger) are permissible and expressive of the aggressive style.	14. Across the ethnic barrier are people, perhaps disturbing, especially in large groups, perhaps economically threatening (and if so, probably disliked as a group), perhaps a little strange, a little odd, even a little upsetting, but not enough to do anything about, not enough, on an individual basis, to bar friendship (when the strangeness ceases), and entitled anyway to their rights. Good form avoids offensive jokes and terms—even out of "their" hearing.

These items are intended to sample the political concepts and expressions of the aggressive personality as opposed to the nonaggressive.

One could add more, of course; on political processes a special and readily available "dictionary" gives the appropriate terms: a compromise is a "sellout," an agreement is a "deal," every proposal has a "gimmick," an unsecured promise is "a bit of blue sky." Nothing is straight; which is, perhaps, just as well, for what such a mind would consider "straight" is likely to be romantic, distant, heroic, the triumph not of the heart or mind, but of "the will."

If this list seems reminiscent of the theme of the authoritarian personality, the similarity should not surprise; after all, one of the features of the authoritarian syndrome is "authoritarian aggression"; another is "power and toughness," and a third is "destructiveness and cynicism." The theoretical argument is different, and the political expressions of aggressive thought are not intended to reflect conventionalism or submissiveness or exaggerated concerns with sex (though perhaps corruption takes its place);[3] but the overlap is important.

The overlap is even greater with political cynicism ("Money is the most important factor influencing public policies"; "In order to get nominated most candidates for public office have to make basic compromises and undesirable commitments").[4] Cynicism is destructive; its very essence is that "nothing and nobody is any good." As it turns out in the United States, it is *not* more characteristic of one party than another. On the other hand, it is "class-conscious," for cynicism is the unstructured radicalism of the uneducated and the poor (with education controlled) and the old. Nor is it merely a political pose, for it is related to a general view of life ("There's a sucker born every minute"; "Men won't work hard unless they are forced to do so") and to a sense of personal ineffectiveness—just as findings indicate is the case for aggressive personalities. Fortunately, the cynical are less likely to talk politics with their friends, and, especially among the better educated, to become active in party affairs. Moreover, since the research I have been reporting on cynicism employed items that had been extracted from the writings of Machiavelli and put together as a "mach scale," one might extend their implications tentatively to the exponents of *Realpolitik* or of *force majeure* in politics. It has much in common with the politics of alienation among the Boston electorate and politicians as well, as these are described by Levin,[5] or the politics of misanthropy analyzed first by Morris Rosenberg[6] and then put to the test in five nations by Almond and

---

[3]T. W. Adorno, Else Frenkel-Brunswik, Daniel Levinson, and Nevitt Sanford, *The Authoritarian Personality* (New York: Harper, 1950).

[4]These items, and the discussion of the correlates of a cynicism scale, are taken from Robert E. Agger, Marshall Goldstein, and Stanley Pearl, "Political Cynicism: Measurement and Meaning," *Journal of Politics,* 23 (1961), pp. 477-506.

[5]Murray B. Levin, *The Alienated Voter* (New York: Holt, Rinehart & Winston, 1960).

[6]Morris Rosenberg, "Misanthropy and Political Ideology," *American Sociological Review,* 21 (1956), pp. 690-95.

Verba: the Italians, highest in misanthropy, had the most hostile view of their own government, the Americans and British the least hostile.[7]

But surely defining the politics of aggression as a political behavior predominantly marked by a desire to injure or humiliate or denigrate some objects important in the ongoing affairs of political life embraces much more than the kind of plainsong for the undemocrat presented in the above analysis. Consider the themes of nazism, fascism, communism, and anti-colonial nationalism as reflected in these brief excerpts—and these come from statements where the themes are, so to speak, prettied up for public consumption:

From Hitler's *Twenty-Five Points:*[8]

None but those of German blood, whatever their creed, may be members of the nation. No Jew, therefore, may be considered a member of the nation.

We oppose the corrupt Parliamentary custom of filling public offices merely with a view to party considerations, and without reference to character or capacity.

We demand a ruthless campaign against all whose activities are injurious to the common interest. Oppressors of the nation, usurers, profiteers, etc., must be punished with death, whatever their creed or race.

From *The Fascist Decalogue:*[9]

Know that the Fascist and in particular the soldier must not believe in perpetual peace.

Days of imprisonment are always deserved.

The rifle and the cartridge belt, and the rest, are confided to you not to rust in leisure, but to be preserved in war.

For a volunteer there are no extenuating circumstances when he is disobedient.

From *The Communist Manifesto:*[10]

The bourgeoisie, wherever it has got the upper hand, has put an end to all feudal, patriarchal, idyllic relations. It has piti-lessly torn asunder the motley feudal ties that bound man to his

---

[7]Gabriel Almond and Sidney Verba, *The Civic Culture* (Boston: Little, Brown, 1965).

[8]Reprinted in Michael Oakeshott, *The Social and Political Doctrines of Contemporary Europe* (New York: Macmillan, 1947), pp. 190-91.

[9]Reprinted in *ibid.,* p. 180.

[10]Karl Marx and Friedrich Engels, *Manifesto of the Communist Party* (New York: International Publishers, 1932), p. 11.

"natural superiors," and has left no other nexus between man and man than naked self-interest, than callous "cash payment." It has drowned the most heavenly ecstasies of religious fervour, of chivalrous enthusiasm, of philistine sentimentalism, in the icy water of egotistical calculation. It has resolved personal worth into exchange value, and in place of the numberless indefensible chartered freedoms, has set up that single, unconscionable freedom—Free Trade. In one word, for exploitation, veiled by religious and political illusions, it has substituted naked, shameless, direct, brutal exploitation.

From *The Wretched of the Earth* by Frantz Fanon:[11]

The existence of an armed struggle shows that the people are decided to trust to violent methods only. He of whom *they* have never stopped saying that the only language he understands is that of force, decides to give utterance by force. In fact, as always, the settler has shown him the way he should take if he is to become free. The argument the native chooses has been furnished to him by the settler, and by an ironic turning of the tables it is the native who now affirms that the colonialist understands nothing but force. The colonial regime owes its legitimacy to force and at no time tries to hide this aspect of things.

I do not, especially with reference to the last selection, raise the question of the merits of the aggressive (injurious) theme; there is, however much it is abused, such a thing as "righteous indignation." But the selections take us out of the parochial mimicry of the curdled Westerner, especially the American. Great thoughts and matters of high sentence are also aggressive—or conciliatory.

Lest one confuse the aggressive dimension with the left-right dimension, let us recall two things. First, Eysenck, in an attempt to isolate a tough-tender-mindedness dimension from a radical conservative one, found that these were, in fact, quite independent of each other. His "toughmindedness" includes a lot more than aggressive behavior and thought, but it does include aggression ("The so-called underdog deserves little sympathy or help from successful people"; "Crimes of violence should be punished by flogging"; "European refugees should be left to fend for themselves)."[12] And second, if one reviews the thought of some great conservatives, as well as great liberals, one finds a very mixed picture, one that, with much ellipsis, might be illustrated as follows.

---

[11] Translated by Constance Farrington (New York: Evergreen, Grove Press, 1968), pp. 83-84.

[12] H. J. Eysenck, *The Psychology of Politics* (New York: Praeger, 1954).

	Left (for change in an equalitarian direction, at least economically)	Right (for the values of a privileged, stable, more or less hierarchical order)
Aggressive (marked by many hostile references to the opposition and destructive goals)	Karl Marx Nikolai Lenin Mao Tse-tung Frantz Fanon	Herbert Spencer National Association of Manufacturers (with no distinguished spokesman) Joseph Chamberlain Barry Goldwater
Nonaggressive (marked by hope for the education of the opposition and reduced conflict in the real and proximate world)	Thomas Jefferson John Stuart Mill Mohandas K. Gandhi	Edmund Burke George Santayana Michael Oakeshott

It is a spotty list, and there is no place in it for the Nazis and Fascists (radical right), but it might satisfy those who believe that inequalitarians or equalitarians are, according to taste, the only aggressive group. Yet, in spite of this, I shall have something to say about the aggressive quality of my respondents and their rightist tendencies.

THE SOURCE OF AGGRESSION

Why should politics be so laden with aggression, political thought so saturated with hostility and anger? Or, given men's nature, how is it that aggression is so often contained and politics occasionally so peaceful? One hardly knows where to expect a natural balance. What is the state of nature in this respect? Animal studies reveal that species vary enormously in their habitual aggressiveness, even among primates; hence one cannot derive from these studies any particular level of expectation for man. Furthermore, both naturally pacific and naturally aggressive animals may be educated to be either more or less aggressive.[13] But, since it is true that sex differences and experimentally induced differences in the amount of male hormone in an animal affect aggressive behavior, it would be well to limit to the human male any inferences to be drawn from our case material. On the whole, however, theories based on inherited characteristics (instincts) do not help us interpret the relation between aggressive feelings and political thought.

There is a second theory of aggression that has nothing to do with instincts, but rather accounts for aggressive behavior through a normal learning process of imitation and repetition of rewarded behavior. Children, seeing their fathers treat others as "objects" who should be aggressed against when they get in the way, learn an aggressive style of behavior. Once started on such a course, they may learn that aggression is rewarding, that is, it helps them to get what they want (and they learn to want what can be gained through aggressive acts).[14] It helps them in competitive situations, in achieving dominance within their corner of the "jungle" of schoolyard or marketplace. Aggressive thought, permitted where aggressive behavior is not, may equally be learned, as the following comment by Rogers, an aggressive Adams junior, reveals:

> When I lived with my grandparents during the war, one of the strongest recollections I have of that period and of my grandfather, since deceased, is that of my grandfather continually complaining about Jews in his business and how they were controlling all the finances in Washington. Upon visiting Miami and seeing the way that the Jews behave out on Miami Beach toward natives of the area, it only served to make my hatred grow even stronger.

The man who pounds the table and complains about tyranny from Washington is likely to have a son who engages in the same kind of aggressive political thought.

But most current theories of aggression give a predominant place to the formulation that "the occurrence of aggressive behavior always presupposes the existence of frustration and, contrariwise, that the existence of frustration always leads to some form of aggression."[15] Let us not argue the universal nature of this proposition, the merit of the term "al-

---

[13]For a review of the findings on aggression in animals as these relate to human problems, see a fine small volume by John Paul Scott, *Aggression* (Chicago: University of Chicago Press, 1958).

[14]Neal E. Miller and John Dollard, *Social Learning and Imitation* (New Haven: Yale University Press, 1941). A later review of this literature is available in Ernest Hilgard's *Theories of Learning* (New York: Appleton, 1956).

[15]John Dollard, Leonard Doob, and others, *Frustration and Aggression* (New Haven: Yale University Press, 1939), p. 1.

ways." Our purposes are served by exploring the uses of the theory in explicating aggressive political thought. As recently modified, the general theory goes something like this: Frustration of goal-directed activity by some agent (which could be the self) creates an emotional state, anger, which in turn prompts a tendency toward aggressive behavior, directed, if possible, at the frustrating agent. The amount of aggression developed in this sequence depends upon (1) how intensely the person wanted that goal, (2) how completely he is prevented from achieving it, and (3), in part, how often he had been frustrated before. It also depends upon his habitual (characteristic) responses to frustrating situations, and, according to more recent theory, the way in which he interprets the situation.[16] This last qualification permits one to explain the difference in aggressive behavior following an "arbitrary" frustration and one that is "understood," differences following anticipated frustrations compared to those that present a surprise, and differences between behavior following frustrations that seem to the individual to be an "affront" (a slap at the tender ego) and those that seem more or less impersonal.

This question of the interpretation of the situation goes further, for it must include anticipation and speculation. A man who imagines that his future road to riches and power will be blocked by government taxes is frustrated, even when the government has done nothing to him as yet. In the same way, a young radical who feels that his vision of a socialist society is made unlikely by the power of the capitalists is frustrated from a happy consummation of his pleasant dream. Like "power," the concept "frustration" must allow for potential and reserved and fantasied uses. In our political material, there is very little mention of actual experienced frustration: the isolationist cannot say that foreign nations have frustrated him, but he hates their "selfishness"; the man who has derogatory things to say about the Catholic church has not had any real goal thwarted by the church, but he thinks he might. The concept "anticipated frustration" is often more useful in accounting for aggressive political ideas than actual experienced frustration. Moreover, the symbol of the potential frustrator may quickly become a ready stimulus to aggressive thought. If the frustration-aggression theory is to have much application to political thought, it must be in this extended sense.

While the reward-and-punishment theory of aggressive styles of thought does explain individual differences in the ways people respond to an irritating situation, the simple frustration-aggression theory does not. To do this one must examine the theory of the aggressive personality, that is, the

---

16 The inclusion of the emotional state "anger" in the theory is Berkowitz'; it is not in the original. Berkowitz also stresses the interpretation of the situation by the frustrated individual. See his *Aggression*.

person who is more than usually ready to respond to some frustrating situation with an aggressive response. Genetically, it seems the aggressive personality emerges from a situation of emotional deprivation, or, more specifically, from a situation where dependency needs have been developed and then frustrated. (If they had not been developed in the first place, a passive, withdrawn personality might have been the result.) When these emotional frustrations are combined with punishing parental disciplinary methods, as contrasted to love-oriented (guilt-producing) methods of maintaining discipline, the aggressive personality is hardened and tempered in his ways. He is marked not so much by a chronic state of anger as by a low threshold to anger, a kind of standardized angry response to a wide variety of life situations.[17]

It has been found that as children mature, two things happen: diffuse aggressive responses become more specific, more closely linked to the sources of their current frustration; and their extrapunitive behavior decreases while their intrapunitiveness increases—they learn guilt and learn to feel guilty about aggression. These findings tend to confirm the original Freudian idea that when destructive and punitive behavior has become pleasurable in itself, the person has regressed to an infantile stage of life.[18]

Work with aggressive children and with adults tends to show that aggressive personalities have weak ego strength, low frustration tolerance, and low estimates of themselves.[19] In much of our data, it seems, the men whose politics is most filled with aggressive terms and ideas (aggressive personalities) seem to be those who have status frustrations. Others may have low estimates of themselves, sometimes to a painful extent, but the most aggressive and hostile thinkers are those who feel this low estimate could be corrected by social status, prestige, some external sign, not by achievement, earned through hard work. *A sense of chronic status deprivation (at whatever social level) seems to make for political thought filled with aggressive sentiment.*

WHY GOVERNMENT INVITES AGGRESSIVE BEHAVIOR

Government everywhere "invites" aggression in the sense that it has the stimulus properties of a good target. At the same time Western democratic

---

[17] *Ibid.,* Chap. 10.

[18] At least as Freudian theory is interpreted by Otto Fenichel in the *Psychoanalytic Theory of Neurosis* (New York: Norton, 1945), pp. 73, 86.

[19] Fritz Redl and David Wineman, *The Aggressive Child* (New York: Free Press, Macmillan, 1957).

governments do not, as do the dictatorships, inhibit the expression of aggressive thoughts; they do not easily scare people off the target and they do not suggest that criticism, however cathartic it may be, is futile. Thus people are "agin' the government" and say so. But this is not self-explanatory, either.

First, consider how the government is a frustrator in a variety of areas. It collects taxes (frustrating desires for alternative expenditures, and demanding the frustrating rituals of filling out the forms). Almost no one escapes this form of frustration, even employees, even customers (where there is a sales tax). Furthermore, it regulates acts that by their nature are affectively loaded: sex, drinking, aggression itself. Constraint or the threat of constraint in these areas may be expected to be more than usually frustrating, because they are more than usually taxed with difficulties in internal restraint. Then, too, the government stands athwart a number of long-term goals and life purposes: the licensing of a profession or a trade, and hence the possibility of denying the fruits of application, long hours of study, a parents' dream for an aspiring but wayward boy. There are the affectively loaded minor goals associated with driving (and the hovering threat of the policeman with punitive powers and capacity to humiliate), or the employment of one's property as one pleases. As taxer and regulator the government is in a position to frustrate at many turns in life.

As servant, the provider of roads, schools, sanitation facilities, the government may deny some request; as grantor of social security, veterans' benefits, crop-reduction payments, the government requires the beneficiary to meet certain specifications, and in its impersonal way may seem dry, meticulous, and unfeeling in the process—dehumanizing in the very situations where everyone wants and needs a *re*humanizing experience.

The government is coercive; it has, we sometimes say, the monopoly of legalized force. As such it is threatening to some whose poise is shattered by force and to others made uncomfortable by authority. As a monopolist, the government can make the search for alternative courses of action futile; it can preempt all the alternatives.

The government tends to delay action beyond the time when many people think it is needed; parliamentary democracy is a talking government with consensus as its aim—not just majority consent—and consequently it frustrates those who, early in the debate, feel the time is "now," it is "ripe," the situation has "matured." The frustration of rising expectations is not limited to the developing nations.

The government is, in the minds of many, responsible for what happens: war, depression, inflation, pollution. Early action, different action, planning and intelligence always might have forestalled the evil. With this point of view, a point of view expressed by the Eastport common man's sense that there was nothing the government should not do, all widespread frustrations can be interpreted as government failures, for the government might have prevented them.

Politics is partisan; national leaders are elected by one part of the society in a contest with another part. The defeated are frustrated almost by definition: an ongoing goal-directed process, the election of their man, was frustrated by the victory of the other side. The victors, their hopes raised by the promises of the campaign, are in a position to suffer disappointments; nothing is so simple as the campaign talk would have us believe —a frustration, sometimes a major one.

As Lasswell says, politics invites conflict because it is the area where the irrational basis of society is exposed.[20] This is true because it is just here that goals and ends are brought into question, and although there are ends-means logics, there is none for the validation of one value or goal as superior to another. Conflict at this level, like the organization of narrower partisanship in a more superficial way, implies the defeat of some goals, the failure of some values to be achieved, be it those of an equalitarian society, a more military one, or a more anarchic one.

There are political forces working to inhibit aggression, as well. The forceful, authoritative character of the government itself may inhibit aggressive statements, partly because of the fear of punishment, partly because of what is called inhibition generalization. Those "targets" similar to whatever originally inhibited criticism will inhibit criticism in proportion to their similarity. In some homes the authorities (parents) cannot be criticized; children are made to feel that criticism is either dangerous or immoral. Since government figures share this quality of authority with parents, they may also share the immunity from criticism built up around the parents. Objects less like the parents (if they were the original inhibitors) will receive the brunt of aggression, perhaps some weaker ethnic group.

The government is increasingly a source of nurturance (grants, pensions, medical assistance). While the denial of assistance is frustrating, the award of benefits may induce something not usually talked about, gratitude generalization. This represents a kind of credit of goodwill on which the government may draw when things go wrong for a client-citizen.[21]

Moreover, the government is moralized in its own right. At an early age children cannot discriminate between patriotism and piety.[22] The gov-

---

[20]Harold D. Lasswell, *Psychopathology and Politics,* in *The Political Writings of Harold Lasswell* (Glencoe, Ill.: Free Press, 1951), p. 184.

[21]Compare David Easton's concept of "diffuse support" in his *A Systems Analysis of Political Life* (New York: Wiley, 1965).

[22]David Easton and Robert D. Hess, "Youth and the Political System," in S. Martin Lipset and Leo Lowenthal, *Culture and Social Character* (New York: Free Press, Macmillan, 1961), pp. 226-51.

ernment is represented by sacred symbols (flag and shield), sacred cere-
monies (Veterans' Day, Independence Day), sacred heroes, and much more
that immunize it from aggression.

The first posture of children toward politics and political leaders is
that of someone expecting only kindness and protection from "the benevolent leader." [23] The growth of critical attitudes is slow, and a bit of the
sense that any occupant of the highest office is benevolent persists into
adulthood. [24]

These comments have to do with the stimulus properties of the government, but the world is full of other political objects available and inviting.
They are satisfying objects for attack when they are already disliked,
whether or not they are frustrating any current purpose, when moral sanctions exist which permit aggression (religious themes against the Jews, for
example), when there are allies who will support the attack (and defend
against a possible retaliation), when one can remove them from the scene
by an attack, causing their noxious presence to disappear, and, of course,
when they can't easily strike back. All of this is embodied in scapegoat
theory; it is equally relevant to politics.

For all of these reasons, it is inevitable that many people would attack the government and its agents and policies, and that many more might
if they were not inhibited from doing so. Furthermore, the nature of politics
is such that a host of politically relevant objects abound, ready for pluck-
ing by anyone with an aggressive feeling looking for an object.

THE POLITICS OF AGGRESSION IN THE ADAMS MAN

It is now time to consider the case material to see if it can be made to
illuminate the problem of aggressive (injurious) politics. First I shall show
something of the similarity in tone which those who have aggressive
things to say about their fathers also display when they talk about elements
of the political scene. It is only a demonstration at this stage, but it makes
a point.

Trumbull:

Personal,   I distinctly remember my father as a person whose entire
Immediate   life was oriented around being unfair and punishing in every
trivial instance which could be manufactured. . . . It is indeed
ironic that at the time when I most needed love and affection,
he had little to offer.

---

[23] Fred I. Greenstein, "The Benevolent Leader: Children's Images of Political Authority,"
American Political Science Review, 54 (1960), pp. 934-43.

[24] Lane, *Political Ideology*, pp. 147-52.

Public,   Politics is a dirty business, just as "politician" is a dirty word.
Distant   . . . No one today wants to be thought of as a politician, and
the most effective way to be thus branded is to have formulated and expressed various opinions concerning the opera-
tions of our state or national governments.

I feel that Catholics as a group are objectionable, but I refer
only to their religion, not their persons; I feel that Jews are
personally obnoxious, but not inferior as far as range of intellect is concerned.

Novak:

Personal,   The artificiality of my relations with my father . . . was
Immediate   created (in part) by my father's unconsciously "being" and
consciously "seeming." . . . My father has always abhorred
intensity. . . . This contrasts with the intensity which unconsciously surrounds him when he is working. He always
has admired scholastic distinctions and urged such for me. He
considered himself a scholar but never published a book. I
equated publication with an important scholar.

Public,   I feel we should wage war directly on Russia at the earliest
Distant   opportunity. . . . I have few Jewish friends and am suspicious
of the motivations of those. I do not attack groups at Adams
which are strong, institutionalized, and widely accepted. I
attack the unaccepted and the out-group representatives.
[But are these representatives symbolic of the public and
distant, or embodiments of the personal and immediate?]

Rogers:

Personal,   There has always been in our family a strong pattern of dis-
Immediate   cipline and I can remember numerous incidents when this
discipline was enforced by the belt. Both my sister and I, I
guess, lived in slightly constant fear of our father, who at
many times appeared solely as the instrument of authority,
one which we could never really love. . . . My mother has appeared in a somewhat reversed position, although I was never
very close to her either.

Public,   My love for the South [Rogers is a northerner by birth and
Distant   upbringing] is perhaps more a dislike for the North, which I
consider atypical of my family. I have adopted the South
solely because I dislike to hear something criticized by some-

one who has equally as bad conditions to attend to but is more intent upon proving his neighbor at fault. . . . At this time I could be classified as the strongest type of anti-Semite character. . . . Let them [foreign nations] come through with concrete evidence that our aid is not being wasted, or I would venture to say that our policy should be that of "get tough."

Taking all the targets of aggression into view, one sees a varied list of political and social objects toward which hostility is expressed. In almost no case is it an object or person or policy that has, in fact, frustrated any of the students' real life goals, though possibly some few alleged deprivations to the family could be so interpreted. But for the most part, the hostility is toward a symbolic policy or person or group, "politicians," "Russia," noncooperative allies, intransigent labor leaders, "wealthy business interests," "selfish" social groups, anti-Semites, America-firsters, isolationists, Jews, rarely "the Church," sometimes Negroes, infrequently Communists and those who "threaten our way of life." There is, in general, not much imagination in delineating a hateful target; after all, part of the pattern of aggression is stereotyping and bluntness and confusion. Moreover, the level of aggression is generally low in this group, as one would expect from the fact that these are just the demographic reverse of the cynics studied by the political scientist Robert Agger, for they are young, well educated, relatively well off.

Of this biographical material we can ask certain questions. First, what is the relationship between the expression of hostility toward parents and its expression toward public objects? Second, how are aggressive feelings employed in the "rational" conflicts of the everyday world? Third, what is the nature of the restraints imposed on these aggressive feelings, and how do they color political thought? And fourth, can we say anything about aggressiveness and liberal or conservative inclinations?

Political Aggression and Aggressive Feelings Toward Fathers.   In passing it may be noted that two aspects of the theory of the genesis of aggressive personalities mentioned above are illustrated (and thus reinforced) in what these men say about their fathers. Almost to a man, the aggressive personalities complain of both emotional deprivation (coldness) and punitive discipline: "When I most needed love and affection, he had little to offer" (Trumbull); "On his infrequent leaves from the service in the latter part of the war he would appear solely as the punishing instrument and not at all as the love symbol" (Rogers); "I have a fear of aggression itself created by my father's unpredictable and severe punishments, which frequently occurred because of his 'headaches'" (Novak). In each case, the boy reports how he believes his father's punitiveness has interfered with his own emotional (including love) life, but, unless he received something special from his mother, he does not see how these feelings made him quickly and easily angry at the world, including the world of politics and group conflict.

As it happens, the three men quoted above are all reactionary, that is, anti-equalitarian, anti-Semitic, anti-welfare state, but before leaping to conclusions, let us look at the views of some liberals or apoliticals about their fathers.

> I have numerous memories of physical punishment administered by my father in an effort to maintain discipline. I reacted to this usually by a temporary retirement into phantasy, imagining various ways of getting revenge. My father is generally undemonstrative of emotion, and I received little affection from him. I can recall even at a tender age of about five a feeling of repugnance when asked to "kiss Daddy." . . . My father's dealings with me invariably carried, to my way of thinking, a marked injustice and incapacity for understanding.

Svenson, the author of these comments, is a weak Democrat, an internationalist, and a champion of civil rights.

Then, too, there are Cohen's remarks about his father, written, it will be recalled, as though told to him by a third person, one "Alex Rosenfeld": "Mr. Rosenfeld often accuses his son of being a 'traitor' if he does not agree with his father and side with him; now Alex rarely speaks to his father about anything of importance, dreads staying home for any length of time, and loses his appetite sitting at the same table with him." Young Cohen is a Republican, it is true, and indeed, hostile toward unassimilated Eastern European Jews (a prejudice he deplores in himself), but he supported Stevenson in 1956 and identifies with what he takes to be the liberal leanings of his professors.

One could not say that father hatred makes conservatives. But it does seem to make "aggressives," that is, it does seem to be associated with a high level of abusive and denigrative language. Thus, in addition to the hostility toward public objects shown by Trumbull, Novak, and Rogers, one finds Svenson saying, of *his* opposition:

> Such incidents as the Nevada governor's objecting to "United Nations Day," and suggesting instead "United States Day," invoke more than a little actual wrath and a great deal of disgust. My attitude toward patriotism in general is one of cynicism and distaste.

He puzzles over this, because in almost all other areas of politics he is, he says, trusting and easygoing, without firm views. He resolves this by concluding that "My beliefs seem a curious combination. One aspect of them is relatively strong and can be traced directly to hostility toward paternal authority and unfairness." (His father is an isolationist and xenophobe.) "The remaining portions exhibit indifference and lack of commitment." Thus, either by building up an aggressive personality through frustration and emotional deprivation, with a readiness for responding to public objects with hostile words, or by creating a disliked model to react against, *father hatred gives political thought a special (but selective) aggressive quality.* The targets are likely to be partisan opponents, lower status groups, abstractions and symbols ("socialism," "the system"), but not heads of state.[25] Novak gives us one key to this: he equates power with goodness.

But, of course, since aggressiveness can be learned in many ways, aggressive politics need not come from father hatred. Consider Buenello, an eldest male grandchild who "enjoyed privileges not granted to other grandchildren," and who exhibited his aggressiveness, among other ways, as the "sole disciplinarian" of the neighborhood gang. Buenello believes that all current parties are so corrupt that nothing can be done with them. He is an aggressive in politics who learned his aggression from an admired parental model in an "authoritarian family" (his term) and in the gang warfare of the streets.

The Uses of Aggression in Rational Conflict.   What we have here to consider are the ways in which aggressive tendencies, the desire to "play rough," are enlisted in political conflicts and made to serve rational purposes, that is, to energize men's efforts to overcome certain real obstacles before them. In conflict situations, men often need an "irrational"—that is, unconscious and emotional—reinforcement to their conscious, rational plans. Here are two such situations.

Goldberg, a tall, almost fair-haired young man of pleasant demeanor, and Demming, shorter and fatter, and apparently more serious about life, are both engaged in quasi-political conflicts—Goldberg in defense of his Judaism, Demming in an aspiring struggle for "reform" at Adams. The emotion they invest in these struggles seems at first "appropriate" (to use an ambiguous word that psychoanalysts employ ambiguously) to their situations, and the target groups seem rationally selected in the sense that they are the groups frustrating the men's desires. But, as it develops, two other processes may be observed, as well. One is that the hostility toward the frustrating group *generalizes to other social causes,* so that a much

---

[25]*Ibid.,* pp. 277-79. The *kind* of paternal behavior that caused the estrangement is most important in determining its political outcome, as may be seen in Chap. 15, below. There the reader will observe that fathers who overcontrolled their sons produced citizens who sought strong personalized government!

wider scope is given to the original impulse—and this is not surprising in view of the known tendency of people in the grip of aggressive feelings toward response generalization. The other is that the simple, direct, "appropriate" emotion turns out, on examination, to be a complex thing, fed by secret springs and sluiced into this "rational" cause by the promptings of partially analogical interpretation of other experience.

Goldberg's Inferiority, Hostility, Judaism, and the Democratic Party. Goldberg, to take his case first, seems to have his hostilities and aggressions well under control, and indeed, for a young man, he does. We are talking about a normal person responding well outside the range of anything that would be called "pathological." His father was an immigrant from Eastern Europe, somewhat remote, highly moral, a model of Old World behavior not quite appropriate to the circumstances of his American son's struggle for maturity. The Goldbergs lived in a large eastern industrial city, in an area marked by religious-ethnic conflict. The first cause that Goldberg espouses, then, is that of Judaism, the defense and protection of "his people." In this he is openly aggressive, but he balances his aggressiveness with some restraint and, indeed, an adoption of the American assimilationist view, having abandoned his father's orthodoxy and adopted the conventional goals for success in the multi-ethnic American environment. Some of these themes are best developed in his own words:

> My first experience with anti-Semitism occurred when I was about six or seven years old. Our neighborhood had been almost entirely Gentile, but over the years after we moved in, many more Jewish families joined the influx. The children of these families were divided into two main groups which were constantly fighting: the Cleveland Avenue and the West Jackson Avenue gangs, which ranged in age between five and nine years old. Probably because I was the best fighter in the West Jackson gang, I was "democratically" elected general. . . . I especially felt the religious nature of these fights since I had begun Hebrew school during the first year of battling. I was being versed in the tradition of the Jews and their persecution at the hands of the Gentiles. Even as late in my growth as my twelfth or thirteenth year a blinding rage would come over me whenever I was called a "dirty Jew." I felt I was the champion of my people and proceeded to glorify all their traditions. . . .

Gradually Goldberg comes to dislike his Hebrew school and to drift away from his religion, but the ethnic identification still means a great deal to him, for in his summary he speaks of himself as "one who cherishes his American and Jewish traditions" and has now a "strengthened in-group identification."

So much is simple: when a person is attacked or feels threatened, he responds with defensive strategies of his own, including solidarity with his threatened group and, when he can do so without too much loss, with a counterattack. He does not need to legitimize his hostilities; they already seem right and necessary to him. But, of course, the world is not a street-gang fight; Goldberg was accepted in mixed groups on many occasions, was accepted into Adams College and did well there, rejects the Old World orientation of his stiff father. He must muffle his hostilities, contain them, put his case in a different perspective, allowing for much more than his championship of his people. It is not easy, and inevitably the development of these constraints is complicated by other considerations, many of them much more important than his ethnic wars.

At one period in his life the family left town for a few months, and when he returned he found that he had lost his position of leadership and peer-group acceptance. He reports that his aggressive feelings during this period somehow got out of control: "At the same time a sadistic drive became dominant in me—a drive which I believe was displaced from the group of which I had been (but was no longer) a member. I enjoyed hitting fellows of my own age and playing very rough in football." This "sadism" was exacerbated by his frustrating problems of status and friendship loss. He cultivates the older boys whose acceptance he seeks and the younger boys whom he can dominate. He discovers he has two distinct personalities, one for occasions when he feels socially accepted and superior, a friendly leadership style, and one for situations where inferiority feelings come into play, when he is passive and withdrawn. "I am," he says, "a different person as the inactive self: quiet, shy, and inhibited because of my inferiority, and *am hostile to the group and myself.* I do not turn my aggressions outward to a weak group, but am intrapunitive for my weaknesses in such situations." (My emphasis). The aggressive impulses, then, which we saw as appropriately developed and directed in his espousal of the cause of his Jewish group, are now seen to have these other components: a history of quasi and muted brutality, not wholly erased by time, and an intrapunitiveness in those very situations where his religious status is likely to be silently questioned, that is, in the presence of a "superior" status group. The Jewish cause, even its muted form, simultaneously helps Goldberg to do two difficult things. First, it helps to legitimate those residues of his wish to "hit fellows my own age," and "to play very rough" on occasion. It is an escape valve for that explosive and hard-to-control anger that first developed in his intrafamily war for independence from his immigrant father. And second, it helps him in his feelings of oversubmissiveness, of inadequacy. Of himself at an earlier age he says:

My acquiescence to the authority of a "superior" group does not mean that I am content in playing a passive role. However, because of my inferiority complex in such situations and my fear of saying the wrong thing, I tend to be quiet even though I may be capable of producing the proper judgment. In my passive role I often feel hostile both to the authority or opinion of the group and to myself for being so fearful of expressing an opinion.

When he has proved himself "capable" in the eyes of the group, then he loses his hostility toward it. But in the meantime, as he says, status loss produces hostility, and, as he does not say, his own sense of inferiority cries out for compensating beliefs and actions. Among these is the belief that he belongs to an oppressed group, his status loss is due to this group membership, and so he must rise to champion the group in a just cause, rather than to fight an inferiority feeling in privacy and humiliation.

I said earlier that not only has enlistment of emotion in such an "obvious" cause a subtle etiology, but it also has ramifying consequences. An obvious one here is the linkage of the championship of Judaism with the post-1930's Democratic party. But even here, the course of life is more subtle than that of theory. Both of Goldberg's parents are Democrats, but in 1940, at about the age of five, he was an "independent," wearing both Roosevelt and Willkie buttons. In 1944 he was a Democrat, for "I had learned by this time that my parents supported Roosevelt because he was believed to be good to the Jews. I recall feeling that a Jewish Republican was literally a traitor to his people." In 1948 he was still a Democrat, actively campaigning for Truman, but at the age of seventeen he takes the "traitorous" step and becomes a Republican, converted by a favored history teacher. Shortly thereafter he returns to the Democratic party and says with relief, " I was saved." He reports:

> Thus, because I was involved in personal religious conflict and hence strengthened by my in-group identification as a Jew, because I have retained my love of Jewish tradition and Roosevelt as part of that tradition, and since my family is Democratic, I am socially predisposed to the Democratic party.

Moreover, those old status insecurities reinforce these loyalties, for he has "feelings of inferiority in certain social situations which subconsciously I may think would arise more frequently in my dealings with members of the Republican party, whom I probably associate with a 'superior' group."

The simple aggressiveness of a member of a group that is discriminated against turned upon the aggressor and shaped into a social cause turns out, on examination, to be infused with the complexities of an aggressiveness not always under adequate control and a self-aggression that requires justification. And the simple ethnic basis of a cause picks up, tortuously and curiously, political and ideological overtones not part of the original situation by any means.

Demming: A Counterelite Struggle Leads to Ideological Revolt. Demming comes from a lower-middle-class background with highly conservative values and a profound suspicion of the New Deal, "socialist tendencies," government interference with private enterprise—all values and suspicions that Demming shared until the fateful turn of events which made him a progressive Democrat. He is, to borrow Nancy Mitford's phrase, definitely "non-U"; that is, his clothes and manner and style of address are marked by the lower-middle-class origins from which he came to Adams. This is true in spite of the fact that he went to a superior private boarding school—but as a day student. The principal of the boarding school, in fact, told Demming he thought it would be better if he applied to a state university, instead of Adams, a bit of counsel that hurt Demming at the time, but which he ignored and which he now remembers with bitterness, having, in fact, done very well at Adams. At Adams, Demming had to work for his room and board, something that became relevant in the contest that brought him full circle into the liberal camp. It happened this way:

> In the spring term of my freshman year I became a leader in a movement which was directed at a change in the system of trying out for the major extracurricular activities at Adams. This system requires a great deal of time, sometimes ranging over forty hours a week, and seemed to prohibit many people from gaining membership in these organizations. I felt that the group especially affected were the working scholarship students, who already had an extra work load. . . . It appeared that the ABS, [Adams Broadcasting System] represented the extremely elite group and, most important, an economic in-group. This was my reaction to a meeting with many members of the ABS, who seemed to me to be a group into which I *and my* [social] *class* could not gain admittance.

This struggle was a turning point in Demming's ideological life, an event that caught up many latent feelings about which he had been barely aware. But the groundwork had been laid earlier. He says:

> At this point a great change occurred. Several members of the ABS attacked our organization, and when I met them, they directed some extreme remarks at me personally. *At this point my hostility began to spread to other college groups which seemed also to represent this same elite group.* This included such organizations as fraternities, certain societies, and so forth. I became

hostile to everything elite or "in" and quite expressive about my sentiments. This naturally provoked reactions which merely made me all the more adamant about conformity at Adams. This seemed to me to be very harmful (I ignore any conformity in out-groups), and I began to conform to nonconformity. [My emphasis].

The reorientation in his thinking spreads to other areas of life; it affects his concept of himself, where and with whom he belongs, what goals are worth striving for. He says, "If I wasn't going to be accepted, I might as well make a point of it," and goes on to strive in new directions: "It seems much better to be a leader of one side [the out-group] than to be an also-ran on the other." For Demming the change "affected every facet of my thinking . . . it affected the way I dressed, avoiding the Ivy League uniform," common at Adams. He attempts financial independence, agitates for reforms of the school calendar, finds new friends, reviews his personal history and discovers incidents that now seem to have been a kind of "persecution" by adult members of the elite, sees in the refusal of the richer boys to give to a Christmas fund for college waiters new evidence of elite indifference or oppression, organizes opposition groups in several areas of college life.

But, as with Goldberg, Demming's "noble cause" (that is his ironic phrase) has multiple roots in a sense of inferiority and in hostile aggressive feelings. Demming is aware of this, for, close to the situation as he is, he can report of his changed attitudes: "They did not arise purely out of in-group—out-group distinctions, but were intimately connected with a deep sense of inferiority." He describes these:

> I have had a deep sense of inferiority since childhood. When I first started school, I can remember living where there were no children of my own age, and I had to play alone. When we moved to another neighborhood, many of the boys were older and bigger, and it seemed to me that you weren't popular unless you were a good fighter. I wasn't. Thus I felt I was in an out-group of another sort, not economic. I attempted to conform, to talk and act tough, to hate school, but I never became a member of the in-group.

Later, as a day student in a boarding school, he finds himself isolated with few friends; "Again I felt alone and inferior." And beyond these circumstantial contributions to his sense of loneliness and exclusion there is a somatic one: "I was always very fat, and this contributed more than anything else to my feelings of inferiority." And (one is tempted to say "of course") "This feeling of inferiority also extended into my relations with girls."

One could only conclude, therefore, that into the emotion that burned within him as he set out to challenge the "in-group" there was infused a strong struggle against feelings of inferiority. Such things make a man touchy about slights, quick, as he says of himself, to see persecution, eager to see "justice" done. And so the causes he espoused, as in all such cases, were mixed defenses of self and others.

> This was not really a question of the persecution of the particular (out-) groups with which I identified myself. It was a question of what I felt were injustices directed at myself. Then when I did identify myself with these out-groups, I could look upon what seemed to be my experiences as the experiences of the group. My own experiences then made me tend to look at life as this in-group—out-group struggle. Because I clearly identified myself with this group, I could transfer my feelings of persecution to feelings of group persecution. Once this idea had been formed, I was very receptive to any experiences which seemed to confirm it.

Out of this identification came a kind of liberal orientation; he espoused the causes of underdogs who in some particular seemed to embody his own experience. How was this adoption of a liberal cause useful for Demming? He puts it well: "In this way I transferred my own personal feelings to those of a group in order to feel that I was fighting for a noble cause."

But if these college and political causes were useful to express and justify a struggle against inferiority feelings, what about the aggressive and hostile feelings they reflect? The causes certainly helped to express and justify these, too. One might have supposed that the frustration of Demming's goals was the source of his aggression. But we have heard him say that at an earlier period he felt out of things because he was not a good fighter. However inadequate their expression in fighting, these aggressive feelings are there, and in abundance. He describes them in words quite similar to Goldberg's:

> In sports I was extremely competitive and had a desire to "pile on the score." I thrive on competition of any sort when I think I am going to win, but am very liable to spells of depression if the outlook is not very good. Thus I try to overcome this shyness and sense of inferiority by extreme methods. I try to act as anything but shy and often seem very aggressive. *Aggression seems to be an attempt to prove that I am not really inferior.* To hide shyness, I would become overbearing. [My emphasis.]

The new politics permitted Demming to attack the elite groups in the name of various ideals of equality and justice and at the same time to even some old scores at home:

> When I am home, certain incidents increase my feelings of inferiority and result in resentment. My parents make remarks about how I drive [aggressively?], how I study, what I do in my spare time at college, etc., which make me feel like a child and embarrass me. . . . I have found that these liberal principles, so opposed to the extreme conservatism of my parents, act as good media both to express hostility and to show that I have a mind of my own. This may explain why my ideology is often based on the New Deal and Franklin Roosevelt, because it is in these fields that my parents show their greatest disgust for the Democrats.

An ideology is indeed a multiple-purpose tool; in this case it permits Demming to justify his own resentment at the social order in which he lives, to aggress against the elite groups that seem responsible for his dissatisfaction, to express an enduring set of hostilities and "pile on the score" against his enemies, to convince himself that he is not inferior, and, not least, to strike at his parents in a vulnerable spot.

Is the ideology a "rationalization" of these resentments and hostilities and identification? Perhaps, but, like many such political elaborations, it is a reasoned conclusion from certain newly discovered value premises as well:

> The Democratic party always represented to me the party of change and of the poorer classes. It has always been presented to me as the party which was changing the values of American society. Since I had not been able to satisfy my needs within what I considered the embodiment of this society, I was able to accept the ideas of this other party. The Republican party seemed to embody the group in which I wanted to be accepted and couldn't, and so I accepted the Democrats as the opposite.

But such a realization and change occurs only under favorable circumstances, the kind of circumstances that college, with its fluid social structure, its distance from home, and its tolerant attitude toward all points of view, can easily provide. It is too little realized that the function of certain kinds of education in college is to provide material with which people can work out an ideological rationale for the outcomes of much more intense struggles going on inside. Demming, insightful and candid to the last, sees this:

> Before Adams I had very little contact with the ideas behind a liberal political ideology. My home life provided only the ideas from a conservative ideology. . . . Thus when I came to Adams I had accepted the usual conservative clichés as the answers on politics. However, Adams provided an *intellectual exposure which could justify my new ideas.* Without exposure to this other

way of thinking, the other factors could not have, by themselves, caused the change in my political thought. [My emphasis.]

Thus after the metamorphosis, in sharp contrast to his ideas only a few years before, Demming expresses "distrust of 'business' and that American ideal, the businessman." He is opposed to the philosophy of "less government in business and more business in government." He feels "that labor has not achieved the influence it deserves in government." And he is a solid and partisan Democrat. The direct and reasonable aggression against the elite group that froze him out of the Adams Broadcasting System, tapping latent feelings of inferiority and aggression, generalized to other elites and underdogs, and, informed by a discussion providing a previously neglected arsenal of ideas, stimulated a train of thought leading to a thoroughgoing American welfare-state liberalism.

Here, revealed in some complexity but still simple compared to the revolutions and conflicts of the larger society, we see four processes at work. (1) Both Goldberg and Demming generalized their dislike of certain elites (high school elites and Gentile groups for Goldberg, college in-groups for Demming), and in this generalization embraced certain (for them related) political groups and symbols. (2) Both developed political rationales—that is, elaborated arguments why this was "right"—which went much beyond the original conflict. Goldberg, fearful of the status advantages of the Republicans, found that the Democrats were the party of both the New Deal and conservation of the current status quo; Demming discovered a new sensitivity to labor and ethnic underdogs which he had not previously experienced and found this equalitarian posture to be rooted in a concept of the public interest. (3) Both found that their earlier aggressive personality tendencies, especially their tendencies to play rough, were usefully enlisted against their opponents in these struggles. And (4) both believe that these same aggressive tendencies were partly efforts to overcome their feelings of low self-esteem and low status.

There is, however, a fifth process: rational calculation of how best to advance certain real-life goals. The emotional and, up to the time of self-analysis, unconscious forces of the personality are harnessed to a deliberative process that is neither at the mercy of rage nor inhibited by crippling aggression anxiety. It makes no sense to say that Goldberg's moderate conservatism or Demming's strong new liberal tendencies are either "rational" or "irrational," for each is both.

9

The Inhibition of Aggression

Not all frustrating situations produce visible aggressive behavior, certainly not of the same strength. Something within the individual often inhibits the aggressiveness of his response. There are three important inhibitions of this sort, of which the most common is the anticipation of punishment, in effect a fear of the consequences. The frustrated person may feel anger, but his aggressive behavior will be stifled. The punishment may be social disapproval, or withdrawal of affection, or failure of a larger purpose; whatever it is, it may erase all public trace of aggressive behavior. Anonymity helps a person to avoid punishment, as does aggressive behavior so disguised as to fool the punishing agent, or so an angry man might believe.

The second inhibition, of course, is the moral code of the individual, the way in which a violated conscience prevents some tempting aggressive act, or aggression more generally. Other people play a part in this conflict between conscience and aggression, for they may release or tighten the code or modify its application in a specific case, as in certain intellectual circles where it is all right to aggress verbally against Catholics but not Jews, or against low-status but not high-status people in the drawing rooms of the rich. The inhibition plays a part in the sequence of acts in which aggression takes place, for guilt over an act of aggression may lead to compensatory propitiation; even an unperformed act or an aggressive but unspoken thought may lead to such "undoing" or counteraction.[1]

In the third place, there is the matter of self-control. "It is difficult," says Berkowitz, "to exaggerate the importance of internal controls as a determinant of aggressive behavior."[2] By controlling his emotional reactions

[1]See Anna Freud, *The Ego and the Mechanisms of Defense,* trans. Cecil Baines (New York: International Universities Press, 1946).

[2]In this discussion I rely heavily on Leonard Berkowitz, *Aggression* (New York: McGraw-Hill, 1962). The quotation is from p. 275.

an individual is capable of devising alternative strategies for surmounting the frustration, for minimizing its effects, and indeed for developing alternative goals. This is that capacity so difficult to measure, and yet so important in political thinking, ego strength,[3] and it is exactly this quality that aggressive personalities so notably lack. For a variety of reasons, such personalities have a low frustration tolerance because they cannot mobilize these internal controls in time to devise alternative strategies. They cannot cope with the insecurity and threat posed by frustration; they cannot postpone indulgence; it must be all or nothing, now or never. They are, in their most severe forms, chronically ready for rage.[4]

FEAR OF CONSEQUENCES

My first thesis is this: *Politically conscious upper-middle-class people whose aggression is inhibited solely by fear of consequences are more likely than others to be reactionary.*[5] The corollary, more dubious, is that politically conscious working-class people whose aggression is likewise inhibited solely by fear of consequences are likely to be radical critics of society—populist, anomic, or Marxist, according to their cultural backgrounds. There are some good theoretical reasons for this, as well as some illustrative case materials bearing on the proposition.

The upper-middle-class reactionary is saying, in effect, that he wants to be free of governmental restraints so as to exploit the world as best he can—and he thinks that he can do well enough if let alone. He believes in a world where ability, especially his, should be rewarded without considerations of equality, protection of the weak, the welfare state. In international affairs, he believes the strong should dominate (at least, this is the view of current American reactionaries, as it was once true of the French reactionaries (De Maistre), the British (Joseph Chamberlain), and the Germans (Nietzsche, Fichte). Thus the reactionary view of the world is one in which aggression has moral support, empathy and consideration for the weak are considered dangerous to the public good, and, most important, reaction promises to release the rich and powerful, and those whose ambition it is to

---

3See, for example, my *Political Life* (New York: Free Press, Macmillan, 1965), pp. 147-55; and my *Political Ideology* (New York: Free Press, Macmillan, 1967), pp. 53-56, 122-27.

4See Fritz Redl and David Wineman, *The Aggressive Child* (Glencoe, Ill.: Free Press, 1957).

5In the next chapter there is a further discussion of various kinds of moral restraints and moral reasoning. Following Lawrence Kohlberg, we may identify a morality based on fear of punishing consequences as the most primitive stage of moral development. See his "Development of Moral Character and Moral Ideology," in M. L. Hoffman and L. W. Hoffman, eds., *Child Development Research*, Vol. 1 (New York: Russell Sage, 1964), pp. 383-431.

join them, from a variety of legal restraints that now curb their appetites. The restraints on aggression posed by considerations of what is best for the self are quite in keeping with the reactionary conscience, while aggression anxiety is not.

Of course, everyone is somewhat restrained from aggression by consideration of the consequences for himself; but for nonreactionaries there is a mixture of restraints, which embrace, in some part, an empathic consideration. In the biographies of the three reactionaries quoted above in Chapter 8 (Trumbull, Novak, and Rogers) there is some evidence of the fear of the consequences of their own aggression as these affect their own plans and feelings; *none* indicating a concern for the effect of their aggression on others. Two of these three reactionaries, Trumbull and Novak, show just this kind of self-oriented concern about their hostile feelings.

In a comment revealing the source of the aggression he now feels, Trumbull says: "I can plainly recall an endless chain of angry explosions issuing forth from him [his father] whose contents were that I certainly had little or no chance of leading a successful life and that I was nearly foredestined to ostracism from the human community." Thus his father, as so often happens with aggressive personalities, both frustrated his son and showed him how to behave when angry. Trumbull is aware of this and of the dangers connected with such behavior:

> I think that signs of repressed aggression are evident in my personality. I can remember in my youth reacting in a violent physical manner at the least disturbance. I have, however, gradually learned to control my temper so that any annoyance is dispelled by an outpouring of sarcasm combined with a high degree of physical exercise with the results that at least my more obviously aggressive tendencies have been partly submerged.

Two things seem apparent: First, the level of aggression and hostility is extremely high, hence the restraint would have to be commensurate. Second, the restraining force is not guilt, but a sense of the personal disadvantages of revealing his explosive aggressive feelings. Sarcasm is better than a tantrum, not because it wounds less, but because it is more socially acceptable and personally less embarrassing. It is true that he mentions some sense of guilt for having engaged in "what appears now to resemble a planned campaign to literally pound my younger brother into the dust," a campaign that he believes was "an attempt on my part to revenge myself upon my brother, whom I felt was receiving the lion's share of parental love and affection. . . . I do remember that I was unjustly persecuted to the advantage of my younger brother." But, he continues, *"I would not have given more than passing consideration to this struggle* had my brother developed along the lines of what is termed a 'normal' child." It is the fact that his brother is mentally sick, not that he waged aggressive war against him, that creates the trouble, no doubt a guilt partially prompted by embarrassment and a clear sense of how this can be used against him. But his anti-Semitism, his view that "any movement which should arise whose tenets are hostile to the basic beliefs of our capitalistic society must be *ruthlessly* and completely eliminated," and his concept that "politics is a dirty business" without relief, all reveal an unusual—for this group—lack of restraint due to a consideration of the victim, a lack of tolerance. (In both of these quotations the emphasis is mine.)

Novak's problems are different, and yet they have the same self-centered quality. He reports that in grade school he feared fights: "The second smallest in my class, I backed out of a fight when chance afforded it. When having to fight, I cried during it and for some time afterward. This continued into secondary school." More than that, Novak developed an intrapunitive streak, but it was not because of any guilt feelings; it was rooted in shame over his own weakness:

> My anti-aggressive streak may have come from my fear of aggression created by my father's unpredictable and severe punishments which frequently occurred because of his "headaches." I became very submissive and could not translate any aggressive tendencies into my own age group. I was not accepted by the in-group—I was, myself, at an early age, the out-group. Hence "aggression" turned inward. At an early age I became very introspective and self-blaming. Feelings of guilt assailed me. I "talked too much" in order to gain attention. When this lost me friends, I blamed myself severely. I came to idolize the "leader" of every in-group. He seemed to have powers which were beyond my grasp.

The account is a good one, because it outlines the course that Novak took in becoming "reactionary" (his own term). A strong, rich, and able young reactionary leader appeared on the Adams scene when Novak was trying to "make it" in extracurricular activities. Novak sought out and followed this leader to what proved to be his academic doom. But for our current interests it is more important to analyze the nature of these feelings about the failure of aggression and its restraint. Why was Novak intrapunitive and self-blaming? Not for fear he might hurt someone, or for shame at breaking the moral code, or because hostility was a bad thing. On the contrary, he was blaming himself for his submissiveness, for his ineptness in exercising leadership, for his failure to "translate any aggressive tendencies into my own age group." He felt guilty about not being aggressive enough.

Thus it seems that the reactionary tendency comes not only from a high fund of hostility and aggression, stemming in part from uncompensated father hatred; it may come also when the restraining mechanism is not guilt about the damage to others done through hostile acts, but rather a desire to avoid damage to one's own purposes, or shame at failure to show off to good advantage, or failure to lead, dominate, and assert oneself. Or, as in the case of the third reactionary, Rogers, there may be no reference to any restraining mechanism at all, let alone a concern about the object of one's hostility, or the justice of it, or the consequences of aggression. These mechanisms are very different from Goldberg's shame about his early "sadism" or Demming's embarrassment over his tendency to compete aggressively only when he could win, or, as we shall see, Coleman's argument with himself about his guilt over an early childish cruelty. The reactionary shows none of these.

Now, the tendency to be reactionary under the circumstances just described is limited to a socioeconomic group, the upper middle class, whose "natural" opponents are unions and government, that is, the agencies that can and do limit upper-middle-class income and freedom. A working-class aggressor has a different set of "natural" enemies, of course, although he may identify with the rich and powerful if he thinks he can rise to meet them, if not actually to join them. If he does not so identify above "his station," his enemies are likely to be more diffuse: "the system," "the capitalists," or perhaps just "they." For the reasons mentioned in Chapter 8, the government is a useful target for such a person as well, but with a difference: he may want to work for the government, and he receives more "help" from the government.

With our sample, we cannot illustrate the motivational basis of the aggressive working-class person, but an examination of some of the themes in De Vita's case, given in some detail in Chapter 1, may help. What they illustrate, I think, is the channeling of aggression in a liberal direction, not because of empathy with the underdog or the victims of aggression, but because of a set of career interests, unspoken ethnic identifications, and a sense of being an outsider in an upper-middle-class setting. The restraints on this aggression, and they are substantial, are indeed a fear of hurting others, but this is not so much because of empathy with others as because of the fear of consequences to the self. The difference in ideological consequences in these two strata of society lies in the different avenues each has for achieving the power and status he wants. For Novak, "Capitalism represents possibilities and opportunities for [my] rising in that society . . . and acceptance by the in-group." For De Vita the situation is different: "I would like a career in the State Department as opposed to any kind of elected office, because, for one reason, I see no real competition on the way into the executive branch." But the sociological and career differences do not fully account for the political differences of these men. It is important to show how De Vita's restraining mechanisms, as well as his aggression, led him into the liberal camp.

Early in his analysis De Vita uncovers two needs he regards as fundamental: his need for affection and his fear of competition. But this does not satisfy him, as we have already seen. To provide the background for this analysis I shall repeat here two passages from his biography.

> On the basis of these two drives alone, I could not fully explain my liberal political idealism. I searched further and finally uncovered a highly repressed but nevertheless very strong drive for power, control, prestige. . . . My attack upon the status quo is perhaps the most important outlet for my repressed power drive.

This attack is quite general:

> I am against any policy which seeks to preserve a status quo that has been of no benefit to me. I can't support things as they are, because I myself fit nowhere into the present system. From the point of view of an outsider looking in, all I can do is to criticize—that I do.

The hostile, aggressive component is quite as great in De Vita's view of things as it is in the cosmologies of the reactionaries, but the targets are different. He has overcome his ethnic prejudices (with some difficulty) because they are anti-intellectual and he has adopted the view that the intellect is the right instrument for the seizure and exercise of power, his instrument. He has, however, a kind of contempt for the masses, and does not believe labor unions should be allowed to share in the power of government since they do not represent informed public opinion, but more especially, "In my attitude toward labor, the generally repressed hostility incorporated in my drive for domination is unleashed. . . . They are usurpers . . . " and so on. He attacks "the bullheadedness of nationalism" and other policies with considerable vigor and relish. The aggression throughout his paper is indeed substantial.

What then restrains this aggressiveness? It is a fear of making people angry at him, of losing their respect, and, above all, of losing their affection. This is true both in his personal relations and, projectively, in his thinking about foreign affairs.

> My desire to dominate is not, I believe, a drive toward the physical destruction of those over whom I exercise control. In destroying a person I would destroy also the source of admiration I really seek. I turn, instead, to a form of intellectual domination.

This is not, I think, conscientious concern for the well-being of the object of his attacks; it is concern for a source of narcissistic supplies. And it is a general pattern and a constant problem for him. He pulls his punches not for fear of injuring, but for fear of giving offense. "In all cases . . . I much prefer not to offend anyone [rather] than . . . to exhibit my desire for power. In fact, some of my experiences in power positions have not been completely successful for this reason." The restraint, therefore, is both a competing need that forces a repression of the aggressive impulse and a calculation of the consequences of aggression in self-oriented terms.

The ideological outcome is, in a sense, predictable, but De Vita, an extremely intelligent and candid person, spells it out for all to see. He says:

> My ideas on government are no doubt externalizations of my drive to control. . . . As I attack the status quo, then, I am building in my mind a government that will embody more intellectually founded policies. I am creating a system that I can control. . . . I look for the day when my claim to power will be the only recognized and admired claim to rule over people.

In that last sentence, apparently the product of megalomania, De Vita intends to say that the general claim of intellect to power should be recognized, but the phrasing is certainly revealing.

More specifically, in foreign affairs one sees the personal problem of aggression and control magnified and reflected. De Vita is a strong internationalist, believes in foreign aid on a large scale, and in this sense wants to see the United States exercise great influence in the world. But it should not antagonize other nations.

> Antagonization [sic] results not only in the withdrawal of affection but also in the provocation of aggression, the beginning of conflict, victory and alienation or defeat and humiliation. When I recently read *The Ugly American,* I was terrified. As I've dealt with my parents and with those around me, so the United States should deal with the world. We want above all that the people of the world will like us.

There is the restraint against aggressive acts: such acts risk counter-aggression, and above all they cut off supplies of affection.

Given their personalities, would Rogers, Novak, and Trumbull have been anomic or radical leftists had they been ethnically different and born on the other side of the tracks? Would De Vita have been reactionary had he been an upper status person with economic leverage to begin with? I think so.

MODERATE OTHER-EMBRACING AGGRESSION ANXIETY

The second point I want to make on this matter of the restraint of aggression, perhaps the obverse of the one above, is this: *Those who are restrained in their aggression because of an other-embracing aggression anxiety, empathy with the intended victims, or guilt will tend to be moderate liberals or apolitical.* Again, there are theoretical reasons for this. As I employ the term here, and as it is commonly employed in the United States, "liberal" means a modestly equalitarian orientation, which, for middle-class people with little to gain personally from this movement, means a consideration for others who are in some respect less well off. Moreover, liberalism is inclusive, while reaction is exclusive; that is, liberalism embraces minority groups in a larger range of things, considers them as people with rights and dignities. Further, the ideal society that is implied in the liberal doctrine is not one of the victory of the strong over the weak, but of the conciliation of conflicting parties in the best mutual arrangement. Conciliation, not domination, is the goal. All of these themes are "other-embracing" and both teach and reflect a consideration of others. Thus they are naturally congenial to a form of aggression restraint which is also "other-embracing," empathic, concerned for the victim.

But there is a set of counterconsiderations. To challenge the going order is to aggress against the values, the symbols, the leaders of things as they are. For middle-class sons, very likely, it is to aggress against parents embedded (enmeshed, some would say) in the pattern of roles and duties of an ongoing order. The middle-class person who shrinks from aggression and worries about what his words and acts will do to others is pulled back from the brink of liberalism and becomes instead either a moderate or a neutral. Aggression anxiety tends to keep people away from extremes of any kind.

Our data permit us to illustrate how this works out in one situation where both the aggressive drive and the moral inhibition are strong. Perhaps one reason for this visible externalized conflict is that in this case, according to its author, a vigorous young man by the name of Coleman, the aggressive drive is learned from one parent, the inhibition from the other. In contrast with most such situations, here the mother seems to be the model for aggression and the father the model for inhibition.

Coleman is a moderately athletic native of the Southwest, the son of an evangelical minister married to a dominating woman. From her, Coleman says, he learned assertive techniques (which he needed in order to maintain some autonomy against her), but at the same time he learned from his father the contents of an "other-embracing" conscience. Today he asserts himself against his roommates, "playing the angry young man" in their company, against competitors for political office in the Adams community, and against all comers in a race for precinct chairman back home in his native state.

But, he says, it was not always that way. Because of early asthma and parental admonitions, for many years he thought of himself as a coward. "I was," he continues, "constantly overcompensating for this by acting the 'big man' and by arrogance . . . [Later] I found that I had the ability to draw people around me and command their unquestioning allegiance. At this point in my life, I used this ability to make up for the inferiority I felt." One would say, in sum, that aggression anxiety was not his central problem.

But there are genuine moral, guilt-laden restraints. The following story gives the flavor:

> I remember being quite cruel to one little boy who adored me. I recall storming away after he had accidentally torn my shirt, exactly as my mother would have withdrawn affection, and later finding an envelope on my door with a dime in it and a note saying, "For the Shirt, from Jimmy." I cried when I realized what I had done and ran to apologize. I was always sorry when I had hurt someone. This probably shows a strain of my father's influence. He is a very peaceful man who hates nothing more than conflict and hurting anyone.

But the internalized father runs into the internalized mother, for the next sentence is "Yet it was natural for me to strike out at people to prove I was stronger than they."

Coleman's politics shows something of the same mix. As reported elsewhere, Coleman's main interest is in achieving some striking political victory in line with his sense that there is a great destiny waiting for him somewhere ahead. Hence his beliefs are tailored to expediency: "In regard to integration, expediency dictates that I take a fairly liberal position. . . . My aspirations go beyond the state level." But also, "My actual feelings on this issue are liberal. My father has always taken a liberal view in race relations." And once again the conflict: "I can recall being incensed when I saw a Negro boy making love to a white girl in France, but I also recognized the irrationality of my feeling." On the welfare-state issues, Coleman takes the middle road; on labor, he is generally conservative: "I have never had reason to identify with the working class and therefore could never see their struggle for power in terms of my own." But then again, in a revealing phrase: "Perhaps my feeling toward labor is analogous to my treatment of my friend Jimmy. I want to be strong *vis à vis* the unions, but do not want anyone else mistreating the working man."

Coleman makes the point well. He is assertive and even aggressive at times, intensely political, chiefly for career purposes, but he has a point of view all his own. His drive for power, like most such drives and missions, is compensatory, a monumental effort to quell persistent doubts, but there is something that keeps this drive from being ruthless; it is a concern for the victims of aggression, his own and others'; it is an "other-embracing" conscience.

STRONG AGGRESSION ANXIETY

The third point on the nature of the restraint of aggression has to do with the more exaggerated cases of aggression anxiety. Theoretically, and according to some research, aggression anxiety tends to make for a diffuse set of targets, a general leaking out of aggression in a variety of small ways, with, of course, much "undoing" of the aggressive acts. Inevitably this means that political targets will share these characteristics; that singleness of view which comes from a few dominant hatreds (Wall Street, labor leaders, etc.) is missing. Thus, *those who have an exaggerated aggression anxiety tend to have a diffuse unfocused political outlook (eclectic moderation), or tend to withdraw from the field.*

This is all the more true since, as we have said, politics is the arena in which social conflict (aggression) takes place; the government is an inviting target for aggression, as are political opponents and their policies. Under the strain that this conflict-laden field creates for the person anxious about his aggression, he must search for a strategy that accommodates him to these threats. He may borrow bits and pieces from all sides, or employ such labels as "independent" and "bipartisan" to confuse and hide his position, or seek compromise as a way of life, or, indeed, give up and get out. We see some of these tendencies in two of the cases that have been examined briefly before, Lamb and Trueblood. Lamb's case, moreover, might be employed to illustrate another point: the reciprocal interference of several needs in the expression of aggression. His need to be liked inhibits his aggressive statements; his need to criticize others (aggressiveness) inhibits his pursuit of the friendship of others; and his need for achievement (an internalized standard of excellence) inhibits both. Some of these ideas will appear between the lines in the following account.

Lamb: How to Avoid Hurting Others.   In general it is the case that people inadvertently reveal their fear of aggression but do not talk about it, even when they sit down to speak candidly about themselves; therefore one must rely upon inference and exegesis, in some ways a less convincing procedure. But Lamb both indirectly reveals and directly says something about his concern lest he hurt, embarrass, assault the people who are close to him. The theme is most clearly revealed in an account of his conflict between his need to be liked and his high standards, principles, or "perfectionism." This perfectionism seems to imply holding people up to standards of conduct which they often fail to meet and hence produces a critical (hostile) attitude toward them. Lamb's account of this conflict makes confusing reading because of the inner struggles going on.

> I have learned that one should set high standards for oneself and if it is at all within one's power, live up to them. This poses a dilemma because as a perfectionist among nonperfectionists, I have become very irritated with other people, because they do not set high standards for themselves. However, because it is part of my beliefs to be tolerant of the mistakes of others, I have not criticized them openly for what I vehemently consider short-comings. During high school I used to blow my top at home rather than tell people what I thought of them.

Observe here both the "vehemence," the almost overpowering temptation to tell people off, and the enormous effort going into restraint, the result of which he says "did not teach tolerance." He grows critical of his schoolmates, the headmaster, "and almost everything about the school." And, as one might expect:

> Because no one lives up to my standards, this has meant that I have never had great enough respect or trust for anyone to have more than [casual] friends, never have I had a close friend. Quite obviously one cannot object to people the way I do, express it very often, and still expect to be liked. Because I think it is wrong to criticize others and because I want to be liked, I never tell people what I think is wrong with them, though my perfectionism tells me that they are worthy of criticism.

But in the next few sentences, Lamb indicates that he does indeed find fault with his friends and allows his critical (hostile) impulses to show through.

> This poses the problem of the conflict between being honest, which is a very important virtue to me, and not telling the truth and therefore being liked. The desire to be liked outweighs perfectionism, because I am not honest with others. Yet in the long run I withhold a greater degree of commitment of friendship from people who I am more dishonest with. Ultimately, I suppose, it could be said that I am honest [i.e., critical] in that I have no close friends.

In this curious way, Lamb first says he compromises his "principles" in order to win friends, yet argues that because he has no close friends, he must be living up to his principles. Because, in a man as bright as Lamb, and as candid and lucid, this kind of thinking is highly exceptional, there must be more to it than meets the eye. He slowly reveals what this is, first by another curious argument: If one likes one's fellow man, one must, in turn, want to be liked. Since Lamb wants to be liked, it "follows" that he likes his fellow man: "I have a great desire to be liked, because I have learned that is a good goal and is inevitable if one likes one's fellow man, and therefore, being a perfectionist, I strive to completely fulfill this goal." He seems to be insisting, against discordant feelings and evidence, that he does like people, he does, he does! But, on the other hand, "At times it could be said that I am scared of people . . . I am hurt very easily." Is he scared because he might do or say something hostile—not very hostile, of course, but frightening to him? Gradually, more of the story comes out.

> This same combination of traits contributes to my avoidance of close personal relations. I don't feel that I am worthy of them, and I also feel that they would lead to the likelihood of being hurt more deeply. *I have often lain awake nights worrying whether things I have said to people hurt them,* and I suppose I fear that in a close relationship there would be more chance of this happening. This lack of self-confidence means not only that I don't have any close friends, but also that I have a desire to have the security of a greater number of friends as compensation for not having close friends. Thus, for instance, at Adams meals I often pass up eating dinner with people I know well and like in order to eat with those I know less well. [My emphasis.]

Furthermore, in high school, as we observed in a previous discussion, Lamb was voted the "most generous" member of the class, a phenomenon he interprets now as an attempt to buy friendship. Much goes into this, of course, but it would surprise me very much if probing did not find something like the "undoing" complex that Anna Freud reports, the acts of ostentatious and "gratuitous" kindness performed in order to "undo" the subliminal and unconscious hostile thoughts or wishes that one cannot acknowledge or accept.

In college the same problems bother him, for, as it turns out, he has more or less incompatible roommates, with no outlet for "blowing off steam" at home. "This meant," he says, "that I would either have to bottle up my dislike of other people or tell them what I thought of them. . . . I kept my true feelings to myself."

Some of the political consequences of this fear of one's own hostilities, this inhibition of aggression, this riveted lid on the steaming caldron, have been examined earlier when we examined the need to be liked, that is, the need for reassurance on this troublesome matter of love and hate. Lamb, it will be recalled, is a liberal-conservative. He is liberal in a way congenial to his own special problem of restraining hostile feelings: "My goal of being good to my fellow man and *avoiding hurting others* is liberal, as is my belief that no man should have his choices made for him by others." [My emphasis.] Moreover, this has a reference in personal experience, for, as he speaks of his experience with members of the working class on a maintenance crew, he shows a kind of sympathy with their cause— sympathy of a special kind:

> My liberalism means that with people who are of a lower educational level or of a lower income level, I am always *careful not to hurt them by showing my superiority in these areas.* However, I believe that I do not make this fact obvious, because I feel this would be almost as patronizing. [My emphasis.]

His ethnic and class tolerance and his desire for the welfare of others arises, according to Lamb, in this way: "The fact that I want to be liked can be applied to my relations with all peoples regardless of income, religion, or race." But, as we have seen, this desire to be liked comes partly from a wish to reassure himself that he does not, in fact, have uncontrollable hostilities that might hurt and damage, as he reveals above. One might, then, infer that a fear of one's own aggression can lead a person in a liberal, even a radically equalitarian, direction. Sometimes it does, but there is a caveat in Lamb's own case:

> I feel that the best and most effective way to accomplish these liberal ends is the use of conservative means. . . . Even though the status quo may be contradictory to my principles, I have always gained security in my private life from order and planning, and I therefore feel that in world matters slow change is preferable.

Radicalism is aggressive; rapid and momentous change involves aggression against established interests; it makes people angry (dangerous) and hurts certain groups (frightening). Therefore, liberal ideals, good interpersonal relations, *and* moderation, balance, and reason (since emotion is likely to get out of control) are the keys to a gratifying belief system for those marked by such aggression anxiety.

Trueblood: The "fear of using my whole strength." Lamb's social anxiety seemed to emerge inadvertently from his fear of aggression, the fear that he might reveal his hostilities. Trueblood's social anxiety may have a similar base; and hence, in developing further the cases of these two men, I am looking at a set of causes of ideological behavior which may be a rather basic one. In both cases the social anxiety and the inferiority feelings have multiple causes; this fear of aggression is not the only one, but it is an important one.

Trueblood, it will be recalled, is bothered, like Lamb, by a kind of perfectionism: his motto is "Be ye perfect in all things," and this causes a kind of paralysis of the will and withdrawal from choice. Could it be the case that this problem of willful behavior is, at the core, a fear of aggression, just as the problem of choice is rooted in a fear of being wrong and thus losing respect? Let us see.

The reader will recall Trueblood's feelings of inferiority arising in part from his early sickness, which gave him a sense of being not quite so strong as others. At the same time, and incongruous but not improbable, is his fear of damage to others if he should assert himself. He puts it this way:

> Sometime between the ages of three and five, at least two occasions stand out in my mind where I was severely chastised for hitting things and breaking them. This instilled in me a fear of using my whole strength to hit or attack something— a fear which lingers in part to this day. The combination of these two factors (inferiority feelings and fear of aggression) hindered me in taking my own part in fights with older boys who were my playmates at that time (about five years old). That is, the fear of striking made me afraid to hit others and the belief of my weakness made me feel I would *and should* lose anyway.

Observe (I have italicized the words) how Trueblood believes not only that he will lose if he is aggressive, but that he ought to lose, that it is a dangerous and horrid thing to strike out, and that the consequences can be disastrous: destruction of something valuable. Not only fear of reprisals, but guilt over the act, is the restraining element, and anticipation of the *just* punishment that will follow. Moreover, the matter is complicated by a home situation:

> My first sister was quite aggressive and daring, and often became involved in my battles. I recall my parents berating me for my lack of spirit in combat and comparing my attitude with my sister's daring. Of course, I felt keen disappointment at my situation, but did not seem to be able to do anything about it.

From his father Trueblood receives what he regards as authoritative but ambiguous guidance, making rebellion and assertion difficult; indeed, it seems to be a variation of Gregory Bateson's "double bind": "Do as I say but don't be so damn submissive."

> In most cases, my father refrained from stating his preference authoritatively—especially where he feels that the decision should be mine (e.g., in selecting a college or vocation). But even still I seem acutely tuned to any vague hints he may give out, trying to discover his opinions and employ them.

An outspoken and more regulative father might have produced a more assertive and willful son. There was, it seems, the incentive but not the opportunity for generating a rebellious spirit. His own aggression, therefore, was bottled up and curdled for want of air.

The result we have seen: a tendency to avoid decisions that might prove wrong. But earlier we said this was because Trueblood feared losing respect, losing status, upsetting his elaborate compensatory apparatus for proving to himself and others that he was not "inferior." Now we add another motive: he fears to assert his views because he might give offense, he might hurt someone. There is not so much evidence that he wants to hurt someone as there was in the case of Lamb, but that may only reflect a more carefully concealed hostility. What is clear is that the training in self-control went awry at an early age, and "the fear of using my whole strength to hit or attack something" does, as he says, "linger in part to this day." And the resulting political thought is anemic, timid, indecisive, withdrawn.

DENIAL OF AGGRESSIVE FEELINGS

Finally, we come to the fourth point, the working through of something that is more aptly termed aggression denial than aggression anxiety. It refers to *a tendency for someone in the grip of relatively strong aggressive feelings that he cannot accept to develop a philosophy of opposition to aggression.* It is the ideology of reaction formation; it is the syndrome of the belligerent pacifist. In the case to be presented here, for reasons that admittedly are obscure, the unacceptibility of the young man's own aggressive impulses does not lead to anxiety or paralysis, as with Lamb and Trueblood, but rather to a forthright and direct political statement of a position that is at the same time a manifest call for peace and unity and a latent embodiment of aggressive tendencies. Donaldson provides the example.[6]

Donaldson is one of the least introspective and self-aware members of the group. An active, athletic person, who comes to class dressed in a combination of work and sporting clothes, clean but suggesting that he is about to do a day's work as a telephone lineman or truck driver over a mountain route, Donaldson identifies with labor, with the New Deal, with the cause of all minorities who are discriminated against, with justice and fair play for all. His father is a scientist and both parents are college educated and moderately well off; they are liberal, but Donaldson has grounds for differing with their brand of liberalism. His views are clear and he expresses them without the doubts and qualifications that others in our group show:

---

[6]Donaldson's case also illustrates the way in which impression-management morality affects political thinking. See Chap. 11, below.

I support the socialistic approaches to bettering the plights of the worker (i.e., wages, conditions, etc.). Moreover, I support the unions in particular because I believe that they have contributed a great deal to these goals. . . . In analyzing my feelings about civil rights and prejudice, I cannot help but find that I feel a true compassion for minority groups or individuals. . . . The goals of the welfare state are not only just, but virtually mandatory if we are to build our country and the world toward a materialistic Utopia. Furthermore, I see no other goal worthy of our efforts.

The tone is affirmative and occasionally dogmatic; Donaldson sees himself as working toward the ends he espouses. But, curiously in a group where everyone else searches for his own motivations, Donaldson is strongly silent about his own inner life. Let us explore the clues he provides.

He entitles his essay "A Study in the Personality of Cooperation." Time and again he refers to the advantages to men's cooperating with one another, to their joining together to tackle social problems:

I believe that labor and management should work together toward applying these principles [of cooperation] with politically directed efforts. . . . The most obvious theme is that of cooperation, the scope of which can be expanded almost indefinitely to help build a more productive and capable world. . . . The spirit of cooperation which I emphasized so strongly in my discussion of labor has emerged again in my discussion of individual and civil rights. . . . It is only through cooperation among men that the goals of a country can be secured. . . . Through cooperation these wasted resources can be applied to our country and to the world to provide an increased standard of living.

But whence comes this idea of cooperation and avoidance of conflict, particularly atomistic or individualistic conflict? There are several clues in the following interesting statement:

I have always been taught the value of cooperation and unity by my parents. The importance of this has been impressed upon me in regard to little and great projects and it is to this feeling that I attribute my most fervent support of unions over unorganized forms of labor. In the unions I see dignity of unity for a great body of men, without which they would all be groveling together. My image of this extends to the personal, and when, in the last few years, I have considered entering labor as a profession, *I have often imagined myself speaking almost vituperatively to a surging mass of men,* asking for cooperation and unity in the pursuance of goals. The importance of this unity and cooperation cannot be overemphasized, because if it is properly directed it will heighten the successes of mankind on earth. Division into atomized militant opposition cannot help but lead to wasted productive force and in most cases to destruction. [My emphasis.]

Clearly the theme of cooperation and unity, tirelessly repeated, has some special symbolic significance to him, for he cannot see that in unions he is organizing men for the purposes of conflict against other interests in society, and he expresses an extravagant fear that the failure of cooperation leads "in most cases to *destruction*," not merely to the condition of most men in most unorganized industries. But the statement reveals more than this extraordinary premium upon cooperation, for it suggests the special meaning and sources. One of them is that this is a theme learned from his family. In that sense, cooperation has behind it the ethical sanction of ideas moralized in early life. But in evaluating this, consider also the following views, expressed early in the essay:

> My parents do not like unions as they have emerged. I can recall my father shaking his head and saying that it is too bad that unions use such petty methods. . . . He feels strongly that the unions have led to further waste and extravagance. . . . My own personal beliefs are in a great sense considerably different. . . . I firmly believe that the unions have achieved great successes. . . . It is also my experience that unless forced to do so, the management of a great many businesses will not and do not suffer vicariously with the plight of their employees.

Donaldson is not a father hater, like some of our men, but it is a fact that in all of the panorama of liberal ideals which his parents support, he has selected the one theme to emphasize, the one career motif, where he is certain to run head on into their opposition. Like all counterideologists, he must work with the ideas of the particular culture in which he has been raised to attack the orthodoxy of the status quo. In the age group to which Donaldson belongs it is hard to differentiate between a thoroughgoing rebel and someone who merely needs to distinguish himself from his parents, to establish his independence and autonomy. Donaldson, it seems, is a bit of both.

But now consider that curious and revealing image of himself "speaking almost vituperatively to a surging mass of men, asking for cooperation and unity in the pursuance of goals." One sees a small figure on a distant stand, almost lost in a crowd of bewildered men, who seek a leader and find him in young Donaldson, merging their petty quarrels for "the cause." This cause, it seems, is mostly a "materialistic Utopia," planned, orderly, free of strife, and controlled by just such a scientific planner as—well, as Donaldson himself. The theme is the exercise of power, dramatic presence, heroism, and domination over others—for their own good, of course. And the language is "vituperative," that is, aggressive, addressed against some enemy or evil, not at all free of conflict. In this one touch of fantasy, Donaldson may be revealing something he does not care to say directly about himself.

As we reconstruct the situation, is it not plausible to conceive of it in the following way? Donaldson, who likes his parents and especially his father, nevertheless is a rebel, and harbors aggressive feelings against his father which he cannot admit because they are too "dangerous" for him. Further, as in the other cases we have seen, these aggressive feelings have been generalized to many political objects, hence his radicalism, his socialism, his total identification with labor. But nowhere does he admit to aggressive feelings or desires to assert himself *against* others, or any lust for power. These feelings and desires, quite clearly revealed in his discussion, are not openly inspected; rather they are left in the unconscious, where it is hoped, they will not threaten the conscious mind. But these forces are all working: the aggressive feelings toward the father, the aggressive feelings toward society, and the desire to dominate others. What better way to solve this problem than to take up a posture and even a career certain to annoy the father and, under the father's own slogan of "cooperation," engage in a bitter conflict against the managers of society, stirring up the masses and leading them to battle?

10

The Need to Feel Moral

All men are moral. This is true even of the most delinquent, hatred-filled children, for, as Redl and Wineman say, there are ethical "value islands" in that ocean of impulsive hostility in which they live.[1] Societies need belief systems with moral reference; individuals need them, too.

THE NEED FOR MORALITY

The moral beliefs of social groups serve to explain why that group's purpose deserves support, hence why sacrifice is necessary, why service is called for, why obedience is something other than subservience. By moralizing their codes of behavior, societies exact a higher standard of conformity to laws and customs and enable their members to work and live more easily together than they otherwise could, since the expectations of each about the others are more likely to be fulfilled. Coordination is easier. That a group's way of doing things reflects the highest morality becomes an article of faith in most ideologies and belief systems, for it maintains morale by supporting the self-esteem of group members; it enhances loyalty and provides sanctions and the grounds for sanctions against defectors, heretics, and deviants of all kinds. Moreover, since all society is conflictful and racked by strains of one kind or another, belief systems provide moral rationales for reducing conflict and relieving strain. They explain why, when it is necessary to frustrate one group and to exploit another, these actions are just.[2]

---

[1]Fritz Redl and David Wineman, *The Aggressive Child* (New York: Free Press of Glencoe, 1957), pp. 201-05.

[2]See, for example, Talcott Parsons, *The Social System* (New York: Free Press of Glencoe, 1951), pp. 326-83; Francis X. Sutton and others, *The Amer. an Business Creed* (Cambridge: Harvard University Press, 1956), pp. 303-25.

Mentioning these social functions in this way suggests some of the cogent reasons why any man who finds himself in a position of authority tends to invoke moral arguments for his demands and tends to reinforce his instrumental statements with normative ones. Leaders find it useful to do this; followers, whether or not they see behind the statement to the reasons for it, find it useful to agree. Moral reference makes obedience, which group members might have to give anyway, so much easier. As Fromm said once about social character, moralized beliefs help the members of a group to *want* to do what they *have* to do.[3]

But, of course, there is very much more behind the individual's tendency to seek moral justification for his thoughts and acts than the psychic costs of deviance. If he wants to be liked, as most people do, he must reveal himself as a man guided by the common moral code. If he wishes to express aggression and hostility, he must rationalize his hostile acts in moral terms to make them acceptable to himself and others. If he seeks power *from* others *over* others, he must show that he can be trusted, that is, he must show that he is trustworthy. These are instrumental uses of moral justification; but a sense of rectitude may be a value in itself, for human maturation in most cases implies acquiring a conscience, superego, or internalized moral guardian with the power to give pain (twinges of conscience, guilt, remorse) when a person transgresses against a moral norm.[4] Further, since the central issue in all moral questions is "self versus others," and since men do have the capacity to empathize with others, to enter into their feelings and experience vicariously what another experiences, it follows that there is a satisfaction in giving the balance of rewards, here and there, to others. Not only that, but the self is not an entity bounded by the person's skin; rather it embraces much that he thinks is his, reflects on him, that with which he identifies. He will be morally judged, and will judge himself, in accordance with the narrowness of this definition of the self, in terms of the selfishness, self-centeredness, self-interest he feels and seems to feel. Thus the need to be moral, to feel moral, and to seem moral is rooted in the human situation.[5] But for some, for reasons and causes we shall explore, the need is exaggerated.

---

[3]Erich Fromm, *Escape from Freedom* (New York: Rinehart, 1941), pp. 283-84.

[4]Jean Piaget, *The Moral Judgment of the Child,* trans. Marjorie Gabain (New York: Free Press, Macmillan, 1965); H. Hartshorne and M. A. May, *Studies in the Nature of Character,* Vols. 1-3 (New York: Macmillan, 1928-30).

[5]*Ibid.;* also Robert J. Havighurst and Hilda Taba, *Adolescent Character and Personality,* Science ed. (New York: Wiley, 1963), and Lawrence Kohlberg, "Development of Moral Character and Moral Ideology," in Martin L. Hoffman and L. W. Hoffman, eds., *Child Development Research,* Vol. 1 (New York: Russell Sage, 1964), pp. 383-431.

MORAL DEVELOPMENT

In the first place, let us distinguish between moral conduct and moral judgment. Moral conduct, often tested by behavior under temptation, has to do with acting out, with overt behavior.[6] Moral judgment has to do with a person's verbal and ideational behavior, with what he thinks is moral or good, and especially his *reasons* for thinking so. The two are related but separate, for a person can conform to the customs of conventional morality for the "wrong reasons," such as fear of punishment or a general state of anxiety. Our interest, of course, is in moral judgment, moral thinking, for it is there that political ideologies and moral ideologies intersect.

What we are talking about here is the set of beliefs in "right and wrong" which a person uses to evaluate others and, to some extent, evaluate himself, and the reasons he gives for these evaluations. He learns these in a variety of ways. Perhaps, mnemonically, one could first mention the four "i's": imitation, indoctrination, identification, and internalization. The individual acquires values and moral judgment to some extent by *imitating* those he respects or fears, or who for some reason serve as models. Thus he may acquire a neighborhood delinquency code, or he may learn from his parents' acts that cheating the authorities is slyly honored. There is considerable evidence that these things happen.[7] In some sense, then, there is something to that cliché about "setting a good example." Furthermore, he may be taught or *indoctrinated* with some set of beliefs about good and bad. In general, it seems the indoctrination of moral principles by churches and Boy Scout leaders has no effect on overt behavior, but reasoned indoctrination in moral choice by a patient and loved teacher does make a difference.

Identification is the main ingredient in this process of moral learning; the theory is that the child learns moral codes through identifying with a warm and responsive adult person (the person, not merely a role occupant). In one version of this theory, at least, the process is considered to be one of *internalization*. In this version the child accepts the moral strictures of the parent, gives up some portion of his amoral impulse life in return for parental approval, makes the parent's views his own—that is, internalizes them —and from then on is subject to the guidance of this internalized parental view. The internalized parent is his conscience or his superego.

The instrument that this internalized parent (or other identified-with model) or superego employs to enforce its demands is guilt, a painful feeling

---

[6]In the following discussion I shall rely heavily upon Lawrence Kohlberg's review of his own and other research on moral development, cited in n. 5.

[7]See Kohlberg, "Development of Moral Character," pp. 412-15; Redl and Wineman, *Aggressive Child,* p. 202.

that one has done, or in anticipation might do, wrong. This has a bearing on judgment as well as conduct, because "bad thoughts" are equally subject to the painful flagellation of guilt. Yet the status of this long accepted doctrine is still somewhat uncertain, for it seems to be the case that the acceptance, for example, of some highly demanding concepts of honesty is not causally associated with feelings of guilt, and, in any event, there is very little evidence of the development of guilt in children under twelve—a feature of contemporary research findings that casts doubt on the Freudian concepts of guilt as primarily the internalization of a parental code. On the other hand, guilt does appear to be a force in children over twelve, and to continue to develop in older children. Thus, although personal identification does seem in most accounts to be part of the process of moral development, the concept of early "internalization" of parental views as the prime source of guilt, and guilt as the prime source of moral behavior, is more dubious.[8]

There is another route to a self-critical attitude toward a transgression of some personally accepted moral code. This route is through the *reasoning* process, whereby a person is instructed in the consequences to others, or to some accepted value, of a course of conduct. This, then, is our first hint that moral judgment is primarily a cognitive phenomenon. Moreover, it appears that the development of moral conduct, at least—and probably also moral judgment—is in some considerable degree the product of things that are sometimes lumped together under the term "ego strength": a prevision of the consequences of an act so that long-term as well as immediate goals may be taken into view, correct inferences about how others will respond and feel (empathy), control over aggressive fantasies, capacity to maintain stable, focused attention, and general intelligence. The importance of these qualities of intelligence, foresight, empathy, and control, together with what is perhaps the most important quality of all, high self-esteem, argues, as Kohlberg points out, that the essential ingredient in moral conduct—and, by extended inference, since the two are related, moral judgment —is not so much superego strength as ego strength. Further, when one adds to this the evidence that moral decisions, like other decisions, emerge from a capacity to synthesize experience, and that moral judgment is related to both experience (age) and intelligence, it seems even more likely that moral judgment is in large part a cognitive skill. It is a reasoning process based on experience; it develops as these skills develop. At least, this is true in substantial part.

We have used the term "moral development" without explaining it. Basically, as the concept has been worked out by Piaget and his successors,

---

[8]Kohlberg, "Development of Moral Character," p. 409-12.

and especially by Kohlberg, it is an abstraction from the kinds of moral reasoning children actually reveal as they grow older. But of course it is more than that. There is implicit in the concept of "moral development" an evaluation by the authors of the term, for they mean that the later stages are also higher stages of development, and morally better. Certain of Piaget's concepts of development turn out to be cross-culturally validated, so that it is possible to think of age and experience as the prime elements in the change, as contrasted to those changes that simply occur in a particular place at a certain time, or which accompany age and experience but are in fact due to specific cultural pressures pertinent only to some special group (as the shift from parent orientation to peer orientation is said to be). There are six such truly developmental features:

1. A shift from moral judgment based on the consequences of an act to moral judgment based on the intentions of the actor (accidentally breaking five teacups while trying to help Mother do the dishes is not so bad as breaking one while trying to steal cookies!); a movement towards *intentionality.*

2. A growing capacity to see that a moral problem looks different from the perspectives of the various people involved, and therefore that there may not be only one moral judgment possible; a growth in *relativism in judgment.*

3. Growing appreciation of the fact that the *morality of an act is independent of the sanctions applied;* realizing that there is such a thing as an immoral act that is not punished, and that punishment does not necessarily imply that the act must be morally condemned. Children reason, "If I am punished, I must have been bad"; moral development, among other things, implies the relaxation of this connection.

4. Development of *empathy,* the capacity to put oneself in the position of another and appreciate how he must feel. From this stems a growing use of standards of *reciprocity,* so that a person feels that sacrifice by one party to a situation may "in fairness" demand comparable sacrifice from another party, notably the self.

5. In an earlier chapter we contrasted two concepts of justice, an aggressive one and a conciliatory one. The aggressive one was this: "Justice as revenge and retribution; talonic law; sentence as punishment." And the conciliatory one was this: "Justice as future-oriented, reconditioning of a personality."[9] Piaget finds that children's concepts of punishment develop from the aggressive one toward the conciliatory one; increasingly they tend to think of *punishment as a device for restitution and reform.*

6. Finally, moral development is said to encompass a view of *mis-*

---

[9] See above, p. 146.

fortune as sometimes attributable to impersonal, "natural" causes. It need not be the product of malevolence. There may be no one to blame. Perhaps it was nobody's "fault."[10]

These six elements of moral development represent, as we have said, those elements of a larger scheme which have proved to be genuinely cross-cultural and which cut across class or status; they omit several others that have been specific to a given country. Taking off from these ideas and re-search findings, Kohlberg presents a portrait of moral development as a set of stages characterized by an invariant sequence: in order to go to a higher stage, one must go through the lower stages in a given order. One learns the judgmental process by stages without skipping; at any one time one is ready to learn the moral reasoning only of adjoining stages, and not the moral reasoning processes separated by more than one stage. These stages can be defined by characteristic stances on a variety of moral issues, such as "motivation for rule obedience or moral action," and "basis of moral worth of a human life." Here are the stages, with their characteristic pre-scriptions for rule obedience:

I. Premoral

Type 1. Punishment and obedience orientation. ("Obey rules to avoid punishment.")

Type 2. Naive instrumental hedonism. ("Conform to obtain re-wards, have favors returned, and so on.")

II. Morality of Conventional Role Conformity

Type 3. Good-boy morality of maintaining social relations, approval of others. ("Conform to avoid disapproval, dis-like by others.")

Type 4. Authority-maintaining morality. ("Conform to avoid censure by legitimate authorities and resultant guilt.")

III. Morality of Self-Accepted Moral Principles

Type 5. Morality of contract, of individual rights, and of de-mocratically accepted law. ("Conform to maintain the respect of the impartial spectator judging in terms of community welfare.")

Type 6. Morality of individual principles of conscience. ("Con-form to avoid self-condemnation.")[11]

---

[10]Kohlberg, "Development of Moral Character," pp. 396-98.
[11]*Ibid.,* p. 400.

An examination of these stages and levels reveals something not fully brought out in Kohlberg's discussion, but important to a discussion of moral choice: the location of conscience, or more precisely the answer to the question "Who shall decide what is right and what is wrong?" In the literature of political philosophy the answers to this question vary greatly, some of them pointing to religious authorities, others to legitimate state officials (especially if they are called "philosopher kings"), some to conventional wisdom (tradition and its qualified interpreters), some to public opinion (not a popular choice among philosophers), and many to the individuals of a society who should be endowed with capacities of their own for moral judgment. Simplifying these choices, one might say there are three locations for conscience: (1) the authoritative rules, orders, and conventions from legitimate sources, which are to be understood and followed; (2) the guidance of friends, associates, others whose opinions one values and whose cues and advice one follows; (3) the promptings of one's own conscience, the synthesis of one's own experience and values, the internalized codes of right and wrong, whose private voice one follows.[12]

Reviewing Kohlberg's stages, one does not see this aspect of moral choice neatly laid out, yet it is clear that Types 1 and 4 corrrespond closely to the first of these alternatives (following external rules), Type 3 corresponds to the second alternative (following group opinion), and Types 6 and probably 5, jointly labeled "morality of self-accepted moral principles," correspond to the third alternative (individual conscience). Since men who follow the first alternative, the morality of external rules, reveal many of the qualities of the less developed of Piaget's children, scoring low on the dimensions of moral development, and since those who make their own conscientious judgments without much reference to conventional morality score high on moral development, I shall attempt to interpret the results of the case studies that follow in terms of both Piaget's work and Kohlberg's levels, adapting them to this simpler threefold scheme. We thus begin with a set of categories reflecting, with some small variations, the concepts of moral development laid out above. Further, we can begin to see just what it is the man who needs to feel moral is trying to convey as he opts for each of these moral levels and principles. With ellipsis and a little bluntness, we can set forth these moral levels and statements of moral messages as follows:

---

[12]These three categories have something in common with David Riesman's typology: tradition-directed, other-directed, inner-directed. On the basis of the Piaget and Kohlberg studies, one might argue that Riesman had the sequence wrong: that individuals (and perhaps contemporary history) moves from guidance by tradition through guidance by peers to guidance by conscience. If that should be the case for societies as well as individuals, we would have a curious piece of information with which to confront those who mourn the loss of individuality in mass society. See Riesman's *The Lonely Crowd* (New Haven: Yale University Press, 1950).

I. Primitive morality

Morality of external rules

"I know the rules; I obey them; they license my actions and thoughts. Indeed, what seems to be selfish is really not that, but rather behavior guided by divine authority, traditional wisdom, authoritative moral law."

II. Intermediate morality

Morality of impression management

"As you can see, I am a self-sacrificing, loving, kind person. I give of myself; no one knows the many little things I do to make life better for other people. I am dedicated to the proposition: Others before self."

III. Mature morality

Self-generated principles

"I am principled, have high standards, live up to them, judge myself more harshly than others. I consult an inner code, not the opinions of others. I often fail, but I am working to make myself a better person."

When the moral levels are put this way, one begins to see the missing feature of moral analysis: self-awareness. By this I mean an awareness that moral choices are often self-serving, that the rules one follows allow considerable manipulation and do not confine one's actions closely, that moral appearance may be more important than moral consequence upon occasion, that one's high tone of principled choice can arise from insecurity and serve to silence doubts about one's sorry, sinful behavior. Without some insights of this kind, morality becomes moralism, and the moralist becomes something of a prig. If moral development serves as one axis of our scheme, self-awareness must serve as another.

The extent to which self-awareness and the level of morality or location of conscience are independent of each other is not clear (and we shall return to the question), but I think they are partially so. The most refined moral sensitivity may coexist with very little sense of where it comes from, how it benefits the self. On the other hand, I am doubtful that in Western societies true self-awareness could coexist with a willingness to abdicate one's own right to develop one's own moral principles and accept the rules handed down by authority. There is something incompatible there. As a consequence, I must regard the moral typology emerging from the intersection of moral development and self-awareness as merely a scheme for purposes of illustration and mapping, and nothing more. I use it here to locate the cases I shall analyze in a moment.

Level of Morality	Self-Awareness		
	Little	*Some*	*Much*
I. Primitive morality			
Morality of external rules	Buenello	Silver	
II. Intermediate morality			
Morality of impression management			
Self-conscious humanitarianism	Donaldson		
III. Mature morality			
Morality of self-generated principles			Lamb

MORALITY AND POLITICAL THOUGHT

The question we must somehow clarify is this: Does the need to feel moral, expressed in primitive or mature form and either self-aware or not, have a relationship to political thought? I shall argue that it does. First, I shall make a case for the belief that the primitive unaware moralism, relying on external rules, is congenial to a closed belief system, inequalitarian in emphasis, ethnocentric in form, static in design, conservative or reactionary in substance. Second, I believe that the morality of the unaware impresssion manager leads to a plastic, direction-free political belief system, but that the particular version we have here, the self-conscious humanitarian, is likely to be closed, equalitarian, and liberal to radical.[13]   Third, I shall argue that the politics of the aware, mature moralist tend to be open, incrementalist, moderate, humanitarian, and, I think, paralyzed. These political conse-

---

[13]I am speaking here of the way in which primitive moralism or self-conscious humanitarianism serve *political* arguments. One can well imagine how a conservative or reactionary might speak of his charity as a counterweight to his somewhat uncharitable view of economics and politics. Thus he might have developed a picture of himself as kind and devoted to his family, or servants, or employees; he might portray graphically his sacrifices for others, or even speak of the humanitarian feelings he has to trample down in order to maintain a "sound" view of economics and political realities. But these do not moralize his political sentiments; they moralize other aspects of the man who holds them. He is, he insists, humanitarian *in spite of them.*

quences follow from some of the "internal dynamics" of moral thought, that is, the force of logic or consistency (dissonance reduction), and the force of personality factors lying behind the choice of moral themes. These forces tend to operate to make one form of political thought more congenial than another. The thought of political philosophers is not immune to these forces, but the thought of the ordinary man or even the exceptional student is more clearly marked by these strains and tensions, especially when he has an exaggerated need to feel moral.

Four of the biographies reveal the need to feel moral in some substantial degree, two of them (Buenello and Silver) expressing this need through an unaware primitive moralism of rule correspondence, one (Donaldson) exhibiting that special version of morality of impression management which we have labeled self-conscious humanitarianism, and one (Lamb) reflecting the aware morality of self-generated principles.

MORALITY OF EXTERNAL RULES

The general message of all the moralizers is this: "I am not sinful." The point of the message, of course, is to relieve their own doubts on this score and to show others, too, how moral they are. As some men need to relieve doubts about their strength, their virility, their importance or status, so these men are concerned about their own moral condition. Men enter the ministry, write moral tracts, say grace for these reasons; here they write their intellectual autobiographies so as to reveal themselves in a moral light.

The special message of those whose primitive morality relies upon external rules is, as we have suggested above: "I understand and obey moral rules." It is our duty first to reveal the special themes of the two men who reveal this kind of moralism, Silver and Buenello, and then to analyze its sources and consequences.

Silver, a small, sober young man with a serious face and some reluctance to talk about his inner life, defines himself first as a "social conservative," by which he means a kind of Burkean philosopher with a respect for tradition, a reluctance to change the going order, and, in addition, a strong preference for capitalism, private property, and a belief in the inequality of man. In his discussion of conservatism he illuminates his ideas about the moral order: "As a working premise, one can observe that the essence of social conservatism is preservation of the ancient moral tradition of humanity." Beyond that, conservatism is (as we noted in an earlier chapter):

> . . . belief that a divine intent rules society, as well as conscience, forging an eternal chain of right and duty which links great

and obscure, living and dead. Political problems at bottom are religious and moral problems. . . . The only true equality is moral equality; all other attempts at leveling lead to despair, if enforced by positive legislation. . . . "Providence" is the proper instrument for change, and the test of a statesman is his cognizance of the real tendency of "Providential" social forces.

A little later in his discourse, which, however "sincere," is being written partly for the record—the very symptom we are examining—Silver lays out a program for the contemporary American conservative:

1. An affirmation of the moral nature of society. Family piety and public honor must be shored up.

2. The defense of property—property in the form of homes, pensions, corporate rights, and private enterprise.

3. Preservation of local liberties, traditional private rights, the division of power and national humility.

He says it and illustrates it: Politics is primarily a problem of morality.

Like Silver, Buenello leaves little doubt about his constraining moralism. "The code of ethics to which I adhere," he says, "requires stringent observance of its principles as the only means of attainment to a desired goal." He continues:

It is, perhaps, the uncompromising attitude of this "system" of ethics which I attempt to follow that prevents my identification with any political party. . . . No party being consistently motivated by the same principles as mine, I am unable to enroll.

As a youth, he says, "I determined to follow the code of social and political ethics in keeping with the teachings of . . . St. Thomas Aquinas and the Apostles." And "once a person has been educated in Christian ethics . . . there is no room for neutrality." Scattered throughout his discussion there are frequent references to the scriptures and to the writing of St. Thomas. Like Silver, he communicates the messages directly and indirectly: "I am not sinful, I know the rules"—perhaps even, if I may put words in his mouth, "Only I (among my friends) know what is good and right and pious, and only I follow the path of righteousness." Silver finds his Jewish friends to be apostates, his liberal friends unfamiliar with the right and moral ends of politics. Buenello believes there "exist in this country a great many people who possess a similar ideology, but who have not, as yet, formed a political party dedicated completely to Christian living and the principle: 'In hoc signo vinces!' (sign of the cross)." Others, then, he seems to say, are corrupt or morally ignorant; I am neither.

How shall we account for this moralism in these two men? Is there a connection between their moralism and their extreme conservatism? Has it further consequences for political thought?

Orthodox Religion.   There seems to be a connection between the primitive moralism of reliance on external rules and training and membership in an orthodox religion, though our material permits only some speculative guesses on what it might be. Silver explains his background in this way:

> My parents are religious and have made an extreme effort to raise me in a semi-orthodox Jewish background. I attended Hebrew school simultaneously with grammar school from the age of eight until I was confirmed at the age of thirteen. I have more or less accepted most of the doctrine of the Jewish faith, although I have had to block some of the ideas of evolution, geology, etc. from my cognizance. . . . It has been a great desire all of my life to attempt a crusade for the Jewish people and faith, because many of my Jewish friends either have become agnostics or have frowned upon many of the doctrines which I hold to be sacred.

Thus, although the external rules that he acknowledges as guiding his morality are those of secular tradition and convention, he sees them through semi-orthodox religious eyes.

Similarly, Buenello accepts religious sources for the rules he adopts and the morality he espouses:

> I grew up under strong religious influences. My father's family was devoutly religious. . . . Mother made certain that my sister and I attended church every Sunday and religious instruction for Holy Communion and Confirmation during the week. This period of my life had a profound influence upon the direction of my later life, for I was asked by a priest to become an altar boy and to serve at mass for him every day of the week.

As a result of these experiences Buenello "soon became interested in joining the priesthood," but his father's illness made him decide this was economically impossible (his mother needed support), and in any case he was uncertain of his "vocation" for that way of life. Nevertheless:

> I continued to read the works of leading men of the Church and came to adopt St. Thomas Aquinas as my guardian and guiding angel. I soon decided that the writings of this saint and of the Apostles were the best visible principles for guidance and aid to "walk in the image of Christ." Accordingly, I determined to follow a code of social and political ethics in keeping with the teachings of these men.

There are five Jews in the sample and three men from Catholic backgrounds. Of these eight, only Silver and Buenello are in any sense "orthodox" or think of themselves as defenders of a faith. The other six are apostates, or, at the very least, humanistically tolerant of the variety of religious views at Adams. Indeed, most mention religious beliefs as something they have set aside—a feature of their past. Religion is significant to only a few of the Protestants. One of them, Lamb, a man with an active conscience, as we shall see, finds the significance in his decision *not* to go to church, as his parents do, because he does not believe in God. There are no other moralizers among them, hence they do not talk much about the sources of their moral guidance. Religious training does not necessarily make a man need to feel moral; orthodox religions are not necessarily associated with the primitive morality of external rules; but in our small sample only those with orthodox religious training, and only those for whom this remains salient as adults, adopt this more primitive form of morality.

Conservatism.   There were glimpses of Silver's and Buenello's conservative views in what we have quoted. Both resist change, Silver stating his belief "that change and reform are not identical. Society must alter, for slow change is the means of its conservation; but 'Providence' is the proper instrument for change." Buenello scatters his views:

> I support the American status quo in that I am against innovations with unsound foundations. . . . I would resist social change if I thought those who clamored for it thought of equality and fair play with regard only to their own interests. . . . If I had to choose between our two major parties I would choose the more conservative one. . . .

Both favor private enterprise, both support the profit motive, both defend private property. Silver says, "Separate property from private possession and liberty is erased." Buenello reports, "I am in favor of our capitalist society, which rewards initiative." Both oppose unions, both have ethnocentric elements in their philosophies, neither is greatly concerned about underdogs. But unlike Trumbull, Novak, and Rogers—three reactionaries with aggressive ideologies—neither Silver nor Buenello favors restrictions on civil liberties, and indeed both speak positively of "diversity."

Lack of Self-Awareness.   In all of this, one finds only traces of that kind of introspection which would alert these two men to the way their political views served their own careers, their own ambitions for wealth and status. These politicoeconomic views are, almost without exception, set forth as general statements about the public interest and the laws of nature and society. Moreover, there is little insight into the way in which the primitive morality of external rules shored up the crumbling ledges of a moral self-image and rationalized an economic view of things that would be hard to defend from other moral points of view. For these reasons, it is fair, I think, to characterize these men as unaware.

On the basis of this evidence, then, we may characterize these men and their belief systems as (a) unaware, (b) primitive moralists relying on external rules, (c) religiously orthodox, and (d) politically and economically conservative. Can we find some relationships among these elements?

Religion, Morality, Politics.   There are two ways we may show the relationship between different features of a belief system: (a) by revealing a pattern of congruence and consonance, constrained by the power of logic; (b) by revealing a pattern of functions such that holding one set of ideas is "functional" for another, that is, serves common interests or provides premises or supports a rationale for the second set. Let us try these different ways, first examining briefly the parallel elements of orthodox religion, primitive morality, and conservatism (as shown in Table A), then turning to the functions of a primitive morality for a conservative.

TABLE A

Dogmatic Orthodox Religion	*Primitive Unaware Morality of External Rules*	*Political-Economic Conservatism*
A way of thinking by chapter and verse and holy text.	Moral judgment based on correspondence of act to law or moral rule.	Opportunity for the elite instead of protection and "a leg up" for the underprivileged.
Reference to external authority instead of reliance on the synthesis of experience and the judgment of conscience.	Reluctance to examine own motives; lack of reflection on own experience; low self-awareness.	Low personal responsibility for social ills.
Belief that matters have been settled beforehand; closure against novelty, discouragement of experimentation.	Low obligation to alter status, power, wealth arrangements, however "unmerited." Thus, although there may be independence between morality of a situation and rewards and punishments, one need not do anything about it.	A sense of exclusiveness; defense of privilege.
Opportunity to earn moral credits either by humane and sacrificial behavior *or* by "devotion," ritual, knowledge.	Absolute moral codes, unmodified by circumstances.	American primacy, dominance.

TABLE A (continued)

Dogmatic Orthodox Religion	Primitive Unaware Morality of External Rules	Political-Economic Conservatism
Attention to the past as the source of tradition, scripture, authority.	Projective tendencies to see others as corrupt, selfish.	Fear of "big" government; reliance on the justice of the market.
Absolute moral truth; denial of the possibility of plural truths, relativism in judgment of faith.	Low empathy; reciprocity for gain, not justice.	Continuity, stability, tradition preferred to reform, change.
Divine or Providential sanctions always merited; rewards always earned; inscrutable justice.	Punishment as retribution, not restitution.	Identification with symbols of business, capitalism, property, management.

Could it be said that in some respects there is a common underlying idea or theme, with only the substitution of referents or terms in the domains of religion, morality, and politics? If so, something like this might serve as a kind of simplified operational code to cover the three domains:

Authority for an act comes from outside the self.[14]
Men (especially others) are selfish; they must be restrained.

These restraints must allow me to get mine.

Because men are selfish:
Punishment deters through fear, and should not attempt to change men's nature—an impossibility.

Injustice is inevitable. If someone else were in charge, injustice would continue; only the beneficiaries would be different.

External moral authorities must be strong, and their codes inviolable.

An economic system harnessing selfishness is the only workable system.

Change and reform will only serve to advance the interests of the challenging parties, serving *their* selfish interests.

[14]The complexity of reliance on self (self-actualization) and reliance on outside authority deserves further attention. Compare, for example, the discussion of reliance on the approval of others in Chap. 7 and of reliance on the authority of scholarship and "facts" in Chap. 15.

Loyalty, responsibility, identification are primarily to self, family, and people like the self in whatever properties one values. Beyond that, justice should be left to God, Fate, the Market, the Jungle.

If something like this "code" is at work among Silver, Buenello, and others who share their combined need to feel moral and their unaware primitive morality of external rules, there is at work an underlying logic that links these moral themes to their retention of orthodox dogmatic religion and to conservatism. Similarly, their early training in dogmatic orthodox religion prepares the way for primitive morality and for conservatism by training them in the substance of the operational code. I speak of a recursive system of ideas here, an intertwining of cause and effect, a pattern with feedback and mutual and reciprocal influence. Now, however, let us see if primitive morality, fed by a need to feel moral, is functional to a conservative view of life, serves to rationalize it in moral terms.

THE FUNCTIONS OF PRIMITIVE MORALISM
FOR CONSERVATIVES

Let us recapitulate the argument. Society provides incentives for leaders to moralize their statements and for followers to moralize their conventional (and, *a fortiori,* their unconventional) acts and beliefs. Beyond this, individuals require moral evaluations and codes to carry on their daily acts of living—but for some individuals these requirements are more than normally salient and they must reassure themselves that they are indeed moral. Such individuals employ moral appeals to justify their political and economic beliefs. They have an option among moralizing beliefs: they may rely on the authority of external rules; they may select some theme appropriate for impressing a special audience; they may attempt to generate their own codes out of the "smithy of their souls," synthesizing their own experience. Buenello and Silver have opted for the morality of external rules.

It seems to me that the morality of external rules serves a special function in the conservative's political thought, a function not easily (logically, compatibly) served by other kinds of moral argument. Liberalism, with its equalitarian theme, its tolerance of challenging views, its openness to conflict, with all the irritations and personal upset these things may imply, suggests some sacrifice by the man who is already favored by the going order. He seems, at least, to be giving up something, some bit of status or power or wealth or privilege or harmonious condition of life. Conservatism, espoused by the prosperous, has no such sacrificial implications. If a conservative refers just to the political-economic elements of his belief system, he cannot argue that he is giving something up; that is, in the central moral dilemma of self against others, he comes down on the side of the self. The stain of selfishness is hard to erase.[15]

For this reason, moralism—the infusion of social thought with references to right and wrong—may be tempting to the conservative as he works out his ideological problems, and especially he may feel the need for an extrinsic morality offering moral credits in some way not requiring references to sacrifice, but instead for following moral rules. Silver does this by a shift from conscience to divine intent, just as the theory suggests he would: "To me there are . . . [these] canons of conservative thought: 1) belief that a divine intent rules society as well as conscience, forging an eternal chain of right and duty which links great and obscure, living and dead. Political problems, at bottom, are religious and moral problems." As it turns out, these religious and moral problems favor the going order, which allows people like Silver to enrich themselves without worrying too much about those who lack their opportunities or skills.

Buenello converts conscience to a following of external rules in a comparable fashion. After speaking of his "determination to follow a code of social and political ethics in keeping with the teachings" of the saints, he says, "I continue to attempt to follow the dictum, The eternal law is the supreme exemplar to which we must always conform. . . . In this sense I do not find the term 'conform' passive or repulsive." But he is careful to remember that part of that "eternal law" is "Render therefore to Caesar the things that are Caesar's, and to God the things that are God's," and that he by no means implies "that I have therefore chosen a life devoid of conflict or contact with things material and worldly." In short, he has decided to conform to an eternal law that licenses his search for power and wealth.

Compared to Silver, Buenello seems a little more sensitive to (but not consciously aware of) the dangerously self-serving character of conservative thought for someone in his position. As it is to all moralists, the idea of self-interest is alarming to him. One line of defensive argument on this point is to attribute selfishness to the opposition, a task often accomplished obliquely in the phrase "politically inspired legislation." Buenello does it (as we have seen) this way: "I would resist social change if I thought that those who clamored for it thought of equality and fair play with regard

---

[15]Some of these "problems" and solutions are taken up in Sutton and others, *American Business Creed*. The point of these authors' interpretation of the growth and function of an ideology is compatible with our own: an ideology rationalizes difficult choices, reduces dissonance, and relieves strain. The strains and conflicts they analyze are role strains; with our case material, we have an opportunity to analyze individual needs and strains.

only to their own interests . . . [and] if I believed that such clamoring was politically motivated." Similarly, it is the self-interestedness of union leaders that disturbs him (not the social consequences of their acts): "Organized labor of today is really a disorganized, factional body of workers manipulated by self-concerned individuals who take every advantage of their position and the powerlessness and even ignorance of their 'fellow members.'" The opposition thus is self-interested; that is, selfish; that is, immoral.

What of the managerial class and the profit motive? It is a problem. St. Thomas had some rather critical things to say about "profit seeking" and this disturbs Buenello, but he finds St. Thomas' approval of "production and exchange for use" a possible vehicle for conveying the moral intention of what it is he would like to do. Furthermore,

> I support the American status quo in that I am against innovations with unsound foundations. . . . On the domestic front I am in favor of our capitalist society, which rewards initiative. . . . Initiative is the heart and reward the blood of the capitalist system, and the privation of either leads to the death of the system. [Buenello was against "socialized medicine" because it destroyed doctors' initiative.]

The selfishness of others, the corruption of politics, the necessity of profit for property owners and of large enough rewards to promote efficiency among managers—both necessary to avoid "the death of the system"—provided an argument sufficient to give moral justification to Buenello's conservatism. There are no sacrifices here; Buenello yields little to underdogs, the poor, the working classes, the medically indigent. There is little in his social policies with which to clothe a naked moral sense. The morality must come from outside. And for him there is available an ancient moral orthodoxy whose rules and codes, while occasionally inconvenient, are really quite well fitted to the purpose he has in mind.

Rationalizing "Unearned Status." There are, it is widely said, two paths to status and privilege: ascription and achievement. Some men inherit wealth and status or seek these through cooptation, marriage, or ingratiation; others "earn" status and wealth through manufacturing, trading, inventing, leading—providing something that society admires and pays for. Silver, from a prosperous family, in spite of his good grades says he has no "dynamic qualities," and seems oriented toward the first of these, a pseudo-ascriptive position in society. Buenello, from a poor family, seeks achievement.

The problem of rationalizing the privileged position of the pseudo-ascriptive conservative is partially solved through several features of the primitive moralism of external rules. The low empathy helps, of course, as does the reliance on an absolute (and therefore uncriticized) set of values and moral truths emphasizing the wisdom of the going scheme. Furthermore, the ascriptive moralist, in emphasizing the wisdom of tradition, need not accept the concept of reciprocity, the idea that privilege is justified by effort or sacrifice or contribution to society. On the other hand, he will probably find congenial the view that somehow, through mysterious forces, it is fair for those who are poor and disadvantaged and lacking in the respect of others to suffer these burdens, since there is a Providential guidance in these matters which is responsible and, in its own way, "just." Thus he can identify the sanctions of Providence or Nature with morality. He can employ the naturalistic fallacy with impunity and convert the "is" to the "ought." "Man must put his faith in tradition," says Silver, and "Providence is the proper instrument of change." In any event, he could say, "Whatever happens, I am blameless."

Rationalizing Status Earned Through Social Aggression.   The second kind of privilege, that which seems to society to be somehow "earned" or achieved, may come to a man in a number of ways, some of which might, by an unfriendly critic, seem to be cases of piracy, the work of a robber baron, the rape of national resources, the employment of unfair competition. The businessman is often sensitive to these charges, whether or not there is any merit to them, and is very likely to help himself to certain rules and arguments justifying these acts. Buenello, not yet a businessman, though oriented in that direction, has some personal characteristics that would encourage him to take on an aggressive social role in business or any other field:

> I am aware of the fact that I am in many respects an authoritarian personality. . . . As the leader (and the biggest boy) [of the neighborhood gang] I was the sole disciplinarian in the group and discipline involved physical coercion. . . . My relationship to discipline and hierarchy (in which I have always been near the top), on both religious and temporal levels, has been deeply ingrained in me and cannot be ignored with regard to my motives, decisions, and actions.

He needs a morality that will justify these aggressive characteristics, and he finds it in the principles of primitive moralism. He need not take the part of the weak, for he is not required to empathize with them. Punishment and deprivations, which he believes he will administer to others, rather than vice versa, can be properly used to impose *his* will. He need not worry about alternative moral codes, for he possesses the final word, divinely authorized.

In any event, it is the others who are corrupt, selfish, rationalizing—not he. And finally, what he takes from society is the proper reward for his initiative and leadership; without such rewards, he says, the social order dissolves.

The Resolution of Conflict. Let us return to something said earlier about the need to couch in moral terms the resolution of internal conflict. A person seeks to gratify some wish at the expense of another person but feels uncomfortable about it: he argues that he had a "right" to his selfish act. It was a moral act. Having convinced himself, on the surface of things, anyway, he feels better about it. The moral argument reduces shame, guilt, anxiety, regret, dissonance. In the same way, the resolution of a conflict between two principles, both "valid" for the individual (as where an emphasis upon achievement conflicts with an emphasis upon equality), may be reinforced, "prettied up," rationalized by appeal to some moral argument: the achievement theme is "consonant with men's right to express themselves," or, conversely, equality is the higher principle because "in God's eyes we are all equal." Moral argument may be employed, then, to resolve conflict, but it is more likely to be used to reduce dissonance regarding a decision made on other grounds, and to rationalize it for easier moral consumption.

Both Silver and Buenello reveal some rather painful conflicts, some conscious, others remaining unconscious, though, I think, operative in their moralizing strategy. Silver says he has "more or less accepted the doctrines of the Jewish faith." More than that, as we have seen, "It has been my great desire all my life to attempt to crusade for the Jewish people and faith." On the other hand, he seeks assimilation in a predominantly Gentile group, wants to avoid "the wrong crowd," and avoids in thought, deed, and dress any suggestion that he is "different."

He is greatly conflicted regarding his attitude toward Negroes. "My only prejudice," he says, "and I am quite ashamed that I have such a prejudice, since I belong to a minority group, is one which deals with the Negro problem. I am still an advocate of the old 'separate but equal' doctrine." Struggling against this prejudice, he joined the National Association for the Advancement of Colored People, but remained unconvinced and prejudiced. He cannot help himself and remains embarrassed.

He finds the question of individualism versus conformity difficult.

> At college the big problem for me would be conformity. Coming as I did, from an unknown school in the Midwest, being Jewish, and not having any real dynamic qualities, I was faced with the problem of friendships. . . . I quickly decided that I must fit the proper typology [at Adams.] . . . . Soon I realized that in

order to show some comparable achievements [to those of the big men], I would have to brush aside my feelings of inferiority with a secondary desire to be better than the next guy as far as schoolwork was concerned.

How can he show his distinctiveness and special worth and at the same time succeed by fitting "the proper typology"? How can he be like everybody else (in the "right social circles") and still be different?

These three conflicts over his Jewishness, his Negro prejudice, and his individualism have a bearing, I believe, on his moralized view of social and political life. But before analyzing them, let us examine Buenello's conflicts, a rather different lot.

As we have pointed out, Buenello is conflicted over the degree to which it is appropriate for him to engage in politics. On the one hand, it interests him. He says, "It can be seen that I seek a life of political participation"; he loves power and expects to have it. On the other hand, he thinks current politics is corrupt, the motives of politicians are "unworthy"; he has no party identification, says he is awaiting the emergence of a "party dedicated completely to Christian living"—an event unlikely enough to excuse him from politics for a while.

He is conflicted over his own hostilities (as most people are) and especially, like Silver, his hostile feelings about other ethnic groups—in his case, other nationalities. "I have, to my knowledge, a lack of any deep and active prejudices," he claims, and seems to bear this out by his choice of roommates, a French Catholic and a Jew. On the other hand, in reviewing his ideas on foreign policy, he mentions, among other evidences of ethnocentrism:

> The French, particularly, seem to maintain a consistency of political ineptitude . . . and the Syrians, Israelites, and Egyptians appear to be playing a little game of their own in which each, believing that the rest of the world "owes him a living," attempts to play the East against the West in order that each may further its own interests.

The Finns, he believes, "might be better off under the control of some strong directing power." He claims a tolerance he does not have.

And on the profit motive and self-interest generally, as we have seen, Buenello believes, quoting Aquinas, that any "form of exchange [which] is carried on for the sake of profit . . . is rightly condemned," but, on the other hand, "initiative is the heart and reward the blood of the capitalist system, and the privation of either leads to the death of the system"—a disaster.

The situation is, I think, clear in each case: Silver must, in the interest of acceptance, forsake his commitment to Judaism; in the interest of high status, indulge his anti-Negro prejudice; in the advancement of social acceptance, lose his individualism or exercise it almost secretly in his struggle for academic excellence. Buenello, unwilling to serve as a mere citizen beginner in politics (waiting to be called as a "leader," perhaps), fails to take up his civic duties; unable to face his ethnocentrism, he assumes the facade of tolerance, attacking covertly the national or group symbols of his roommates and lashing out at foreign nations; and while giving lip service to service motives in production and exchange, he proposes a life of profit-seeking for himself and others.

In most cases, the choice having been made in the service of some rather special selfish need, a moral argument is called forth to reduce dissonance and rationalize the choice. Thus Silver argues, with respect to Negroes but not to Jews, "I believe that men segregated themselves in society according to race in obedience to a basic natural law which decrees that like shall seek like." With respect to his attempt to fit the Adams traditions and "typology," he argues the case for tradition and custom as the sources of wisdom in any society. Buenello makes of his civic withdrawal a virtue, for it reflects his unwillingness to soil himself in the dirty business of current politics; he defends his ethnocentric belligerency in foreign policy ("I do not support the United States' tradition of waiting until the first physical blow has been struck before retaliating against an enemy") with assumptions of the moral rightness of the American position. And profit-seeking, he says, is necessary if the elite are to be fairly rewarded for their extraordinary contributions to society. Throughout, moral themes are employed to make "right" what seems like a selfish choice in a dilemma of principle. And because they serve the self, and are used to embellish prejudice and exclusiveness, and to indulge hostilities rather than contain them, they are borrowed, not from the arsenal of higher morality, but from the primitive morality of the child who has not yet learned how to be self-critical.

The Control of Impulse.   Finally, the control of forbidden impulses may be mentioned. It is relevant to moral thought, for morality is, in large part, society's way of controlling men's unsocialized impulse life. The problem emerges here because of the way in which Buenello's aggressiveness and Silver's concepts of the dirtiness of human nature call forth moral constraints and rationalizations.

Buenello is a fighter; in college he was a wrestler. Though he seeks to "walk in the image of Christ," he says, "I still find it difficult to turn the other cheek in any type of conflict." But, after citing this trouble, he immediately says, as we noted earlier, "Render therefore to Caesar the things that are Caesar's, and to God the things that are God's," as though this quotation licenses his unmeek posture toward life; and later he develops, as we have seen, an economic morality that requires some men to seek and earn large rewards. His morality both constrains and licenses his aggressive impulses.

Silver argues the case for tradition as a "check upon man's anarchic impulses." What these are is unclear, but something, he says, has given him a "hatred of filth." On sex, he has the classic "good girl on a pedestal, bad girl for pleasure" syndrome:

> I feel that an attempt to ruin the virtue of a girl because of lust is a shameful and inexcusable act. Yet I recognize that there are many girls who fit into the prostitute pattern, and I have no qualms about spoiling their virtue or furthering their degeneration.

For both men the impulse world is dangerous, with its hostilities, lust, filth. On the other hand, tradition, order, control—these things are not merely attractive to them, but the very conditions of their well-being, perhaps of their self-control. They must be made a part of the divine or Providential scheme of things, enforced by moral codes. Thus they are moralized. A conservative, changeless, traditional society, with clear limits to the freedoms it permits, is a better instrument for that purpose than an open, indulgent, liberal one. Thus these men are conservatives. And who is to say they are not right? Men who are afraid of themselves may indeed be better off in conservative, moralized societies.

11

Toward a More Mature Morality in Politics

IMPRESSION-MANAGEMENT MORALITY

The need to convey the message "I am not sinful" may, as we have seen, find its expression in an elaboration of the way one appreciates and follows ethical rules sanctioned by tradition and religion, but there are other modes of expression. Piaget found that as children mature they tend to shift their frame of reference from adult-given rules, traditional norms, to the ethical opinions of peers; that is, the source of authoritative interpretation of moral rules changes in this "democratic" direction. Although there seems to be some question regarding the universality of this trend,[1] there is considerable evidence that increasing peer orientation takes place in the United States,[2] and it does seem to be an inevitable consequence of growing up. I would not think that this increasing peer orientation, except as it is necessarily associated with increased age and experience, should be appropriately interpreted as *moral* growth; but its attitudinal concomitants may be so interpreted. Along with this shift in reference, there is an increased attention to the motives or intentions of the moral actors, an ap-

---

[1]Lawrence Kohlberg argues, partly on the basis of research among Israeli children reared in a kibbutz, that Piaget's findings regarding the shift "from an authoritarian to a democratic ethic" are culture-bound. Consequently, we may prudently confine the relevance of the tendency toward increasing peer orientation to cultures where children are reared in nuclear families—but this is a broad arena, and notably includes the United States. See Kohlberg's "The Development of Moral Character and Moral Ideology," in Martin L. Hoffman and L. W. Hoffman, eds., *Review of Child Development Research,* Vol. 1 (New York: Russell Sage, 1964), p. 399.

[2]Robert E. Lane and David O. Sears, *Public Opinion* (Englewood Cliffs, N.J.: Prentice-Hall, 1964), Chap. 3.

preciation of the plurality of judgments possible in a given situation, an increase in reciprocity and empathy, a new emphasis upon punishment as educational, and some sense of "injustice," that is, unmerited punishment and uncorrected wrongdoing.

The general characteristic, then, of the intermediate morality we wish to explore is the calculation of what is moral or immoral according to its anticipated effect on some particular audience of friends and associates. I have used Goffman's term "impression management"[3] because the criterion for framing a judgment is the impression it creates on others, not the correspondence of an act with a set of predetermined rules or with some aspect of a developed conscience. All morality is in some measure "other-directed," of course, even that of the saint; but what we have to examine here is a more exclusive reliance on the opinions of others. Under these circumstances we would expect the ideological direction congenial to an impression-managing morality to be whatever wins moral credits with a particular audience. In itself, it is direction-free.

MIDDLE-CLASS IMPRESSION-MANAGING HUMANITARIANISM

We have in mind a special variation of this impression-management morality, the morality of self-conscious, but not self-aware, middle-class humanitarianism. The theme that the impression-managing humanitarian seeks to convey is one of service to others, of unselfishness, of dedication to an ethical cause. Such expressions are gratifying to the person in doubt about his moral status, for they help him to quell those doubts that, *sotto voce* but insistently, query him about his ambition, his self-indulgence, his pride, his appetites. For reasons that may be obscure to the individual himself, and which are not revealed in depth in our biographies, he cannot accept these aspects of self-interest as part of that very thing he claims to prize, humanity itself. He cannot accept the idea that among those he serves, his own self, too, has rightful claims. These are denied, not because they are necessarily more overweening or exaggerated than others', but because even in a modest form they are more frightening. This self-conscious humanitarianism, then, like primitive moralism, is likely to close the windows on the self, rendering the unconscious opaque. But, of course, the ambition, the interest in the self, does not then disappear because it

---

[3]Erving Goffman, *The Presentation of the Self in Everyday Life* (Garden City, N.Y.: Doubleday Anchor, 1959), pp. 208-37.

remains unexamined; hence it must be "interpreted" in moral terms, and, as Freud explained, the unacted-out private wish or thought must be publicly "undone" in some sacrificial act or expression or pose.[4]

I have argued that the primitive moralist is likely to be a conservative, and the middle-class conservative is likely to find primitive moralism congenial to his moralizing needs.[5] In the same way and for the same reasons, the moralizing liberal, or more likely the moralizing radical, is likely to find self-conscious humanitarianism congenial to his needs. After all, for the middle-class person, the themes of reform are those of elevating the lowly to those statuses and privileges and economic advantages that he, the reformer, now enjoys. To do this is to give up something or at least to share privilege, and so to dilute it. Thus it is not surprising to find that the most radical equalitarian in the Adams group, and the one man who wishes to make a career of his radicalism (he wants to be a labor organizer), is the one who most clearly represents this theme of self-conscious humanitarianism.

The politics of impression-managing humanitarianism reflects its genesis in an insistent need to reassure the self it is not selfish, for it argues discreetly: "I am not ambitious for myself, only for others. I love mankind more than most. I sacrifice myself for others. None are too lowly to merit my attention." Thus it focuses on political and social obligation—what one owes to the community. It develops ideas of responsibilities, rather than rights. It is equalitarian in one sense—the poor and miserable must be helped—but I think there is often a reticence about the distribution of *power* to these same poor and miserable, for its essence is that "People like me should be good to the unfortunate and disinherited." If they were as powerful as the impression-managing humanitarian, his moral platform would dissolve. It contains many Christian themes (ones that Buenello hardly acknowledges), and emphasizes goodwill, cooperation, faith in the goodness of mankind (reflecting one's own trusting nature). Proudhon, not Marx; T. H. Green, not Mill; Russell, not Laski, are its spokesmen.

What is surprising in the sample of biographies spread out before me in this analysis is the paucity of cases of this kind. About a quarter of the men have some kind of socialist or strongly equalitarian orientations— positions, as I said, congenial to this moralizing humanitarian argument. Moreover, we are dealing with men in a culture that is often given to moral argument, as Max Lerner has pointed out. "In few civilizations," he says, "is there so constant a sense of moral crisis . . . [and] much of this anxiety

---

[4]Sigmund Freud, *The Problem of Anxiety* (New York: Norton, 1936).
[5]See Chap. 10, n. 13.

focuses on the young." [6] These days only the Germans are so concerned about the contemporary state of moral behavior of their fellow country-men. [7] It seems, however, that among the needs of the "chosen" young men of the 1950's and early 1960's, so far as our sample is representative, the need to present the self as "humanitarian" was not very strong. Perhaps, indeed, it is the obverse that one should be wary of, the need to present the self as, if not "bad," at least a little alienated, or as able to see the worst in oneself and to tell all, or, in the end, as suffering from a sickness of soul, a malaise that can only be suggested. "Humanitarianism" is so square.

Donaldson. In contrast with the others, Donaldson, the athletic son of a natural scientist, the young man who so cleverly disguised his aggressive feelings in the language of cooperation, writes about himself with many little self-serving, self-congratulating references:

> My personal life has always existed outside the bounds of want, and consequently I have never felt the desire or need for security. Therefore it is only through observations and imagination that I am able to understand the necessity for programs such as these [proposed humanitarian reforms]. I realize that all men are not equal in ability or determination, and yet it is a degrading thing to force these [impoverished] people to lead a beggarly existence. . . . In analyzing my feeling about civil rights and prejudice, I cannot help but find that I feel a true compassion for minority groups or individuals. I do not believe it is pity I bestow upon people so situated, but a mutual understanding that they are alone in an alien culture. . . . I can recall numerous instances at parties where I will seek out the individuals who are unknown or of foreign descent to make them feel welcome. . . . My feelings toward the individual are so oriented that I bear no animosity or ill will to start and I only develop these if I feel that I have been greatly wronged or in some way mistreated. . . . By working toward my political views, I have helped to spread the benefits of comfort and lessen the agony of pain throughout the world.

The main theme, of course, is the "Dr. Jekyl" presentation of the self, all good, somehow enlightened, and, without overdoing it, bearing a certain noble stamp; better, in any event, than others. We have seen how Donaldson made a case for himself as a nonaggressive prophet of "co-operation." In a sense, however, the most enlightening features of this

---

6Max Lerner, *America as a Civilization* (New York: Simon & Schuster, 1957), pp. 666-67.

7Asked the question "On the whole would you say that you are satisfied or dissatisfied with the honesty and standards of behavior of people in this country today?" the following percentages of samples in each country said "dissatisfied": Norway, 20 percent; France, 39 percent; Britain, 47 percent; West Germany, 51 percent; U.S.A., 58 percent (Gallup International, interviews July and August, 1963).

tale of kindly goodness by a self-conscious humanitarian are the omissions. There is nothing about the way in which the high ideals are self-serving, little on the play of ignoble impulses in these noble causes; one is not taken into a confidence that includes the hostilities, the needs to be liked, the desire for fame or attention, which, perhaps adventitiously but nevertheless truly, shape a political philosophy. Authoritarians are not the only ones who are reluctant to look into their own motives for fear of what they will find. The self-conscious humanitarian does this, too, and with perhaps a greater obfuscating skill. By contrast with Donaldson, the two men who think of themselves as authoritarians, and to some extent are, reveal much more about themselves than he does. Nor is this reluctance merely omission; to some extent it is also denial, for when one is exposed to the literature on the way in which private emotions find their ways into politics, and asked to write an answer to the question "Of what use to *me* is my liberalism (conservatism)?" the matter is hard to overlook. In the entire biography Donaldson makes only two references to such personality-generated social views. The first touches on the possibility of a desire to be accepted:

> On the conscious level I do not consider it a duty or a chore, but rather an enlightenment, to meet . . . [an outcast] person and attempt to draw him into a circle of my interests or project myself into a similar circle of his interests. But in the subconscious, perhaps, I am motivated by a desire to be accepted, appreciated, understood. If this is true it is not, however, accompanied by an equal feeling of rejection from my own more common areas of influence.

However much credit these sentiments reflect on Donaldson, he loses much by his patronizing account of his excursion outside his "more common areas of influence." Nor does his reference to the possibility that he may be, in some fashion, "narcissistic" do much to make one think that here is a man in communication with his deepest self:

> Politics serves a particular function for me. By working to implement my views and thoughts, I feel that I can make the world somewhat less painful. Perhaps my desires are narcissistic and motivated simply by identifying the world with myself. If this is true, however, [here, as in the above paragraph, he admits such a thought only conditionally, in order to deny its importance], I am certain it is not the whole truth. If the world is deprived of beneficial activity [such activity as he has engaged in], it simply drags along on a dog-eat-dog basis.

In short, he would have us believe that he is a liberal only because he is moved by the suffering of others and by his insight into the need for cooperation and unity among men. Under these circumstances, he can respond only with liberal sympathy and "beneficial activity."

We have suggested that among those seeking to earn moral credits, it is the middle-class liberals or the radicals who will justify their political views with self-conscious humanitarianism. For the working-class person, support for the welfare state or the socialist society is, or may be, a kind of self-interest, indeed a kind of ethnocentrism. The middle-class conservative is blocked by the logic of his argument from a thoroughgoing equalitarianism, especially in economic matters. In political and economic thought only the middle-class person, with something to lose by greater equality, is likely to find this impression-managing humanitarianism congenial.[8]

MATURE MORAL JUDGMENT AND POLITICAL IDEOLOGY

The man with mature moral judgment is endowed with a better machine for moral decision-making than the morally less mature. The elements of that machine are, in general, those things that make for good decision-making in any field: high intelligence, a capacity to draw inferences from experience, a capacity for stable, focused attention, control and acceptance of impulses (something Silver and Buenello found difficult, in certain respects), ability to predict how other people will react to the relevant features of a new situation, and a self-esteem high enough so that one's honor or reputation is valuable but not irreproachable. These things come with growth and age, but they come more quickly to those who have an education and some social status in their own communities. They are, in large part, cognitive; they have much in common with ego strength.

But now, cutting across this analysis, come two other concepts: (1) the need to feel moral, the moralizing syndrome, and (2) self-awareness, the capacity to see in one's own moral drives elements of self-interest, even of selfishness, and the strength necessary to analyze, balance, and interpret these self-interested motives. I suspect that the first of these, the need to tell the world "I am not sinful," is that flaw in the ego strength that is

---

[8]When one tries to place Donaldson along the Kohlberg-Piaget dimensions, one runs into difficulties. It is true that he has a much better empathic sense than Silver and Buenello, a clearer grasp of reciprocity, a more vivid concept of injustice, a more advanced view of punishment. But he is absolutistic in his political-economic ideology, and he is clearly very much concerned with impressions as contrasted to results. I think these difficulties reveal a weakness in the Kohlberg-Piaget developmental analysis: they do not adequately provide for the *functions* of a moral idea, either in a larger ideological scheme or in a total personality. That is, they do not analyze how a moral theme supports and reinforces some pattern of ideas, reducing dissonance, or how it may fulfill some personality need, reassuring a man that he is, after all, not weak, not stupid, not sinful.

necessary to reveal to us the operation of the moral judgment "machine," and not at all a feature of mature morality. Probably many of the twenty-four men in the group had mature moral judgment, but I do not know, because they did not sufficiently reveal their moral thinking in their essays. This is a defect in our method, and of any method asking subjects to define for themselves the matters close to their hearts.

The second relevant concept, the self-awareness of a moral thinker, is different. Everyone was asked to search his deepest motives; some could do it, others could not. In the single case we shall examine, mature moral judgment and self-awareness go together, but (as we noted earlier) I suspect that this association is partly accidental. Some of the most original, developed, and empathic consciences in the world are likely to coexist with relatively little self-awareness. I would guess, for example, that moral philosophers throughout the world are unlikely, as a group, to be more aware of their own motives than other kinds of philosophers, or other social thinkers. On the other hand, I think that true self-awareness does inhibit those immature forms of moral judgment we have examined: the morality of external rules and of impression management. Moreover, while I do not think self-awareness is a *necessary* condition for moral maturity, it does make a powerful contribution to refined moral thought, and thus might be said to approximate *sufficiency*. One might imagine a distribution of cases in the following simplified form:

Proportion of Self-Aware Persons with High and Low Moral Maturity

	Self-Awareness	
Moral Maturity	*High*	*Low*
High	All	Few
Low	None	Many
Total	100%	100%

We now have these concepts and sets of relationships:

1. The moralizing need is a condition for our observation of the character of moral judgment in the material we are analyzing. It is irrelevant to a theory of moral development.

2. Cognitive skills (a good decision-making machine) and ego strength are causally related to mature moral judgment.

3. Mature moral judgment is a comprehensive term for an appreciation of motives and intentions, reciprocity and empathy, the independence of sanctions and morality, punishment as education, natural causation, and plural moral perspectives.

4. These elements, taken together, cause and are otherwise associated

with (defined as) a refined working conscience, the agency of moral judgment.

5. Self-awareness is logically (definitional overlap) and psychologically related to this refined working conscience; like cognitive skills, it is causally related to conscience and mature moral judgment, but it is not a necessary condition.

Let us examine one other aspect of this fifth point, the relation of self-awareness to mature moral judgment. Self-awareness itself takes cognitive skills: focused attention, abstraction from particular experiences, "getting the point," seeing relevance in an event. Thus both mature moral judgment and self-awareness have some sources in common. Second, the successful interpretation of one's own experience requires relatively few areas closed to insight. If the individual cannot see himself clearly, or unconsciously avoids facing up to his own "sordid" motives and other moral defects, the self-critical functions will atrophy or miss their mark. This is important because the sanctions against moral transgression are self-condemnation or guilt. But for this to work, a person must be able to see himself relatively clearly, without panic or abasement; that is, with a true awareness.

This interlocking complex of elements, a need to feel moral, decision-making skills associated with moral maturity, and self-awareness, will, we are arguing, shape a political ideology. What should we expect?

1. *The ideology emphasizes the rightness and wrongness (not the efficiency, causes, history) of policy.* This follows, almost tautologically, from the interests and needs of the ideology's author. He thinks in terms of right and wrong, moral and immoral; he brings to bear his own sense of personal conduct upon official conduct. He is concerned with the moral consequences of action as well as the moral principles of legitimacy, consent, obedience, duty. But—and here he differs from the primitive moralist—he judges the intent and the consequence of an act rather than the rules and conventions that might apply to it.

2. *The ideology is open, allowing for alternative views.* A mature morality allows for "relativism in judgment," that is, for situations in which it is likely that one person (a teacher) sees morality one way, while another person (a student) sees it another way, and neither way excludes the rightness of the other. This is one reason why the accompanying political ideology should be tolerant, open, pluralistic. Another reason is the influence, once again, of self-awareness. One of the things that tends to create a closure against new ideas and change or modification of an ideology is the fear of exposing the self to the self (and to others), that is, panic over the possibility of revealing a repressed wish, a hidden motive. The man who is already consciously aware of his own needs and motives, the seamy

side of the self, is less likely to fear such exposure. Or, from still another point of view, Erikson suggests that the force behind total or exclusive ideologies is the superego, while behind open and democratic ideologies is that more benign feature of personality, ego identity.[9]

3. *The ideology is humane, empathic.* This follows partly from the definition of mature moral judgment: it includes empathy. But the empathy affects the rest of the elements. "For self-criticism to be guilt," says Kohlberg, "the child must 'take the role of the other' in a deep or internalized sense, regardless of whether the other knows about his transgression."[10] Thus guilt or self-condemnation relies both on knowledge of the self, as we have said, and on the capacity to see oneself from the perspective of another. And this, too, is a cognitive skill.

One of the things that makes ideologies "external," concerned with social categories such as sovereignty, class war, social contracts, the state, is a reluctance to explore that which is human, psychological, intimate. The reluctance often stems from a basic aversion to any inquiry into the self. Furthermore, the self-aware person, or at least the person seeking self-awareness, is already working with the categories and concepts and material of individual human life: he seeks to know why men believe what they believe, enjoy their enjoyments, respond to poverty, duress, acceleration of status, and other experiences as they do. And the ideology of self-awareness is likely to be empathic because the instrument for understanding others is, basically, the self.

4. *The ideology is relatively unrationalized, "honest."* To rationalize is to set forth "better," that is, more socially acceptable, reasons for an act or belief than is warranted. One may rationalize more easily if the cognitive machinery works erratically. But also one rationalizes because one fears to examine or to reveal the real, "honest" reason, since this exposes the self to view, making conscious the material that all the forces of repression seek to hide from consciousness. Thus, when repression is relaxed and when one has already explored the seamy side of the self, the need to rationalize is weak. There is no need to project the bad side of things onto others, so as to assure the self that it is none of those bad things. That the self should be bad is regrettable, but not terrifying.

5. *The ideology emphasizes individual responsibility, obligation.* In part this follows from the nature of moral thought applied to civics: the substance of that thought has to do with human rights and duties. In part it follows from the reciprocity theme in moral maturity: one cannot expect

---

[9]Erik Erikson, "The Problem of Ego Identity," *Journal of the American Psychoanalytic Association,* 4 (1956), pp. 58-121, reprinted in Maurice Stein, A. J. Vidich, and D. M. White, eds., *Identity and Anxiety* (New York: Free Press of Glencoe, 1960), p. 82.

[10]Kohlberg, "Development of Moral Character," p. 413.

others to carry on their civic duties without an equivalent "contribution" by the self, a return for benefits received. In classic language, one might say that included in the concept of a social contract is the concept of individual obligation.

6. *The ideology eschews violence, makes change incremental.* The relative absence of taboo subjects implies high thresholds of tolerance for alien ideas and foreign ways, little suspicion, slow resort to nonreasoning devices, little violence. Because the weaker, more sinful side of the self is known and balanced against the stronger, better side of some kind of rendered account, men create conscious doubt (tolerating ambiguity): "a change in policy *might* be effective"; "*perhaps* men will work as well under conditions of greater equality"; "it is *possible* that military escalation will create the conditions for peace." Under conditions of conscious and accepted doubt, men are likely to adopt the experimental method, incremental change, modest deviations from the going thing. Certainty in these matters is sometimes built on repressed doubts and leads to overcommitment; conscious doubt permits tentativeness. Furthermore, the bluntness of total solutions is often the consequence of inadequate powers of discrimination. The superior cognition of the mature moralist should reduce this bluntness.

7. *The ideology, relying on human plasticity, emphasizes education.* This is implied in the idea that punishment is properly a form of education: if one believes this, he believes men are educable. Moreover, the belief that "you can't change human nature" goes badly with the idea of self-improvement, self-examination, self-awareness. It is, indeed, the counsel of despair of someone who has tried this process of self-change and given up, or, more likely, fears to try. If the door to social reform is locked by the incapacities of men and their leaders, then education is the key to this lock. The ideology of the self-aware moralist is likely, indeed, to suffer from an excessive faith in personality change, and thus to fail to appreciate the need for institutional change.

8. *The ideology risks paralysis; it may be all anchor and no sail.* The emphasis on cognition may be at the cost of volition. The failure to embrace unrealizable utopias may deprive men of a necessary *elan* and motivation for risk-taking. The conscious doubt that prevents overcommitment may also prevent commitment. Concern with the self may stem from anxiety, a condition in which people tend to ignore political affairs, civic obligations.[11] Awareness of one's own moral infirmities may lead one to believe that one is, after all, a poor instrument for social change. Paralysis may result.

These eight features of an ideology of moral self-awareness rest on

---

[11]Morris Rosenberg, "Self-esteem and Concern with Public Affairs," *Public Opinion Quarterly,* 26 (1962), pp. 201-11.

inferences of varying reliability, backed up by research of varying relevance and cogency and by logic with some tenuous links. It is a kind of model, or ideal type. Let us see how closely Lamb fits the model.

LAMB, A SELF-AWARE POLITICAL MORALIST

Lamb is a moralist; he says he is, he speaks in terms of moral categories, and he illustrates in his reflective analysis of his life the way in which moral categories of right and wrong were given primacy, even when he was a child. Much of this moral discussion is subsumed under his term "perfectionism," by which he means that he sets high goals, many of them moral, tries to fulfill them himself, and asks others to do the same.

> Because I see things in black or white terms, I have reached the point where I now think perfectionism is morally right and therefore cannot see back to some basic insecurity that may underlie it. . . . [I have a tendency] to see almost all issues, even minor ones, in black or white moralistic terms. . . . I have always thought that to study was morally good, and I think, speaking objectively, I overdo my homework. . . . As a little boy I was called "the judge" because people thought I was so mature, but what I think they must have meant was that I judged things in moral terms. I judge my personal affairs in moral terms and I also judge national and international problems, even ones with minor consequences, with respect to right and wrong. This is true in all the matters I have discussed, i.e., labor, integration, religion, size of government, etc.

The statements are convincing, the illustrations even more so; as he himself says, he is overconscientious about his homework; when he takes on assignments for extracurricular affairs, he carries them out scrupulously; he takes responsibility for every act: "I will never drink even beer before driving because I know that if an accident occurred and anyone was hurt, I could never forgive myself." But (or and) he does not go to church because he does not accept the Christian theology (only its moral precepts), and "I feel that I should believe the things that I say in church . . . hypocrisy is very wrong."

In the light of the theory of moral judgment discussed above, one must, I think, give Lamb credit for a mature morality, as contrasted to Silver and Buenello's primitive moralism. Lamb is concerned with men's intentions and motives, including his own. The test is not so much the relationship of the act to the rule as it is the intention to live up to a principle, to set high standards. It is true that he is hard on his friends when they do not do this, and when they disagree with him on what is right, and in this sense he fails to reveal that relativism in judgment that characterizes a mature morality—indeed, his parents have urged him to mellow a bit in this respect. But, unlike Silver and Buenello, he does not believe at all that there is any necessary justice in the current distribution of rewards and punishments in society (independence of sanctions), and he believes in a kind of ideal reciprocity, often imagining how it must be to be in another's position. He certainly believes that if there must be punishment, its purpose must be educative, but he punishes himself much more than he would punish others.

But if it is relatively easy to establish that Lamb is a moralist, can one also show that he is introspectively conscious of the sources of his moralism, the imperfections in his moral record, the cost and consequences of moralist thought and behavior? I think so. First, then, as to causes. It would be too much to expect a moralist to "explain away" his emphasis upon moral categories; to do that is to destroy altogether their moral force. But Lamb does ask whether his perfectionism could be "a reaction against insecurity," and tentatively accepts the view that "this might well be true of me, especially in my relations with other people." While dismissing this for the moment, he implies it later when he reports finding "security in knowing that by my standards I am 'right' " and when he says that if he loses his self-confidence "this causes me to redouble my efforts to live up to my standards." Moreover, he candidly and with more courage than most moralists admits, toward the end of his paper, "I think that having perfectionist standards gives me a feeling of at least moral superiority over others, and thus a kind of security." Finally, he sees one other competitive advantage in applying his high standards (among them moral capacities) to others: "To recognize ability in others would tend to subtract from my own standing." He sees the hostilities as well as the competitive spirit behind some of his moral criticisms of others (as we saw in the discussion on aggression), and generally opens his mind to receive the evidence that his moral and other perfectionism is self-serving and not wholly unselfish.

Further, he is aware of the costs to himself of his effort to impose these high standards on the world, including himself. The most important of these is the way it impedes his other main conscious drive, his need to be liked. Part of the story is the chain of events: impossible standards → inevitable failure → loss of self-confidence → "a desire to be liked in order to assuage my lack of self-confidence." But the high standards frustrate his need to be liked, because, as we have seen,

> As a perfectionist among nonperfectionists, I have become very irritated with other people, because they do not set high

standards for themselves. . . . Because no one lives up to my standards, this has meant that I have never had great enough respect or trust of anyone to have more than [casual] friends; never have I had a close friend. Quite obviously one cannot object to people the way I do, express it very often, and still expect to be liked.

Moreover, not only do his high standards and criticism put people off; his loss of self-confidence reduces his capacity to make friends: When "I have a lack of self-confidence . . . [I] can see no real reason why anyone should be very interested in me." His moralism and generally high standards cost him his self-confidence, his capacity to reach out toward others, and, because his lack of confidence generates an irritable posture toward others, they cost him the warmth and reassurance of friendship—a high cost for Lamb.

There is another cost: "One of the consequences of this perfectionism is a fear of ever being associated with anything that is 'wrong' or imperfect." It is somewhat paralyzing. It impedes cooperative effort, for in an impure world where all causes represent compromises, Lamb says, "I will not be a party to any action which I feel is wrong, even if my friends put considerable pressure on me." Here, I think, he joins Donaldson, entering the world of the self-consciously pure, good, impression-managing moralists.

Finally, his high standards make it impossible for him to pay people compliments, yet, "Though I am reluctant to pay compliments, I need to receive praise, and because I don't give many compliments, I don't get many." He needs these compliments, he says, more than most, again because of the high costs of high standards. "I think that because I strive to fulfill high standards and often fail, it means that praise is often necessary to repair an ego lacking in self-confidence." He does not preen himself on his preservation of high standards in the face of these costs; rather, in an analytic spirit, he assays the balance, wondering, it seems, whether or not the whole thing is worth it.

In general, Lamb's politics correspond to the pattern anticipated for the self-aware moralist, but there are a few surprises. His belief system has a *moral emphasis:* Just as "I judge my personal affairs in moral terms . . . I also judge national and international problems, even ones with minor consequences, with respect to right and wrong." Lamb's political outlook is *open and undogmatic,* in the sense that, although he favors much in the status quo, he finds that "socialism is appealing in that it might satisfy some of my liberal goals . . . but would result in the loss of another of my liberal aims, freedom." In this sense, he entertains and weighs an alternative before he rejects it. His politics is *humane* and empathic, in the sense that Lamb "wants to see all people given an equal chance for good housing, good education, job opportunities, and a multitude of other things." It is relatively *unrationalized, "honest,"* in the sense that Lamb faces the contradiction between his liberal goals and his conservatism, saying rather awkwardly in one place, "The association of conservatism with a desire to maintain the security of the status quo applies to me," and at another place, "Even though the status quo may be contradictory to my principles, I have always gained security in my private life from order and planning." He therefore tends to support much of it.

Lamb's belief system emphasizes *individual obligation,* duty, responsibility. Although I cannot show this in terms of career plans or civic activity at Adams College (he was head of the student council in high school), it is revealed in the principled behavior toward others:

> I have worked with a group of maintenance workers at school . . . and judge them as people rather than as members of a class. . . . When I say that I do not judge people or discriminate against people because of race, color, religion, income, or education, it means that because of my perfectionism I do not permit myself to deviate in the slightest from this standard.

It is nonviolent, *incremental*: "In world matters slow change is preferable. . . . A slow but constant change is best in the school integration issue." It emphasizes *human plasticity, education*: "Though I believe that income should be based on ability and application of one's self to one's work, I feel that everyone should be given an equal chance to develop ability. I want to see . . . improvement and increase in education and the chance for the poor to get a good education." And, in some ways, the ideology *risks paralysis*, with everything weighed against everything else, and the entry of unanalyzed emotion impeded: "My whole life is regularized and organized and I have shown that I find it very difficult to do anything that has not been planned. My setting of high standards and trying to follow them involves a striving for the security of having a set pattern of life."[12]

I have suggested that one of the important needs experienced by modern man is the need to feel moral, and that men seek to gratify this need in several ways. Drawing on the theory and research on moral development, I have found that one of the ways illustrated in the small group of

---

[12]I have argued that "paralyzed" or over cautious political decision-making follows from several different situations or qualities: (a) the need to be liked joined with self-conscious intellectuality (Chap. 6); (b) aggression anxiety (Chap. 9); and (c) a need for moral self-imagery joined with a mature and sensitive conscience (Chap. 11). Since Lamb figured in each of these discussions, there is a risk that the interpretation has confused association with causal sequence. Our hope is that we have correctly identified three different dynamic forces even though they work together in the same personality. (In the next chapter we discuss further sources of uncertainty, a discussion in which Lamb does not figure.)

men who reveal this need to feel moral, the reliance on external rules, is cognate to and implied by the concept of a primitive morality, the morality of young children and the poorly educated. This primitive morality, moreover, seems to rest in part on and to imply low self-awareness, a reluctance to examine one's moral motives. It is congenial to and supports a conservative view of life by middle-class individuals.

A second way of proving to the self and others that one is moral is through trying to manage one's beliefs so as to impress some particular audience. One of the ways of doing this is to seek to convey one's humanitarianism, one's sacrificial nature. Moreover, although it is not self-aware, this form of morality seems to embrace more of the elements of moral maturity than the morality of external rules; it displays an attention to motives, a sense of reciprocity and empathy, an ability to divorce the rewards and penalties of life from moral credit, and an interest in doing something about social injustices. For the middle-class person, this view is most congenial to and supportive of a liberal or radical point of view.

Finally, we come to a still more mature morality combined with very considerable self-awareness. We suggested reasons for believing that the political ideology associated with these qualities would, in addition to its moral emphasis, be humane, open, unrationalized, stressing individual responsibility, education and incremental change, while avoiding violence. Yet something is missing: vision, drive, action.

12

The Struggle against Feelings of Inadequacy: General Comments and "Body-Mind" Problem

Men seek to assuage their feelings of inadequacy and inferiority through compensatory striving fortified by a supporting social and political rationale.[1] We have seen this process at work where men felt they were deficient in popularity or likableness and where they were worried by doubts about their own morality and obedience to moral law. There are many other kinds of inadequacy feelings, among them (a) feelings of physical unattractiveness, weakness, poor health, awkwardness, and low athletic ability, (b) a sense of low social status or of economic deprivation, (c) belief that one is inadequate "as a person" or as a personality, especially in those qualities that make for "success" in school and life, among which assertiveness (but not aggression) is important. These inferiority feelings affect strategies of behavior and strategies of thought, these strategies being generally designed to restore one's self-esteem, the property one values most.

TYPES OF RESTITUTION AND COMPENSATION

The effort to restore that self-esteem of which one has been robbed by these feelings of inferiority is a dominating influence in the life strategies of

---

[1]Although most of the discussion in this chapter and the next deals with striving for wealth and status and some vaguely defined "success," the literature on the need for achievement is relevant. See David C. McClelland and others, *The Achievement Motive* (New York: Appleton-Century-Crofts, 1953); and also McClelland's *The Achieving Society* (New York: Van Nostrand, 1961). Yet it should be borne in mind that I am not talking about some internalized standard of excellence, but rather, in most cases, some external symbol of status.

the men we are here considering. Indeed, for some of them this is what life is all about. It affects their choice of career, their human models and group references, the audiences for whom they perform and to whom they "present the self," their values and beliefs about what is worthwhile, their relations with other people, their attitudes toward status, social class, wealth, and inevitably, therefore, their political belief systems.

The first "choice" is whether or not to face up to the deficiency, confront the allegation, and admit this "knowledge" to the conscious mind. If the answer is "no," the person may deny the attribution, repress the observation, look the other way. No doubt much of this has occurred among those who are not mentioned in the discussion to follow; they are working out some sense of deficiency of which their conscious mind is unaware. Just as Donaldson is unable to see how his impression-managing moralism is an unconscious device to tell people how kind and humane he is, and, with all his candor, Mintz does not mention the fact that he is Jewish, so also many of the men ignore hurtful senses of deficiency in one respect or another while striving unconsciously to assuage those very hurts. Coleman reported that when he was younger he would rather deny that there was anything wrong with him than to get braces for his buckteeth or try to control his weight. In spite of the denial, these deficiencies were, he says, "critical in the formation of my personality," and, according to his report, led him to value strength and aggression and develop leadership qualities as a form of compensation. Thus repression and inattention are no solution; rather the effort to repress something forces the reconstitutive efforts into channels less accessible to the conscious mind.[2]

Given the fact, then, that some form of conscious or unconscious striving for relief is inevitable, a second choice opens up: should these men lower their aspirations to avoid failure or increase their striving to increase the rewards? In general, men who fear failure not unreasonably lower their aspirations and reduce their goals.[3] And since much of what we have to say

---

[2] Joseph A. Kahl finds that frank avowal of striving for success and of ambition is "most characteristic of a person in the lower middle section of the status hierarchy," and that the middle and upper middle sections are more likely to assume wealth and some form of success, concentrating their aspirations on broader community status. Within this high-level group, however, we find no difference in the economic backgrounds of those who are more likely to admit their success striving. All of them are, in reality, striving for a fairly general form of recognition, but those most in need of "recognition" are likely to see money and status, rather than achievement, as the vehicle for their purpose. See Kahl's "Some Measurements of Achievement Orientation," *American Journal of Sociology,* 70 (1965), pp. 669-81.

[3] R. A. Clark, R. Teevan, and H. N. Ricciuti, "Hope of Success and Fear of Failure as Aspects of Need for Achievement," *Journal of Abnormal and Social Psychology,* 53 (1956), pp. 182-286; Eugene Burstein, "Fear of Failure, Achievement Motivation, and Aspiring to Prestigeful Occupations," *Journal of Abnormal and Social Psychology,* 67 (1963), pp. 189-93.

deals with men who suffer various kinds and degrees of feelings of inadequacy, we might expect them to have limited goals. Yet this is not the case. At this stage in their lives they are aiming high. Indeed, those who feel least adequate and report the most severe feelings of inferiority are engaged in the most intensive striving. Apparently in a highly intelligent, young, and prestigious stratum of the population, feelings of inadequacy may serve to increase striving rather than to reduce aspirations.

There is a third set of choices: whether to seek relief from feelings of inadequacy in the same value domain, through winning increments of the lost value, or in some compensating value domain. The first is not always possible, but one can see some of the men seeking to *win increments of the lost value*: the nonathletic Trueblood finally learns to swim, the "cowardly" Coleman learns to fight, the economically and status-deprived Novak determines to make money and associate with the important people on the campus. And we can see others *selecting a substitute value domain* where they may earn compensating increments of self-esteem—as Mintz, aware of deficiencies in athletics and good looks, becomes intellectual, advertised (to his disgust) by the label "intellectual" (along with "revolutionary") inscribed by his picture in the school yearbook when he graduated. And Simpson, unable to be aggressive enough to satisfy himself or his mother, takes some comfort from his success in gaining "popularity as a result of not antagonizing anyone."

But, of course, it is the nature of inferiority feelings, almost like moods, to generalize to values and aspects of the self far beyond the original domain within which they were learned. Indeed, the men report general feelings of inferiority: "I have had a deep sense of inferiority since childhood" (Demming); "Once started on this physical inferiority tack, any further incidents which seemed to aggravate the inferiority were seized upon and emotionally magnified to terrific size" (Trueblood). And as a consequence, they may choose some generalizable symbol of worth, like status, wealth, or "success." Thus Cohen, speaking in the third person about his respondent self, says, "Alex told us that he feels very insecure. . . . Although Alex has a great obsession to be successful in whatever he does, he is somewhat pessimistic about his future and does not know what he will do after being graduated from Adams." And Simpson, somewhat discouraged by his record at Adams and his continuing failure to be assertive enough, says, "I have acquired a somewhat obsessive reverence for wealth and social prestige." Thus, a third restorative strategy, arising partly from the generality of inferiority feelings, is to *select some generalizable asset*, like wealth, status, "success," to show the world that one is not, after all, an inadequate person.

To support these strategies (the term suggests more conscious selection than I mean) of restoring one's self-esteem—that is, to win through in the original domain of inferiority, or to find some specific compensating value domain, or some general symbolic value—men develop rationales and explanations, fragments of an ideology. The function of these beliefs and values is partly to reduce their sense of deficiency, partly to make their choices seem to be the best in large, nonselfish terms, partly to give direction to their further striving, partly to explain to themselves their own strenuous efforts. Inevitably in this search for a rationale, the nature, breadth, and source of the denigration will shape their thinking.

BREADTH, SEVERITY, AND SOURCES OF INADEQUACY FEELINGS

Part of the individual's efforts to restore his self-esteem will be shaped by his perception of *who* it is that is causing him these hurtful feelings in the first place. In general these will be either parents or peers.[4] What would we need to know, as a minimum basis for analysis? Something like the following would help.

Does the denigration fall within a generally supportive relationship? For example, does a generally supportive father make his son feel inadequate in sports or some other specific arena, or is the denigration much broader and therefore more hurtful? King's father always made him feel clumsy on camping trips, which invariably ended in a great quarrel; but King says his father was supportive in most important areas of life (though there was a crisis over ROTC). MacGregor says his father "demanded perfection and I could not live up to it." MacGregor develops a more comprehensive and tougher ideology to account for his striving than King does.

Does the denigration come from more than one source? Does it come at a time when the child has lost other support? Unable to win self-esteem from parents, can an individual win it from peers? Can he turn from one parent to the other? Has he an alternative social basis for his self-esteem? Trumbull felt that his father's denigration was especially destructive during his years at preparatory school, when he felt himself to be unpopular and socially unsuccessful. There is little humanity in Trumbull's ideology; it was squeezed out of him at an early age.

Is the denigration so widespread, inclusive, and intense that it inhibits

---

[4] On the general question of the sources of low and high status, see Herbert Hyman, "The Relation of Reference Group to Judgments of Status," in Reinhard Bendix and S. M. Lipset, eds., *Class, Status, and Power: A Reader in Social Stratification* (Glencoe, Ill.: Free Press, 1953), pp. 263-71.

corrective striving? Striving comes from uncertain, but possible, success. If one discounts this possibility too greatly, the costs of striving are too high and the rewards likely to be too small. Trueblood, who speaks of his "marked inferiority feelings," suffered from a sense of inadequacy regarding both peers and parents. When he "tried to gain superiority through brains," he felt this made people think of him as a sissy. He felt his father's disapproval but could not figure out what was expected of him. As a consequence:

> No matter how much I compensate, the inferiority feelings somehow manage to rise up to that level. In every situation where I can be compared with other people, I seem constantly to be seeking possible areas where I may be inferior. . . . The possibility of creating more inferiority and of not compensating perfectly may lead to a desire to avoid taking the step which may give this additional sign of inferiority and add to one's disgust with oneself. Paralysis results.

Is the deficiency differently evaluated by different valued sources of esteem? A conflict is created within the individual when one valued group favors a certain quality and another valued group disfavors it.[5] Rogers could preen himself at home on his family standing, but this did not go down well with his friends, for whom wealth was more important and useful. Goldberg's father, clinging to the orthodoxies of the Old World ghetto Jews, criticized his son for his lack of piety, but Goldberg found his secularism quite congenial to his teachers at school. The most common conflict, of course, comes from parental emphasis upon achievement values (good grades) and peer-group emphasis upon sociability, athletics, good looks.

Is there a discrepancy between subjective feelings of deficiency and the judgments of others? This discrepancy could be reflected in subjective perceptions of the self as "too low" or "too high" as compared to the way others see one. Trueblood's self-estimates are too low (I know he is intellectually capable, personable, and able to make those decisions that, to date, have given him a promising start in life). On the other hand, Coleman started life at Adams with expectations for himself that were too high, based on a high school career that gave him, he says, "the position and recognition that I needed." But at Adams "I cannot easily be at the top of my class and my athletic prowess did not meet the competition. . . . I have thus tended to seek strength in 'rebelling against the system.' "

---

[5] See Leonard Broom's discussion of status inconsistencies: "Social Differentiation and Stratification," in Robert K. Merton, Leonard Broom, and Leonard S. Cottrell, eds., *Sociology Today* (New York: Basic Books, 1959), pp. 429-41.

These are the matters about which questions of status in any society revolve: mobility, competing reference groups, status ambivalence, differences in objective and subjective status,[6] the custodianship of status credits, and attitudes about what shall be done about (for?) the low-status person, the underdog. One might think of those who have been made to feel deficient or inadequate in some way as deprived of internal status.[7]

In general these inadequacies create in the individual feelings of ambivalence about himself. These are striving men, after all, not apathetic or withdrawn individuals who have given up. Ambivalence and doubt, as we have said, are the sources of striving, hence the sources of political and social rationales growing out of striving, ambition, and proving something to the self.

A SENSE OF WEAKNESS, AWKWARDNESS, UNATTRACTIVENESS: THE POLITICS OF THE OUTSIDER

Let us look first at those feelings of inadequacy based upon the shape, condition, or skill of the body. There is a book yet to be written on the somatic basis of belief systems, for our material gives us many clues that a substantial half-hidden force is here at work. The most obvious ingredient is *athletic ability*: "I was a poor athlete, and, with grade school criteria such as they are, was never very popular" (Simpson). "In high school, athletics, good looks, success in being an 'all-round guy,' and popularity with the girls became all-important. Unable to meet the challenge, I withdrew into myself" (Mintz). "I was afraid to relax in the water . . . depressed by my lack of [swimming] progress, I resigned myself and chalked the failure up to my 'innate' physical weakness. The high school boys who were leading the swim classes grew tired of me, made fun of me, and eventually suggested I stay home" (Trueblood). "I have always been shortwinded. Even when I was in grade school I did not very often go out and play with other boys. . . . Whenever I was in a position in which I had to participate in a game or stand awkwardly on the sidelines, I always tried to be the equivalent of a right-fielder in a baseball game. There I had few chances to look bad" (King). In every case, the athletic shortcomings led to some compensatory activity—either to do well in school or to find

---

[6] Heinz Eulau brings out some of the political implications of the differences between subjective and objective status in his *The Behavioral Persuasion in Politics* (New York: Random House, 1963), pp. 55-60.

[7] See Herbert Hyman, "The Value Systems of Different Classes," in Bendix and Lipset, eds., *Class, Status, and Power*, pp. 426-42.

some other basis for self-respect. The self-images of these boys and their striving patterns were affected in critical ways.

Size and shape are important, and not only because of their effect on athletic ability. The *fat* ones suffer their brand of agony. Caplan says, "I rather think I have almost neglected the most obvious factor which would affect my personality as well as my political beliefs. This is my size and shape. I have always been short and fat. . . . There is what some people call a 'Napoleon complex' which seems to seize us short ones, which makes us more aggressive individuals. I have always been of this type." For a period of time, as suggested above, Coleman suffered this way:

> The ages of ten to twelve were particularly critical in the formation of my personality. First, I became unattractively fat and was characterized by two prominent buckteeth. Both of these factors were matters of considerable concern to my mother and she did not hesitate to bring them up as subjects of conversation. . . . But for me to submit to braces or to try to lose weight would be to admit that there was something wrong with me, and I could not do that. I would rather deny that there was anything wrong with me.

And Demming: "In addition to this feeling of loneliness, I was always very fat, and this contributed more than anything else to my feeling of inferiority." All three of these fat ones now are assertive people; each mentions his fatness as a source of his assertiveness.

The *small* ones have their problems: "With my feeling of being an outsider, of being too inferior in size, and of being of a minority group, I felt that I had to grasp onto the ideas and mores of the 'big men'" (Silver). "The second smallest in my class, I backed out of a fight when chance afforded it. When having to fight, I cried during it and for some time afterwards" (Novak).

These physical shortcomings are related to feelings of cowardice or weakness, but fears of weakness are common among the larger boys, as well. Novak's fear of fighting is partially explainable by his size, but Coleman is by no means undersized; his problem was precipitated by asthma:

> I was asthmatic until I was twelve and my mother was overprotective. I was constantly warned not to exert myself, to "be careful." This constant admonition to be careful had the effect of making me afraid, and for many years I thought myself a coward. I was constantly overcompensating for this by acting "the big man" and by arrogance.

Strength becomes a paramount value in his scheme of things. Trueblood's problems also had a source in illness: "In infancy I was sick rather frequently . . . and was made to feel that I was weaker and did not quite have the strength of others my own age." This, combined with punishment for "hitting things and breaking things . . . hindered me in taking my own part in fights with older boys who were my playmates at that time. . . . I recall my parents berating me for my lack of spirit in combat." Trueblood finds compensation first in artistic achievements, then in intellectual ones. Ransome, vividly recalling a wound in childhood, believes this has had a direct effect on his foreign policy: "I believe that I would be quite afraid of fighting a war. . . . A principal aim of my internationalist position is thus the prevention of war."

As implied in some of the above comments, infirmities due to illness (heart conditions, asthma, rheumatic fever) take their toll not only on the body, but on one's sense of strength and vigor, and hence on one's self-esteem. Lamb, like Coleman, had buckteeth and suffered from a sense of being unattractive. Trueblood had to wear braces, as well as being the first in his class to wear glasses. And in every case, the young man shapes a strategy for restoring in some way his sense of adequacy, through denial, or overassertiveness and aggression, or achievement in some compensating area where the young man can achieve—often "intellectuality"—or perhaps in some principled view of things that makes his weakness a virtue. Not infrequently these are world views about society, human nature, violence, the good life.

Sex, as everyone knows, is both a form of interpersonal relations and a physical phenomenon. There were many expressions of a sense of inadequacy in meeting and relating to girls, most of which were merely extensions of general interpersonal problems: "My sex relations have not been entirely satisfactory because I fear that an advance on my part will meet with disapproval and withdrawal of affection" (De Vita). "I have never been able to give affection to any girl and yet my great desire to be liked shows itself most clearly in relation to girls" (Lamb). "I find it difficult myself to demonstrate emotion. I have had few sexual experiences, and my relations with the opposite sex have always been characterized by varying degrees of inhibition" (Svenson). But two of these expressions seem related not so much to feelings of inadequate personal relations as to worries about the body: Is it adequate? Is it properly oriented? One of these problems, Mintz's, was cited before. He says: "For years prior to adolescence I was disturbed about the diminutive size of my genitals. . . . Occasionally I am troubled by fears that I might possibly have homosexual tendencies." Cohen's worries, milder in expression, center first on his obsessive collecting tendencies, which he thinks indicate "anal traits," and second on his relations with girls. His father, he says in his third-person account, "lectures the subject on going out with girls more often; the subject resents this very much and worries about being 'abnormal' in this respect." No doubt others are worried about their masculinity as well, but do not reveal it. In a *machismo* culture, these worries would be less expressed and more troublesome—but we have something of the *machismo* strain in our non-Latin, northern society. Perhaps an ideology can help repair the damage.

How does it feel to experience oneself as physically unattractive or weak, and requiring special consideration in a boys' world of physical prowess, endurance, skill; or awkward and lacking in that very quality that makes one wanted on a team, an asset for the school? There is a term that captures some of the emotional perspective that seems most relevant here: it makes one a bit of an *outsider*.[8] This kind of hurtful experience, where the hurt comes from a sense of not measuring up to one's peers' expectations, of being in their eyes not quite good enough, puts a kind of distance between them and the target individual. This sense of being an outsider, of experiencing a distancing between self and others, has several facets.

Greater Individuation.   In the first place, and most generally, employing pain as a lever, somatic deficiencies contribute to the *individuation* of the individual, discouraging the quick and unthinking acceptance of all that he sees and hears and might otherwise imitate. He tells himself sorrowfully, "I am different." Growing up is, in any event, a cutting of many silver cords; here, as in birth itself, the separation is involuntary and painful. This sense of difference, then, opens up the possibility of a genuinely individual perspective on life, including one's own, a carefully worked-out view of society and politics. And, curiously, this means that when these men who have been hurt in childhood through their physical inadequacies seek conventional views, they have often developed reasons for their views which are more consciously articulated and "philosophical" than those of others who merely absorbed them from the culture.

The psychological separation is sometimes reinforced by physical separation, voluntary or enforced by "protective" parents. King, whose rheumatic fever left him with a "feeling of weakness," says, "When I was little I played by myself a lot, and read a great deal. Even when I was in grade school I did not very often go out and play with the other boys, but instead climbed the tree in my backyard or ran around with my dog." Trueblood, failing in athletics, says, "My efforts to compensate produced a good deal of introversion as I tried to withdraw from as many contacts with others as possible." Novak, small and given to crying, says he was not allowed to go far from home to play with other children and "rarely did

---

[8]For a related discussion focusing on social as contrasted to psychological causes, see Howard S. Becker, *Outsiders: Studies in the Sociology of Deviance* (New York: Free Press, Macmillan, 1963).

any accept an invitation to visit me." His desperate efforts to integrate with other groups, even in college, reflect the uncertainties of this early experience, but for all of that, he does not accept the conventional views; rather he prides himself on his difference, his authoritarian and reactionary ideas.

This individuation is rarely that of a strong, self-confident sense of identity. Based as it is on feelings of weakness and rejection, it tends to reflect an uncertainty about the self, expressed in an overeagerness and overcommitment or withdrawal and uneasy apathy. Much more is involved in "success," however defined, than would have been the case without these early feelings of inadequacy.

The source of inadequacy feelings based on the body is ephemeral even if the feelings it generates are not. This is true for two reasons. First, athletics are much less important in college than in high school, and, as one anticipates adult life, they are seen to have little bearing on success. The mind takes primacy over the body; perhaps this is also partially true of dating and relations with girls. And second, the freckles disappear, the buckteeth are less noticeable as well as less noticed, weight comes under control. Thus the awkwardness, feelings of weakness, feelings of being unattractive often recede, although they may never wholly disappear, leaving their mark on the personality and belief system as these developed through childhood and youth.

An Opening to Outside Views. It is often said that marginal men, men who belong to groups not wholly integrated into or accepted by a culture, serve as importers of new ideas or inventors of change.[9] This has been the contribution of the Jews in many cultures, of the Scottish in England (*vide* John Knox, Adam Smith), of the Chinese in Southeast Asia, of the Indians in Africa, and so forth. The person who is an outsider, not for ethnic reasons but because of his "ugliness," awkwardness, weakness, may have some similar role to play. He has no common culture with others who are merely "different," no social support for this role, but nevertheless he may, on his own, be more open to the nonconventional idea than others. Feeling not quite a member of the group, he may be more ready to hear other views, befriend members of other minorities. Something is working in him to encourage this openness. It was only after Demming decided at Adams, "If I wasn't going to be accepted, I might as well make a point of it," that he began to "hear" his professors. "When I came to Adams, I had accepted the usual conservative cliches as the answers on politics. However, Adams provided an intellectual pattern which could justify my new

---

[9]See Everett E. Hagen, *On the Theory of Social Change* (Homewood, Ill.: Dorsey Press, 1962), pp. 91ff.

ideas." Silver, physically small, with "no real dynamic qualities," develops an elaborate Burkean philosophy for the views that Trumbull, Rogers, and Niven, also very conservative but physically more impressive, share without such philosophical support. Mintz, feeling himself unattractive and unlovable, prefers, like Demming, to attack the group: "In demonstrating my hostilities against the school, I began criticizing the traditional customs and ways of doing things . . . and became much impressed by equalitarian political theories." I do not think these men are more tolerant of differences than others; they are more open to deviant views, which they may then espouse with dogmatic conviction.

From Body to Mind: an Emphasis on Intellectuality. King, in his retirement due to his "feelings of weakness," says he "read a great deal." Mintz says that "because of my apparent preoccupation with studies, and my inactivity in sports and extracurricular activities, I became known as an intellectual." Trueblood, unable to compete in sports, bothered by early illness, argued to himself, "If I was physically inferior, I could excel in intelligence, or some other skill," but retreated from this line when he thought it was giving him a bad reputation. Cohen, small, worried about his relations with Gentiles, also has something of a sex problem, and "worries about being 'abnormal' in this respect." His father "cannot understand why he likes to listen to classical music and read the books that he does."

It is an obvious point and an obvious alternative means of establishing oneself as an important person, an adequate person. But it has consequences for a belief system. What has been called "bookishness" is associated with liberal, equalitarian thought, at least in the American culture.[10] Perhaps this association has a somatic basis; perhaps the bookish ones, the Mintzes, Truebloods, Cohens, Kings, turn to books as a relief from their sense of physical inadequacy. It is that sense of being an outsider because of their bodies that makes them both "bookish" and liberal. But equally it seems to work the other way around: since most writers of history, at least, and probably of fiction, are liberal and equalitarian in outlook, these readers ingest liberal ideas in their retreat from the physical world.

Ambivalent Attitudes Toward Elites. The elites of childhood and youth are very often those who are the best athletes, the best fighters, the best looking. There is much hero worship in childhood: very often these qualities define the hero. The outsider, however, has a problem: he cannot be a hero on these terms, or even share in the heroism. He thus may envy the heroic (somatic) elite, seek their favor, hate them for their share in making him an outsider, resent their position, challenge the basis of their

---

[10]Gardner Murphy and Rensis Likert, *Public Opinion and the Individual* (New York: Harper, 1938). See also the discussion of "intellectuality" in Chap. 6.

superiority through emphasizing the value of nonsomatic qualities; in short, experience a set of ambivalent attitudes and feelings.

King reveals something of this problem in his account of his political success in high school.[11] There is a fraternity clique, he says, that has been running things: "Because of their control over social life, a tendency to rally behind certain agreed members, and their inclusion of most of the athletes in the school, these two [fraternity] groups were able to control elections. . . . Even though I wanted to displace the clique, I did not attempt to crusade against it, for *that would have made me stick out and classed with the 'odd balls' of the school.*" (My emphasis.) He organizes the "plain folks," uses his job as editor of the school paper for political purposes, and wins an election, a happy ending for an outsider who used to play by himself with his dog in the backyard. But the ambivalence toward his relations with elite groups, reflected in his comment on being an "odd ball," is illustrated in a less happy way in his political career at Adams. In the Debating Society there, as we have seen, he joins the Conservative party, whose platform is out of sympathy with his own liberal Democratic views, explaining this odd behavior by saying it was "to avoid the extremism which I felt might be prevalent in the Liberal party. Even though I am a liberal, I have a fear of extremism. In specific matters of policy, it usually works out that I do not vote with my party." At Adams, the elite are conservatives, or so King thought. His fear of being an outsider, because he has been one, creates a tension regarding appropriate relations with the leaders of the dominant order.

Mintz is more explicit, as we have seen in an earlier account: "I envy those who seem to perceive their needs and desires without difficulty. Yet at the same time I have a strong suspicion and dislike of the ultra-enthusiastic, purposeful, 'well-rounded' individuals who act as if they knew exactly where they were going and how to get there. I consciously avoid the BMOC's [Big Men on Campus], because, while I cannot always detect it, I feel they must somehow be phony." Silver tries to get close to the "big boys" but fears their rejection. Novak totally identifies with and submits to a strong reactionary leader on the campus, but later feels this was a sign of weakness. Caplan, as a freshman in preparatory school, first challenges the seniors to political debate, and only later, as he says, relaxes this challenging attitude. Demming switches early in his Adams career from intensively seeking acceptance by the leaders of what he calls the "in-group" to a posture of intense hostility toward that group, becoming, instead, a leader of his own "out-group."

---

[11]For a fuller exposition of this incident and the general problem of the symbols of acceptance and the substance of power, see Chap. 7.

The men who are embarrassed by their fatness, their smallness, their awkwardness must somehow come to terms with their ambivalent attitudes toward the elites in their own lives. Similarly, they may be hero worshipers in politics: Caplan was devoted to Henry Wallace; Novak read the biographies of great men when he should have been attending to his studies; Cohen was swayed from his Republican stance by the fact that he had recently met some distinguished and successful men who were Democrats; Mintz, in summarizing his political views, uses as a caption "passivity and dependence," under which he puts, "Roosevelt seen as protector." Or, on the other hand, they may solve this problem of ambivalence toward elites by indecision, withdrawal, hostility toward all political authority. The one thing they cannot easily do is to take a relaxed, instrumental view of elites in politics.

Uncertainty and Overcertainty. What we said about those who felt a deficiency in likableness holds here, with a difference: they are either uncertain about their political outlook or they are dogmatic. It seems to be difficult for this group to decide easily what social ends are congenial to them and what political means will best serve these ends in a framework of relaxed inquiry: the matter is fraught with tension and difficulty. Thus:

> There are times when I appear to myself to be devoid of motivation and direction, like floating on a cloud buffeted to and fro by the winds. Neither past, present, nor future seems terribly real to me, and I do not feel that I have really come to grips with life and the world . . . One of the greatest difficulties, even in seeking to locate a source for political opinions, arises from the inconsistency and confusion which attend virtually all my thinking [Mintz].

> Because of no real rational synthesis on my part of the basic tenets of conservatism, an environmental change could create a superficial change in ideology, but no real change in my relation to authority upon which I am dependent [Novak].

> Most of his instructors at Adams seem to be Democrats to him; these are successful, distinguished, and important men for Alex and he finds himself identifying with some of them. He is tempted to become a Democrat. . . . We believe that the subject could change his party affiliation without too much difficulty. [Cohen].

And elsewhere we have commented on Trueblood's inability to decide what party to support because all decisions are fraught with peril for him, and we have observed how King tends to hedge his position so as not to appear extremist or "odd ball" in the eyes of others (and himself).

On the other hand, there are the vigorous assertions of the three men who, at the time of writing or earlier, felt that they were too fat. They serve as a dramatic contrast.

> My political ideology involves, first of all, a distrust of "business" and that American ideal, the businessman. . . . I do not feel that capitalism is a good system. . . . I firmly believe in a more progressive income tax, finding no justification for fabulous incomes which go far beyond the most extravagant needs of the people involved. . . . [I have] a feeling of hostility toward the wealthier business class [Demming].

> From the age of fourteen I have had a feeling of destiny in my life. . . . The possible conflict between . . . [my political ambition and my liberal ideals] is resolved largely by my belief in an inevitable destiny in which my actions are largely determined, a belief that justifies whatever I do to advance myself as being for an ultimate good [Coleman].

> As for my aggressive, attention-seeking . . . personality, I think I need only say that the past term was a fair indication of this. It's been that way for many, many years. To sum this all up, I would say that I stand today in the liberal wing of the Democratic party. . . . I feel of course that the government should be a positive force. . . . I hate . . . the Joe McCarthys and Bill Buckleys, the Fulton Lewis Juniors and the Westbrook Peglers, but the best way to fight them is with facts and logically reasoned arguments [Caplan].

There is a hostility theme in Demming's and Caplan's assertive statements; Coleman's is marked by his self-confident sense of mission, a mission he was beginning to carry out while still at Adams. Perhaps feeling rejected because of fatness is different from being rejected because of a sense of weakness or athletic deficiency—none of these men reported any athletic failures, and Coleman had considerable success. Whatever the truth may be, there is something that marks most of the men who felt rejected because of their bodily inadequacies, either an uncertainty and doubt or an assertiveness that does not leave much room for casual give and take in political discussion.

BODY ACCEPTANCE AND SOCIAL THOUGHT

Going much beyond the evidence, is there something more general, as well as even more speculative, that we can say about the relationship between the body and the belief system? Could it be, for example, that those who feel secure in their own bodies feel more secure interpersonally than the physically inadequate, and hence:

(a) are more likely to have a feeling that others can be trusted (because they are less threatening);

(b) are less likely to overreact (to be submissive or assertive) to local elites and to distant authorities;

(c) are more likely to focus on the here and now, where they experience a feeling of inner security and confidence;

(d) are less likely to deal with things symbolically, enjoying the tangible, manageable nature of things;

(e) are less likely to have the "intimacy complex," that is, are less likely to prefer distant and symbolic affectionate relations to close and personal ones; but are they also

(f) less likely to need people to reassure them they are "all right," and

(g) more likely to be unconscious accepters of their environment, conventional for conventional reasons?

There are, perhaps, additional special insights into the way the body affects experience, hence generalization, knowledge, rationalization. Two men, Goldberg and Buenello, were gang leaders because they were larger than others and better fighters. Each of them indicates that in many settings he expects to be the leader, the dominant figure. Buenello develops a political philosophy emphasizing a leadership principle, but Goldberg does not; he is a partisan Democrat who favors the party, in part at least because it is for "the little guy," who is, in his mind, symbolically associated with his own minority group. It seems doubtful that the experience of physical dominance based on size and fighting prowess makes for elitist thinking in any way. But Buenello as compared to the other Italian, De Vita, and Goldberg as compared to the other Jews—Mintz, Cohen, Silver, and even Caplan—reveal a kind of confidence in themselves, an assurance of tone, an anticipation of a secure future. And this is true in spite of Buenello's moralism and Goldberg's feelings of insecurity vis-a-vis "superior" social groups.

Dobb is rich and wellborn, athletic and good-looking, but he is in a state of mild rebellion against his parents. He feels that he was less favored than his brother and that he lost out in the struggle for affection at home. He is, contrary to parental directions, a Democrat and a moderate liberal. Moreover, he is vigorously determined to "stand on his own two feet," to be nobody's man, to make his own way. One of the things, I believe, which facilitates this liberal indulgence and rebellion is his security in his own body. For one thing, he can, partly for physical reasons, afford to be independent vis-a-vis others:

> The particular feeling of independence was evident in an example taken from school when I was about ten. There was a class bully in that year who required only that I yield to him and follow in his "gang." Many fights occurred, but to this day there has been no question of yielding on my part. On account of this defiance I was able to make a place for myself in the class.

And for another thing, he is able to be "self-contained" because there is opportunity on the field of sports for him to prove himself against others and to work off his feelings of loneliness or self-pity: "I became, like my father, very self-contained. My outlets for emotion were confined to sports, in which I participated wholeheartedly, and still do."

Good looks are an ascriptive value, and serve in the same way as other ascriptive values for which people do not have to work and about which they do not have to worry lest they fail to "make it." It is as though there were some physical remnant of aristocratic society deposited in the midst of this contractual, achievement-oriented society. Dobb was good-looking; so was McDonald, the adopted boy who tempered his socialist inclination to remain in the more popular Democratic camp; Goldberg says, "I am told I was a beautiful baby as well as an only son," and today he is "fair-haired" and good-looking. Their personal acceptability, as children and as young men, makes them anticipate acceptance. They are neither radicals nor reactionaries. There is something secure and humane about their views, but each has a tendency to soften the unpopular statement, temper the interesting idiosyncrasy.

13

Striving for Wealth and Status
and the Sense of Inadequacy

We cannot, as we have seen, say that all feelings of inferiority and inadequacy lead a man to value wealth and status;[1] he might choose, as the value
domain in which to restore his self-esteem, achievement, friendship, interpersonal leadership, knowledge. Neither, of course, can one say that all
striving for wealth and status stems from a feeling of inadequacy; that kind
of striving may come from a variety of other sources, such as the simple
pursuit of an easily available means of livelihood, long established as a
family tradition. But is there, nevertheless, some connection between feelings of inadequacy and striving for wealth and status, fortified, as usual,
by some social and political belief system? Let us explore this problem.

THE VALUE OF WEALTH AND STATUS

There are good reasons why wealth should be an attractive value for those
seeking to restore their self-esteem, lost in childhood either because of a

---

[1] On the meaning of wealth, see Georg Simmel, *The Philosophy of Money* (Leipzig:
Duncker & Humblot, c. 1950).

There are many discussions of status relevant to the discussion below. I think Weber's
concept based on "honor" is too narrow. I prefer Parsons' idea of status "in its valuational
aspect" as "the ranking of units in a social system in accordance with the standards of the
common value system." Nevertheless, most of the men who employ the term in the following
discussion have in mind the kind of ranking Lloyd Warner was getting at when he asked
people in Yankee City who was "higher" and who was "lower" in that community, and who
went with whom. See Talcott Parsons, "On the Concept of Political Power," in Reinhard
Bendix and S. M. Lipset, eds., 2nd ed., *Class, Status, and Power: A Reader in Social Stratification* (Glencoe, Ill.: Free Press, 1966), pp. 240-66.

sense of economic deprivation or for other reasons. In many ways wealth and status are just exactly those values that most clearly meet the needs of those who feel, on a variety of grounds, somewhat inadequate. In the first place, they permit ostentation, they have ways of being worn on the sleeve; indeed, the sleeve itself may reveal expensiveness. This is not true of special talent or achievement within a professional group. Second, wealth is a fungible asset; it buys power, deference, even popularity. Third, wealth is widely admired; there are few people who would not like more of it for themselves. Thus it is easy to set up those invidious distinctions that the insecure person often needs to restore lost increments of self-esteem. Along the same line, wealth is likely to impress both parents and peers, whom we identified earlier as the two most important sources of denigration. Fourth, wealth gives security; it is characteristic of those who feel inadequate that they also feel insecure. Fifth, it is earned in many ways, including speculation, luck, and marginally moral dealing. Thus almost any person may be able to see some avenue to wealth congenial to his interests, skills, and moral development. Professional achievement, while not without its politics and luck, is still different in these respects.

On the other hand, there are some reasons for ambivalent feelings about the pursuit of wealth, or at least its public acknowledgment. There is a social ambivalence about making money; the wee small voices in the mores along with the mock thundering of the church against materialism complicate the search for status through wealth. Other voices join this chorus: the steady declamation from the respectable left against special privilege, the equalitarian themes expressed by those who speak for the American tradition, ideals of "service" in competition with the ideals of "success," and much more, equally intangible, equally important. Skill is not treated with such gingerly affection, nor is beauty, but wealth invites it, as the proper names Midas, Croesus, and Mammon suggest, as the phrase "The love of money is the root of all evil" implies, as the problem of the rich man getting into heaven portends, and the blessedness of the poor, but not the rich, allows. All this opens the door to ambivalence, but hardly forces it upon people; most people in the United States revere wealth, consider it earned, merited, even if it is the gift of fortune.[2] Perhaps it is for these reasons that only a little over a third of these striving Adams men mention or clearly indicate that one of their major goals in life is to be or become rich.

How, then, does the need for wealth and status (they are usually conflated by these men, although much of the theoretical literature, including

---

[2]See Robert E. Lane, *Political Ideology* (New York: Free Press, Macmillan, 1967), pp. 65-67.

the work of Weber, Tönnies, and Warner, clearly separates their criteria and social functions)[3] serve these men's life strategies and larger needs? And how, at the same time, do they argue the case for a society in which they may hope to prosper?

EARLY INADEQUACY IN STATUS AND WEALTH

The sense of inadequacy arising from bodily deficiencies encourages, for the most part, compensatory restitution in other value areas: wealth, achievement, status, friendship and social acceptance, moral superiority, or education. One cannot plan a career so as to restore self-esteem, lost through early weakness or awkwardness, in the same value domain as that in which the loss occurred: the conditions of success change, the body changes. But, when one has been made to feel inadequate because of lack of status or money, one can indeed plan a career to restore one's self-esteem in these very value areas, and can begin early to develop a rationale for one's striving, showing that self-interest joins nicely with public interest.

Direct Restitution of a Missing Value. The ranking of people in terms of some kind of social standing, deference owed, starts early in the individual's life. For children, as for adults, it is a confabulation of wealth and "family," sometimes differentiated, sometimes not. People can be made to feel inferior on both counts; people who feel inferior on one can seize upon the other, as a kind of compensation—but never quite enough. Here we shall examine three young men who experienced this kind of deprivation: Novak, Rogers, and Niven.

Novak says, "My friends had houses larger than mine. I recall once at the age of ten I invited a girl friend to visit me. She left soon after arriving. I blamed it on the house. When my father bought an electric vacuum cleaner it was smaller than those I had seen in my friends' homes." He believes that his drive for wealth and status (and defense of capitalism) is rooted, in part, in these early feelings of social and economic inferiority. Novak self-consciously reports how his political rationale serves these purposes, allowing him to achieve some increments of self-esteem by becoming rich. He says, referring to his activities at Adams:

> My wide participation in extracurricular activities points partly to the striving to raise myself in the hierarchy of my social environment. One important element in society allowing such mobility is flexibility in income and purchasing power.
> Capitalism represents possibilities and opportunities for ris-

---

[3]See the discussion by these authors in Bendix and Lipset, *Class, Status, and Power.*

ing in that society. My relationships at prep school and at Adams with members of the upper economic strata have enhanced the earlier concept of "bigger houses" and "vacuum cleaners" which money provides. The having of such objects represents a symbol of assimilation into and acceptance by the in-group.

Similarly, one can discern some of Silver's drive to be accepted by wealthy and high-status people in his comment on his changed views when he was invited to join a fraternity in his private school:

> At that time my views on social and class distinctions were to be altered. The boys who were members of the fraternity were a cliquish group and tended to look down on "the lower middle classes." . . . I was forced to drift away from my former friends and although *at the time my family was not the economic equal of the families of my new prep school friends*, I also began to take on a snobbish air. [Emphasis mine.]

Silver's parents were Democrats; "Now, however, since I have made an attempt to analyze my political beliefs, I feel that I am a true believer in the Republican party. All my friends at prep school as well as at Adams have been Republicans and are supporters of any and all policies which have aided big business."

Niven, like Silver, reveals the importance of early economic comparisons. He starts his report by saying, "I was born the son of lower-middle-class parents in Newark. . . . At the time of my birth both parents were working—father as a bookkeeper, mother as a stenographer." His father then steadily improves his economic position until, as Niven says, "For the last ten years we have lived in a neighborhood where the average income is considerably below ours." Niven, however, who is very, very sensitive to relative standings of this kind, does not forget the early years, for even in this more prosperous situation, he says,

> Being a Republican helped to overcome a slight feeling of inferiority in grade school contacts. In my neighborhood [during the past ten years] I remained aloof from those of my age group, due to our better social position and my private schooling, which I transformed into a desirable thing in this connection. Being a Republican in this Democratic district helped to complete this scheme.

Restitution through a Substitute Value. These three men, Novak, Silver, and Niven, experienced mild relative economic deprivation in their childhood; in two cases it was ephemeral, but, so we are told, it influenced their patterns of striving, and consequently their political orientations. But what of the others who experienced economic deprivation? How do they solve their problems of self-esteem? The general pattern is to find another value and to erect a political and social philosophy to which that value is central.

Buenello, probably the least prosperous of the group, emphasizes, as we have seen, his moral values, leaving the way open for financial and political success ("I seek a life of political participation"). Furthermore, he claims powers of leadership and develops a rationale for a society in which all of these qualities are valued and in which he will have a preferred place: "At the top of the ideal hierarchy should be those human beings who are best qualified, both mentally and physically, to provide for the welfare of the nation."

Rogers, like Novak, did not suffer real economic privation (his father being a professional man), but he compared himself unfavorably with others. Although his parents told him that "blood is everything in the modern social strata," he suffers pangs of economic envy: "I have always been in the position of being envious of those who are more fortunate than I in respect to material wealth. . . . I can remember my mother being sorely distressed because she was not able to keep up with her friends." Moreover, "This envy of money has perhaps led to my chief prejudice in life, that which I feel strongly toward the Jews." But, although in many ways, he is very reactionary (a member of the "States' Rights party"), he does not ever say he plans to be rich to restore directly the self-esteem thus stolen away. Rather, perhaps naturally for the son of a professional man engaged in the educational process, he gives himself increments of status in another way: "I guess that I have been privileged in receiving a better education than the average. I feel that I am in a position where I can place myself above those of less education and feel that leadership should come from this class of educated individuals."[4]

Demming, the product of lower-middle-class parents, a day student in a boarding school, working his way through Adams, says, "I resented the limited financial resources of my parents." He reports a pervasive and enduring "feeling of inferiority," but he does not at all aim to become rich. On the contrary, he strikes out against the rich and well-to-do and aims in college at leadership of what he calls "out-groups." He adopts a liberal stance, switching to the Democratic party, which, he says, "seemed to me to be an out-group and to represent economic out-groups." He finds, in this opportunity for leadership, some relief from his feelings of inferiority.

De Vita, also from the lower middle class, adopts, as we saw in Chapter 1, a different basis for relieving the feelings of inferiority engen-

---

[4]On belief in the magical properties of education, see my discussion in *Political Ideology,* pp. 324-25.

dered by a low-status background: he opts for intellectuality and knowledge. He therefore erects a philosophy of society in which only the well educated, the professionals, the knowledgeable have a right to determine policy.

Thus real, or only relative, economic deprivation with its lower status and occasional blows to pride and self-esteem can indeed lead to an effort to restore one's good opinion of oneself through becoming rich and of high social status. When that is the case, men find conservative rationales for their striving, often becoming ethnocentric in the process. But there are opportunities for restoring one's self-respect in other ways. One can pride oneself on one's moral qualities and develop a moral ideology, or one can assume that one has special leadership qualities, receiving and anticipating some increments of self-esteem for these, developing (like Buenello and Rogers) philosophies that accord the self positions of prestige and power. Or, along with such leadership philosophies, one can emphasize education and intellectuality and knowledge, leading to support for a kind of meritocracy in which one sees a place of honor for oneself.

Still, there are others who do seek directly to be rich and achieve high status. If it is true that only a small portion of the drive for wealth and the status it buys represents a direct attempt to win increments of self-esteem in the same value domain as that in which it was lost, what are its origins?

INADEQUACIES AS A PERSON OR PERSONALITY

The striving for status and wealth might come, not from loss of esteem in these value areas, but from some severe parental criticism or control, causing a person to doubt his qualities of assertion or, more generally, of competence and worth. We shall examine two variant forms of this type of situation. In one, the youths come to wonder if they have the qualities of strength or assertiveness necessary to succeed as their fathers (or mothers) succeeded—a specific allegation that would have to be proved false. Under these circumstances, status and wealth would prove to the individual that he was not weak, not without spirit, not "weak-kneed," as he thought he might be. In the other variant, produced by more inclusive denigration, status and wealth serve to silence certain doubts about personal worthlessness.

Ambivalent Subordination-Assertion Relations with Parents. The boy from a business home who struggles, like others, with parents whom he loves and hates, admires and rejects, and from whom he demands both freedom and respect, is in a difficult position. If he rejects his parents' values, he forfeits their respect, yet one of their values is competitive assertion, perhaps the very quality that made the father a success. In one sense the father (or perhaps the mother) may be creating an impossible bind for his (or her) son, saying to him: "Be aggressive, assertive, 'hard' like me, but don't use those qualities against me." Since the youth must learn and exercise these qualities at home if he is to have them at all, an intrafamilial conflict is ensured, and so is an intrapsychic one. This seems to be the case with MacGregor, Simpson, and Novak; MacGregor and Novak face this kind of double bind [5] with their fathers, Simpson with his mother. All three speak of themselves as in some respects authoritarian, MacGregor and Novak saying they learned this quality from their fathers, Simpson from his mother, who, he says, dominated his home. All three need to impress the dominating parent with their ambition and assertiveness in order to win parental respect and therefore self-respect. All three think of winning respect through business success which will give them wealth and status and thus prove something their parents' criticism and constraint cast in doubt, their real worth.

MacGregor's father was a hard-line conservative, a self-made man, a dominating figure in the household. MacGregor says, "My [paternal] grandmother dominated my grandfather, and my father has a very deep respect for her. My grandfather he scorns, because of his weakness, both physically and ambition-wise." It is up to MacGregor to prove to his father and to himself that he is not weak, and therefore that he deserves his father's respect, which will enable him to respect himself. But when he tries to prove his strength in the home by some assertive act or some degree of deviance from his father's hard line, he says, "My dad claimed I was trying to flout his authority on purpose. . . . He accused me long enough until my every energy was involved in trying to make him mad at me."

Unable to take his father's strictures, MacGregor was sent away to boarding school, where he assumed a "flaming youth" character and adopted radical ideas totally at odds with his father's business philosophy. One sees him here struggling both for autonomy and to overcome any impression in his father's mind that he might be weak. His account of his return to the conservative fold and to the business world reveals more of this identification with his father than the young man knows:

> During the three summers while I was at prep school, I worked in the business world. I began to see that not all people in the business world were like my dad. I saw that it was possible to be successful and still maintain a very different philosophy of life. . . . They [successful people] realized that cash value was

---

[5] Gregory Bateson's paradigm of the "double bind" is characterized by the position of the boy whose father says, in effect, "Do as I say, but don't be so damn compliant." See the discussion of "normlessness and uncertainty" in the home in Chap. 15.

not the essential net worth of a person. Thus, the pendulum had stopped swinging away from the conservative Republican orientation of my father, and slowly but surely I stopped seeing things in an "either-or" proposition manner. I became able to identify myself with their conservatism and big business foundations without identifying myself with my father.

Now, after two and a half years of college, he says:

> As I came out of my liberal idealistic shell, no longer did it have to be "I versus my Dad." I was able to recognize and accept him for what he is. . . . The fact of the matter is that his business associates liked him. They found him fair both as a worker and as a boss. Perhaps I was all wet. . . . Now, if I will pay lip service to him for the sake of expediency, things go wonderfully well.

MacGregor says he is insecure ("As my father grew up insecure, so did I"), and he prizes this insecurity as the source of his ambition and initiative. Indeed, he believes one of the merits of capitalism is that it makes people insecure.[6] He is determined to be a success in business, like his father, though more humane, like his mother. Can it be doubted that this insecurity, a product of these father-son quarrels, drives him to compete with and, if possible, outdistance his money-making, businessman father? Certainly his new-found defense of capitalism and adoption of a business philosophy were developed to justify the new direction of his striving.

Simpson's father is also a businessman, though not so successful; more to the point, his mother was in business before she married and was rather more successful than the father. Often she prodded young Simpson about his lack of assertiveness, his mediocre record in school, indicating to him that he was "a great disappointment to her" at times. He dismisses his father as less important in framing his personality and political orientation, accounting for one side of his uncertain orientation this way:

> I consider my mother to be an authoritarian. . . . I feel that her dominance in the home has made me both weak and respectful. This has probably been the cause of my lack of aggressiveness. . . . As a result of this personality trait, I have come in recent years to feel a certain frustration as a result of a lack of an assertive personality, and tried to be more assertive. But in so doing I have acquired a somewhat obsessive reverence for wealth

---

[6]MacGregor says: "By rejection of the welfare state, farm subsidies, and the like, I wish everybody to be in an insecure or in a nonguaranteed position. It's my feeling that security breeds complacency. This takes away all initiative and ambition, robbing society of the results of creative work."

and social prestige. Wealth and social prestige have come to mean for me both symbols of assertion and the reward for assertion. For this reason, I have an affinity to the Republican party, which traditionally is symbolic of the financially successful men in the nation. It is because I am trying to climb that I tend to identify with those who have already "climbed" and reached the top. I tend to favor legislation which will make it easier for me to become wealthy.

Then, stating directly the need for wealth as a form of restitution of lost self-esteem, Simpson says: "In my eyes, I was unsuccessful when young, rose to positions of considerable distinction among youths. I think I have declined from those heights, and wealth has become my symbol of success in adulthood."

Novak's arguments are more explicit, as we saw earlier in our report of his discussion of the way in which wealth and status helped him restore the self-esteem lost in his comparatively disadvantageous economic position as a child. Yet beyond this is his struggle to find some means of asserting himself against his father, some means to show to himself and to his father that he is indeed a man. True, there is not so much evidence here of ambivalent feelings toward his parents, but there is some. His father, he says,

> . . . has always been a distant force in my life. He early represented strength, authority, and its concomitant punishments. His punishments were severe and unpredictable. His affection always has been balanced by a sharp temper. He is a vaguely religious and highly moral person. . . . He has been very consistent in his work.

Against this force, without maternal support, Novak could not successfully assert himself. As a consequence, he says, he "came to have something of an anti-aggressive trait," which he thought was "created by my father's unpredictable and severe punishments. . . . " As a result, he says,

> The capacity for conscious or strong rebellion may have been eliminated. I not only submitted to my father but came to depend upon his authoritarian manner. I adopted many of his mannerisms. An example . . . can be found in my copying his handwriting. I not only idolized my father but began to respect his severity in dealing with me. . . . I was dependent against my wishes.

The consequence of this submissive pattern has been a tendency to idolize the strong, rich, and successful men and groups wherever he found them, with, says Novak, an occasional "weak-kneed rebellion." He assumed this dependent posture while at Adams, especially with a rich and magnetic young conservative, but also as a general policy: "I do not attack groups at Adams which are strong, institutionalized, and widely accepted. I attack the unaccepted and the out-group representatives." He believes that if a group is powerful it must be good, and therefore "I associate with the prestige-powerful elements at Adams." With them he expands, becomes talkative, and draws attention to himself. Is it any wonder, therefore, that he identifies with the going order, seeks success wholly within its terms and in such a way as to impress the rich and powerful? Even his defense of capitalism takes this form: "I feel capitalism is the only proper form of economy today. . . . I feel the individual should be permitted to exercise 'conspicuous consumption' to the extent that his capabilities allow him. Only capitalism allows such freedom." Ashamed of his submission to his father, but unable to adopt an independent assertive personal style, he seeks, by his association with the rich and powerful, and by his anticipation of being rich himself, to reveal himself as a worthy individual, a real man. In Novak's case it is not so clear that he respects his father, but he does want to impress him with these achievements and to beat him at his own game, as his constant comparison of his own achievements in college with his father's college achievements indicates. By his anticipation of later success within a conservative order of rich and successful men, he wishes to prove his own worth, about which so far he is quite uncertain.

Often, then, behind the drive to be successful in business and to achieve wealth and social prestige is this ambivalence about assertiveness complicated by overassertiveness or underassertiveness against the very parent who conveys this criticism. There follows from this situation an internalization of a dominating parent's norms and the conversion of ambivalence about the self into a determination to resolve these doubts by achievement in the business world, or at least in the capitalist world, where wealth and position will prove, once and for all, that one is worthy of respect and self-esteem.

Although it is true that Simpson has some doubts about a life dedicated to the pursuit of wealth and status, he joins with the others in certain features of their political and social rationales. All three defend capitalism as a system in which able men can rise to the top (directly reflecting their own ambitions). All three have special respect for rich, high-status men, men who have "made it." All three are drawn to the Republican party because it represents and symbolizes these rich and successful men. All three mention their support of policies that favor the market system of allocating rewards according to ability as contrasted to central-governmental allocation according to need. And, as I shall elaborate in a moment, all three are somewhat anti-Semitic, regarding the Jews as something of a threat to their own striving.

Wealth and Status as Alternatives to Parental Approval. While MacGregor, Simpson, and Novak were, I believe, much interested in earning increments of self-esteem through improving their position in their parents' eyes, something else seems to be going on in the cases of Cohen and Trumbull. While Simpson said of his mother that he "turned to her for help and advice," and MacGregor's theme was one of a return to a *modus vivendi* with his father, whom he felt he resembled in many ways, and Novak says at one point he "idolized" his father, Cohen and Trumbull reveal little of that warmth or even ambivalence. Cohen "loses his appetite sitting at the same table with" his father, and Trumbull says, "I never had a friendly relation with my father." Both emphasize the criticism they had to endure from their fathers; neither mentions his mother as a softening force in this harsh, denigrative environment. Surely wealth and social status, or success of any kind, would provide a welcome alternative basis for security and self-esteem after these identity-destroying experiences.

With more or less explicit reference to this problem, in words sometimes quoted before, these men tell us of their struggle. Cohen, who feels he cannot talk about anything with his parents and goes home as little as possible, says of his respondent self, Alex:

> At present he has a particular love of money; this near obsession to be rich has been greatly intensified since attending Adams. . . . He says that he has thought about and may go to graduate school to get a Ph.D. or to law school; but he has no strong desire to do either one—the end is success in almost anything and the means do not matter very much.

But he comes back to money and repeats his "obsession to be rich and have large quantities of money."[7] Although an admired aunt and uncle are Republicans (like his parents), he discounts their influence and believes his political choice is based on the fact that "The Republican party has been described as the 'rich man's party,' and Alex, whose family is already 'financially comfortable,' considers membership in this group as part of

---

[7]The complexities of the drives that produce a striving for wealth and status, especially when they come out of the crucible of general and severe parental denigration, are reflected in some of the contents of Cohen's "obsession" with money. For example, he says, in his third-person account: "Ever since Alex can remember, he has collected something; one of his earliest childhood memories is that of collecting pieces of candy in a drawer of his mother's desk with the idea that once his collection were large enough, he would have a great feast. But his mother would always destroy the contents of the drawer before he could eat them. . . . The enjoyment or gratification seems to come from the act of collecting and possessing and has little to do with the object itself. At present, he has a particular love of money."

being rich (which he hopes to be) and part of being successful." Of course, there are other causes, but with very little conjecture one can see how this young man, called a " 'traitor' if he does not agree with his father," bereft of other sources of ego reward at home, might seize upon money and success as an alternate basis for a frail self-esteem in need of external support.

Trumbull, as we have seen before, suffered at the hands of a critical father, who, he says, "at a time when I most needed love and affection, had little to offer." On several occasions he refers to his sense of insecurity, going on to give this a political implication: "In summary, then, my Republican membership serves as a mechanism with which to combat my insecurity by proving to myself that I hold the same views as the leaders of our society and that I am therefore entitled to as high a position as they." But more than that is at stake:

> I have discovered from association with those of the "Long Island estate group" and others of considerable financial means that wealth is mainly with the Republicans, and therefore, by claiming to be a Republican, I can acquire at least one of the characteristics of the group of which I wish to be a part.

He is, in his set, surrounded by Republicans with conservative ideas, like his own, and it would take a degree of "individualism" he claims he does not have for him to go against these views. But, of course, he does not want to. Too much is at stake, including a future self-image embracing wealth and success, an image that helps to restore the self-esteem lost in childhood.

ALTERNATIVE SOURCES OF STRIVING FOR WEALTH AND STATUS

Lest it be thought that the sources of striving for wealth and status always lie in either relative economic deprivation during childhood or in some parentally inspired sense of inadequacy, one must note that others, quite attached to their parents, also seek these values. Niven's drive was much more a product of his desire to be successful like his father than of his sense of early economic deprivation, discussed earlier. He greatly admired his parents, especially his father, who worked his way up from a lowly position; yet, he says:

> Somehow, I had become an extreme daydreamer and builder of castles in Scarsdale or Bronxville par excellence. I wanted material prosperity desperately and counted this as my goal in

life. I had always dreamed that someday I would be extremely wealthy and I wanted to act as a member of the upper class.

And Gardiner, who gives an account of his parents' solicitous guardian- ship and instruction, which still left room for a certain amount of rebellion, speaks of his "affinity for the well-to-do segment of my class," and says, with reason:

> I have been fortunate to be included in the upper society bracket of Cosmopolitan City. . . . I thoroughly enjoy attending debutante parties and the like. . . . These parties are, to me, a visual representation of the wealth and power of this country. This leads me to be even more interested in preserving this coun- try to the utmost of my ability.

Thus men may seek wealth and status because they identify with their parents, because this is the way of life they know and can move into easily, because they are hedonists and want what wealth can bring, because, like Gardiner, their fiancées encourage this way of life, and for many other reasons. It is the quality of tension, the intensity of desire, the ambivalence about success, the thirst for praise, the need for self-validation that cues the careful observer to look for sources in a earlier sense of inadequacy.

Note on the Rejection of Wealth as a Value.   I said earlier that in this allegedly materialist culture there were still some reasons for rejecting the struggle to get more money. Simpson, who in the end will almost certainly try to prove his strength and assertiveness by seeking wealth, nevertheless reflects this ambivalence:

> I am beginning to develop two sets of values. On the one hand, I have a strong desire to make a great deal of money, to achieve social prestige, and to have my children have the best of everything. Yet on the other hand, I realize this is a very super- ficial set of values and the real accomplishments of life are not dependent upon wealth. I want to leave the world a better place than it was when I arrived.

Others, achievement-oriented, or currently preoccupied with their problems of acceptability and popularity, no doubt share this hesitation about a single-minded pursuit of so self-serving a value.

The case is even clearer for Dobb, the athletic son of wealth and lineage who stresses his drive to be an independent, autonomous man. At the moment of writing, at least, he was in a state of rebellion against parental pressures:

>   Though my father would like to have me go into international business and try to earn some money, I am going to and have intended for years to try to get into the Foreign Service. In this last conflict I am rebelling against the idea of the necessity of money in favor of my own idealistic ideas, which maintain that money is not the only criterion of happiness. . . . My mother also feels that money has a great deal of importance.

He makes this rather special pleading more plausible as he goes along:

>   The feeling about money is an obsession which I have had for years. When I was young I remember that I used to hate to ride in my grandmother's chauffeur-driven car. At that point I was associating with boys who have since graduated from high school and are now working. I was extremely conscious of our class differences and riding in that car to me symbolized that difference, which I did not want to emphasize.

As a consequence of these equalitarian feelings, these sentiments of guilt, and his somewhat self-conscious rebellion against his parents, Dobb is a Democrat, the only one in his family. "This," he says, "is significant because it gives me the opportunity to rebel. . . . It is a rebellion against money."

The point reflected here, the social and therefore personal ambivalence about wholly selfish striving for money and status, is important, for it is reflected in most of the men's ideologies. Perhaps it is their conventionalism and their sense that the going order, including certain protections against the worst hazards of life, that make them reject a truly dog-eat-dog ideology. But perhaps, too, it is the fact that even the most reactionary, even the most insecure, even those who need desperately to find a source of self-esteem and for whom wealth represents that source, embrace some policies of social security, pensions, welfare allowances, even, occasionally, minimal union protection. Even though, like MacGregor, they may be led by their own insecurities to justify insecurity as a principle, or, like Trumbull, may feel that any policies that threaten capitalism should be stamped out, there are personal and ideological restraints on their selfishness, on their pursuit of money for themselves.

Striving for Wealth and Status—a Source of Anti-Semitism.   All of the men striving for wealth and status, except Dobb and Gardiner, are anti-Semites. This is very rarely true of those seeking other values. Novak attributes his anti-Semitism to his desire to associate with in-groups, and hence, he says, "I reject members of the out-group in striving to enter the in-group and . . . I am suspicious of the motivations of my few Jewish friends." Niven says, "I became rather anti-Semitic in the course of my upbringing," an attitude that, in context, seems to be associated with his upward striving and his desire to be a member of the upper class. Cohen, whom one might think immune to this disease, says that since coming to Adams he "has had the desire to disassociate himself from Jews," even though "he finds himself more at ease with Jews"—a formidable problem of ambivalence. Trumbull says that out of his own "admitted feelings of inferiority and insecurity" he has become ethnocentric and believes that "Jews are personally obnoxious, but not inferior." Simpson, a rather mild-mannered young man, says, "I have borne a hostility and contempt for those who threaten my position or who may present competition to my aspirations. I have little hostility against Negroes as a group, but find that I am generally hostile to Jews, particularly those who present a threat." And MacGregor, without interpretation, says, "I cannot stand the so-called clannish traits of the Jews. It turns me against some Jews before I can get a chance to know them."

From such evidence one might gather that persons who seek to restore through wealth and status a self-esteem eroded in childhood either by a sense of competitive disadvantage or from parental denigration try to stifle competition in any way they can. Status (more than wealth) is a scarce resource, since it is built on comparative rankings. In the tense and uncertain striving for status entered upon by most of these men, a convenient, if unfair and unworthy, weapon lies at hand to reduce the competition: discrimination backed by prejudice and calumny.

Striving for Wealth and Status and Ideological Conservatism.   In the most summary terms, one could say that striving for wealth and status, for whatever reason, encourages the elaboration of an "ideology" or elaborated rationale, and that this is always conservative. This is not true about striving for earned achievement, for popularity and affection, for autonomy or dependency or other values and needs. These are neutral with respect to some vague left-right dimensions such as we have used in this book (but, of course, these other strivings shape the style and texture and assurance and imagery and inclusiveness and so forth of a belief system). But wealth and status are so clearly ideologized and politicized, there must be social and psychological forces working in this direction. Some of these may be set forth as follows:

1. Wealth and status are not really more "selfish" or "self-regarding" than popularity, autonomy, achievement, or bodily satisfactions, but religion, literature, folk culture, and popular media characters and plots often argue in effect: "It is good to be rich but bad to strive overtly for money"; "Service is more acceptable than status"; "There is more morality in poverty than in wealth"; "Pride goeth before a fall." I touched on this before, but it is relevant here because it helps to explain why the

man who acknowledges his striving for wealth and status is under some pressure to rationalize, ideologize, moralize his striving. He must answer these criticisms and make his striving "all right" to himself and to others.

2. In spite of a generalized "mood" of abundance in the group, there is probably a sense that the rules of the game in this value domain of wealth and status are "zero-sum" rules: what one man gets he takes from another. There is only so much wealth and especially status to be shared. This is not so clear with respect to, say, bodily enjoyments, or friendship, or freedom from constraint, although, if we were to study the need for power, we might find even greater moralizing, because it is even clearer in that domain that what one gets another loses. The men striving for what they call "leadership" always have in mind leadership for the good of others.

3. Wealth and status are organizable "interests"; wealth is always organized, status sometimes. As such they play a larger role in politics than the relatively unorganized values of morality, friendship, beauty. Skills, of course, often organize, as do power interests, but very often in defense of economic privileges. Organization means the development of a rationale for a collective unit, something to keep men working together, to account for joint sacrifices, to give a handle to leadership. Thus those striving for wealth and status have, ready to hand, a body of ideas to explain their efforts in public-interest terms, something less true of many other values.

4. Political parties "aggregate" interests, simplify their multiple demands, and around the world these tend to have a dominant poor-versus-rich dimension. Almost all of the Adams men (and all of the Eastport "common men" I reported upon in *Political Ideology*)[8] believe that the Republican party is for business and the Democratic party for labor. Thus not only are those striving for wealth and status caught up in party politics; they have taken a side, are partisan, and often feel impelled to defend past decisions of their adopted party, as well as to engage in old polemics. They have, by this means, adopted a history of argument. Those striving for other values are not necessarily less ideological or partisan, but they have a wider set of choices from which to select.

5. While government policy in a sense affects the distribution of all values—indeed, that is its business—this is most obviously true of power and wealth (but in the United States it is not so true of status). There are two main mechanisms for distributing wealth: the market and governmental allocation. Encroachments of the second on the first seem to threaten the success of the men who seek great wealth, especially as this may be affected by tax policy. Thus their striving takes place under conditions of

---

[8]Lane, *Political Ideology*.

"threat," and they must protect their field of endeavor from government regulation and taxation. In order to do this, they must explain why it is better for society that they be permitted to enrich themselves.

It is for reasons such as these, then, that we find the strivers for wealth and status more clearly ideological than others, and, once in this net of arguments, more clearly conservative.

14

Identity Continuity and
Identification with the Family

During their college years young men may seek and value a continued identification with the family, or they may seek above all to break relations with the family; both patterns of behavior are forms of striving that do not reflect precisely any of the needs we have been discussing.

On close examination we find that these two forms of striving are energized by composite rewards. Those who seek to maintain their identification with the family may be rewarded by associating themselves with the high status of their families, by gratifying their needs for affiliation, by help in continuing to "work through" old psychological conflicts, by clinging to enduring paternal models. There is, nevertheless, one theme that seems to be common to these various rewards: *a continuity of older and earlier efforts to develop an identity* (including both social placing and individual conflict-reducing efforts).[1] Similarly, although the effort to dissociate the self from the family has several rewards, they all embrace a kind of *autonomy*. Because both identification with the family and dissociation from the family have very important political consequences, they must be examined as energizing sources of political thought, even though they violate the neatness of the scheme laid down earlier. We shall call them "motives" instead of "needs," and see what we can learn from a textual examination of the biographies as they deal with these areas.

When De Vita reports that "my parents were always loving, warm, and permissive," and then later says, "I tried to carry the domination-submission relationship which I found in my relations with my parents into

---

[1]Perhaps some concept of the meaning of family identification may be found by contrasting it to "homelessness," as discussed in Robert E. Lane, *Political Ideology* (New York: Free Press, Macmillan, 1962), Chap. 11.

my relations with other children," we take the two statements together and are not persuaded by the first. When "Alex" Cohen says he "finds himself glorifying his parents and attributing to them the characteristics which he knows his uncle and aunt [whom he greatly respects] have," but later reports that he "rarely speaks to his father about anything of importance, dreads staying home for any length of time, and loses his appetite sitting at the same table with him," we suffer with him in his *wish to believe* and his dreadful disbelief in parental glory. Not everyone who says he loves his parents can be believed. How, then, do those who can be believed express themselves?

We take our cues from certain expressions: "understanding" is more persuasive than "love," for example. A tendency to go home rather than to stay away from home as much as possible is indicative. Emphasis on the way the family "believed in me," and evidence that parents were supportive when the son was defeated or depressed, as well as proud of the son's victories, help the case. Some casual mention of conflict and rebellion is persuasive; these matters are not, then, too dangerous to mention. Where there is evidence of tolerance of dissent, this evidence weighs heavily. In all of this, the indirect revelation of the case through accounts of specific incidents is more persuasive than bald statements of affection.

INTERPRETATIONS OF IDENTIFICATION WITH THE FAMILY

It is important that the concept of the need for identity continuity at this late but crucial period of postadolescence and early manhood be understood, for it illuminates the problem of the historical as well as individual continuity of political thought and values, and the question of the inheritance of party identification, sometimes referred to as the "Mendelian law of politics." There are eight possible interpretations of this desire for continuity of family identity which I believe are inadequate or false. The first is that this is a case of the need for *succorance,* reflected in help-seeking behavior. In an examination of comparative child-rearing practices in six cultures, succorance and self-reliance are opposed: "Given a situation in which an individual encountered difficulty, whether he asked for help or solved the problem himself would indicate the relative strength of his succorance, or, in contrast, his self-reliance."[2] Rather than encouraging dependency, the parents of the four men in our group who identified with their families gave emotional support for self-reliance, that is, the men

---

[2]Beatrice B. Whiting, ed., *Six Cultures: Studies of Child Rearing* (New York: Wiley, 1963), p. 7.

were encouraged to believe that they could overcome obstacles in their own paths, and usually they did, whether the obstacles were to better grades, or winning school elections, or solving interpersonal (girl) problems.

The second possibility, the one I originally believed would describe these cases, is that identification with the family would reflect a *need for dependence*. Sears defines dependency behavior in children as: (a) "negative attention seeking," including disruption, resistance to rules, ignoring demands—such behavior as provokes special attention by a teacher; (b) "positive attention seeking," including seeking praise, seeking to join ingroups by cooperative behavior; (c) "touching or holding," a tendency to cling to others; (d) chronically "being near" some authoritative or admired person; (e) "seeking reassurance, comfort, or consolation." Sears finds such behavior to be disruptive to the healthy maturation process for boys (but not for girls), an impediment to the development of self-reliance and later independence.[3] Ignoring the first of these items, negative attention seeking (for boys it is unrelated to the other items), one might interpret the behavior of the late adolescent who clings to the family—who needs to be near them ideologically, or who agrees with their views—as a kind of search for reassurance and a residue of early dependency behavior. I do not doubt that this is partly true in several of these cases; they do derive comfort from their basic agreement with their parental values, and although they differentiate themselves at various stages of their lives, they emphasize the satisfactions of agreement and closeness of family ties. But if the behavior is similar in some ways to that described by Sears, the inference that they are "dependent personalities" in a more general sense is false. They are notable for their qualities of leadership, even if this leadership is within more or less conventional bounds. This is the paradox: one of the family values is independent achievement: in absorbing this family value they "overcome" most of their tendencies toward passivity, acceptance of things as they are, the role of second fiddle.

Third, I do not believe they would score low in tests for the *power motive*; that is, they do not avoid mentioning "the maintenance or attainment of the control of the means of influencing a person" or of power relations between people.[4] They are conscious of it and seek actively to influence others. Their identification with their families is not a means of "passing the buck" to the family or of avoiding responsibility, nor is it a means of cloaking themselves in the power and authority of their parents. On this they are explicit. They do battle with and for their families' ideas,

---

[3] R. R. Sears, "Dependency Motivation," in M. R. Jones, ed., *Nebraska Symposium on Motivation* (Lincoln: University of Nebraska Press, 1963).

[4] See Joseph Veroff, "A Scoring Manual for the Power Motive," in John W. Atkinson, ed., *Motives in Fantasy, Action, and Society* (Princeton; Van Nostrand, 1958), p. 219.

most of which they share. In this sense they are not more fearful of the use of power than is the man who shares loyalty and beliefs with his country-men, the patriot.

Fourth, these men are not *"compliant personalities"* in Horney and Mulcahey's sense. The compliant personality "shows a marked need for affection and approval of a 'partner' on whom he can lean, an inability to stand alone, a tendency to subordinate himself, to feel weak and helpless, to feel that others are stronger, superior, more attractive . . . "[5] We have here men who have been presidents of their class, who seek to command industrial empires, who aim at professional success, who have in mind ways to change the world. In these endeavors they feel the support of their families.

Fifth, while it is true that these men, in Sullivan's terms, seek conjunc-tive relations with their families, such relations are, with one possible excep-tion, not marked by low self-esteem. Hence they do not develop the *pas-sive dependency* that Sullivan describes as follows: "What happens is that a person who has a low opinion of himself develops a relatively suave way of manifesting, if not inferiority to significant people, at least such blatant hints of inferiority that he becomes more or less an object of philan-thropic concern on the part of the other person." Such persons, says Sulli-van, are likely to fall within the orbit of domineering others for whom "domineering and vassalizing their fellows is their source of security."[6] Among the twenty-four men we have under scrutiny, there are those who develop such a vassalized relationship with a parent (Trueblood) or a fellow student at Adams College (Novak), but these are not the ones who make a point of their identification with their families.

Sixth, these men are not *submissives* in the sense that they have no influence in the home and believe it is appropriate for them to have no in-fluence. Submissives of this variety tend to be apolitical, and this is not true of these men.[7] Nor, seventh, is it true that they share in the syndrome described in *The Authoritarian Personality, "authoritarian submission*: submissive, uncritical attitudes toward idealized moral authorities of the in-group."[8] While their tendencies to "glorify their parents," a feature of authoritarianism, does alert one to this possibility, their glorification is not followed by "a note of complaint or self-pity," as is the case with the authoritarians,[9] and they are not uncritical of moral authorities (with the

---

[5]Patrick Mullahy, *Oedipus, Myth and Complex* (New York: Grove Press, 1955), p. 232.

[6]Henry Stack Sullivan, *The Interpersonal Theory of Psychiatry* (New York: Norton, 1953), pp. 351-52.

[7]Robert E. Lane, "La Maturation politique de l'adolecent aux Etats-Unis et en Alle-magne," *Revue Francaise de Sociologie,* Numéro Spécial, 1966, pp. 598-618.

[8]T. W. Adorno, Else Frenkel-Brunswik, Daniel J. Levinson, and R. Nevitt Sanford, *The Authoritarian Personality* (New York: Harper, 1950), p. 228.

[9]Nevitt Sanford, "The Approach of the Authoritarian Personality," in J. L. McCary, ed., *Psychology of Personality* (New York: Grove Press, 1956), p. 278.

possible exception of Gardiner, who views the capitalist industrial establishment uncritically).

Finally, their acceptance of their parents' views might suggest that they were unusually *persuasible,* in the sense that Janis and others have used the term. Persuasibility, in these studies, is measured by a tendency to change one's views according to the "authoritativeness" of a statement, and is related (as in Sullivan's concept of the passive dependent personality), to low self-esteem.[10] The feelings of inadequacy and the social inhibitions that Janis and Field employed to measure low self-esteem seem to exist in one of the four, Lamb, but not in the others, and Lamb is tenacious about his agnosticism in the face of his parents' modest piety and his Democraticness in the face of their Republicanism. He absorbed their basic values, but was not persuaded on two important interpretations of these values. The other three escape entirely from this measure.

Self-conscious identification with family norms, ideas, and values, and open gratification from the emotional sustenance of the family, then, need not imply dependency, excessive needs for succorance, persuasibility, submissiveness, or estrangement from the uses of power. If this were not true, we would need to look to the family rebels, those who seek drastic independence from their families, for social leadership, a situation implying some threat to social continuity and stability. What is important here, however, is that the basic values of the family are usually employed as a premise for social criticism and change or, in one case, defense and leadership in the system. A man can feel that where he has been is good but not perfect, that his nuclear family and all it stands for is "right" but not enough, that the family is a platform and not a cage, that whatever there is in him that is his family's is acceptable, at least in substantial part, but that he is, nevertheless, a separate individual. Thus the political thought and behavior of such a person may at the same time cement family bonds, inviting emotional support from the family members, *and* serve as guides to reality, provide him with narcissistic supplies, give status and compensate him for his inadequacies, serve as vehicles of his aggression, and help him to be popular among his peers.

THE FORMULA FOR POLITICAL IDENTIFICATION

If identification with the family does not represent dependency and submissiveness, but rather is a source of one kind of strength in dealing with the world, we should examine how this comes about and then look at the difference it makes in political expression. Family identification helps

10 See Carl Hovland and Irving L. Janis, eds., *Personality and Persuasibility* (New Haven: Yale University Press, 1959).

clarify a person's social identity (social placement and sense of group membership) and his political and ideological identity (how he thinks of himself in these contexts). It seems to me that there are seven features of this identification process that are worth attention.

Communication. The members of the four families at issue here *talk* to one another. The process starts early with confessions of misbehavior, proceeds through frankness about sex and religion, and moves on to politics, though not necessarily in that order.

On political matters, McDonald says:

> Both my parents are politically verbal and in the past have been quite active in various community organizations. . . . Thus the intellectual growth in the family has been centered about the social sciences. In this work they have come to certain conclusions about the nature of man and social and political institutions, conclusions which they have directed me toward.

More explicitly on topical issues and party preferences, the conversations have opened the way to mutual exploration, both liberal and conservative in tone. While McDonald, who comes from a professional family, says his parents "have seen in the Democratic party the political vehicle for this [humane] philosophy, as also I have," Gardiner, from a wealthy middle-western family, says, "The first thing I can remember of a political nature was hearing my father condemn President Roosevelt and his New Deal legislation." Over the years, says Gardiner, his father "explained to me the basic differences between the 'New Deal' and the laissez-faire system, and pointed out the advantages of the latter." For the most part, these were dinner-table conversations, and while Gardiner was first only a listener, he gradually came to "interject my own views to a greater extent," sometimes challenging his father.

From other studies we know that families in which political conversation takes place are more likely to transmit a political inheritance to the children and less likely to encourage political rebellion.[11] Moreover, in Nazi Germany, children who were allowed to speak up were not likely to become Nazis, perhaps reflecting parental as opposed to the then dominant societal values.[12] A "ventilated" opinion is an interpersonally tested opinion; without conversation, such political ideas as a person may have

---

[11] Russell Middleton and Snell Putney, "Political Expression of Adolescent Rebellion," *American Journal of Sociology,* 68 (1954), pp. 527-35.

[12] David M. Levy, "Anti-Nazis: Criteria of Differentiation," in Alfred H. Stanton and Stewart E. Perry, eds., *Personality and Political Crisis* (Glencoe, Ill.: Free Press, 1951), p. 155.

are likely to be unrealistic, "sour" or inhumane, with great personal reference.[13] A common ingredient among the family identifiers was their general practice of talking to other family members about intimate things and also about political things, a practice that made their political views more realistic and more resistant to outside pressures than the views of the family disidentifiers, with less self-reference and more social reference.

Openness to Challenge; Tolerance toward Difference. It seems that in families, as in society generally, tolerance of small differences and open discussion prevent larger differences and rebellion. When one hears that Gardiner's father's "criticism of Roosevelt and his policies went on for many years before I ever came to think for myself," the possibility for Gardiner ever to arrive at an opinion of his own seems dim. Not so. Gardiner says, "When, at the age of approximately eleven or twelve, I began listening to news broadcasts and at least glance at the newspapers, the discussions took on a new light." He began to speak up and "occasionally to bring up a point which was not so easy for my father to explain. This gave me new confidence in myself, and encouraged me to try to find out more things on my own." Later he learns from his teachers about a point of view different from that of his parents, and, he says, "I found that on occasion I was more informed about a situation than was my father. This encouraged me even further in my independent thought and reading."

Similarly, Ransome deviates from his parents' Republicanism and reports that "when I was young I was always 'for' F.D.R.," although he is now, like them, a liberal Republican. McDonald was a socialist for a time, while his parents are Democrats. Lamb is a Democrat, while his parents are Republicans. Yet each of these men, like Gardiner, stresses his basic agreement with his parents' political values, and now, in college, only Lamb differs even in party identification from his parents. In spite of this party difference, he makes a point of saying, "My parents are conservative in their ways and this has had a great influence on me," giving him, he says, "the conservative side to my personality."

The sense of choice, the feeling that an opinion that coincides with family opinion is one's own, independently arrived at, is an important ingredient in this formula we are stating. The process is complex, but embraces much that is known about opinion formation. In the first place, young men of college age who feel that their parents were either too strict or too lenient (indifferent?) are more likely than others to rebel and choose a party different from their parents'—in both directions.[14] Thus,

---

13Lane, *Political Ideology,* pp. 99-104.
14Eleanor E. Maccoby, R. E. Matthews, and A. S. Morton, "Youth and Political Change," *Public Opinion Quarterly,* 18 (1954), pp. 23-39.

parental expression of a political philosophy combined with tolerance of dissent seems best to fit the model of direction and concern, on the one hand, and permissiveness and latitude for exploration, on the other. At the same time, the fact that the children were encouraged to state their ideas brings into play two other processes. One of them is the "saying is believing" phenomenon, discovered in role-playing experiments, especially the finding that a position a person is asked to take for purposes of debate is particularly self-convincing if he has had to develop the argument himself, rather than merely to espouse an argument already formulated for him.[15] These men believed that they developed their own arguments. Further, it appears that a "fact" is more likely to be accepted as such if an individual discovers it for himself; other people's research is less persuasive.[16] Lewin found that communications were much more persuasive if they were argued through with the groups whose ideas were to be changed and difficulties were rehearsed aloud, compared to situations where the audiences were merely exposed to arguments made by others.[17] Finally, and most generally, it is plausible that ideas and standards and behavior are more enduring if they are "internalized" as contrasted to merely indoctrinated and enforced. After the preverbal stage, for a person to internalize a point of view so that it becomes, so to speak, a part of the character structure (as values are), imitation is rarely enough; it must be adopted as part of an identity-formation process that includes a sense that this is "mine," achieved through effort and not merely absorbed through convention.[18]

Political Activity (Commitment). "In the summer of 1952," says Ransome, "I came home to find my mother working at Eisenhower convention headquarters in Chicago. It looked exciting, and so upon request she got me a job and I became happily involved in the work of the Young Republicans." In the same year Gardiner, at the age of fifteen,

> . . . was working passing out literature at a polling place in Midwestern City. This event ties in closely with my dislike for the action of the Democratic party in Midwestern City, for it concerns the action of this party's "machine." As I was passing out my literature a car stopped and two men got out and told me to "beat it." I rose upon my toes and refused. At this point one of

---

[15]See Carl I. Hovland, Irving L. Janis, and Harold H. Kelley, *Communication and Persuasion* (New Haven: Yale University Press, 1953), pp. 215-40.

[16]See "Problems of Re-Education," ed. Kurt Lewin and Paul Grabbe, special issue of the *Journal of Social Issues* (August, 1945), especially pp. 33-37.

[17]Kurt Lewin, "Studies in Group Decision," in Dorwin Cartwright and Alvin Zander, eds., *Group Dynamics, Research and Theory* (Evanston, Ill.: Row, Peterson, 1953), pp. 286-301.

[18]See Ernest R. Hilgard, *Theories of Learning* (New York: Appleton-Century-Crofts, 1956).

them swung and managed to break my nose. This was the final blow, so to speak, in my estrangement from and lack of respect for the Democratic party.

McDonald remembers accompanying his professional father in a study of the poor farmers and miners of the southeast. "Thus," he says, "even at this early age there was an intellectual and *experiential* reinforcement" of his commitment to egalitarian views. (Nevertheless, he declined to act them out by handing out socialist leaflets in college.) Lamb's political experience is limited to colorless high school politics (in which he became head of the student council), but he works with a maintenance crew in the summer and makes a point of being one of the guys and has "gotten along well with them and enjoy[s] visiting them during vacations." These experiences, he believes, help to reinforce his equalitarian and humanistic ideas about race and religion and social class.

Action of this kind, supported in all cases by parental endorsement and in many cases by parental invitation, is a kind of commitment; it costs time and energy and implies a rationale. One must have reasons for these choices of action to account for what one gives up by acting in this way. At this point, then, the need to minimize the attractiveness of alternative courses of action, to give good reasons for sacrifice, to reduce any feelings of ambivalence one has had, comes into play. These forces of dissonance reduction follow from any course of commitment.[19] When the commitment takes place with family blessing or under family aegis, as in these cases, the dissonance reduction may be said to reinforce the family political values that are the premises of such action.

Developing a Family Culture. To identify with the family implies that among competing group loyalties, the family group takes precedence, and among competing beliefs and values, those of the family tend to dominate. Without exception these men trace their beliefs more to their families than to college reading, friendships, or anything else.[20] One reason for this, I believe, is the development in each of these families of a sense that there is a family way of doing things, a family point of view, a specialness about this family. And a condition of this development, of course, is harmony between the parents. Ransome's father was a Republican lawyer with political connections, while his mother worked at Eisenhower headquarters; he always mentions them in the plural when he reports conversations and advice and support. Gardiner too always speaks of his parents

---

[19]See J. W. Brehm and A. R. Cohn, *Explorations in Cognitive Dissonance* (New York: Wiley, 1962); and Leon Festinger, H. W. Riecken, and S. Schacter, *When Prophecy Fails* (Minneapolis: University of Minnesota Press, 1956).

[20]For a comparable analysis of students in a girls' college, see T. M. Newcomb, *Personality and Social Change* (New York: Dryden, 1943).

together, and reports that his mother's social and political philosophy, "though nowhere near so profound as my father's, followed the same lines." McDonald, as we have noted, says, *Both* my parents are politically verbal . . . *they* are *both* professionals. . . . *They* have come to certain conclusions about the nature of man. . . . This is *their* basic philosophy. . . . *They* have seen in the Democratic party the political vehicle of this philosophy." [My emphasis.] And Lamb constantly refers to what his parents believe, differentiating between them only on one occasion, when he mentions the special harmonizing effect of his father's sense of humor.

If parental agreement and a common philosophy are important, so is the sense of the specialness of the family. Gardiner stresses this as a matter of status and importance: when his family bought a large farm, "we became, as a result of this farm, the recognized leaders of the neighborhood." Meanwhile, back in the city, "I have been fortunate to be included in the upper society bracket of Midwestern City." He completely accepts this; more than that, he defends it and the system that supports it. Through his identification with his family and all it stands for, he takes on the views of the executive committee of the ruling class.

McDonald speaks of the family philosophy and the family's intellectual growth. Ransome, in speaking of the closeness of his family, says it is "one that I would surmise from conversations with my friends is quite out of the ordinary." The family philosophy is one of hard work, reward for industry and skill, consideration for the unfortunate, and support of the going American system. As we shall see, he identifies with his father, and finds that this gives him a "philosophy of how to attain" success. Lamb imbibes his special mixture of moralism, liberalism, and conservatism from the special philosophy of his parents. "I feel that much of my perfectionism has come about as an influence from my parents, who are themselves perfectionists." This is true also of his "respect for the individual and his right of free choice" and the conservative way of doing things. Like all inherited culture, much of this training is unspoken. Lamb says, "My father and I have never had what I guess would be called long man-to-man philosophical talks, but there is such a basic similarity and agreement between us which we both realize that problems do not have to be thrashed out." And again the hard-work theme: "My parents apparently set such an influential example that this [instruction in the value of work] was not necessary because I knew the importance of working."

In these several ways, the men reveal the presence of a strong, harmonious, and usually moralized family culture that in most cases is regarded as distinctive, at least in emphasis. For the group reference to be meaningful, it must be instructive, and in these cases it is instructive, for there is a content and a code to which reference can be made. From what we know of the resistance to change of interpersonally reinforced cultures, of the problems of assimilation of groups who live in ghettos, of the tendencies of like to seek like in marriage, of the interlocking and mutually reinforcing nature of culture items (belief systems), of the enduring nature of codes and values laid down early more by induction than by instruction, especially when these have roots in preverbal learning— from all these things we would expect the ideas of college students who emphasize their agreements with their families to comprise a stable philosophy that will alter little.

Yet, as with the young radicals that Keniston interviewed, one might find that the values espoused in the family culture led to variations in implementation.[21] Indeed, some youths might choose to carry out these values through explicit policies that turn out to be relevant for the new generation but which were never conceived in the philosophies of the parents who established the premises on which they rest. One cannot rule out espousal of changes latent within the value framework of the parental philosophy.

The Father as a Model. All of these four men admire their fathers.[22] The son of a lawyer wants to be a lawyer, the son of a businessman wants to be a businessman, the son of an academic family wants to teach—the identification is occupational as well as ideological, behavioral, stylistic. More than that, it seems to shape political strategies and beliefs. In an earlier study I found that those adult sons whose relations with their fathers were severely damaged in youth tended not only to be tense about authority, but to be unable to criticize political authority directly, although indirectly they might show their suspicion and hostility. Further, they were unable to conceive of a benign and tolerant authority; rather they spoke in terms of respect and power. They did not believe that "we were moving closer to an ideal society," although those without such damaged relations tended at that time (1957) to believe we were moving in that direc-

---

[21]Kenneth Keniston, *Young Radicals, Notes on Committed Youth* (New York: Harcourt, Brace & World, 1968).

[22]Jennings and Langton find that when parents' political identifications conflict, the mother tends to have more influence than the father over their children's choice, and further, that even when they agree but one is more interested in politics than the other, the mother's superior interest has more effect on children's choice than the father's superior interest. Under these circumstances one might wonder about the selection of the father for special treatment in this discussion. Our findings, however, are not in conflict with those of Jennings and Langton. We all might agree that in general the father is more interested in politics than the mother, and, as our evidence shows, when the mother dominates or challenges her husband she also dominates her sons. Beyond this my cases show that if such a woman spoils her son's identification with his father, she has done much to shape and perhaps sour his general social outlook. See M. Kent Jennings and Kenneth P. Langton, "Mothers versus Fathers: The Formation of Political Orientations among Pre-Adults," *Journal of Politics,* forthcoming.

tion.[23] Other research suggests that good relations with a tolerant father encourages a capacity for independent social criticism and gives a basis for independent political action.[24]

Thus, on the basis of their identification with their fathers, these men might be expected to take a hopeful view of society, offer criticism without rejection, believe in the possibility of benign authority, and engage in political action. These things they do.

Emotional Support: the Creation of Self-Confidence.   Much of what we have said so far would lead one to wonder how, if ever, the umbilical cord would be severed. The answer lies in the paradox of good socialization: a supportive family creates the means for *self*-support. Ransome, Gardiner, and McDonald are clearly self-confident young men; Lamb is an achiever with grave self-doubts who nevertheless believes in his capacity to master and control events and forge for himself a successful career. Not in task achievement, but only in getting along with others does he doubt himself. To show how these families give their sons the strength to strive and the belief that they will overcome obstacles, only a few glimpses into the early years are necessary. Ransome, an only child, says with humor and pathos:

> Like Gabriel Marcel, "my illnesses, my successes and failures at school were given an absurd importance." But more important than the mere attention for my personality formation was the very great love given me by both my parents. I can remember once describing this love in a bad prep school theme as two great spotlights shining on me. But the love was (and is) of a much warmer kind than spotlights, and infinitely more vast.

He then goes on to explain the reassurance he received in the crises of his life, the confidence his parents showed when he confronted obstacles, and their guidance when he needed it. "I have always had the feeling," he says, "that my parents would support me in whatever situation, and though they guide me, they always value my judgment and decisions too." He strives; he overcomes obstacles; he thinks the social system ought to reward people who strive and succeed; he believes the capitalist system does this.

Gardiner finds similar support for his waxing ego. His father makes a point of treating all of his associates as equals, even though he seems, in his son's eyes, to be financially more successful and better educated. More important, he allows his son to "win" political arguments, at least to such

---

23Robert E. Lane, "Fathers and Sons: Foundations of Political Belief," *American Sociological Review,* 24 (1959), pp. 502-11.

24Middleton and Putney, "Political Expression of Adolescent Rebellion"; Levy, "Anti-Nazis."

a degree that the son is encouraged to challenge him. As a consequence his son says, "My admiration never became fear; neither did it cause me to revolt from any feeling of frustration."

McDonald, an only child in his home of adoption, reports his "favored position" in the family, and the help his parents gave him through their love to "rationalize and intellectualize the anxieties that had been present previous" to his adoption. Indeed, he associates the welfare state, or even socialism, with his "long striving for social security and the warm loving relationship of his parents." Similarly, Lamb, the recipient of "a great deal of love and understanding," finds his parents' eagerness to help him "relax" and "mellow" a source of support in his striving for success and demand for high standards in all things.

What these men share, then, is the emotional support for ambition. From the beginning they have been encouraged to believe two things: first, temporary failure is not the end, hence purposive action is not too dangerous to undertake, for the love of the family is not wholly conditional on success; and second, each has within him the means to succeed. With this kind of support, they have overcome obstacles in the race of life (including the admissions hurdle for Adams College), and these experiences of success have reinforced their own beliefs in themselves, giving them a sense of personal efficacy. When their attention is turned to politics (and with their family backgrounds this is likely: Ransome's mother worked for Ike, Gardiner's grandfather was a politician, McDonald's parents were active in community organizations), they also have a sense of political efficacy, that quality which studies of American and European electorates reveal to be a condition for political activity. [25]

Beyond this, even in a group generally believing in the dominance of man over nature, there is a special sense that events yield to effort: hence they are controllable, hence the world is not running down or need not, hence either government can solve problems or, if that is the wrong instrument, industry and "social forces" under the control of men can do what must be done. I have argued elsewhere [26] that the belief that men are dominant over nature (for modern men nature = society) flows from personal experiences of self-control and mastery over situational forces, that is, from ego strength. Here, conservative, liberal, and "radical," each in his own way, reveal this fundamental premise of political thought and action.

The Non-Phasing Out of the Family. What originally led me to suspect that these expressions of identification with the family would, on

[25]See Gabriel A. Almond and Sidney Verba, *The Civic Culture* (Princeton: Princeton University Press, 1963), pp. 180-257.
[26]*Political Ideology,* pp. 94-97, 123-27.

inspection, reveal a pattern of dependency, succorance needs, and submissiveness, was the young men's failure to cut the cord at the "appropriate" time. Now I see that this is not a necessary condition for political action and for political thinking of an increasingly independent nature. My confusion on this point is grounded in three errors.

First, the idea that independence and self-reliance require a severance of family ties is culture-bound, and even within the American culture it is myopic. The closely-knit but extended family (something Tocqueville "missed" in America) was the vehicle of politics in ancient Rome, and the same pattern has prevailed in all aristocratic societies. One has only to think of the great English political families, the Churchills, the Chamberlains, the Pitts, the Walpoles. Nor is this true only of aristocratic societies: America has its Roosevelts, Kennedys, Rockefellers, and Stevensons.

Second, the idea that there is such a thing as self-reliance devoid of group reference and the anchoring of opinion in *some* association with others is a part of the mythology of American "individualism" which we now know to be false. Without wholly accepting the "other-directedness" hypothesis of American character, one can accept the idea that few people, if any, make up their minds on matters outside their immediate experience without some kind of subliminal or explicit group reference.[27] It is not necessarily more "independent" to employ peer-group references than family references for this anchoring and validation process.

Third, there is some confusion on the meaning of identification with the family which Keniston has helped us to clarify. The young radicals he interviewed were leaders of that process of critical agitation against American foreign policy which was known as the "Viet Nam Summer," and came from well-educated, upper-middle-class, and liberal homes. They were not, in their own minds, dissociating themselves from parental values; rather they were implementing them with policies that seemed to them a closer approximation of what was implied by the values held at home. Furthermore, they were doing this while remaining loyal to their parents in substantial part, and asking for and receiving parental "understanding" of what they were doing. Keniston further points out that for the most part they had already been through their adolescent "identity crises"; that is, they had come to terms with their own personalities, they did not have major sexual problems still to work through, they did not doubt their own capacities. Thus it was fully possible for them to seek an identity continuity that embraced both their sense of being a separate but loved and loving part of their family and political independence or radicalism.[28] It so

---

27Hovland, Janis, and Kelley, *Communication and Persuasion,* pp. 134-73.
28Keniston, *Young Radicals.*

happens that none of the four men here examined have such radical views; they are older (historically earlier) by ten years. But, like Keniston's young radicals, they have the sense that if they deviate from any particular "family line" they do not forfeit emotional support from their families.

FAMILY IDENTIFICATION AND POLITICAL INFERENCE

The biographies have permitted us to see something of the process of identification; now we shall see how they illuminate the ways in which family identification affects political beliefs. For these men, inferences regarding strategies of belief and preferable political postures flow from the "premises" of their family identification. They flow, that is, in some loosely logical sequences where some of the premises are implicit and where some of the inferences rest on the son's own special concepts of cause and effect, or at least entailment.

Ransome.   Ransome had a "close family relationship" and felt that his family "would always value my judgment," which produced in him "a feeling of confidence and worth and a great desire never to betray the value my parents placed upon me." His "belief that I could attain a measure of success . . . led me to enjoy competition and to place value on it." Moreover, his father was a model for him in many ways, not least in providing a model of hard work and a philosophy to support it. As a consequence, Ransome, like his father, believes in a social philosophy of competition, hard work, acceptance of risk, reward for industry and skill—in short, the popular version of the capitalist system:

> Because capitalism is founded on competition and attempts to give a reward proportionate to industry and ability, this seemed to me to be a fair and beneficial system. The value of work had been shown to me at home and it was experienced in prep school, hence it seemed proper that greater work should produce a greater reward. Socialism, on the other hand, became repugnant, as I could not see the logic in depriving the most able and hardest workers of greater rewards for the sake of equality. . . . A man who wishes to work and believes that his work will be productive, i.e., is confident that his work will bring a measure of success, will wish to compete with others in order to amass as much property as he can and set himself apart from other people.

Ransome is not a Neanderthal man; he "came to realize that a pure competitive system was impossible and probably not even desirable. . . . Government must guarantee equality of opportunity, and social security, and nonmonopolization of competition, etc. etc." and above all he places his faith in good education for everyone. These are not mere details; they reflect a basic humanity that goes along with his desire for competition (a theme that seems a little shrill here and there, especially since this is a lad who fears bodily hurt very much indeed). Psychological sequences are hard to establish because much is latent, interaction and feedback are almost instantaneous, and rationalization confuses the order, since reasons are often discovered after the commitment is made. But something like the following process of "deduction" may have taken place:

My parents believe in me.

Therefore: I believe in myself. I can compete successfully.

Since a competitive capitalist system sets terms favorable to me, it is a system in which I can win.

Therefore: I believe in a competitive capitalist system.

These beliefs about his own competitive skill and capacity for hard work are tried by a situation in which he is challenged by low grades, assures himself that he can make it, buckles down and by great effort pulls up his Latin grades so that he enjoys some recognition. His belief in himself "pays off," is reinforced; a segment of a benign cycle is completed.

My parents' belief in me is both (a) fundamental and irrevocable, and (b) susceptible to marginal change.

I value my parents' good opinion; on this I have built my world; it is the axiom from which other values must follow.

Successful living (following parental codes somewhat loosely interpreted), coping with challenges to "success" (a distracting girl, poor grades), and overcoming them reinforce my parents' belief in me.

The moderate capitalist system offers conditions wherein I can earn such success, preserving my parents' good opinion.

Therefore: I believe in a moderate capitalist system.

This sequence, then, provides Ransome with an incentive to believe in a system that will permit him to go on and receive incremental rewards vital to him, increments of parental esteem and approval. But there is a further route to the same end:

My parents believe in a moderate capitalist system.

"Independent" agreement is rewarded by increments of parental approval.

I will agree with my parents' social outlook in order to gain their approval.

Therefore: I believe in a moderate capitalist system.

Where earlier Ransome had approved of competitive capitalism because it promised him future gains, here he adopts this belief because of present gains. But yet another route to this end is available: identification with the paternal career and imitation of a model:

My father is an admired model of behavior and belief and character.

My father believes in moderate competitive capitalism.

By imitating my father, I approximate his virtues, his strength; I gain guidance in difficult choices, satisfy security needs.

Therefore: I believe in a moderate capitalist system.

Identification is served by many motives, like so many auxiliary engines giving motive power to a train: the belief in the self in a given social order, the belief that this social order provides the conditions for future parental approval, the agreement with parents now for current approval, the imitation of an admired father. And here, at least, working in harness, these auxiliary motive powers move Ransome to believe in what he thinks of as the competitive capitalist system. No wonder he finds that the society is basically just (it promises to reward him for effort), that its rationale is reasonable (it meshes with his "own," that is, the one he is rewarded for embracing by increments of parental support), and that he and his family can "work" the system, for they are working it with some success.

Gardiner.   One might reproduce for Gardiner much of the paths of thought and inference that lead Ransome to identify with the capitalist system, the status quo. Gardiner too has self-confidence, which has been encouraged by patient parents who permitted him to make his own decisions (on choice of school, summer work, etc.) and to differ with them even to the point of winning arguments. This self-confidence permits him to believe that in competitive situations, he will win. He gains credits at home by his basic agreement with parental values; he identifies with a father who is successful in a capitalist world. But still his account of himself spotlights two different paths of reinforcement, two ways in which continuity of his family identity reinforces his identification with the ongoing society.

The first of these is his selective reinforcement in what he "chooses" to see and hear, and especially his selective association with persons like himself, ensuring peer-group support for his views. In this analysis of one route to societal identification, we may start again with the all-important self-esteem, the sense of the rightness of the self:

> With the help of my family, I have come to believe in myself and in the rightness of my own values and preferences.

> Although I get along with "all kinds of people," I prefer the company of like-minded associates.

> What I see and hear from others and in the media of communication validates my sense of the rightness of my ideas; my ideas "work" for me; they help me interpret the world the way I like to see it.

> I have confidence in my values and beliefs, which leads me to implement them in action; I am committed.

> Therefore: I am a Republican, a "capitalist," a moderate conservative.

Curiously, while Gardiner stresses how he learned "the all-important lesson of how to get along with others, no matter what they may be like," he is quick to mark status and ethnic differences, and chooses his friends among those with backgrounds similar to his own. In contrast, Ransome hardly notices the "differences" in status or background of others, and therefore does not have to limit his association with others who differ to merely "getting along" with them; he may or may not make friends with them, according to whether he likes them or not. More often than not, he likes them.

But Gardiner's most important pathway to identification is the status his family membership gives him. As we have seen, he is acutely aware of this. "The economic situation is simple to explain," he reports, "for it is disposed of in saying that I have always had all that I could possibly want and more." His parents' friends were, compared to them, "of inferior standing both socially and economically"; in the area where his family purchased a large farm, "the farm served as a visual representation of the superiority of my family—at least economically," and his family "became the recognized leaders of the neighborhood." In the religiously mixed school he attends he finds that "the Christian group was much more like myself in habits and interests than was the Jewish." His rich cousin, an industrial tycoon, is "the personification of the things that make America great," and has taken the time to "be extremely kind and friendly" to Gardiner. His girl's father, a Republican candidate for governor in his state, was a kind of patron of young Gardiner. No wonder he can say, "I have been fortunate to be included in the upper society brackets of Midwestern City." The flow of benefits from this status are enormously reinforcing for his chosen political position, that of a "progressive Republican" dedicated to "maintain what is good from the past, and improved by additions." (He says "additions"; Ransome, with a similar view, says "changes.")

In this perspective, then, a set of belief pathways that lead from identification with the family through a set of reinforcements dealing with status and wealth can easily be discerned.

> Parental support and encouragement have led me to adopt the family ideology and model, and to accept my family's status and the value placed on status.

> I accept the status and status values. From them I receive a flow of benefits: ascriptive leadership, deference, indulgences, power.

> These benefits serve to validate my parental codes and values, for they prove to pay off.

> Paying off in the present, these values become the basis of my future calculations, the bases for political argument and rationalization.

> Therefore: I am a Republican, a capitalist, a "moderate" conservative.

But, alternatively, one might argue that a family tradition is likely to persist unless there is an opposing force; that is, the strength of the case could rest on some social analogy to inertia and momentum. The kinds of opposing forces that might alter the force of attitudinal inertia would be some inner conflicts, rebellion against paternal authority, an alternative theme from a close family member. Failing this, it is not necessary to suggest that Gardiner is working for parental approval, although he treasures this very much. Rather he is tasting and enjoying the meal that his family sets before him. Where so many benefits flow from a conservative ideology, to say that he *needs* family nurturance is like saying that the diner at Maxim's needs sustenance.

McDonald. McDonald links his identification with his family to his sets of beliefs by yet another set of processes, all of which tend to restrain his tendencies toward rebellion, separation from the social norms, and disaffiliation with his more conventional friends. Here the central theme is this: *Society and government are like the family; their rewards and punishments are based on the same distributive principles that are employed in the family; to be rewarding social behavior must follow the behavioral pattern set down in the family.* Although these ideas are generally unvoiced, sometimes McDonald is explicit, as when he says: "I see in the Democratic party an expression of parental love which is demanding yet permissive." The pattern is seen in three tensions, each of which requires of him some constraint, lest he lose something he has learned to prize: (1) power and authority versus his feelings of aggression and rebellion, (2) affiliation and love versus his feelings of hostility and withdrawal, and (3) structure (rigidity) and security versus his desire for autonomy and freedom. He identifies the authority, love, and structure of the family with the authority, love, and structure of the more general society. In interpreting his views we should keep in mind that he lived for a year with his natural mother, a period of security (he says), then was in a foster home for a few years, a period of anxiety and repressed hostility, and finally, for the past sixteen years, he has lived with the professional couple who adopted him, a period of growing security and healthy development. (He has received therapy and, it seems, has been informed of his earlier years by his psychologically-oriented parents.)

Power and Authority versus Rebellion and Aggression. McDonald says he first challenged authority in the process of toilet training by his foster parents, who he feels were excessively insistent on proper performance. The situation in the home of adoption was much better, for here he met a more understanding set of parents, and he came to identify almost completely with this family; it was, indeed, *his* family. He likes his father, who took him on long trips, but there is still the element of rebellion and challenge to authority. In his biography he tends at first to play down his rebellious feelings: "There has been the normal amount of childish rebellion but this disappeared as I learned that this type of behavior possessed no value in itself." But this understates the case:

> Up to the age of six I had bed-wetting dreams whose content consisted of direct disobeying of the parents' wishes about control of the bodily functions. This was a period of anxiety eventually cured by therapeutic work. At other times in my life I responded to what I thought was extreme family authority by threatening to run away from home. At one point I almost carried through with this threat, with the cooperation of a schoolmate who had the same idea. This happened at a particularly crucial time of my life, namely adolescence, when authority figures are undergoing a transferral from parents to peer groups. As soon as I was able to repress this form of behavior I would be assured of a place in the family.

McDonald sees a reflection in his social philosophy of his experience in learning how to come to terms with authority and power within the family. Clearly authority and power bother him, yet he has experienced the controls of beneficent power, a paternal power he comes to accept and with which he identifies. As a consequence, he says, "I do not find myself expressing hatred or distrust of generalized authority figures, but I accept the status of authority in helping the society in directing itself. But despite the feeling of security I feel in my personal situation, the events of the past still haunt my mind." In a conservative family, no doubt, these haunting problems of authority and power would center on the power of government, but in a liberal-to-radical family it is the power of "big business" that threatens, for "a generalized concept of the authority of big business was formed at an early age. . . . Business enjoyed too much power and in this sense was a 'bad' authority figure." Yet the constraints on rebellion are at work, as well as the balancing views of intellectual parents, for "big business was not hated as such, just as authority was not hated as such; mainly because I made a proper adjustment to the authority of my parents. In this way a rationale could be formed which was liberal and leftist evolutionary, but not destructive."

Speaking more generally of society, McDonald sees within himself the extension of his family attitudes toward authority and regulation:

> Within society there are norms and rules which should be obeyed, but the society does allow variations of behavior as long as they are not dangerous. Over the years I have been able to take advantage of this laxness; I have patterned my behavior in order to gain the love and acceptance of my peers and superiors, but I have rebelled at what I thought was overbearing authority.

And the same thing is true of the Democratic party, for, he says:

> The Democratic party is a heterogeneous party which allows varied points of view and behavioral differences, while most parties to the left demand too much rigidity and formalism. This is ill suited to my situation. . . . The Democratic party, while satisfying my basic philosophy, is not a strict hierarchical structure, making it a relatively easier task for me to identify with this party.

Thus, in a brief paradigm of McDonald's pattern of inference:

Society rewards and punishes like the family; the behavior and attitudes which are rewarding in the family are properly and naturally transferred to social behavior and attitudes.

Control of aggressive and rebellious feelings and more or less compliant behavior toward paternal (good) authority is rewarding; it produces a reinstatement of love and acceptability.

Generalized social rules and norms are desirable, legitimate, not too constrictive, hence I accept them and rebellion is unwarranted.

Big business is a bad authority and hence criticism and challenge of it are not dangerous; socialist dogmatic authority is too constrictive, hence unacceptable (yet "something I intellectually need").

The Democratic party allows latitude for deviance, hence is acceptable and rewarding.

Therefore: I follow social rules and norms.
I am against the power of big business.
I am not a socialist.
I am a Democrat.

Affiliation and Warm Personal Relations; Love versus a Desire to Withdraw, Criticize, Be Deviant.   Much of the tension between the need for affiliation and the desire to deviate from the conventional social norms is implied in the discussion of authority. Nevertheless, the differences are important. McDonald's first experience in the disruption of affiliation came with his separation from his natural mother (a "happy state") and placement in a foster home: "From this position of security I went to one that was frightening. This lasted for about a year until I found that I could regain the security and obtain the love of the foster parents by repressing resentment toward the uprooting that occurred." When he was taken from his foster parents and adopted by his present family, he again was frightened and responded (together with the "childish rebellion" reported earlier) by "extreme efforts to gain dependency satisfaction by striving for love and learning to do the things which were connected with parental love." More generally: "My socializing experience has been one of anxiety and loneliness; I have found that to relieve the tension caused by conflicts between myself and society my behavior had to be patterned so that I would be acceptable to my peers and superiors."

Thus the stage is set for two interrelated ideological dramas: the struggle between identification with the socialists and the Democratic party on the one hand, and the more general struggle to make peace with what seems to McDonald to be an impersonal and rather cold social order. On the first issue, McDonald feels an intellectual need to identify with the socialist cause, but against this he weighs the fact that the Democratic party is "accepted by the American people," and then wonders "why the concepts of loyalty and conformity to the general patterns of American thought and behavior are so important to me." The answer lies in his view of the socialists as unloved and lonely—conditions that, as we have seen, he greatly fears. "I see the socialists as people without a country. They are cut off from society. When I see them on the street corners passing out handbills, they appear to me as lonely men without friends save for their political associates." This is frightening for him, but the conflict is real:

I was at the crossroads. In one direction was a situation whereby I could follow my philosophy and alienate myself from my friends (at the same time seeking to destroy the old society), in the other, follow the old conventional patterns to avoid punishment and secure acceptance. The adjustment difficulties I [had] experienced forced me in the direction of conventional behavior. Thus I identified with the Democratic party. . . . [29]

The second dramatic struggle, the struggle against identification with a cold and impersonal society and an impersonal bureaucratic government, is more diffuse and less easily explained, although the mechanism for resolving the conflict, identification with the Democratic party, is the same. He has, he says, "a dislike of the impersonal society which I see about me," and he worries about the bureaucratic features of the welfare state. "This aspect of seeking love from authority figures," he says, "precludes a figure that is cold and impersonal. Thus I cannot accept the bureaucratic implementation of most political measures." These things frustrate his need for warmth and close personal relations. The solution? He chooses to see one side of the welfare state and of party politics:

> I see in the welfare economics of the New and Fair Deal, i.e., the welfare state, an intense consideration of human problems. It seems to deal with society not as some mechanistic object with which to be toyed, but as a living breathing mass whose interests must be furthered. I see in the Democratic party an expression of parental love which is demanding and yet permissive.

The "logic" of this choice, following the other paradigms, is clear and starts with the same premise.

> In society, as in the family, affiliation and love are conditional on love-seeking affiliative behavior.

> Socialism is not accepted by the American people, and joining the socialists cuts one off from friends, destroys opportunities for love, makes a person lonely.

> Society is cold and impersonal; bureaucracy is an external and cold authority.

> The Democratic party offers an antidote to the impersonality of society and the coldness of bureaucracy by offering something like parental love and satisfying affiliation needs.

> Therefore: I am a Democrat and for the welfare state.

---

[29]In Chap. 7 I described McDonald's "conformity" to social norms as "forcing" him to do something he wanted to do anyway, on other grounds. Here we see some of the other grounds, among them McDonald's sense that rebellion against any kind of authority is dangerous.

Social Structure and Security versus the Need for Autonomy. The insecurities produced by the early changes from natural to foster to adopted families were associated in McDonald's mind with "the social disorganization caused by impersonal marketplace economics," something signaled when he speaks of having been placed on the "adoption market." Further, his adoptive family moved from place to place rather frequently, and his adoptive father had many changes of jobs, which McDonald also associated with the unsupportive and vacillating nature of a capitalist economy. Further still, he was a child of the Depression, and feels that "as such I was a product of one of the greatest examples of social and economic disintegration." Thus, the interweaving of his own life changes with the unsupportive, unstructured, unguided nature of the economy, no doubt aided by some interpretation of these events by his family, led him to fear social disorder and disintegration. He sees around him "a weak society that permits widespread disorganization to take place."

On the other hand, as we have noted, he does not want to be "fenced in" and bitterly resists an imposed order from a source he cannot accept. He has rebelled against the family, rebelled against society, loves the laxness of the Democratic party's doctrine. Yet he says, "I felt so keenly a part of the immediate social structure (friends and family) that any act I committed that was considered asocial I felt to be dangerous to society." The consequence is a further set of inferences based on immediate family life:

Uncertainty and disorganization in family life are analogous to and follow from a weak and disorganized (capitalist) society; both family uncertainty and social disorganization threaten personal security and order.

The Democratic party and the welfare state promise both benign authority and measures to mitigate social insecurity and disorganization.

Therefore: I am for the welfare state and governmentally sponsored social organization, whose agent is the Democratic party.

McDonald comes to the same conclusion by other routes: when he was a small child in the foster home he was reproved for acting superior to a retarded child in the home and made to adopt the behavior and to espouse the doctrines of brotherhood. Although no doubt his sentiments regarding the brotherhood of man and social equality would have been developed by adoption of his parents' views in any case, his early training in the evils of "acting superior" and in the morality of equal rights reinforced these later intellectualized views.

Thus in many ways McDonald assimilated his own family training and experiences to the larger social questions that he came later to confront. By his identification with the family he came to adopt a posture toward all social and governmental authority which contained rebellious features but restricted them, which incorporated his needs for affiliation and love but helped him to use them constructively, and which brought together his fear of social disorganization with his need for freedom from hierarchical imposition. The mechanism for these reconciliations was a belief in the Democratic party and the welfare state.

Lamb. Lamb is a man who believes in "liberal goals," such as the equality of man and freedom of choice for all, but "conservative means," which he interprets as an orderly and cautious program of change. He views the world in moralistic terms, tending to see things as black or white. He is compulsively orderly, anxious about "being liked," yet imposes on himself and others such high standards that he never meets them himself, has never met a girl who measured up to them, and finds fault with his friends because they fail in one respect or another to meet his standards. He believes that his perfectionism, his liberal goals for society, and his preference for conservative means are all derived from his family's views and behavior, a special family culture that he totally accepts. At college he misses family life but sternly sets himself a course of action requiring independence and emotional self-support.

It can be said of Lamb that, like Ransome and the others, his identification with the family means that the family's social and political instruction is favorably received and heeded, that he is tuned to his parents' subtle hints and cues and responds to them, that he imitates them in most important matters, and that the political ideology and behavior he reveals flow naturally from the premises and policies of home.

Like McDonald, Lamb sees in society a large-scale analogy to the family. He says that people generally should be given the latitude of choice that he has been given, a complex freedom that, in essence, gives people the freedom to choose *the* approved moral course, and censures them if they do not. The complexity of this kind of freedom (and source of damage to Lamb) is revealed in the following passage:

> In recent years in discussions with my mother and father about certain issues they have been trying to make me mellow in my way of seeing problems from a drastic right-or-wrong point of view. . . . This shows the liberal belief of my parents that I am an individual and that decisions in my life should be made by me. . . . This liberal element of free choice could lead one to believe that my perfectionism is an imitation of my parents, because I really did not know what they approved of, and so I chose to

follow them as a means toward security. However, this view would discount the closeness of the family situation, for I have always seen quite clearly my parents' example.

Men in society, like men in the family, are "free" but limited by a code not of their own choosing.

Similarly, society should be planned and ordered as a family is planned and ordered: "Another thing which binds our family together is our conservative way of acting. . . . I have always gained security in my private life from order and planning, and I therefore feel that in world matters slow change is preferable." His father makes everyone feel at ease through his easy humor; he makes people like him. Lamb tries the same thing. In international affairs, as we have seen in Chapter 7, he reveals that he believes American foreign policy should be based on such a policy of making friends. Thus, the state is the family writ large; the analogy "works" for Lamb.

The new elements in Lamb's case, however, lie in other directions. They comprise a set of complementary and yet antithetical themes in Lamb's family life. More than the three others (Ransome, Gardiner, McDonald) discussed above, Lamb is torn by tensions and uncertainities about himself, and he needs the family for comfort and solace. The most important function the family serves for him now is to help him to relax the codes taught by the very family that he now returns to for help. This is not like the case of the drunkard seeking comfort for his addiction in more alcohol, for the reason that the parents, being sentient and humane, can seek consciously to undo what they once did, and, from the passage quoted above and other evidence, we may believe that the parents now want to help their well-loved son to adopt a more "reasonable" and tolerant view of the world.

Lamb borders on obsessive thought and compulsive behavior: as a child he set himself tasks of throwing a tennis ball within a square and would not let himself quit until, often with fading daylight, he had done this a specified number of times; he preferred trolley cars to fire engines because they ran on tracks; he works in the summer because he would feel guilty about accepting his parents' offer of a trip to Europe; although his family is moderately well to do, he nevertheless wants to pay his personal expenses in college; he spends days organizing his belongings; he has missed only five classes in three years at Adams "because of a sense of duty, and because I have so ordered my life so that it is not necessary to cut classes"; he constantly keeps lists of things to do; he will not take a beer if he knows he may have to drive a car; his various extracurricular activities are "responsibilities," not fun. "It follows," he says, "that I set one of my basic goals in life as taking a job of a high degree of difficulty and trying my hardest to do the best job possible."

Of his family, he says, "We are all perfectionists in our way and set high standards." Why then would he return to the family for relief from the stern superego that drives him to this compulsive behavior? Because, in addition to the high standards and moral tone of family life, there are other features that serve as counterweights. There are humor and forgiveness; there is "understanding," since they seem all to suffer, though less acutely, from the same problems. He is made to feel important and successful when he suffers from self-blame; there are "narcissistic supplies." He is loved at home, and because the parents' "high standards" include compassion, they seem ready to seek to undo what they did earlier, perhaps when they themselves were less sure of themselves, and to work actively to disarm this monstrously punitive superego. In this sense, Lamb is seeking not so much identity continuity as identity reconstitution, rebuilding; and the best persons to do this, if they can, are those whose early instruction made Lamb so anxious about success and achievement and morality. The "external" contemporary parents become the opponents of the internalized parentally inspired superego.

> Early identification with the family was rewarding in terms of guidance in ambiguous situations, warmth, love, humor, reassurance; it was punishing in developing impossible standards and a punitive conscience.

> Continuing identification with the family into early adulthood offers support for efforts at independence, reassurance that failure to achieve the impossible is forgivable, continued love, catharsis, *and* help in relaxing the strictures of conscience.

> The family political culture (humane, cautious, moral) is reinforced internally by identification with the family, and externally by association and example.

> Therefore: I am a liberal-conservative, increasingly tolerant of a wayward world.

This case, then, reminds us of two things. First, the family of childhood is not the same as the family of young adulthood—parents change as well as children. It is a dynamic situation. More than that, it is a *psycho*dynamic situation, in that Lamb achieves autonomy not by breaking with the family, but rather by working with the family toward his own emancipation. It is the same paradox mentioned before: the family can support a youth in his efforts to become *self*-supportive.

15

The "Autonomy Motive" in an Estranged Family Relationship

When sons are estranged from their parents, particularly from their fathers,[1] they seek in their political thinking and behavior some means of coping with the deficiencies that caused the break with their families: the loss of self-esteem, the lack of power, the coldness of family relations. The striving associated with a need for autonomy from the family is, in this sense, an attempt to repair a missing "part," a reconstitution of the self, or a special case of self-actualization by psychologically deprived persons.[2] This is a process of *restitution* or compensation, and, when politics is important enough to them, these men use politics to help them in their striving to become "whole." The source of the damaged family relations is also a source of political belief.

To clarify the issue we would note at the outset that the search for autonomy described here is only minimally a search for ways to emancipate oneself from current constraints on one's freedom of action. In a number of cases there is indeed an earlier history of rebellion against restrictive authority, and in some few others there is still a war going on over what the son should or should not believe or do. But much more important is the desire to get away from damaging and poisoned interpersonal relationships of various kinds. The sons desire freedom from the influence of the family community, the family culture, and the rewards flowing from this freedom are opportunities for self-esteem, love, guidance, assertion. The situation is more complex than a simple "rebellion against authority," and to analyze

---

[1] See my "Fathers and Sons: Foundations of Political Belief," *American Sociological Review*, 24 (1959), pp. 502-11.

[2] Carl R. Rogers, *Client-Centered Therapy* (Boston: Houghton Mifflin, 1951), pp. 487-88; Gordon W. Allport, *Becoming* (New Haven: Yale University Press, 1960), pp. 27-28.

it we must find answers to three questions: Autonomy from what? Autonomy for what? What capacity has the individual to restore the missing parts of his life?

This last question is especially important for an inquiry regarding the relationship between a child and his family, especially a son and his father, for this is a struggle with its own special difficulties. One of these, obviously, emerges from the special nature of paternal authority. The father's role is saturated with authority: the authority of genuine physical power (up to a point, anyway); the authority of legitimacy, for law, morality, and religion give to the father such legitimate authority; the authority of precedent and habit, going back to the earliest experiences of the child; the authority of superior knowledge, experience, learning (on most matters); the authority that comes as a product of the connections with the extrafamilial world, for the father, like all elites, communicates with relevant others outside the group, in this case with school officers, fathers of friends, officialdom, in a way that the child does not—although in this respect, as in the matter of knowledge and experience, the father may not match the mother. All of these things, and an infinite number of smaller things (like driving the car, controlling the family funds, mediating disputes—if the father is not a party to them) give him authority and power in the family. It is not surprising, therefore, that in discussions on youthful conflict with parents, the element of authority is often stressed. But it is not enough.

There is a second aspect of all father-son situations which tends to complicate the problem of analysis and interpretation beyond all simple solutions: the father is at the same time the source of the grievance and, as represented in the character of the son, the means of responding to it. The historical internalized father meets himself in current conflicts. This has a ghostly sound to it, and of course the son is much more than a copy of his father; he is the reaction to the model, not its form and mold. But the point reveals an important truth: often it is the very traits the father hates in himself that provoke his anger when he finds them in the son. At this point counsel passes in the guise of helping the son to avoid the father's mistakes, but this "help," as we shall see, often comes in the form of inappropriately harsh criticism. It is thus an uneven conflict in many ways: the son is struggling to find an identity that is inevitably partly that of his father, and in this struggle, like an underdeveloped country quarreling with a former colonial power, he must use the ideas and qualities he has learned from the "oppressor" (or his wife).

The third main point (illustrated by Lamb's problems, analyzed in the previous chapter) is that we are dealing with a developing situation, one that emerges from a past in which both father and son were younger, and which therefore is the precipitate of personal history and experience. It is the nature of these quarrels, or of the harmony that some relationships show, that each person responds not only to what the other does, but to what he did in the past. MacGregor, as we shall see, responds "inappropriately" to his father's current suggestions and advice because once upon a time the father acted as though he "owned" his family, especially his dependent son. The son above all sees in his father a multilayered stereoscopic version of a man, protector, critic, disciplinarian, provider, an intermixture of all these and more. The father is today a contrast to but also an embodiment of what he was yesterday, back to the beginning of time, the son's time.

SOURCES AND POLITICAL CONSEQUENCES OF FAMILY ESTRANGEMENT

What are the features of this estranged relationship as we see it in the young men of our group? I think there are five specific kinds of deprivations in the historic family relationships: (1) belittlement or the deprivation of self-esteem, (2) constraint or the deprivation of choice or power (especially without a "fair hearing"), (3) coldness or the deprivation of love, (4) normlessness or the deprivation of guidance and security, and (5) dependency demands or a deprivation of self-fulfillment and sense of independence. Of course, these deprivations often come in clusters, so it is hard to prove that one kind of deprivation is associated with a given kind of political thought and action. But the detailed accounts of these lives help to reconstruct the processes of thought and to connect them with their sources in the damaged family relationships.

Belittlement and the Deprivation of Self-Esteem.   One of the themes in the cases of Ransome, Gardiner, and McDonald was the experience of acceptance and of guidance toward maturity in such a way that at each stage in growing up, these young men were permitted to feel good about themselves. The contrast to this is the experience of belittlement, of being made to feel less important, less adequate, less satisfying to others than is necessary for growth. This unpleasant and damaging experience comes in a number of forms, some of them extending across a broad range of experience, as in Svenson's case. A sandy-haired young man who would generally prefer not to get involved in political discussions, Svenson has this to say about his father: "There was an abundance of criticism and little praise. Even at the present I am always belittled for one thing or another, seemingly just so my father can have something to criticize. If any cognizance is taken of my [positive] attributes, it is never voiced." It is small comfort for Svenson to find that this parental attitude reflects a generally critical and suspicious attitude toward the world: "My father also seems to think that the world is made up almost completely of chiselers and 'phonies,' who exist for the express purpose of cheating him. This includes almost all politicians."

Trumbull recalls his father's punishments and criticisms in a smiliar way, as we noted in an earlier chapter on aggression. He remembers his father as someone "whose entire life was oriented around being unfair and punishing in every trivial instance which could be manufactured." The punishment, demeaning in itself, was made worse by the "endless chain of angry explosions . . . whose contents were that I certainly had little or no chance of leading a successful life and that I was nearly foredestined to ostracism from the human community, not to mention my family, unless I changed my ways." As a consequence, Trumbull says he "feels scared and insecure," although he covers his uncertainty with a "veneer of self-sufficiency."

Often, as might be expected, the sense of inadequacy arises from failure to meet the expected standards at school. Rogers, like Trumbull an aggressive and ethnocentric young man, says "Neither my sister nor myself have shown the brilliance expected of us. This has hurt my father very much and has always been the biggest trouble in our family." Simpson, an overprotected and somewhat insecure person who had some successes in high school, says of his early days, "In grade school, I was of quite high intelligence, but never really exerted myself. . . . I wasn't a poor student—just mediocre. . . . My mother would sometimes admonish me for my mediocrity. I think I must have been a great disappointment to her in those years and on into high school." It is his mother's views that count; his father he considers to be "a weakling."

At other times, it is lack of spirit or "personality" that invokes parental criticism and belittlement. Simpson feels this is so in his case, and so does Trueblood, who says he recalls "my parents berating me for my lack of spirit in combat and comparing my attitude with my sister's daring. Of course, I felt keen disappointment at my situation, but did not seem to be able to do anything about it." For others it is a kind of nagging criticism, as when Demming, on going home from college, finds: "When I am home, certain incidents increase this feeling of inferiority and results in resentment. My parents make remarks about how I drive, how I study, what I do in my spare time at college, etc., which make me feel like a child and embarrass me." Rarely mentioned but frequently there is the question of the boy's attitude and behavior toward girls. Cohen, writing in the third person, says his father "lectures the subject on going out with girls more often; the subject resents this very much and worries about being 'abnormal' in this respect."

The response to these deprivations of self-esteem is twofold. First, there is anger and resentment: Cohen says his father is a "slob"; Simpson says his father is a "weakling"; Rogers implies that his father is a failure and that he thinks of his father only as "a punishing instrument"; Trumbull speaks of his father as an "authoritarian personality . . . who was either too old, too busy, or too annoyed to play the role of the devoted parent, much less a friend"; Svenson agrees with his mother that his father is constantly making "inane and stupid remarks."

None of these belittled sons have father models; all of them have difficulty in relating easily to authority. But most characteristic of their response to these particular experiences of belittlement is their search for restitution of that which has been taken from them: their self-confidence, their self-esteem. Earlier (Chapters 12 and 13) we talked about the problems of coping with low self-esteem for those who suffered from feelings of physical inferiority or inferiority in athletic ability, or who suffered in childhood from a sense of lower status and wealth compared to their friends. Although some of the men are the same in the two groups, the processes of restitution and compensation are different. Feelings of physical or athletic inferiority led men to strive for a substitute value, often intellectual or aesthetic. In this way they could withdraw from the peer-group competition in which they did so badly. But it is hard to escape from parental belittlement in this way, and hence intellectual and aesthetic pursuits offer less escape and less compensation for deprivation of self-esteem from this source. On the other hand, it does seem that those who are belittled by their parents seek wealth, power, ambition as a compensation, but of course, since they are still students, these values serve mainly to inform their fantasy life, and it is still in their imaginations that they fulfill the purpose of compensation and restitution. Further, compared to the pain of low status or wealth relative to friends, the pain from parental belittlement is much deeper and the relevant responses much more bitter, permeating more of the men's lives and thought.

The loss of self-esteem in the family affects social and political beliefs in several ways. The most obvious is through invidious distinctions made between themselves and others. Thus, Trumbull, Rogers, and Simpson are all anti-Semites, a "philosophy" with many roots. Cohen shares some of this feeling of anti-Semitism, and this disturbs him. One reason we may appropriately regard anti-Semitism as a restitutive maneuver arising from the hurts of parental belittlement is that these young men see it this way themselves. Trumbull, having said that his father made him feel chronically inferior, says, "Probably as a reaction against and a shield for my admitted feelings of inferiority and insecurity, I have developed a trend I would classify as ethnocentrism," and mentions his prejudices against Catholics and Jews. Simpson, who was made to feel inferior because of his lack of assertiveness, says, "I am generally hostile to Jews. . . . It may be a deep-seated envy of . . . [their] aggressiveness which is partially responsible for my hostility." And Rogers, in a curious statement, says:

> Because of this continual pressure by my father that money means absolutely nothing, I have come around to the position where I oftentimes am very jealous of those who can put up a better appearance than I. This envy of money has perhaps led to my chief prejudice in life, that which I strongly feel toward the Jews.

But more than the complications of dealing with authority, and more than the ethnocentrism, the main outcome of the belittling experience is to put politics in the service of ambition.[3] Demming was determined to be a leader and to restore his damaged self-esteem at Adams College. When he found he could not "make it" as a conservative, he became a liberal and a leader of the out-groups. Cohen and Trueblood both say that their party identifications will be decided by whichever group seems to have the highest status and promises to give them the standing they desperately need. Trumbull says the Republican party is the party of the elite, to which he belongs, and especially the party of the "Long Island estate group," to which he aspires. Only Svenson seems free of this explicit and often dramatic choice of political outlook grounded so clearly in status considerations and obsessive needs for success, apparently because he is "opting out" in a sense, and thinks of himself as "easygoing"; hence, in politics: "I do not make positive decisions and identifications and remain essentially indecisive and uncommitted." But the main point is this: Those who are deprived by their parents of the kind of status represented by self-esteem seek to achieve this in any way they can, and more or less consciously employ politics as one of the means to this end.

Constraint and the Deprivation of Power. Some of the accounts of estranged family relationships focus not so much on belittlement as on control, regulation, lack of free choice. It was this feature that we had anticipated would be the main source of the drive for autonomy, but, as it happens, this is only one element of a larger, more inclusive estrangement process. Again, some of the son's criticisms are quite general, especially where there is an "overbearing" father or an "authoritarian" mother whose will generally dominates the home. Rogers suggests this when he says:

---

[3]Compare the discussion of the way in which political beliefs serve those who feel that they have done less well in college than in high school, failing to fulfill early promise. The process of restitution for them, too, is one of making political ideas serve more clearly the purposes of their ambition for "success."

There has always been in our family a strong pattern of discipline and I can remember numerous incidents where this discipline was enforced with the belt. Both my sister and I, I guess, lived in slightly constant fear of our father, who at many times appeared solely as the instrument of authority, one which we could never really love.

Svenson speaks in the same vein:

The punishments always seemed to me to be administered almost indiscriminately in an attempt to maintain parental authority. I was denied things with no reason given for the denial. It was always "Because I say so, that's why." It seemed that anything I wanted to do was automatically wrong and that was that.

MacGregor, the son of a self-made and prosperous businessman, speaks of his father as a "domineering authoritarian-type person," and recalls

. . . how relaxed and relieved I felt whenever my dad went on a business trip. I used to be so afraid and fearful of him that I would spill my milk all over the table at dinner because I would be watching him instead of what I was doing. . . . Although my father is a rational man, if one did not conform to the pattern he set down, he would use any means possible to return one to this pattern.

Finally, accused of flouting his father's authority on purpose, MacGregor settled down to doing just that, and, he says, "I kind of reveled in the punishments he gave me as this reinforced my belief that he was a wicked individual."

And Trumbull, scion of an elite family, came later to realize that his father's strictures "were merely reflections of his unfailing desire to wield my character into a more nearly perfect mold," leaving little room for free choice.

These fathers, one gathers, were stormy and willful; but there are other ways of controlling youth. Novak's father was a more scholarly individual, but both inconsistent and demanding. Novak says, "My father has always seemed a distant force in my life. He early represented strength, authority, and its concomitant punishments. His punishments were severe and unpredictable." Novak especially remembers how limited were his movements away from home and how severely he was punished for masturbation or any suggestion of sex play with other young children. Trueblood, whose father was also unpredictable, was apparently overcontrolled in another way:

My father's control over me has not relied heavily on corporal punishment, but it is strong without it. Disapproving glances, cross words or inferences have sufficient strength. As an example of his control, I remember one time in my elementary school days when I had started a "club" with a few select friends. I was very proud of this "club" and spoke of it at home. My father mentioned offhand that my methods of selecting members were not democratic. I resigned from the "club" the next day at school.

Rogers, MacGregor, Trumbull, and Novak (but not Trueblood, with his anxieties) suggest the paradigm situation for rebellion against authority. It was this struggle whose unequal terms in Germany were said to lead to the authoritarian personality.[4] More generally, Murphy says it is the origin of a desire for power as a widespread social motive: "Prestige and power problems in very early childhood are evident in the battle with the restraining figures, especially the parents, over objects to be had, privileges to be obtained, training to be submitted to." As the child grows older, *"power*, which was earlier simply the thrust of the individual against obstacles, becomes a struggle for relative control of the situation in the competitive atmosphere of the home or school or playground, and success in achieving power enhances the self."[5] Where power becomes the central issue in the household, we may expect that a desire for power or a fear of power will follow. This seems to be the case.

It is often said that the subject matter of the study of politics is the uses of power, and that the practice of politics is defined as the exercise of power, and that government is to be conceived of as the legitimate monopoly of power.[6] Hence, those for whom power becomes a central and perhaps frightening value ought to reveal this in their political thought. Let us see, recalling the difficulty with few and overlapping cases of connecting family cause and political effect.

Novak speaks of himself as an authoritarian, is ashamed of his own inadequate response to his father's dictatorial ways (a "weak-kneed rebellion"), and goes on to identify the cause in the fact that "the early impossibility of opposition to my father created an equation between strength and goodness." It is this identification of strength with goodness that leads him to support Joseph McCarthy, at that time a prominent figure. Rogers, an advocate of the States' Rights party (Southern autonomy) and conservatism, argues the case as follows. One of the clues to his thinking, I believe, is in the frequent use of the word "strong." He says:

---

[4]See Bertram H. Shaffner, *Fatherland: A Study of Authoritarianism in the German Family* (New York: Columbia University Press, 1948).

[5]Gardner Murphy, "Social Motivation," in Gardner Lindzey, ed., *Handbook of Social Psychology* (Cambridge: Addison-Wesley, 1954), p. 623; my emphasis.

[6]See Max Weber, *The Theory of Social and Economic Organization,* ed. Talcott Parsons (New York: Oxford University Press, 1947), p. 154.

I think that a *strong* central figure is essential for the working of the government, yet I do not want this figure to encroach upon my own private preserve and those rights which I believe should be left to the states. It is necessary, I further believe, to have the *strongest* state government possible. . . . Principally this *strong* central figure, to return to the original thought, is to be *strong* only in the field of foreign relations. . . . I think for the price of world prestige we should not pay with policy from a body which is so often and easily split but should put up the *strong* front headed by a *strong* executive. . . . It is not that I want a dictator, yet I feel that there must be this *strong, all-powerful* executive who can solely determine the policy of the country.[7]

He then goes on to argue for a *"strong* sense of local autonomy" as well, since he does not want the federal government intruding on the rights of his adopted South. One reason, incidentally, why he can believe in such strong government without fearing too much for his own "private preserve" is because, as he says, "I feel that I am in the position where I can place myself above those of less education and feel that the leadership should come from this class of educated individuals."

Trumbull, a conservative Republican, says, "I happen to believe that the ideal form of government would be something along the lines of a benevolent despot who would rule with absolute power, but only for the good of the nation as a whole." MacGregor, who finally established an uneasy truce with his father and is now a more or less liberal Republican, following a radical period, says, "I believe the government should be so geared that a strong man, with the best interests of the country in mind, can operate as quickly and effectively as a totalitarian government." This strong man should, however, be controlled in his judgments by "the enlightened few," of which MacGregor is or will be one.

There are, of course, exceptions, for one cannot expect a single feature of family life, even so important a one as the use of power, to shape all political views. Thus Simpson has personal tendencies that might have developed into a worship of power in government, but does not take this stand. He says:

I consider my mother to be an authoritarian. I would not say that I have become an authoritarian as a direct result of her influence, but I have been more susceptible to authoritarianism. I have little respect for weakness [he calls his father "weak"], and I am contemptuous of those who are given opportunities and fail to take advantage of them.

---

[7]The omissions in the text represent only a few sentences in each case; my emphasis.

Nevertheless, his political views are divided: "I am 'internationally' broad-minded, tolerant, and humanitarian, while domestically intolerant and self-seeking."

In the same way, Trueblood, overcontrolled at home, but less by the willful acts of his father (or mother) than by anxieties caused by other factors in the home situation, totally withdraws from political decisions and refuses to talk about politics lest he make a mistake. In one sense, he is reacting to a set of constraints in the home by this fear of power, openly admitted (recall the discussion of his "fear of using my whole strength"). But since the controls in his case are different from those of the others, the response is also different.

Most of these men, then, clearly seek and value what they were deprived of in the home: power. Furthermore, in their political beliefs this value becomes a central theme and, more than most, they see government as the exercise of power, limited only by the most tenuous concepts of popular sovereignty, moral codes, minority rights, and collective decision-making.

Coldness and the Deprivation of Love.   It is not the case that each of the kinds of deprivation we are dealing with here is somehow parallel to the others in the processes of political thinking it stimulates. The resentment of the kind of authority that has deprived men of their early freedom of choice or power can be expressed not only as overvaluation of power in politics, but also in seeking to exercise power. The very elements of the deprivation situation provide an example of the use and abuse of power. The family provides a learning experience in power relations. This is not true of the deprivation of love, for in the loveless family there is no model; it is not a learning experience in the uses of love. At the beginning of this chapter we stated the question of autonomy as tripartite: Autonomy from what? Autonomy for what? What capacity has the individual to restore the missing parts of his life? Here, the search for the missing part, love, is hampered by the fact that the individual has had his capacity for love stunted. He may seek love, but being loveless himself, he is unlikely to be able to find it.[8]

Some of the men speak of their families as loveless, others reveal this lack in their family life in other ways. Cohen, as he interviews himself, is explicit: "As a child, the subject received little in the way of companionship

---

[8]This is in line with the findings in Douglas P. Crowne and David Marlowe, *The Approval Motive* (New York: Wiley, 1964); also compare Harry Stack Sullivan's discussion of exploitative attitudes, suggesting that the person who seeks love or sympathy from another but is not himself capable of friendship is likely to find himself in situations that "are apt to be somewhat unpleasant and complex for the other people involved" (*The Interpersonal Theory of Psychiatry* [New York: Norton, 1953], pp. 351-53).

from mother or father. . . . He therefore never asks his parents' advice on personal matters," reports hostile feelings toward his father, and says he "does not like his mother very much, either." So is Svenson:

> My father is generally undemonstrative of emotion and I have received little affection from him. I can recall even at the tender age of five a feeling of repugnance when asked to "kiss Daddy." In fact, my family is particularly loveless. . . . Seemingly as a result of this atmosphere, I find it difficult myself to demonstrate emotion. I have had few sexual experiences and my relations with the opposite sex have always been characterized by varying degrees of inhibition.

Rogers, whose father was seen as the punishing instrument and little more, says, "I have never been particularly close to either of my parents and to my knowledge have only very seldom gone to them with any troubles that I might have. . . . I think the strongest feeling that I have is that of independence from my parents, my relations, and my home life." Trumbull, who does not mention his mother at all, says of his father, "It is indeed ironic that at the time when I most needed love and affection, he had little to offer." Demming mentions his parents only to criticize them and to express his resentment regarding their postures of sacrifice and their nagging criticism. Simpson respects his mother but is contemptuous of his father. Novak ridicules his father's hypocrisy and fears him, while he says his mother's "affection toward me has seemed shallow" and complains about her "periods of moodiness and 'tiredness'" and her lack of protection against the punishing father. Of the six men who come from loveless homes, all but Rogers mention their difficulties in relating to girls.

What is distinctive about the political thinking of those who are estranged from their families because of the cold and loveless nature of family life is the way in which they think about the "social contract." Here they divide into three groups. The first group is made up of those who see no obligation on the part of government for a protective or nurturant role. In a loveless world, there is no reason to believe that government should or would take care of the weak or powerless or those needing help. Government officials, like others, would have no such motive. These are the reactionaries: Trumbull, Rogers, Novak. For them, government is authoritarian and punitive; there is little in their experience to teach them to look for more.

Second, there are the two men whose liberal philosophy, they say, is reinforced, if not generated by, a desire to attack their more conservative parents. Thus, although Svenson says, "I have always had a rather trusting belief in the humaneness of society," which he exemplifies with his hostility toward nativism and prejudice, he adds that he believes this reflects his mother's views and "a reaction against my father's hypercritical authoritarianism." At the same time, Demming, as we have observed, says:

> I have found that these liberal principles, so opposed to the extreme conservatism of my parents, act as a good media to express hostility and to show that I have a mind of my own. This may explain why my ideology is often based on the New Deal and Franklin Roosevelt, because it is in these fields that my parents show their greatest disgust for the Democrats.

His liberalism is, indeed, couched in oppositional terms. He introduces the matter on the first page of his biography with a statement of distrust: "Broadly speaking, my political ideology involves, first of all, a distrust of 'business' and that American ideal, the businessman." His father is a small businessman. Both Svenson and Demming are "humane" for a purpose: to oppose their parents. Over time, other reasons develop and the position becomes elaborated and rationalized. The main emotional source, however, seems to be hostility, not love, while the main function of a liberal government is regulation, not service.

Third, there is Cohen's pattern, which is almost totally to ignore all substantive issues (one of the rare biographies so naked of such discussion), and to concentrate almost entirely on himself and where he "belongs." He says, interviewing himself, that "the subject" has "an obsession to be rich and have large quantities of money" and sees "the GOP as the dominant party of his section of the state and the party to which successful people, with whom he desires to associate, belong." Nowhere does he describe just what it is the Republican party might do with the power of office; certainly there is little to suggest that it should employ power to serve others. One reason he does not reveal a belief in a "loving government" is because he hardly thinks about government at all; only his own future, about which he is "pessimistic."

Normlessness and Uncertainty.   Where there is a clear family political culture or agreement on other, and usually more important, values, one may expect that this clarity will produce a clear acceptance or a clear rejection. In the cases in the previous chapter there was a clear acceptance, with certain deviations by Lamb paradoxically designed to prove his acceptance of the family concept of "independence." In the cases of loveless or overcontrolling or authoritarian families, it seemed that a clear rejection, at least of the father's political views, was likely to occur. Yet even in opposition, an authoritarian or cold family can provide something for the child: it can provide guidelines, something to respond to (or against). Ambivalence on the other hand, or normlessness, or divided authority, deprives the child of guidance and certainty. And, just as in the loveless families, this very deprivation may prevent an appropriate restitution, a successful striving for capacities of inner guidance and certainty.

This lack of guidance may occur in three ways: (a) parental uncertainty or failure by either or both parents to provide clear cues to guide the child, (b) parental hypocrisy, where the parents express values or ideals they do not themselves pursue, and (c) hostile division between the parents, where each may be relatively clear but the division of opinion leaves the child uncertain. In each case, the child strives to cope with the uncertainty either by withdrawal of emotion from the conflicted areas (part of the "cross-pressure" syndrome),[9] by eclectic and selective identification, or by intense but changing and confused loyalties. In one of these ways he strives to minimize the damage of uncertainty, or to find some area of certainty to cling to, but he is generally unsuccessful because the confusion is rooted in his personality and he has not the capacities for self-confident choice. As we shall see, these attempts at restitution or compensation have their political expressions, which are not too difficult to discern.

Trueblood exemplifies the condition of uncertainty generated by lack of clear cues from either parent. We noted above that Trueblood in one sense was subject to very considerable constraint from his parents, largely indirect and heavily moralized. This is not inconsistent with uncertainty about the limits of approved behavior and thought. It is as though his parents were saying to him: "Many things are disapproved; you must try to find out what they are." Trueblood states it this way:

> In most cases my father refrained from stating his preference authoritatively—especially where he feels that the decision should be mine (e.g., in selecting a college or vocation). But even still I seem acutely tuned to any vague hints he may give out, trying to discover his opinions and employ them, not necessarily as deciding factors, but at least as contributing ones in making my choices.

This search for cues is complicated by his fear of his father: "My emotions appear to be attached to him principally in the form of fear . . . My relationship with him, while friendly, has never been free and easy." At the same time, although he says, "My relationship to my mother is one primarily of love," he adds, "I feel repulsion at overt manifestations of love accorded me by my mother (such as hugs, kisses, etc.)." Thus the normless-

---

[9]Paul Lazarsfeld, after some criticism of an earlier position, discusses his views on cross-pressures in the penultimate chapter of *Voting* (Chicago: University of Chicago Press, 1954), of which he was a co-author with Bernard Berelson and William McPhee. Since this discussion, the literature on consistency, dissonance, and balance has improved the conceptualization of conflicted mental states, although the later work has some methodological problems, too. See, for example, the criticism of the logic of dissonance theory in Roger Brown's *Social Psychology* (New York: Free Press, Macmillan, 1956), pp. 601-3.

ness of uncertain guidance is reinforced by or based on ambivalent feelings of "love" and "friendliness" and "repulsion" and "fear."

This general state of uncertainty applies to the political area as well. Trueblood says, "Unlike perhaps many other families, political discussions were practically nonexistent in my family life. . . . I think of him [his father] as a Democrat, but he has with one exception not given me any indication of his reasons." He gets no additional guidance from his mother, believes she voted once for Roosevelt and voted Republican in 1944, but he has been given "no reasons for these choices. . . . She appears to me . . . as one who wavers from one side to the other, finding it hard to make up her mind."

Trueblood presents the clearest case of a deep-seated ambivalence and, since the stakes seem high to him, in view of his parents' implicit warning that the world is highly moral and highly dangerous, he prefers to avoid commitment. But there are others who reveal other routes to a similar uncertainty. Novak, as we have seen, is a case of uncertainty flowing from what seems to be parental hypocrisy and weakness. It will be recalled that he thought his father's statements about his own tolerance and freedom from racial and religious prejudice were belied by his offhand prejudiced comments on Negroes and Jews, that his pretensions to scholarship were undercut by his failure to produce a scholarly work when he was a college professor, and that his attitudes toward people who create tension were anomalous in the light of the tension he created among others. Novak's father is a "liberal Republican" who believes in what he calls "controlled capitalism," but Novak thinks his views in support of "socialized medicine" once again reveal the shallowness or hypocrisy in his beliefs. Moreover, his punishments were both "severe and unpredictable," adding to young Novak's anxiety and uncertainty.

Svenson and Simpson both illustrate the third variety of uncertainty in the home and the failure of a family to develop a culture that can give strong cues to the searching child. Simpson says, "There is no doubt that my mother was in charge of the discipline, not only because she was home all day, but because she is a strong woman, whereas my father is not strong." He thinks of his father as a kind of "snob" (as well as "a weakling"). His father's Republicanism, says Simpson, is not thought through, adopted "merely because the Republican party is associated with the businessman" and his father is a businessman. His mother is or has been a Democrat; "unlike my father, my mother is very egalitarian, and is quite proud of it, with a slight 'holier-than-thou' attitude." Simpson has "a distinct disdain" for his father and feels much closer to his mother, but he says he feels "her dominance in the home has made me both weak and respectful."

Svenson's mother is, in his opinion, much more intelligent than his father, whom he cordially dislikes (at least at this stage in his life). His mother is liberal and his father is a nativist and anti-intellectual and, in his words, "probably ripe for fascist propaganda." Even more than Simpson, Svenson is torn by the family feud and identifies with his mother and his mother's views, but also shows some ambivalence toward her.

In all of these cases, the search for certainty and something to rely upon takes the form of escape from the family and emotional withdrawal, or eclecticism, or rapid change. Trueblood and Simpson refuse to commit themselves to a political party or even to take a stand on whether or not they are primarily "liberal" or "conservative." Svenson takes a strong stand on internationalism and ethnic prejudice, as we have seen, but characterizes his political ideas on other issues as "ambiguity mixed with confusion and ignorance."

Among Novak's views are support for Taft, while he cheers for the "liberal accomplishments" of Eisenhower and hopes that Eisenhower can "become as strong a figure as was Franklin D. Roosevelt." He respects Senator Joseph McCarthy and admires his "rugged determination." He believes "we should wage war directly with Russia" and feels that "capitalism is the only proper form of economy today," but this is largely because it offers him the greatest opportunity to achieve status and wealth. If that were not the case, he says, he would adopt another political philosophy. At the conclusion of his paper he says, "Because of no real rational synthesis with the basic tenets of conservatism, an environmental change could create a superficial change in ideology but no real change in my relations to authority . . . [to which] I am respectful and, in my background, submissive."

Without some definition of a common family culture, without strong ties to the father (especially if the mother has an opposing view and family dominance), without clear indication of some values to be pursued, the youth's search for guidance takes him out of politics or erratically over the political terrain.

Dependency Demands, Deprivation of Self-Fulfillment, and Sense of Independence. Since it is necessary in all cultures, and especially in the United States,[10] for children to "grow up" and assume independent responsibilities in society, parents who impede this process deprive the child of something he needs. In depriving him of his growing sense of independence they may create resentments, especially when he looks back upon his adolescence and perceives what has happened. Too much nurturance, too

---

[10]See the discussion of American interpretations of "freedom" in the concluding section of this chapter and in n. 12. Also compare the dependency demands reported here with the helpful guidance toward independence shown by the parents of those who continued their identification with their families (Chap. 14).

late in the maturation process, is not, indeed, the same thing as too many constraints, any more than too much help is the same thing as too many prohibitions. This is true although the same child may experience both.

In striving to find what has been missing, the means of independent thought and action, or to compensate for the feelings of dependency which are experienced and resented, young men may adopt several postures: (a) assertion of separateness and distinctiveness, (b) assertion of their own strength and power, (c) anxious confession of concern regarding their own identity. Of course, the third attitudinal "posture" is likely to permeate, at a subliminal level, the other two. To the extent that a person is interested in politics, he is likely to employ political material in these efforts to cope with his deprivation of independence. But, nevertheless, the political style of those deprived of a sense of independence is likely to be shaped by a search for "the authoritative."

The thrust for independence, the struggle against dependency, is made by rich and poor alike: what the rich parents put up as a bribe, the poor parents put up as a "sacrifice" in order to induce dependency of the young. Both Dobb, a scion of the rich, and Demming, a lower-middle-class boy, are restive under these obligations and reject them, each in his own way. Dobb, handsome and sports-loving, is a Democrat, to the consternation and amazement of all his extended family of Republicans. Some of this effort to establish his independent identity is caught in his badly penned but straightforward account of himself:

> It is a rebellion against money, which I associate and have associated for years with the Republican party. The rebellion goes back to the feeling in the chauffeur-driven car [earlier he had said, "riding in that car to me symbolized that class difference which I did not want to emphasize"]. This feeling has persisted to the present day. The same grandparents who own this car have been very generous to me. And it appears to me that their generosity has almost come to the point of bribery. Consequently, their generosity has been unable to influence my actions, and I have appeared to be very ungrateful. This last point is an important element of my rebellion. It has been necessary to stand on my own two feet. I want no help from anyone.

The declaration of independence is a claim that extends to many areas of life. Dobb would not "yield" to the local bully in school; he "would not go to a teacher after class, though I knew he liked that sort of attention"; he worries about the "protected life behind the ivy-covered walls" at Adams College, and says, "I would prefer to get a job on my own merits rather than have my father or someone help me." But, of course, there is an element of aggression in it too: "I consider myself a Democrat because they [parents] are Republicans." On the whole, however, he insists that he proceed without a crutch (and religion, as well as parental money and help, is a crutch). Several times he repeats the phrase "I have preferred to stand on my own two feet." Thus in politics, as in school, career choice, and interpersonal relations, the main theme in Dobb's account of himself is his striving for independence and autonomy.

Demming is similarly resentful of too much help from his parents; he feels constrained by parental "sacrifice," an offering he does not want, a device for manipulating his guilt so as to carry on the business of control, dressing it in the finery of moral talk. Thus Demming:

> My parents almost had to go beyond their means in educating me. Because I was trying to overcome my feelings of inferiority, I hated to have anyone give up so much for me. This smacked of my being very dependent, which was in contrast to the show I was trying to put up. I went to all lengths to try to send myself to college and to show that I was independent and "standing on my own two feet." Thus, accepting a political ideology different from that of my family could be taken as another way to show my independence.

Moreover, this drive for independence, so difficult to channel among youth, so necessary, and yet so hard to bear, arises from that same mixed matrix of reason and need, resentment and gratitude, which was formed by the layered experience of earlier years. Demming goes on to reveal a glimpse of this irrational source of the movement away from the family. Speaking of his rebellious feeling, he says:

> It may also be related to the fact that I resent the limited financial resources of my parents. My secondary and college education was with boys of considerably greater economic means, and, as this dawned on me, it increased my feelings of inferiority and caused resentment toward my parents. My conscience would not let me express my resentment openly, and thus, I could use the Democratic party as a hidden expression of this resentment.

As in college, where politics became a vehicle for creating and leading an out-group against the oppressive establishment, so in the family, too, political ideas were useful in developing an area of independent, self-created thought and action.

In the first chapter we explored in some depth the case of a lower-middle-class boy, De Vita, who found himself in a kind of sociological no-man's-land when he arrived at Adams College. Unlike Dobb and Demming, he does not openly declare his independence from and resentment toward his family, but we may see these themes in his account of his fear of going against his parents' wishes, lest they withdraw their love, and his efforts to play a parental role with his friends, a role of "dominance." As a consequence, it will be recalled, without his knowing exactly what he was doing, he attempted to contrast his new liberal identity with the old family way of thinking in a variety of ways, such as his emphasis on intellect, on change, on the advantages of "big government," on ethnic prejudice, hope for the future, internationalism, and so forth. Furthermore, he emphasizes his needs for power over others, and his fear of making others angry. For him, more than for others, a sociological gap in status and education help in the new identity and the cause of separateness.

If Simpson's relations with a divided family reveal the problems of normlessness and lack of a family culture, his relations with his mother reveal the problem of dependency demands. As we saw in Chapter 13, she made him "weak and respectful." Yet instead of being repelled, he says, "There is no doubt that I have always felt closer to my mother, have turned to her for help and advice, and have felt far more love for her than for my father." As a consequence of this ambivalent dependency, he feels stifled and believes he has never really lived up to his full intellectual potential: "I think it is largely my dependence on my family for support that makes me intellectually sterile." His pattern, then, combines respect for strength and assertion, which he envies and feels he does not have, with an inability to establish a separate identity, either politically or in other ways. He looks forward to the future when he will be emancipated: "I think that when I am on my own, and old enough to vote, I will probably feel the need to make these political decisions [that is, choose a political party]."

Finally, in reviewing Mintz's case, we see spelled out some of the mechanisms that make the dependency demands potentially very damaging. Mintz says, "My parents' . . . effect on me is best understood in terms of my passive, dependent personality characteristics." In politics, this is exemplified by his father's indoctrination:

> My father has extremely positive political values which have traditionally been heard rather than discussed. . . . On numerous occasions . . . I have found myself advancing as my own arguments those which I had in reality learned from my father. This tendency toward "automaton conformity" has made it increasingly difficult for me to develop independently conceived and reasoned thought patterns. My dependency, of course, extends beyond the family and politics. Indeed, it permeates my entire personality.

But Mintz does not counter this tendency with assertions of his own individuality or of his own strength and independence. Rather he explores how he came to be this way and how his feelings of dependency affect his life and thought. Mainly, he believes, his dependency has given him a deep sense of "inferiority and inadequacy," which in turn make him think of himself as "unlovable and unloving." Further, it has made him think of himself as sexually inadequate, a source of very substantial tension and inhibition. As a consequence, he believes, he substitutes "general and impersonal for personal contacts," and thus prefers idealized abstractions, and rather than carry through his sense of the need for reform, he maintains a disembodied "idealism" marked by "sympathies for underdogs"—if they do not get too close. His analysis (guided by his own psychoanalysis under professional care) is a remarkable achievement, even if one takes it with due caution, for it helps us here to see a process of political idea formation arising from what to the outsider must appear to be a nurturant family situation. From the inside, however, it is experienced as somewhat loveless (he never mentions his mother), somewhat constraining, and designed to induce feelings of passivity, indecision, and dependency. The identity confusion (including sexual identity) is not countered by assertions of individuality and strength, and perhaps that is the trouble.

All of these men worry about their independence and their assertiveness. Dobb and Demming mention their intense desires to "stand on their own two feet" and to be free of family "help"; Simpson worries about his assertiveness, mentioning this as his most important personal problem. De Vita stresses his desire to have power over others and his fear to exercise it. Mintz speaks of his passivity and dependency as "permeating his entire personality." Thus, concern about the independence of which they were deprived by their dependency-demanding families is marked.

Four of the five (all but Simpson) either became lawyers or planned to enter the Foreign Service. One of the characteristics of law and government is that it cloaks the individual in the power of a mighty force, the law and legal authority. An authority and power that might seem to the individual to be missing from his own arsenal of qualities is provided by an external agency. I do not believe that these men were, in fact, "weak," and I suspect that in life as in their biographies (with the exception of Simpson) they have had positive, coherent views and have taken independent stands on public matters; but what moves them is not the reality of their "true" capacities, but rather their concerns about themselves and their capacities.

The point is certainly not established by these career choices, for one might equally argue that the legal profession demands independence and assertion, and that the Foreign Service (and I am not sure that Dobb carried out his intention to enter the Foreign Service) requires negotiation and discretion. But within the scope of the roles and social structures chosen by these men (including business roles, which Simpson very likely chose), I would expect the style of "coping" to emphasize the borrowed authority of an institution, or of law, or of the majesty of government. Two of the lawyers have, at some time, been teachers of law. I would expect them to rely upon the authority of a reputed author, the authority of "facts," not the authority of their own imaginative inference.

COMMUNICATION: "THE TALKING CURE," "THE TALKING SHOP," DUE PROCESS

All of these cases of estrangement from the family, for whatever reason, share one thing in common: the young men feel that they have not had a chance to "talk things over" with their parents. This is in marked contrast to the pattern in the previous chapter, where Ransome, Gardiner, McDonald, and Lamb all talked things over with their parents and felt that their parents listened to them; hence they believed they were respected. We must not confuse cause and symptom; failure of communication itself derives from conflict and estrangement, but it also increases estrangement and the evident resentment of the men who seek to dissociate themselves from their families.

Communication, talking things over, has ramifying effects. Psychoanalysis is called "the talking cure," for through a special kind of conversation, one in which one partner learns gradually to talk about things he dared not think about, he brings the repressed into consciousness and so comes to understand his problems and, if successful, to master them. For the child and parent both, conversation in the family offers some small portion of such a process of "making conscious" the forbidden topics (sex, religion, hostility, dependency, authority). While Ransome says he received his sex education in the home, Cohen complains that he was given a book and only later learned from his friends what sex was all about. Lamb talked over matters of religion as a freely discussable topic on which a variety of views could be entertained; Rogers, on the other hand, was subjected to pious indoctrination by his grandmother, who did not respect the heterodox views of her grandson. McDonald was allowed to express his hostility toward his parents' authority; Novak was persuaded to believe that he was sinful and wrong in challenging them. In framing thoughts about the social and political world, it is useful to have available to the conscious mind one's feelings and beliefs on these topics, for then they are less likely to erupt into self-defeating and socially damaging political beliefs.

In quite a different way, modern (and some ancient and some primitive) societies have come to appreciate the "talking shops," parliaments.

They serve to bring conflicts of interest into the open, to inform authorities of the nature and strength of opposing views and grievances, and to effect a reconciliation, where possible, of these conflicting interests. More than that, they serve to legitimate decisions, for the decisions bear the stamp of a group and a process in which each person can feel he has a stake and his interest has at least been "represented." A family parliament, or town meeting, since it is a form of "direct democracy," would have served to inform Trueblood where his father and mother stood on matters of interest to him; would have given Trumbull a chance to express his grievances regarding his father's shaping of his character; would have permitted Demming to state just what it was that made him desire to earn his own way in college. And, speaking of "interests," such family parliaments would have permitted Dobb to say that he thought his brother received all the attention, and Trumbull, perhaps, to communicate his feelings that his younger brother received "the lion's share" of affection—this, rather than "pounding him into the dust." Moreover, something would have been learned about the way in which community decisions can be shared. Thus the views of Trumbull, Rogers, and MacGregor regarding the advantages of quasi-dictatorial rule might have been modified. But, of course, parental attitudes would have to change before the parliaments or town meetings could have succeeded.

The courts of law, with their protection of due process, offer another analogy. Due process of law is not only a device for arriving at the right decision; it is a device for bringing the defendant into the decision-making process so that he at once feels that he is regarded as an important member of the community and is entitled to have his views considered and, further, can follow the reasoning of the court. So it is in the family. When Svenson complains that "My side of the picture could never be presented," when Trumbull complains that his father "was always quick to criticize and to anger, at which times he completely escaped all bounds of rational discussion; he was right and I was wrong," and when MacGregor complains about his "authoritarian domineering father" and goes on to say that "if one did not conform to the pattern he set down, he would use any means possible to return one to this pattern," much of the pain and resentment expressed has its source in the lack of a chance to be heard, to be considered, to have the constraints interpreted and explained.

AUTONOMY FOR WHAT?

I suppose that in some sense autonomy is something valuable in itself, a terminal value; the very absence of the constraint or suffocation, or whatever, is, at least by contrast, a relief. But even more than most values that may be prized for themselves, autonomy is valued for what it permits men to do, for its instrumental value. Then, of course, the question is this: Autonomy for what? And in answering this question, we can perhaps develop some ideas of the uses of autonomy for these twenty-four men, the attraction it has for them. We can do this best by stating as unproved hypotheses some of the relationships between the source of the drive and the nature of the goal.

1. Those who admire their fathers (MacGregor, Dobb, and, to some extent, Novak), even though they have warred with them in their various ways, seek to impress their fathers in some way. Success comes from excelling in the ways their fathers did themselves or within the same social orbit. The payoff comes from making the old man admit that they, the sons, are worthy, have quality, deserve recognition. To the extent that this is the nature of their ambition, their political rebelliousness will wane with their successes. They want admittance to their fathers' circles of respect and esteem; it is the door to their own self-respect. Once this is achieved, deviant politics loses its value and the aggressive-hostile component fades.

2. Those who hate their fathers seek revenge and injury to them and what they represent. Other goals will become more important, but these revenge goals have no built-in mechanism for redemption. Moreover, the aggressive-hostile component, directly partly at the father, generalizes to other aspects of society. They want freedom to hate, as we have seen in Chapters 8 and 9.

3. Those who were bedeviled by their parents' ambivalent direction, who sought guidance in vain, do not want their autonomy very much. Like Novak, they may find a substitute authority. Like Trueblood, they may withdraw. They wanted freedom *from* the uncertainties of their situation, although they may have preferred to remain within it and receive guidance, but they do not want a freedom *for* expression, because they do not know what they want to express.

4. Those who have found the nurturance they received too sticky want a chance to prove that they can make it on their own. Tempted, perhaps, by the indulgences offered, they want to win their battle against temptation and to provide their own sustenance and support. But concerned about their capacities for assertion and independence, they subtly cloak themselves in external authority.

5. The flight from indifference, coldness, and loveless family life leads to an endless search for better human relations, impeded by an underlying belief that love is impossible, fear of close ties, and a reliance on compensating values. There is nothing to keep these men at home, certainly not human companionship. For them, in a cold contractual world, government must proceed coldly and contractually.

6. For those who serve their sonships in belittling families, autonomy

means searching for conditions that would help them to think better of themselves. They seek a politics of status; their political beliefs are shaped to serve their ambitions.

7. For the most part, those who have suffered from the abridgment of due process, who have not been heard, their voices drowned out by paternal direction, do not seek for mankind the "justice" they have been denied. What they have learned is that it is a hard world and the rewards of life, large and small, go to the strong. The exception to this rule comes when there is something to be gained in the father-son warfare by opposing a "hard-line" dogma put forward by the old man, and when the mother sets forward or embodies an alternative set of views. For those who have been deprived of due process and fair hearings at home, autonomy means an escape from *ex parte* judgment, not an effort to restore to others what has been denied the self. Indeed, in the argument of MacGregor, one of the "best" of these men, "As my father grew up insecure, so did I. Therefore, perhaps, I wish to impose my feeling of insecurity on others." But usually it is rationalized in other terms: "a hard world," distrust of others, justice is the will of the stronger.

CAPACITIES FOR AUTONOMOUS POLITICS

The last point implies a general question that probes deep into the uses of the prized autonomy from the family, once it has been gained: Have these men the capacities to employ their "freedom" in fruitful and expressive ways? Much is made of the negative nature of American concepts of freedom. Erikson says of the American character:

> The [American] individual must be able to convince himself that the next step is up to him and that no matter where he is staying or going he always has the choice of leaving or turning in the opposite direction if he chooses to do so. In this country the migrant does not want to be told to move on, nor the sedentary man to stay where he is.[11]

If the American does not want to be told what to do, has he, then, the *capacity* to make use of the freedom he wins through this resistance to control? Dorothy Lee, in her analysis of the American concept of freedom, implies that Erikson is wrong and that the question Americans now ask themselves is different:

---

[11] Erik Erikson, *Childhood and Society,* rev. ed. (New York: Norton, 1963), p. 286.

I believe that freedom *from,* the condition of the situation, was at one time felt to be supremely necessary but has since been taken for granted. . . . The individual is no longer supremely interested in *what can be done,* but rather in *what I can do.* . . . The emphasis has shifted from a passive potentiality in the situation to a vital capacity in the person.[12]

This poses the problem for the men who have repudiated their family political cultures and must each now forge one of his own. It is a difficult problem to solve under any circumstances, but for these men it is especially hard. The reason it is so difficult, of course, is that the very circumstances they flee from have inhibited their capacities "freely" to employ ideas regarding authority, humanity or humaneness, or dependent relationships in society. Ideas on these matters are dangerous thoughts for these men, having been given in childhood a special frightening meaning that is hard to erase. They can achieve "freedom from" as they leave the family, but can they then make use of what Dorothy Lee says is now the dominant theme of American concepts of freedom, "vital capacity"? This is the tragic dilemma of their situation.

---

[12]Dorothy Lee, *Freedom and Culture* (New York: Spectrum, Prentice-Hall, 1959), pp. 56-57. Compare Karl W. Deutsch's discussion of freedom as a sequence of choices, each widening the possibilities open to the individuals (in C. J. Friedrich, ed., *Liberty* [New York: Atherton, 1962], pp. 301-7). Deutsch stresses the "vital capacity." On the other hand, in the same volume (pp. 274-88), Felix Oppenheim stresses the idea of freedom as lack of external constraint. Evidently, the concept needs two legs to walk on.

16

The Idea of Political Consciousness

Political consciousness is not the same as political knowledge or political interest or "following" politics. The broader meaning of the term embraces an understanding of other things, but the usage I employ here refers to the "self-in-politics" as far as the self goes in that direction, both in action and in thought. Sensitivity, awareness, discernment are all as important as intelligence. The posing of problems is as important as problem-solving.

Political consciousness begins with or must include a knowledge of one's own needs and motives, the sources of striving, and the areas of gratification if the striving is successful or of frustration if it is not. It is one answer to the question "What am I trying to do?" perhaps the most important one, though not the only one. Clinical psychologists of every persuasion regard ignorance of one's own motives as a possible source of sickness and, depending upon the motive, likely to lead to some unhappy feature of a person's life. Such "ignorance" is a necessary element of repression, of anxiety, of parataxic thought,[1] of the character neuroses, of unfulfilled lives, of the failure of growth or self-actualization.[2] And this set of illnesses and failures occurs whether or not the individual is intelligent and whether or not he is informed about the world, educated, cultured, sophisticated, perhaps even wise.

"What am I trying to do?" is a difficult question to answer, as we have seen. Buenello said he was trying to follow the teachings of St. Thomas and "walk in the image of Christ," but there was every evidence that he

---

[1]See Harry Stack Sullivan, *The Interpersonal Theory of Psychiatry* (New York: Norton, 1953). The term refers to a kind of unorganized thought.

[2]As noted in previous chapters, the concept of "self-actualization" means a combination of self-development and self-fulfillment; it is employed by Carl R. Rogers in his *Client-Centered Therapy* (Boston: Houghton Mifflin, 1951), by Gordon Allport in his discussion of the concept of *Becoming* (New Haven: Yale University Press, 1960), and especially in A. H. Maslow, *Toward a Psychology of Being,* 2nd ed. (Princeton: Insight, Van Nostrand, 1968).

cared more for the "image" than the walk, and that he cared more for dominance over others, worldly success, power and wealth, than anything else. Donaldson spoke of his loving human nature and desire to help the downtrodden of the earth, but denied any implication that there were other than altruistic reasons for this. The aggressive men did not speak of their need to express their aggressive feelings; the outside world seemed both cause and reason enough for their anger.

Beyond this level of explanation lies the deeper psychodynamic explanations that would account for the original setting down of a need, its channeling into one area of life striving rather than another, its symbolic significance, and the elaborate analogies that give current experience the meaning and threat of "old, unhappy, far-off things, and [especially] battles long ago." These are important for adequate explanations of individual, and therefore social, behavior and change, but not for us now. Suffice it to say that relatively untrained men can reveal proximate needs and motives to themselves which help them account for their ideas at a level of meaning they previously lacked.

But now let us turn from the need to the product, the political ideas themselves. Asking the question "What am I trying to do?" in the political field often uncovers what seems at first to be an extraordinary poverty of political ideas, values, goals. What each of these men took to be a belief system marked by the richness of a political philosophy turned out on examination to be a set of undigested and unreflected-upon labels: conservatism, liberalism, internationalism, inadequately illustrated by examples from current events. Almost without exception, these highly intelligent and educated men had failed to give much thought to what *they* believed, though they might have done a creditable job reporting the beliefs of Thomas Hobbes, or John Stuart Mill, or Karl Marx. Thus they are at first as surprised by the quick exhaustion of their store of conventional words and phrases as by their lack of self-knowledge. Both sides of the "equation" had to be painfully developed; if their motives were buried in the unconscious, their politics were lost in the great unawareness. And between them (I speak metaphorically or paradigmatically) lies the "thinking machine" outlined in Chapter 5.

One of the reasons why "rational decision-making" in political thought is so difficult, and comes so late in the process of political thinking, is that the thinking instrument itself is the source of a crucial piece of information: the answer to "Who am I?" the consciousness of *identity*. The term is vague, but for our limited purposes we might say that a person's political identity is that feature of his self-image which becomes relevant when he thinks about political matters—a definition that avoids the difficulties involved in giving each man as many identities as there are areas of life (religious, family, economic, societal). What is important here, therefore, is that he know *himself* well enough to be able to integrate his needs and motives without self-deception, thus giving them the priorities that must inform his most satisfying selection of political ideas. It is impossible to make rational calculations on life choices without such knowledge, and the temptation to present a false identity to the world of others—even greater than the temptation to adopt a false (class) consciousness in the Marxian sense— is very great in a society of strangers like our own. Recall how one of the Adams men, Caplan, said he had lost the respect of his friends and equals by the kind of façade he first presented at his boarding school, where he was the "little guy whom all the big boys knew." He had to dig deeper and forsake appearances. Political consciousness, then, as a first step in clarifying needs, motives, and hence goals, requires an accurate identity, including a true self-knowledge of one's tendency toward passivity or activity, of one's real rapport with people or estrangement from them or hostility to them; a fair appraisal of one's capacities, including one's aptitude and liking for "intellectuality"; and an accurate judgment not so much of one's worth, but of one's feelings about one's own worth, that is, one's self-esteem. This is both an effort at accurate self-description and self-appraisal, and since the self is both the instrument and the model for judging others, the more sharply defined and accurate one's sense of self, the more truly can one resolve one's conflicts—and the reverse is also true. The relevance of these judgments to political judgments has been demonstrated throughout the previous discussion; a change in any one of them is likely to imply a changed style of political thinking and participation. Political consciousness implies consciousness of identity.

The difficulties that lie in the path of this consciousness of identity are substantial; one is so immersed in the self, so ready to see the "best of a bad case," to excuse rather than define or explain. Alternatively, one may be disposed to blame, rather than to examine, meditate upon, and correct. Further, it is hard to be conscious of the self without being self-conscious. In spite of the Delphic Oracle's injunction to "know thyself" and the implications of Socrates' pejorative view of the unexamined life, the strain toward self-knowledge and the problem of identity are modern, emerging from the ambiguity and "openness" of modern society. The symptoms and sicknesses of the psychoanalyst's patients in the late Victorian era and the early twentieth century are different from those in recent years. There has been a shift from conflicts based on repression to conflicts based on disorientation and "identity crises," to use the new name.

To ask a person about his philosophical and operational belief system is like asking someone to tell you of his autonomic nervous system. Many of these beliefs and "value orientations" just *are;* they are given. They may be revealed, however, through questioning and discussion, and, since they are usually not repressed but only unperceived, they may surprise their hosts but need not threaten them. Yet they *may* threaten them too, for when the givenness of ideas on which one has implicitly guided one's life is questioned there is a loss of orientation that can be frightening. The questioning of everything, from religion to sacred property relationships, demands that familiar philosophies and operational codes be examined again and again. Growing consciousness of one's own society and culture poses for many people new and difficult questions about matters they had regarded as settled.

Nations emerging from colonial rule find it hardest to bear this total questioning, since the alternative answers bear the equally distasteful stamps of "primitive" and "foreign," but it is never easy in any society. Why is the United States "future-oriented"? And wouldn't it be better if we focused more on "being" than "doing"? Why do we rely so heavily on consensual decisions? Would we not be better off to select greater men as leaders, trusting their better informed discretion? Difficult questions. They make one uncomfortable. They probe the metaphysics, the ethics, the epistemology, the value systems, the moods implied in everyday thought. To be politically conscious is, at the very least, to be aware of the presence of these premises; beyond that, for those inclined to search their own minds, political consciousness implies an examination of and a rationale for these inarticulate premises of belief. Utopian thinking, for example, implies a different time sense from incrementalist thinking, as well as a different realm of political possibility; internationalist thinking embraces a different geographical domain from that of the parochialist or the nationalist; a belief in "the communist world conspiracy" implies a different explanation for the causes of war and empire and causation generally than belief in the possibility of a detente, of the bourgeoisification and conservatism of the Russian elite, of communism as one of the paths to modernism.[3] It is certainly possible to hold and change these specific political beliefs without any idea whatever about the underlying premises. But that is not political consciousness.

Would consciousness of these most fundamental beliefs, imbedded in a cultural matrix of behavior and expectation so pervasive and dense that one mistakes it for the natural environment, give one leverage on his own political thinking? I do not know, but there is evidence in the autobiographies that those who had a sense of themselves in a moving stream of time, anticipating their own differences in position a few years from the time

---

3On this point see Barrington Moore, Jr., *Social Origins of Dictatorship and Democracy* (Boston: Beacon Press, 1967).

of writing, were able to give to their political views a kind of perspective and detachment that was not possible for those who were so immersed in the here and now that they could not see over the rim of their current collegiate experience. Those who were conscious of the high value they put on "order" and continuity and predictability—and they all valued these things —were better able to explain their conservatism or their liberalism than those for whom the value placed on "order" was subliminal. And, of course, those who were aware of the cost of any value pursued in terms of other values—as McDonald valued socialist equalitarianism but feared the coldness and impersonalism of bureaucracy—made a more convincing case for their point of view. We are not asking total consciousness (that is impossible if one believes in attention), but something much less godlike, something closer to sophisticated awareness of the issues of time, place, and community, self and others, moral development, value *choices,* cause and effect, the environment of abundance or scarcity in which events occur.

In asking "What is real?" or "What do I believe is real?" inevitably one uses words to inquire into the meaning of words. One might say that the wisdom of science informs us that words are signs that direct and symbols that stand for and refer to observations and experience. Nothing more. But the wisdom of consciousness tells us that words suggest, imply, set in motion fantasy as well as directed thought. Words are labels for concepts and concepts have penumbras of meaning. To be conscious is to know two types of meaning, the direct definitional referential meaning and the emotive, connotative, associative meaning of terms. To be politically conscious is to understand the power of words like "democracy," "freedom," "imperialism"; to understand that one source of their power is in the emotional charges or valences they carry, the very elements that make cognitions dissonant or consonant, and that another source of their power is their associative meanings, the very ambiguities that permit them, like Rorschach ink blots, to suggest to each person just what he wants to see in them. Political consciousness is wisdom about the nature and meaning of concepts employed in analyzing the nature and meaning of everything else. The philosophical premises will be expressed in terms that help to clarify the political ideas they underlie; metaconsciousness at this level embraces awareness of the opaque, fragile nature of the conceptual instruments of thought. This awareness helps to avoid the "rubrication" or categorizing thinking that, when we are opposed to its direction, we call stereotyping, and which obscures the complexities that lie within a category or under a rubric, and usually transcend it.

If we grant that everything we have been considering here is somehow learned, and if we limit our attention to the learning involved in changes of political beliefs and attitudes, we are in a position to seek limited guidance from two kinds of theory and research: one, shorter in term and more experimental, is labeled simply "learning theory"; the other, longer in term and more observational, is labeled "developmental theory." Since our interest is long-term and our data are biographical, developmental concepts of learning and maturation are more relevant to our discussion of political consciousness. As a person matures, can he become aware of his own political maturation, his own tendencies to select new ideas to meet his changing needs? Elsewhere I have argued that *political* learning in college is heavily dependent on the way men perceive political ideas to be useful to them in their ongoing life struggles, something less true of science, history, and literature. Men can become aware of this feature of their own learning but there are risks involved if the awareness becomes a narrow guideline for learning. It is at this point that political consciousness might prove to be a new form of *un*awareness. If a man asks of every message, every self-generated thought, "Of what use to me is this message?" and rejects the "useless," he mistakes his present, more or less ephemeral character for an enduring, constant, changeless being. Yet nothing is clearer from the men's autobiographies than the changing nature of their needs and motives. We have said they learn what they need to help them with their identity formation, their interpersonal relations, and their task and career progression (Chapter 5). But their self-images change virtually under the observer's eye (the embarrassed "intellectual" blooms as he discovers it really is all right to be bright; the high school "up-and-coming young man" retains his image back home but portrays himself as a rebel at college). Their interpersonal relations change: the academic marketplace may be a job market for scholars, but it is a personality market for students, and one in which men are continuously discovering something new about themselves, as well as about the market. They are at a point in life where their interests change, something De Vita revealed when he spoke of his intense consciousness of moving from a lower-middle-class to a middle-class status and way of life—the interest gap we mentioned earlier. Similarly, their values are changing, as Simpson revealed when he spoke of the strain between an attraction to wealth and status, on the one hand, and service on the other. This emphasis on consciousness of change should provide an alertness to what is relevant in books and lectures to make the present man open to the needs and opportunities of the future man. The question "Of what use to me is this message?" which might have limited awareness, expands it under these circumstances, for it embraces concepts of "another me" at "another time." I am only giving a sharper definition to what is present in the autobiographies, but blurred and out of focus.

Most delicate of all is the aspect of political consciousness which discovers in the social milieu and group reference the means for intelligent and independent choice. Like the immersion in the self that impairs a clear perspective on identity, the immersion in "the world of people for me," the culture they represent, the guidance given without intention and read without awareness similarly impede political consciousness.

There are many parallels between unawareness of one's own identity and unawareness of one's social milieu and group reference, partly, of course, because they are conceptually and psychologically interrelated, as is evidenced in the concept of "social identity."[4] In each case the problem to be solved implies detachment, perspective on the self in a social situation, knowledge of both "me" and "not me," distinction, as though in an experiment, between outside stimulus and inner predisposition. Individuation cannot take place without both some concept of self and some concept of others, individually and in groups, or, indeed, partially reified, as in the concept "society." Since this individuation is both a historical process, as we shall see, and a maturation process, we are dealing with both historical eras and life stages, life times.

To be politically conscious, then, is both to ask and to answer, if only in a minor way, such questions as "What groups do I care about?" and "What does this 'caring' imply?" Implied in these questions are others: What are the group stakes in politics? What are the group opinions or values from which opinions follow? What are the costs and gains for me in allowing such views to guide my own thinking? What weight shall I give these views? Examination of such questions will develop for most people a set of cross-pressures that may be internalized, creating internal conflicts and dissonance. Such conflicting references and guides are handled like other conflicts: opinion domains are established where one group reference dominates another; mechanisms are devised for reducing the sense and pain of conflict—denial, withdrawal of affect, withdrawal of attention, eclectic absorption of defused ideas, confabulation, compartmentalization, and so forth. Most of these processes are unconscious, but one finds glimpses of conscious reporting on these matters in the biographies. MacGregor finds after a struggle that he can establish hierarchies of reference: he takes some career and occupational ideas from the family (father) and refuses to take from the family certain other life values, for which he substitutes values absorbed from admired older friends in recent summer experiences. De Vita reports a conscious search for an eclectic mixture of features of his home culture and his new college (higher status) culture: from the home he selects the warmth of interpersonal relations, while the college culture offers an emphasis on intellectuality and knowl-

---

4See the discussion of "Identity Diffusion and Ideological Caution" in Robert E. Lane, *Political Ideology* (New York: Free Press, Macmillan, 1962), pp. 381-99.

edge, which serve as the basis of his new identity. He denies, as we saw, some of the intensity of conflict, but acknowledges much of it. Men can become aware of their immersion in demanding social groups, can identify points of conflict, can report their procedures for handling the conflicts—at least some men can do some of these things some of the time. Political consciousness of one's own group reference is possible, but it must be taught and it must be learned slowly through "internal experiments."

To be conscious of and so to be able to define a situation is to bring together these elements of personal and social awareness we have been examining. But these are the background knowledges and sensitivities that shape perception; something more is called for in a critique of any current drama in which one has a part, perhaps a part with obliterated lines requiring almost total improvisation. What is it? In the broadest metaphorical language it is the answer to "What is going on here?" and more specifically it is the answer, for each of the actors, to "What is *he* doing here?" "What are *they* doing here?" and then, "What are *we* doing here?" This means at least these things: What are the actors' goals, purposes, ends? What are their means, strategies, devices? Who is with whom for what part of the game? What have we in common to gain and lose? Where do we overlap? Where do we divide? What do they expect of me? What shall I expect of myself? What are the potentials in this situation?

And since "situations" are almost always conversational, the conscious man, political or otherwise, has an attentive ear to words and meanings, discovering group meaning from the various voices of the now orchestrated, now cacophonous group. What is expressive language and what is instrumental? What is the latent message each seeks to convey about himself? What are the meanings *they* attach to their words?

The synthesis of the sensitivities of the political boss ("Who wants what?"), the psychoanalyst ("What emotional charge lies behind that statement?"), the literary critic ("Wherein lies the evocative power of that line and passage?"), the worldly-wise ("Behind the idealism, what?"), and the wise ("Behind the materalism what ideal lies hidden?")—this synthesis lies in some measure in all of the Adams men, for they know more than they know they know. When the subliminal is limned, when the perceptions are made conscious, when the thinking about thought is revealed to the thinker, then some of this unknown knowledge can be revealed in each of us. If consciousness is one computer monitoring another, then we must ask for a third computer to monitor the second. The second computer gives us self-consciousness; we also need knowledge of self-consciousness.

The rational decision-maker, maximizing gain and minimizing loss and employing preferred-risk schedules, might well ask all the questions we have asked, after calculating the information costs (including, I suppose, the cost of giving up the secondary gain derived from "neurotic" defensive strategies). He would want to know how an expressive idea fits an identity, the buried philosophical premises of a political concept, the strategies for learning what is useful for an indefinite set of tasks for an indefinite future for a person not yet fully defined, what the group stakes and group references are for any one domain of political thought, and how, coming to a focus in the here and now, the situation is to be characterized and evaluated. Without this breadth of consciousness he might calculate economic gain and loss, or, if it were defined for him, the gain and loss of any one policy for any one value or group of values; but unless he were also "conscious" in this special sense, he wouldn't be able to calculate the emerging, the latent, the empathic (other-regarding), the conflicted, and the repressed gains and losses. That is why rational calculation as usually defined often seems inadequate to the demands made upon it.

Turning now (later than the paradigm implies) to modes of conflict resolution, we find that political consciousness has preferred solutions to problems of dissonance. In the first place, because of the self-awareness demanded, it rejects those that imply self-deception, especially *denial* and some aspects of *rationalization;* it does not accept the substance of a message while deflecting its evaluative implications, it does not explain "away," or attribute the fault falsely to others, or use euphemisms. The pain of dissonance or cognitive imbalance comes from disturbing a preference for assigning favorable attributes to a favored object and unfavorable attributes to a disfavored object; it is under greatest strain as a rule when the object is the self. At the extreme it is a sorting of the world into black and white. The pain of dissonance is also inflicted by ambiguous situations, although they add another element of pain that pinches some (authoritarians, for example) more than others, the pain of doubt and uncertainty. But consciousness, as we have said, implies the penetration of categories; it is the enemy of rubrication. Once penetrated, most classes of things or people are multivalued, or ambiguously valued, with some of the value signs marked plus and some minus, and some neutral. If they then seem "gray," it is the impressionist's gray, made up of dots of light and dark, gray only to the distant eye. The politically conscious moralist will discover that the corrupt politician (say, James Michael Curley) has voted for most of the things he favors; the politically conscious liberal will find that his "enemy," Robert Taft, was a partisan of some liberal measures, like public housing.

But have we something to say about "withdrawal"—either affective withdrawal ("It doesn't matter which way it comes out; I was never much interested in politics anyway") or effective withdrawal (the privatization of interests and actions where once they had been public)? To be conscious is to be aware of the consequences, to know what you are doing and what will happen because of it. There is wisdom in withdrawing from the pain of a hot stove—unless one must cook over it; the man with sense rarely asks to be stuck with a needle—unless it is to be inoculated. In the same way, withdrawal from the pain of dissonance or conflicting emotions may make sense; it may lubricate interpersonal relations, or, in Abelson's term, cool the "hot cognition"[5] to increase veridicality and logic and reduce evaluation. Similarly, and here is a paradox, the politically conscious man we have been talking about may withdraw from politics if the stakes are low, if his influence is small, and if the costs (say in the disruption of family accord or the destruction of his business) are high. To be politically conscious is not to be single-mindedly political.

To repress is to make unconscious, and the projective styles of both conflict resolution (for the aggressive man: "*We* are a peace-loving nation; *they* are warlike") and reaction formation (for the greedy: "See how charitable I am; take all for your worthy cause") rely upon repression of the motivating impulse and its conversion into something else. It follows that political consciousness implies relatively less repression, relatively more communication with one's deeper self, relatively more self-acceptance.[6]

Consciousness is rewarding in any domain of life or field of striving or strife. Consciousness becomes politically and socially rewarding when a man is engaged in political thinking.

---

[5]Robert P. Abelson, "Computer Simulation of 'Hot' Cognition," in Silvan Tomkins and S. J. Messick, eds., *Computer Simulation of Personality* (New York: Wiley, 1963), pp. 278-98.

[6]I argue in *Political Ideology* that self-acceptance and self-esteem are different from each other and that both are important ingredients in "the democratic personality." See pp. 409-12.

17

Political Consciousness
and Citizen Self-Knowledge

If the politically conscious man has a need to be liked and knows this about himself (as De Vita, Lamb, Mintz, and others could reveal with such poignant detail), he will sooner or later confront certain aspects of politics which become problematic because of this very need. The first of these is the problem of coping with *conflict,* inevitably serious for the man who needs evidence of his likableness in a variety of situations, who indeed often defines situations as tests of this quality in himself. He is characterized by conflict anxiety. When he discovers this about himself, he is better prepared for the ordeal of partisanship. He is warned that his propitiating and ingratiating tendencies will encourage withdrawal or, as a defense against his inner alarm, the bolstering of his fragile defenses with offensive maneuvers. For example, De Vita, realizing for the first time his dependence upon the expressed goodwill of other people, is now aware of his withdrawal tendencies in conflict situations and his more subtle evasions by dealing with politics in utopian terms. Is he not now much better equipped to deal realistically with political argument than before? His political consciousness here will help him, if only marginally.

Political consciousness helps the man who needs to be liked in another way: he must eventually come to terms with his feelings about *deviance,* especially his own. King has been launched on this process of self-inquiry. He seeks the evidence of popularity in elections, worries about his lack of ambition to be more popular at Adams, reports his fear of "extremes" and his exaggerated alarm at being associated with the "odd balls"—but he is now, after his self-analysis, worried about his own conformist behavior. A new conflict has emerged in his life with dynamic implications for his feelings about being in some way, even in his political ideas, different. In a

322

small way he is on the road to a political consciousness that provides, as it must, a tolerance for considered deviance.

Perhaps, too, an increasing awareness of their own thought and behavior by those who need to be liked (a complicating but not a necessary condition) will bring to consciousness the difference between the symbols of people and the people themselves, between scoring in elections and being liked as unique persons, between acceptance and friendship. Svenson, Mintz, De Vita, and Lamb have struggled with these distinctions; if they work them out they will see that Bentham (the greatest good for the greatest number) does not contradict but does not comprehend the worlds of Maslow, Erikson, Sullivan, Rogers, Allport[1] (the greatest growth and development of each individual). Moreover, they will be facing away from that particular form of rubrication which most of us indulge in: analysis by categories of social class, ethnic group, region, urban-rural status—necessary, but often an impediment to understanding.

Finally, we would hope for relief for those who live on ambiguous social grounds, like Cohen, torn between his sense of being at home with Jews and his ambivalent desire to associate with Gentiles. Of course he was "conscious" of the problem, but he had by no means "worked it through" nor seen how it affected his desire for wealth and hence his Republican identification. If he had seen some more congenial way to "validate himself," he might have also seen that for *him* a professional career, which would have called forth his sensitivities and talents directly, would have gratified needs made almost unfulfillable by his ambivalent social identity.

Let each man ask at the appropriate time, "Why am I so angry?" or perhaps "Why am I *not* indignant?" If he can answer the question, much will happen to his political outlook. These are among the most difficult questions a man can ask himself, for the very state of anger blocks out the frame of mind that asks such a question (anger is directed outward), and the very struggle against anger is so fraught with imagined danger that a person fears to loosen his cold control. Nevertheless, Trumbull was able momentarily to ask and answer his own questioning of his anti-Catholic and anti-Semitic feelings in terms of his own insecurities, and MacGregor courageously admitted he was partially wrong to be so angry at his father. Since Trumbull's status consciousness (the way he says he copes with his insecurities) reinforced an unquestioning conservative Republican partisan-

[1]A. H. Maslow, *Toward a Psychology of Being* (Princeton: Insight, Van Nostrand, 1968); Erik Erikson, "The Problem of Ego Identity," *Journal of the American Psychoanalytic Association,* 4 (1956), pp. 58-121; Harry Stack Sullivan, *The Interpersonal Theory of Psychiatry* (New York: Norton, 1951); Carl R. Rogers, *Client-Centered Therapy* (Boston: Houghton Mifflin, 1951); Gordon W. Allport, *Becoming* (New Haven: Yale University Press, 1960).

ship, a glimpse into the sources of the insecurity that lay behind his angry and destructive attitude toward minority groups (whom he identifies as Democrats) might just possibly relax, if only a little, the emotionally charged bonds that linked him thoughtlessly to a political party. Given his friends and career choices, it is reasonable that he should be a Republican (the gains outweigh the costs); but, as a politically conscious friend might say to him, he should "give it a thought."

In the same vein Trueblood asks himself why it is that every act of partisan choice is fraught with one dominant emotion, anxiety. A young man once thought artistic and prematurely intellectual, he is not insensitive to what happens in the world, but when something he should (by his own admission) care about is jeopardized, he is paralyzed lest he do the wrong thing. He does indeed lift the curtain on the early stages of this pallid drama; he learned to fear his own anger lest he destroy something and then be rightfully punished for it. Knowing this, can he now in some small way leak out a little indignation—not enough to frighten him, but enough to taste it, like it, try it again? He is on his way to political consciousness if he can, for even a little indignation would loosen the bonds that keep him frozen, looking back over his shoulder, like Lot's wife.

Three men are angry at society for its failure to give justice to the underprivileged, the underdog: Demming, Donaldson, and, if the underdog is a member of a discriminated-against ethnic group, Svenson. Each expresses his anger in a different way, and the sources of their anger are diverse, but for each of them the anger is in the service of some features of the American ideal. What would happen if, discovering the sources of their anger in their personal lives (their quarrels with their fathers or with some more recent penalizing elite), they were to reflect on this and come to terms with their personal conflicts? Would their liberalism disappear, their causes fade? There is, of course, no way of knowing the long-term effects of the discoveries they have made about themselves, but in the tentative and inconclusive and short-term comprehension of their political orientation available to us, there is no evidence that such was or will be the case.

Actually, I think something else happens: they become aware in their self-analyses of their equalitarian views and their anger against injustice; they also become aware of the roots of these views in family quarrels. And then, instead of changing their views, they change the grounds for their views. It is almost as though Lasswell's paradigm were reversed. He says that political man is the product of private motives displaced onto public objects and rationalized in terms of the public interest.[2] Here we are saying that, once this has happened, and once this particular form of political

---

[2]Harold D. Lasswell, *Psychopathology and Politics* (Chicago: University of Chicago Press, 1930).

consciousness has been achieved so that something of the processes involved are perceived (not exactly in the displacement and rationalization terms Lasswell anticipates), then political man *may* (but need not) keep his views, think them through in the light of his personal motivation, and shift the emotional support to something else, perhaps a genuine empathy for others. There is something serendipitous about this, but one may argue that thinking has an autonomy of its own and that ideas learned under the lash of one set of motives do not die when the motive is uncovered (some would say "unmasked"). Rather, we may well find (I think we do in the biographies) that in the politically conscious man, just as there are motives in search of an idea, there are ideas in search of new motivational support.[3] We find in the studies of the development of moral judgment in children that the rationale for the games they are playing changes from a morality based on hedonic calculations to one embracing reciprocity and empathy. When this happens the children may change some rules, but not the basic game.[4] Political consciousness frees men to grow; we have seen this happen. Might they not then "grow" in this direction: from a love of the underdog based on angry reactions to their overdog fathers to an appreciation of the liberalism thus espoused in terms of a morally more mature understanding?

This last point leads into the discussion of the ways political consciousness affects the need to present a moral image to self and world. The discussion is made easier by the central thrust of theory and research on moral development, for, as we have just seen, that thrust has to do with the growth of consciousness, consciousness of the human source and man-made nature of rules, consciousness of plural perspectives on moral questions, consciousness of the rights and feelings of others and of the difference between morality and punishment, along with the interpretation of punishment as education. Within this framework of ideas it is easy to see that the two men who couched their political autobiographies in terms of the moral or moralized rules of lawgivers (Edmund Burke and St. Thomas) failed in the insights of the politically (or morally) conscious man. I should have followed these reports with the question the analyst always asks following a factual account: "How do you feel about it?" The habits of a lifetime would not be easily eroded, but perhaps they would be over time, especially if one were to turn their political thinking back upon them so that they could see that relinquishing one's conscience even to a philosopher king (even a dead

---

[3]See Milton J. Rosenberg, "An Analysis of Affective-Cognitive Consistency," in Carl I. Hovland and M. J. Rosenberg, eds., *Attitude Organization and Change* (New Haven: Yale University Press, 1960).

[4]See Jean Piaget, *The Moral Judgment of the Child,* trans. Marjorie Gabain (New York: Free Press, Macmillan, 1965).

one) is an invitation to dictatorship and contrary to their own argument. A small seed will, in time, crack a concrete pavement; an idea, if seminal, may also crack the crust of a moral code. Perhaps for the politically conscious man the political implications of a *political* idea have this seminal power.

For the moralizing others, the questions that political consciousness asks are relatively simple, but of course not easy to answer. Morality provides the playing fields for games of impression management, hence the insistent question: "Why do I care if I seem moral to others?" This was the question that Donaldson skirted so successfully, with his idyll of the humane man who embraced the outcasts of the earth and devoted his life selflessly to the welfare of others. Donaldson deflected his own two weak questions about the self-serving nature of his morality rather easily: he was for the underprivileged because he experienced a special empathy for them and because they needed his help. But behind this superficial dialogue with himself, there may have been another inner dialogue in which two ancient sparring partners were engaged, impulse versus control, id versus superego, desire versus conscience. Of course the way to make this conflict tolerable and the dialogue reasonable is to bring the impulse up to the surface for examination, and, equally, to bring the controlling agent into the light of consciousness. But since each of these contestants has his "reason" for avoiding examination, there are resistances. I am not so sure about the case of Donaldson; he might have developed a moral consciousness rather quickly (I thought his "game" with his father was only a superficial one, not embittered or central to his development). But the fact is that when invited to examine the basis for his views, he declined, and, in any event, even if he could go further with this self-inquiry, many could not. Had he done so, finding in his proposed life of dedication to the cause of cooperation among men something in which career aims, his self-assertion against his parents, and his moral showmanship all played a part along with his genuine empathy and kindness, he might have perceived more clearly what he was up to: the use of class conflict in the service of his ideals of cooperation, unity, an all-embracing goodwill. Clarification of thought might, in this case as in others, have followed from clarification of motives, the first step in political consciousness.

While consciousness of aggressive needs and needs for moral imagery reveals conflicts in impulse and control, consciousness of feelings of inadequacy and inferiority does not point so clearly in this direction. The roots of inferiority feelings may be traced to very early experiences, may be difficult to change in later life, may involve controls of impulses with physical bases—for example, a sense of worthlessness or sin associated with early sexual behavior, as with Novak, or a sense of weakness due to moralized admonition against expressions of anger, as in Trueblood's case. But the surprisingly large number of men in the Adams sample who reported inferiority feelings in their youth which had waned in college suggest that feelings of inadequacy, inferiority, and weakness may yield rather easily to maturation and the experience of success. If this is true, the problems of political consciousness in this area are those of working with, rather than against, the life forces that successful men enjoy. (I say "successful" because my sample is made up of men who, whatever their subjective expectations may have been, in the eyes of the world are now "making it.") But like Marxists, who must assist the historical forces working in their favor, we may accelerate the growth of self-esteem in men who are coming to this self-confident state late in their maturation.

In the first place, the man with inferiority feelings is a victim of the invidiousness of comparative evaluation which comprises so strong a theme in modern Western culture. Where society instructs its initiates that each is responsible for his own destiny and thus that a person's status is self-created, where each man's work is "graded" and scored on a curve calibrated by the scores of others, where sibling rivalry has robbed the term "brotherhood" of its earlier meaning, it is inevitable that there should be many casualties who will define themselves as inadequate or inferior. Perhaps it is idle to imagine that some consciousness of the social forces that produce these feelings will give much relief. Still, if a man is reflective, an awareness of the network of influences that have caught him might help him to see that the "inferiority" he feels is a social product as well as a "personal failing." We do not know whether a social or political consciousness would help men in their struggle for self-esteem, for this was not a feature of our experiment, but the relief and "exhilaration" they sometimes report imply some increment of satisfaction with the self.

In that little explored problem of the interrelationship between soma and society, we said that the child who was taught by his friends and parents to feel weak, awkward, ugly (especially if fat) became to some extent an "outsider" in his social group. A direct approach to this problem would require that the child be taken at this bad time in his life and treated then; but to the extent that the feelings linger (and to some extent they do), the development of political consciousness in the young adult implies the examination of what is "outside" and what is "inside" and why. Our Adams men were glimpsing a change in boundaries. Silver, extremely conscious of social criteria, nevertheless defined his area of excellence and differentiation in academic terms; Demming, finding himself outside the college in-group, stopped knocking at that door in his freshman year and created for himself a circle of friends whom he was happy to call the outgroup, and happy to lead in an assault against the portals of the establishment. Some rumor that the athletic high school hero was now selling shoes, some discovery that the handsome boy who laughed at his friend's buckteeth had failed his college boards may have helped in this redrawing of the boundaries. This sense of the shifting nature of evaluative boundaries did much to restore self-confidence to some, changing their political out- look: elites now appeared more like them; the grounds on which groups could be defined as "superior" included that eminence on which they them- selves stood. (At the same time, of course, the three men who remembered the lost glories of high school failed to share in this gain. Rather their new consciousness gave them a few fragile instruments to analyze their malaise and so to penetrate its source, define its limits—usually athletics or popularity—absorb its meaning, and take remedial steps.)

Much more important, because growing up does not here have this therapeutic potential, is the problem of those who seek to remedy their feelings of deficiency by dreams of status and wealth. There is a certain realism in this orientation: professional status and power and the respect that money buys do help assuage many feelings of inadequacy. By the world's standards, men with these qualities and statuses are not inferior. Still, when someone like Simpson feels himself balanced between the ideals of service and the ambition for wealth and status, he might well ask the question: "What is the meaning of buying self-esteem?" For him, of course, it means proof that he has the qualities of assertiveness which he (and his mother) thought he lacked. For Cohen money would "prove" that his father was wrong about him; he *is* a worthwhile person, and moreover, if he were rich he would have the means to bolster his feelings of insecurity. For both these men Republicanism is a property of wealth (it goes along with a well- kept lawn and a Cadillac). If somehow this complex of meanings could be sorted out, so that Simpson could divorce his need for evidence of assertive- ness from his image of wealth, and Cohen could separate out his problems of insecurity from his "obsession" (his term) with money, further choices would open up. Then, if each could see that Republicanism was not simply an attribute of the wealthy, but rather the concept of a party with a set of more or less consistent policies with consequences for society as well as consequences for his own ambitions, another increment of clarity and choice would be gained. Political consciousness, started with the insights these men displayed in their analyses of their own motives for their ambitions to be rich, is here a process of separating out the several elements of the chain of reasoning which leads them to a political decision, or in Simpson's case, an ambiguity leaning toward a decision. One can buy self-esteem; but self- esteem can come in other ways, as the politically conscious come to know.

The next two problems for which the concept of political consciousness has a special relevance have to do with men's perceptions of themselves vis-a-vis their families, in the one case their sense of their own identities as conditional in part on their family memberships, and in the other their sense that they will fulfill themselves only to the extent to which they can win some autonomy from their families. For the first of these, the family identifiers, political consciousness implies above all the question of an awareness of the distinction between self and family, or the distinctiveness of the self in the family, or the risks of total immersion, of the beach-heads they must maintain on the outside world. What is important is that their identification be seen as a *conscious choice,* neither better nor worse than separateness; for because this identification represents a continuity of identity, it might easily be confused with inertia of identity, identity drift. The demands made upon selfhood in this situation are very great, for the family relationships carry into their present status a freight of meaning and emotion burdened with dependency, tutelage, and the archaic connotations of infancy and childhood.

Yet the dynamics of the situation which, so far as I can tell, charac-terize the lives of those who have chosen such an identity continuity favor continued growth rather than continued boyhood. This is because one of the factors that led to the choice of continued family identification was the relaxed quality of the constraints that the parents had employed in helping the young men to achieve maturity. To some extent, though the limits are not clear, they could continue their identification because they were free. The inference is stronger because the experience of the family identifiers contrasts so markedly with the experience of the young men in families demanding dependency as a price for their support. By demanding it they produced rebellion and a counterdemand for autonomy, whereas the families of those sons who remained within the family fold, by granting them their freedom, produced no counterforce to drive them elsewhere. Cautious interpretation is required here; there are silken nets more powerful than iron bars, but the situation seems to be as we have described it.

Political consciousness demands knowledge of alternatives; otherwise choice is meaningless. Those who have chosen to continue their family identity do so at the peril of too narrow a vision of the world, a constituency too homogeneous for adequate reference. Gardiner, the young man born to affluence and status in a part of the country not noted for its heterodoxy or cosmopolitanism, suffers from this impairment of consciousness, es-pecially since he chooses his friends from like-minded men of similar back-grounds. But Ransome in some degree balances his conservatism in scales where the advocacy and evaluation of other doctrines are allowed some weight; McDonald poses one view of the world against another with an open mind; and Lamb, a struggling prisoner of a family culture, nevertheless employs family values to arrive at outcomes different from his parents'. They are all peer-oriented as well as family-oriented. In each case except

Gardiner's there has been a contest; their views are not given but chosen, at least to some extent. Political consciousness under these circumstances must reinforce, often without adequate social support, this determination to see the subtle cues that give guidance in this all too familiar setting, to see the familiar figures as standing out from the accepted background, to see the openings declined, to appreciate other ways of life, and, seeing and appreciating them, to entertain them as possibilities for the old familiar family self. This is nothing less than to imagine the self as something other than what it is.

Finally, we come to the consciousness of those who seek, for various reasons, autonomy from their families and their family cultures. Like national counterideologists or revolutionaries, they must use the values and ideas they have learned from the prevailing culture to counter the prevailing norms, but with a difference. On the one hand, their problem is made simpler than the revolutionary's by the availability of outside sources of ideas. One of the functions of a college education is to provide just this source of ideas counter to the family's. Further, unlike the revolutionary, they need not persuade anyone but themselves. In a sense they are their own cause, leadership, and following. On the other hand, as we noted earlier, their personalities are intertwined with their parents' personalities in such a way that they must often employ the very traits their fathers dislike in themselves to fight for their autonomy. Or, like Coleman and Simpson, they may find themselves enlisted in their mothers' cause against their fathers—or, indeed, they themselves may do this recruiting of allies.

For these reasons and others, the autonomy seekers, like the identifiers, must also ask, "What is 'me'?" and "What is family?" Clarity on this point is crucial, even though the problems posed for the two groups are very different. The autonomy seekers, as we have said, want to repair the deficiencies in their lives, to find a basis for self-esteem denied them, to avoid the loveless routines of the family circle, and perhaps to find elsewhere a better set of friends, to discover freedom where they have known constraint, to find norms and guides not provided at home, and to achieve a sense of independence which family dependency demands have stolen from them.

Consciousness begins when they can answer the questions defining self and family, and develops further as they clarify their malaise, asking, "Who has been doing what to me?" closely followed by the question "What shall I do about it?" To realize at an early stage that "Mother is making a baby of me," that "Father is trying to shape me into a more perfect mold—but it is *his* mold, not mine," that "This is a loveless family"—to realize these things is to know what is poisoning family relations and making this drive for independence so insistent, so central, so much a feature of all striving, and, as we have seen, so important a determinant of political and social thinking. The paradox in this situation is that instead of finding independence and autonomy, the youth in these circumstances is imprisoned by his very flight; his orientation is polarized. True enough, there are more options in going away from something than in going toward it; there are objective alternatives. But whether a person in the grip of an avoidance mentality can be said to be freely choosing, whether he can be said to be conscious of his long-run objectives when he is running away from home and looking back over his shoulder, is not at all clear. He certainly is not in a position to consider the positive values left behind, or to appreciate that what he takes for aversion is really ambivalence (as it usually is). Hence he needs cool answers to the question "Who has been doing what to me?" and reflection on the variety of answers he will get.

"What shall I do about it?" implies that he *can* do something about it and that he can do more than one thing; he has a choice. MacGregor gives us an indication of some of the things he can do. First MacGregor tried to beat his father in argument and to assert himself within the family framework. When this failed, he rebelled and became "wild"—outside the family framework. When this proved no longer satisfying, he came to an accommodation with his father on terms that did not challenge his father and gave young MacGregor the inner sense of autonomy and choice he needed. Further, he did not *need* to disagree with his father politically; he could both agree and feel that his ideas were his own. Svenson, on the other hand, makes disagreement on certain things a principle. The principle is opposition to his father and he has no further area of choice. Novak differentiates himself from his father politically, but finds a substitute authority who is more attractive and more demanding and confining, too. Mintz carries on a characterological struggle with his sense of passivity and indecision, which, as he leaves school, he is on the verge of winning, a secret war of which his parents are hardly aware. Not yet certain that his political ideas are his own, he nevertheless is conscious of the difference between those he has absorbed uncritically from his father and those he has developed for himself. Furthermore, and here lies the victory for political consciousness, he can agree with his father, but need not, and he can disagree with his father, but doesn't have to.

The premise for these victories over "autonomy" is that the world is "out there," not confined in the arena of struggle; it is open, full of possibility, has its own terms. Political consciousness must provide a way of validating beliefs which is independent of the family quarrel and ways of validating the self which do not rest on victory over the father (or mother). The struggle involved in the restitution of the parts of life deprived in the home can be independent of the interpretation of the political and social world. Life's struggles are sorted out and the struggle for autonomy from the home appears in the conscious mind as only one of many struggles, not the single arena in which the campaign for the world is won or lost.

The consequences of this expansion of consciousness so far are still unclear. One must neither expect nor claim too much; the experience is brief, the forces that laid down the pattern and goals of striving are old and ingrained, reinforced by "character" and habit, bulwarked by ongoing social pressures, rewarded by the very satisfactions that brought each man to this point in his life. But in observing the struggle for political consciousness, we might note the following effects, in each case supported by the reports of one or more men themselves.

First, the uncovering *and stating* of enduring needs and motives helped the autobiographers to understand certain of their own nonpolitical behavior patterns (eating with acquaintances instead of friends, indecisiveness in buying a car, feelings of inferiority in certain social groups), and in so doing relieved, if only to a minor extent, some anxiety that had occupied their attention and privatized (personalized) their lives, making them unfree, had they been inclined, to offer their attention to other things. Their insights were liberating experiences, possibly for social thought, possibly for something else. For some, too, the inquiry into themselves brought an unanticipated relief; they had been afraid to look, afraid to try. This might have been even more true of those who did less well, who uncovered least and were less in communication with their inner selves than others. For them, instead of the "Aha!" experience of discovery, which some enjoyed, there was a "That wasn't so bad" experience of nondiscovery. Yet the rivulet of attention in this unwonted channel may become a stream; one such person came to me six months after the event to correct an interpretation in his biography (he wanted to substitute his mother for his father in a certain portion of his analysis).

This general liberating and deepening experience of self-discovery is important in itself, but it is also helpful in answering an important query questioning the very underpinnings of the previous analysis: What happens to the energy source of thought if it is analyzed away? The same question is presented to every psychotherapist confronted by the relationship between therapy and creativity, a process whose sources are even less understood than political thought. The answer, of course, is that analysis of a set of motives may or may not relax their power to move; it depends upon whether, in the larger view that the analysis provides, the motivated act serves a larger purpose. We spoke of the experience of ideological self-analysis as liberating for the reason that it liberates choice, unties a thought from a specific need, and examines its serviceability in a larger context. If the thought is no longer useful, it may be dropped, but the energy to think is not thereby reduced. Rather, because anxiety is thought-inhibiting, the energy to think is increased. Further, taxic or stimulus-bound and need-bound thinking is tiring because energy is expended in warding off dangerous thoughts: the thinking may transcend the need and discover too much. The cockroach and bat may not be tired by their negative phototropism, but human beings must expend energy in avoiding light and seeking darkness. The indissoluble bond between a specific idea and a specific need is an obsession, boring to others, tiring and tiresome to the self. Political consciousness examines and loosens these bonds.

18

Political Consciousness in Man and Society

Asked where ideas come from, most men are as innocent or as misinformed as the child who asks where babies come from. While human reproduction is now the subject of candid, informed, even polite conversation, the production of ideas out of the material of personality and experience is often explained by some equivalent to the story of the flowers and the bees; the process is wrapped in a rationality that does not account for an idea's origins, its private meanings, its power to move and paralyze, its style of expression, the ellipses and lacunae in its uses, and much more. These sources and processes of political ideas can be learned and should be taught. I believe such knowledge is growing in Western societies, and that much of what seems to be postadolescent malaise is, in fact, the pain and uncertainty attendant upon the expansion of consciousness in this new form.

But now let us briefly turn the focus of political consciousness away from the self and onto government and society, not forgetting the *self* in society, but placing the emphasis upon the *society* surrounding the self. Here too, it seems to me, there are signs of an increased sensitivity to the latent, the implicit, the immanent, the emergent ideas in a conventional passage, the hidden emotion in a cold calculation, a sensitivity reaching a little way into the management of government itself. In this extended sense, political consciousness is one form of political knowledge, that form dealing with meanings of concepts, institutions, ideologies, and policies. Often the new meaning comes from penetrating their formal aspects, unmasking them, seeing through their many disguises.

It is a story with a history. For some time now—Fromm says about four hundred years,[1] Burckhardt argues for a turning point in the mid-

---

[1] Erich Fromm, *Escape from Freedom* (New York: Rinehart, 1941).

Renaissance[2]—a process of *individuation* has taken place, whereby men have come to think of themselves as detached from their tribes, families, villages, with properties peculiarly their own. No doubt all elites at every point in history have had some sense of their individual personalities, but the sense of self has gradually come to be a widely shared privilege, until finally it has become a "right" and now most recently a kind of duty. A sense of self is a requirement for the kind of political consciousness we have been discussing, but it is not enough.

The Reformation broke the prevailing institutionalized monopoly on religious thought; heresy led the way to skepticism and humanistic religion: the process of *secularization* has long been under way. The Philosophes in France, the Pietists in Germany, the Nonconformists in England eroded orthodox beliefs;[3] myths were examined and lost some of their mystery. Marxism, while running in some ways counter to the processes of individuation, and through the concept of historical inevitability breaking with the growing view that man, not Fate or History, was in charge of his own destiny, nevertheless helped to launch a discussion of social institutions and especially property relations which opened these concepts to fundamental examination, half "religious" and half secular on both sides. Empirical social science, aided in this century by the teachings of the philosophy of science, carried this process of secular investigation further.

Rapid communication and rapid transit, mass communication and mass travel, the world diffusion of ideas, the world dialogue, however imperfect, confronted one way of doing things, one set of values, with many others. Less culture-bound, men came gradually and defensively to the bar of *relativism,* where institutions and ideas must be evaluated on a comparative basis. Nationalism, racism, ethnocentrism may increase in their persuasive power as they are first challenged; but the challenge brings their implicit assumptions into the light of day, makes them increasingly available to the consciousness of men. They are seen both as aids to political and cultural cohesion and growth and as arbitrary (unreasoned) loyalties to a given set of unselected values. National, racial, and group consciousness have thus been subject to some of the strains placed earlier on tribal and village consciousness. Men with these loyalties are forced to answer the questions "Why the *American* way?" "Why *not* black power?"—questions asking for justifications of the going order and inquiring into matters buried in the unconscious acceptance of things as they are. Political consciousness here takes on new responsibilities.

---

[2]Jacob Burckhardt, *The Civilization of the Renaissance in Italy* (London: Phaidon, 1944), p. 81.

[3]For a discussion of some of the relationships between religion and science, see Robert K. Merton, *Social Theory and Social Structure* (New York: Free Press, Macmillan, 1957), pp. 574-94.

Under the impact of cultural investigation and increasingly searching study, political and social institutions require a new kind of defense. It is no longer enough to refer to their sacred, constitutional, authoritative origins to justify the particular arrangement at a given time and place. Now they must be evaluated in terms of their consequences and in terms of specified values; they are subjected to *functional* analysis (an analysis improved under recent criticism). Moreover, their "functions" are not accepted as completely described by their official purposes; rather the investigator wants to look behind the charter and annual report to see what the institution does for and to all those associated with it, all those in its path, the social and incidental costs of operation, both human and financial. He seeks an accounting in terms of both manifest and *latent functions.*

Under the surface of laws and rules, we now see institutions as patterns of behavior informed by men's interpretations of how to behave and what values to pursue in their respective positions or roles. These interpretations themselves have latent and manifest components, *operational codes* that are only half conscious. The pitiless examination of the premises of behavior, the rules of the game, make conscious political belief systems that the actors could not have articulated for themselves: as when Nathan Leites examines the code of irresponsibility and "buck-passing" among members of the French Parlement,[4] or when James D. Barber uncovers the primitive nonpolitical satisfactions and roles of certain "reluctant" or "advertiser" legislators in Connecticut,[5] or when Lucian Pye exposes the institutionalized identity conflicts of the Burmese politician,[6] or when James Scott discovers the damaging effect on the Malaysian civil servants of their latent philosophy of scarcity or "limited pie" mental set.[7] The political consciousness of the men in politics and government (as well as the observers and critics) gains new depth with the growing awareness of the inarticulate, half-understood premises and codes governing their behavior.

When men in government (or other institutions) ask the questions posed for the politically conscious individual, "What are we trying to do?" and "What is going on here?" they are likely to be referring to the effects of old and new policy, to intervention with money and rules into the ongoing stream of events. The effects of policy are often obscure; like medicine and surgery, policy often has side effects not anticipated in the original plan. Sometimes there are no effects at all. Government now, in some cases, provides for a regular evaluation of the effects of its policy, seeking knowl-

[4]Nathan Leites, *On The Game of Politics in France* (Stanford: Stanford University Press, 1959).

[5]James D. Barber, *The Lawmakers* (New Haven: Yale University Press, 1965).

[6]Lucian Pye, *Politics, Personality and Nation Building* (New Haven: Yale University Press, 1962).

[7]James C. Scott, *Political Ideology in Malaysia* (New Haven: Yale University Press, 1968).

edge of consequences based on information sometimes called *feedback*.[8] Further, it desires to know at what cost these results are achieved. Are there cheaper methods? Are there other ways of achieving these goals? Are there goals of higher priority to which funds and men might better be allocated? A policy-planning budgeting system is instituted to provide the means of answering some of these questions. For society, the new information improves the answers to the question "What is going on here?" At the governmental level political consciousness takes on new meaning as the latent and discrete and accidental effects of policy are made conscious.

Contributing to an understanding of men in society, and of social discontent and capability, the study of personality, as we have seen, illuminates the very nature of thought itself, as well as the processes of perception, motivation, development or growth, fantasy, breakdown. We have been made aware of the pervading influence of the unconscious, and of the complicated interaction of the conscious and unconscious in each individual. Through its capacity to explore interpersonal relations, psychology reveals much of the latent functions of organizational life; many of the unstated sources of tension and conflict in society; many of the implicit criteria employed by leaders to solve at the same time their own personal problems and the social problems with which they are faced. It is precisely this bringing to the surface of the latent, the unstated, the implicit that forms the core of the new social and political consciousness.

Psychology, of course, is only one of the branches of thought contributing to this end. In the sociology of knowledge there is a new attention to the social foundations of belief systems, of ideologies, even of science itself. Modern technological society, whether capitalist or communist, encourages a philosophy and epistemology based on reason and rationality, for such rationality sustains technology, law, postponement of pleasure now for greater pleasure later, economic calculation—that is, the ingredients of "modernism"—just as unquestioning faith sustains the caliphate, and myth and charisma support fascist totalitarianism. The purposes of a society provide it with its own concepts of truth. But relativism cannot endure in this arena: the modernists turn reason on unreason, while science examines myth and faith to give an accounting that has a superior power to control: a more powerful sorcery than any seen thus far.

The sociology of knowledge, the philosophy of science, secularization, and psychology join in the exploration of concepts and human relationships employed in both the attack and the defense of the established order. Myths of natural law, sacredness of contract, authoritativeness of fatherhood, invisible hands, materialistic dialectics all become vulnerable to

---

[8]See the penetrating theoretical discussion of this process in Karl Deutsch, *The Nerves of Government* (New York: Free Press, Macmillan, 1963).

examination. Under these cruel searchlights ideologies are not so much unmasked as unstuck, decomposed into their elements. Further, when they are closely examined, each reveals a superstructure of interests; each has a source in an elite with something to gain from the proposed reform and selective support by those whose consciousness, false or true, tells them their claims are better served by the proposed arrangement of things. Nor does the "exposure" end there, as we now know, for just as social ideas and ideologies have their economic and institutional substructures hidden from the ordinary eye, so the ideas of individuals, including charismatic leaders and sober statesmen, have their unconscious support in little-known, perhaps repressed, needs pressing for satisfaction. On the social and the individual levels the manifest has its sources (and consequences) in the latent and unconscious. Whether the visible figures on the wall of the cave are the shadows of the manifest or the shadows of the latent is never clear.

The future lies latent in the present. As the present is clarified by an examination of the past, the future is "revealed" by projecting change through time, suitably modified by knowledge of parallel, intersecting, and limiting forces and events. The concept of modernization gives us some partially illusory and partially insightful knowledge of where the less developed nations are going, for we think we know the impact of education, literacy, mass communication, urbanization, industrialization. But we do not know, and hardly pretend to know, the influence of the compression of time, of imitation as contrasted to invention, and of different orders of learning. Bluntly we apply historical analogy to current crises, comparing the decline of Rome to the decline of the West, confusing "the appeasement of Munich" with the Geneva accord on Vietnam of 1954. Metaphors dominate our thinking as we speak of "frontiers of knowledge" as though something like the winning of the West were involved; concepts and processes successful in one stage of history with one group are applied without thought to another; when we should be learning about biracial societies, though not necessarily imitating them, we are immersed in the language of assimilation. Analogies and metaphors, such as those underlying social Darwinism, take their power from the partial congruence of one situation with another; to guide our thinking of the future we must know which features of the implied comparison are congruent. To bring to consciousness concepts of the future as it lies latently in the present is part of the development of political consciousness in this broader range of meaning. The synoptic view implies more than the diachronic view of history, the view that reveals the road traveled by certain men between an earlier and a later period of the past; it must look to the future, as well.

If there is a considerable and growing capacity for political consciousness among such young men as those whose fortunes at Adams College cast them in my net, and if these capacities, broadly interpreted to include knowledge of the latent in society as well as the latent in the self, are increasingly prevalent throughout society and in government, there must be some set of causes, some new life conditions that would help us account for this. An accounting scheme for these changes would include many things: the cumulative nature of scientific knowledge, the differential survival probabilities of knowledgeable societies compared to others, the basic "need to know" discussed in Chapter 2, the interaction between wealth and knowledge, and much more. But returning like a refrain to our original theme, the sources of thought in the needs of men, can we discern some changes in the character of these needs?

As we see institutions change we do see changes in human character; they have a complicated but indissoluble relationship to each other. In the developing nations we see the excruciating pain of rapidly altered demands made upon their people, pain comparable to that of the bends, experienced by ocean divers when they are subjected to too rapid changes in pressure. Yet while social change, particularly if rapid, creates painful characterological stresses, and modern society is not notably less stressful than others, something may have happened to the dominant needs of an increasing number of "modern men." Maslow, whose thinking has often stimulated the discussion in this book, suggests that there is a hierarchy of needs, such that some must be satisfied before attention can be given to others.[9] The safety needs, whose satisfaction is required for survival, obviously have priority. These are followed by social needs, needs for love and affection, and the self-esteem needs, needs for a measure of dignity and sense of worth. But when these "deficiency needs" are minimally satisfied, as they may be for many people in a modern affluent society, an emergent drive for something more, for individual growth and development, becomes apparent. Latent in everyone, this desire to fulfill oneself may become ascendant among the more secure and self-confident. In the cases Maslow describes, persons with these "self-actualizing" tendencies are more penetrating than others in their observations, more aware of and tolerant of the diversity of human character, more conscious of themselves in the world. This awareness includes much of what I have been describing as political consciousness, for self-knowledge and the awareness of the latent, immanent, and potential in society represent a form of growth, a development not so much of the powers of reason as of the powers of sensitivity and understanding. The emergent possibility is always obscure, but if it is true that the satisfaction of those needs which can be met by economic security liberates men for personal growth, then political consciousness, embracing both self and society, may represent one important new kind of knowledge now emerging from the background of the unknown.

---

[9]Abraham H. Maslow, *Motivation and Personality* (New York: Harper, 1954) and *Toward a Psychology of Being* (Princeton: Insight, Van Nostrand, 1968).

Index